MW01515721

VIOLENCE INTERRUPTED

BOOK SOLD
NO LONGER R.H.P.L.
PROPERTY

BOOK SOLD
NO LONGER R.H.P.L.
PROPERTY

Violence Interrupted

Confronting Sexual Violence on University Campuses

Edited by

DIANE CROCKER, JOANNE MINAKER,
AND AMANDA NELUND

McGill-Queen's University Press
Montreal & Kingston • London • Chicago

© McGill-Queen's University Press 2020

ISBN 978-0-2280-0099-0 (cloth)
ISBN 978-0-2280-0100-3 (paper)
ISBN 978-0-2280-0238-3 (ePDF)
ISBN 978-0-2280-0239-0 (ePUB)

Legal deposit third quarter 2020
Bibliothèque nationale du Québec

Printed in Canada on acid-free paper that is 100% ancient forest free
(100% post-consumer recycled), processed chlorine free

This book has been published with the help of a grant from the Canadian
Federation for the Humanities and Social Sciences, through the Awards to
Scholarly Publications Program, using funds provided by the Social Sciences
and Humanities Research Council of Canada.

Funded by the   Financé par le   Canada Council   Conseil des arts
Government   gouvernement   for the Arts   du Canada
of Canada   du Canada   Canada

We acknowledge the support of the Canada Council for the Arts.

Nous remercions le Conseil des arts du Canada de son soutien.

Library and Archives Canada Cataloguing in Publication

Title: Violence interrupted: confronting sexual violence on university
    campuses/edited by Diane Crocker, Joanne Minaker, and Amanda Nelund.

Names: Crocker, Diane, editor. | Minaker, Joanne Cheryl, 1974– editor. |
    Nelund, Amanda, 1985– editor.

Description: Includes bibliographical references and index.

Identifiers: Canadiana (print) 20200213504 | Canadiana (ebook)
    20200213539 | ISBN 9780228001003 (paper) | ISBN 9780228000990
    (cloth) | ISBN 9780228002383 (ePDF) | ISBN 9780228002390 (ePUB)

Subjects: LCSH: Rape in universities and colleges—Canada.

Classification: LCC LB2345.3.R37 V56 2020 | DDC 371.7/82—dc23

This book was typeset by Marquis Interscript in 10.5/13 Sabon.

RICHMOND HILL PUBLIC LIBRARY
32972002030114   RH
Violence interrupted : confronting sexua
Oct. 23, 2020

Contents

Figures and Tables

FIGURES

TABLES

Acknowledgments

I'd like to acknowledge the support I have from my family and my friends for indulging me in lengthy conversations about the issues raised in this book. My work on this book also benefited from input by many colleagues and especially those working in Nova Scotia universities.

– Diane Crocker

My gratitude and unconditional love to my family team, Bryan, Ayden, Taryk, and Maylah for always believing in me. I admire so many trailblazing, feminist humans – too many to name – who inspire me. I dedicate our project and quest to end sexual violence to Diane Minaker, my beautiful and strong mother, whose legacy lives on every time we are humble and kind with ourselves and each other.

– Joanne Minaker

I would like to thank Fraser and Abi for their constant support and encouragement. I'd also like to thank all of the students and colleagues who have studied, worked to end, and experienced the violence this collection deals with.

– Amanda Nelund

This work has been a collaborative project from the beginning. We value the ideas and insights that all the authors share here. We want to thank all of the contributors to *Violence Interrupted* – for what you wrote on the page and for what you do in the world to interrupt sexual violence on and off campus.

Big thanks and appreciation to Jessica Burke for sharing extraordinary talents to assist with the planning and implementing of our colloquium. Kudos and gratitude to Larissa Doran for hours on hours of editorial assistance and index help. Funding was provided by the Social Sciences and Humanities Research Council through the Connections funding program and an Award to Scholarly Publications grant. We are also grateful for financial support from Saint Mary's University.

We asked ourselves: can we thank each other in the main acknowledgment? We decided, yes!

It's been such a pleasure to have a project grow from some initial conversations into a huge collection like this. We continually look to each other's research, teaching, and service for inspiration and support on how to build a meaningful academic career. It has been an honour to collaborate with such incredible hearts and minds. Thank you for all you do and your faith in a more just society.

For a world without sexual violence.

VIOLENCE INTERRUPTED

Introduction to Sexual Violence on Canadian University Campuses

New Challenges and Novel Solutions

Diane Crocker, Joanne Minaker, and Amanda Nelund

WHY BRAVE AND CRITICAL CONVERSATIONS ARE NECESSARY

Time's up for complicity, silence, and inaction. The realities of sexualized violence persist. The onslaught of blame, shame, and distrust of survivors – a group that continues to be disproportionately made up of women, girls, and those marginalized by their gender or sexual identity – persists. And, so do we. Brave and critical conversations about these issues are necessary because sexual violence continues relatively unabated while going under-reported, and survivors still suffer in silence. We teach, do research, and work administratively within Canadian post-secondary institutions where we see the impact of deeply entrenched social norms that perpetuate sexual violence. A feminist social fact we learned in our own undergraduate educations – that individuals who identify as women disproportionately experience sexual violence – holds up at the institutions where we work, in the lives of the students who come forward to disclose, report, and seek support after sexual violence. Working to challenge and change systemic, cultural, and social inequities is difficult and meaningful work. Building a culture of consent, respect, and accountability for harm becomes paramount if post-secondary institutions are to truly foster academic growth and transformative education.

In this introduction, we outline the key threads that stitch together the collective conversation inspired by the book's contributors about campus sexual violence. Definitions of sexual violence vary among scholars, community advocates, and universities. The Sexual Violence Policy at MacEwan University (the institution where both Joanne and Amanda work) defines sexual violence as "any sexualized act or act targeting a person's sexuality that is committed, threatened, or attempted against a person without that person's Consent. Sexual Violence varies in severity, can be physical or psychological in nature, and may include but is not limited to all forms of sexual contact, sexual humiliation, sexual exploitation, degrading sexual imagery, sending unwanted sexualized text messages, cyber harassment, indecent or sexualized exposure via electronic or social media or otherwise, Sexual Harassment, Sexual Discrimination, Stalking, and Sexual Assault" (MacEwan University 2018). At Saint Mary's University (where Diane works), the Sexual Violence Policy and Procedures define sexual violence as "any act, attempt to obtain a sexual act, or other act directed against a person's sexuality using coercion, by any person regardless of their relationship to the victim. Sexual Assault is an offence under the Criminal Code of Canada. It is illegal. Sexual assault is any unwanted act of a sexual nature imposed by one person upon another and includes such activities as kissing, fondling, oral or anal sex, intercourse, or other forms of penetration, without consent. Sexual assault can occur between strangers but it can also occur in a dating relationship or between spouses" (Saint Mary's University 2019). Campuses across the country include similar definitions in their policies. They typically include a full range of behaviours, from rape and sexual assault to sexual harassment. Some are included in the Criminal Code of Canada (such as sexual assault), while others are prohibited under human rights legislation (such as sexual harassment). All policies allow students to make complaints without involving police or human rights tribunals.

Despite formal responses aimed at taking sexual violence seriously, rape culture remains a real and salient force in Canadian campus climates and in students' experiences. As we imagine a world without sexual violence, our vision is grounded in academic study, activism, and advocacy that demonstrates so clearly the power of collective action, and it is informed by a deep commitment to realizing a better world – one policy, procedure, and practical step at a time. In this collection, we illuminate the challenges and opportunities of this moment when it comes to addressing sexual violence, supporting those involved, healing harm, and changing not only post-secondary institutions, but the broader cultural spaces in which all of our lives are embedded. *Violence Interrupted: Sexual Violence on University Campuses* presents new, varied, and unique approaches to understanding and addressing campus sexual violence.

Multiple perspectives make for a rich, textured, and nuanced analysis of institutional responses to the problem of sexual violence. As cisgender, non-racialized, settler academic women who bring both our privilege and our experiences with gendered violence and inequity to bear on this work, we acknowledge the need to compassionately listen to diverse voices and hold space for divergent views in our quest for a more just world. As academic researchers, one way we can contribute to change and healing is by stimulating, conducting, and promoting rigorous research and theory-building that represents the diversity of experiences and lived realities of those impacted by sexual violence. We hope that this collective achieves that goal.

WHY NOW?

"Who would you hate fuck?" – an awful question that several male dentistry students at Dalhousie posted on Facebook in 2015. They followed their question with the names of female dentistry students.[1] Months after the public release of the postings, one of this book's editors, Diane, attended a panel addressing the incident and campus sexual violence more generally. She went with a friend who had been active in feminist politics as an undergraduate but had since stepped away from that world and pursued other interests. Leaving the event, Diane's friend turned to her and said, "Nothing has really changed, has it? I could have been at this panel in the early 1990s."

Indeed, the problem of sexual violence on university campuses in Canada is not new. The slogan "No means no" began to circulate in the late 1980s and early 1990s. In more recent years, Canadian campus education programs have focused on "Yes means yes" and "enthusiastic consent." Yet, stories about rape culture's manifestation, experiences of sexual violence and harassment, and misogynist ideologies still proliferate. The problems of gendered violence continue. Post-secondary institutions have grappled with sexual assault, harassment, and other forms of sexual violence for decades, but in recent years the problem has risen to the top of the agenda for many university administrators.

Universities have been widely criticized for failing to intervene effectively or support survivors appropriately. For example, the

Canadian news program *The Fifth Estate* revealed UBC's failure to act quickly in the face of several sexual harassment and assault complaints (CBC 2015). A recent report highlights the lack of adequate responses in several Ontario universities (Buss, Moore, Rigakos, and Singh 2016). Student groups have also been highly critical of universities' efforts (Student Society of McGill University 2017).

This volatile climate may contribute to students' feelings of uncertainty and to concerns among faculty, staff, and university administration about the most appropriate ways to address or respond to sexual violence on campus. This, in turn, leads to the fear or assumption among some that Canadian campuses are unsafe places that do not provide adequate support or protection when students experience any form of sexual violence. It does not have to be this way.

We begin our exploration into campus sexual violence in the Canadian context with a different, though related question, to the one that Diane's friend posed: "What are the new challenges, and how can we work together to create novel solutions?" To address this question, this edited collection brings together researchers working in diverse disciplines, including sociology, psychology, education, law, and social justice studies. Their diverse expertise begins to bridge the gap between practice, theory, and research. The authors are all contributing, in different ways, to the difficult work of making change on university campuses and in our communities to better address the systemic silences around harm and justice. The chapters work from a variety of feminist perspectives, all sharing a commitment to thinking about sexual violence as a social problem that must be examined in an intersectional way.

Our book contributes new empirical and theoretical scholarship to inform and impact ongoing national conversations around sexual violence in post-secondary institutions and what transformative change may look like. While some chapters draw on empirical data from specific institutions, the book is not a collection of case studies. Authors analyze large-scale survey results, data from students and administrators, university policies, and other forms of evidence to explore the broad trends and recurring themes that animate the problem nationally. Indeed, one of our goals is to move away from hand-wringing and debate about specific incidents and particular campuses. Asking simplified questions like "What went wrong?" or "What is the best practice?" obscures the intricate and complex character of sexual violence in the post-secondary context, where bureaucracy, hierarchies, and intergenerational relationships exist, and the choices of students, staff, faculty members, and administrators are constrained by age, gender, ethnicity, sexuality, ability, and other power axes. All of this complicates how harm is handled, formally and informally, on campuses across the country.

Sexual violence cannot be reduced to a hashtag trending on social media. The complexity of sexual violence constitutes one of the book's underlying themes. Returning to the incident at Dalhousie: the Task Force Report produced after the misogynist Facebook posts concluded that the university had appropriate policies and programs (Task Force 2015). And yet, the report also documented a climate of sexism and misogyny permeating the School of Dentistry. In addition, over the past few decades, post-secondary institutions have designed programs that target the problem (Anderson and Whitson 2005; Banyard, Plante, and Moynihan 2004; Berkowitz 2001; Davis and Liddell 2002; Choate 2003; Government of Ontario 2013; Lonsway 1996; McMahon, Postmus, and Koenick 2011; Potter, Moynihan, Stapleton, and Banyard 2009). In Canada, we feel safe in saying that all post-secondary institutions aim to educate students and change their attitudes. But many of these initiatives fall short of changing behaviour. Notwithstanding the reports, inquiries, and action plans arising from high-profile incidents at several universities across the country, we have yet to see real, sustained academic research and theorizing about sexual harassment, violence, or rape culture by Canadian scholars about the post-secondary context.

In Canada we have witnessed a rise in campus activities in response to public pressure, and the enactment of provincial legislation, including the creation of policy, hiring new coordinators, and offering new programming. In 2016, universities in Ontario were mandated by legislation to adopt stand-alone sexual assault policies. Other provinces have followed suit to mandate that universities adopt stand-alone or accessible sexual violence policies.[2] In addition to work on legislation, advocates, student groups, among others are collaborating with governments to create action frameworks for ending campus sexual violence.

With the rise in campus activities and provincial legislation, we ask: *Where is the research and data behind "the solutions"?* As we go to press, we have some hope that evidence-based approaches are on the horizon. Manon Bergeron and her colleagues (Bergeron et al. 2016) have produced a comprehensive survey of francophone students in Quebec. In 2018, the Ontario government commissioned the Student Voices on Sexual Violence Survey (CCI Research 2019). Other universities across the country have conducted campus climate surveys. Most recently, the federal government received a commissioned report on developing a national framework on campus sexual violence (Khan et al. 2019). In addition, the IMPACTS project will be producing data from across the country on how to create sustained change on campuses across the country (McGill University 2019). And, of course, the chapters in this collection will contribute to our knowledge and be part of the emerging evidence on how to create and sustain change.

COMING TOGETHER FOR CONVERSATIONS ABOUT SEXUAL VIOLENCE

More Canadian academic research on these issues is urgently needed, work that promotes creativity, innovation, and inclusion. This book responds to this need. It began with a two-day event that we organized in June 2016 at Saint Mary's University in Halifax. "Conversations about Sexual Violence on University Campuses: New Challenges, Novel Solutions" was the first colloquium in Canada to focus on academic research related to sexual violence and rape culture on university campuses. The gathering combined rigorous and in-depth intellectual exchange with a programme that attracted a wide audience. Unlike other meetings with government and service agencies, we primarily targeted academic researchers. Our focus was how to enhance the ways we theorize and conceptualize both the problem and responses.[3]

Our intention with the present collection is to incorporate new knowledge about sexual violence and rape culture, address some of the gaps in the literature on campus sexual violence, and contribute to the development of responses to the problem, informed by Canadian academic research. This book is the culmination of our efforts, so far. We hope this body of work will increase knowledge concerning sexual violence and rape culture on campuses across Canada, not only offering a better understanding of how institutions are responding and the current research programs, but fostering networks of research and practice to inspire meaningful change.

With only one other related publication from Canadian researchers (Quinlan et al. 2017), it was not surprising that the response to our call for papers was tremendous. The following chapters convey a deep concern about sexual violence and rape culture and express a growing sentiment that addressing such a complex problem requires changes beyond the borders of the university. With each contribution, we aim to provoke thoughtful reflection about how to respond, or to share research findings that university administrators and student service professionals would do well to take seriously when developing and employing interventions.

CHAPTER OVERVIEW

The chapters in this book grapple with contradictions and recognize complexity. The chapters are organized, therefore, according to four main themes or points of departure, rather than by topics. This arrangement better reflects the multi-layered nature of the contributions and avoids imposing a structure that simplifies their arguments. The four themes are: (1) Imagine, (2) Complicate, (3) Problematize, and (4) Interrupt. Instead of imposing an artificial sense of linearity to the problem and solutions, we appointed different chapters into these subsections based on editorial conversations about how different groupings could best illuminate each of the four starting points. But we acknowledge that each chapter is not singular in its thinking about the issue. As a result, readers will encounter chapters in tandem that would not typically be placed together if the topic, rather·than the focus or kind of analysis, was the criterion for organization. With this arrangement, we aim to complicate the conversation in our readers' minds. If sexual violence were a simple problem to solve, then decades of feminist activism and research would already have solved it. Indeed, there is much more at work.

Imagine

The first set of chapters imagines – or envisions – sexual violence differently and encourages new ways of transforming the post-secondary landscape. In "Critical Components of a Survivor-Centred Response to Campus Sexual Violence," Kate Rossiter, Tracy Porteous, and Misha Dhillon highlight essential components of a comprehensive response to sexual violence on campus, and propose innovative solutions that improve disclosure and reporting options, enhance supports to victims/survivors, and increase the competence and confidence of members of the campus community to speak up and break the silence on sexual violence. Post-secondary institutions are responding to this issue with policy, and Rossiter and her colleagues argue that policy must be imagined, written, and ultimately implemented from a survivor perspective. Imagining survivor-focused policies is a good first step to tackle campus sexual violence.

Chloe Krystyna Garcia, Mindy R. Carter, Milka Nyariro, Maria Ezcurra, Lori Beavis, and Claudia Mitchell offer a creative approach to the problem in "'There is a Crack in Everything/That's How the Light Gets In': Reflections on Selected Arts Interventions Used to Bring Awareness to Sexual Violence at McGill University." The authors imagine new ways for art to advance campus reforms to combat rape culture, support survivors' healing, educate, protest, and build community. From these lenses, the authors turn to practical examples of arts interventions that they have been a part of, and reflect on their roles in addressing issues of sexual violence within the university and wider communities.

While the previous two chapters focus on large-scale, organized responses, the next chapters imagine ways in which individuals who identify as women might better navigate and respond to sexual violence on campus. In their chapter, "Alternative Practices and Politics of Care: Women Students' Experiences of Rape Culture and Sexualized Violence on Campus," Marcia Oliver, Rebecca Godderis, and Debra Langan examine the experiences, understandings, and responses of women-identified students to rape culture and sexualized violence. They highlight the different ways that women-identified students engage in alternative practices and politics of care, which are oriented toward cultivating caring relations and collectives that are attentive, responsive, and responsible to the needs of particular others, including oneself.

Daniel Del Gobbo focuses on the use of consensual dispute resolution to resolve complaints of campus sexual violence in "The Return of the Sex Wars: Contesting Rights and Interests in Campus Sexual Violence Reform." The author asks whether consensual processes should be offered as an alternative to campus adjudication at the complainants' request. The chapter argues that schools should embrace the contradictions of the "sex wars" through a more pluralistic approach to campus sexual violence policy that provides for both adjudicative and consensual processes in appropriate cases.

Complicate

The next set of chapters offers different ways to complicate our analysis with more nuanced understandings and approaches toward sexual violence. A number of responses, such as bystander intervention and consent education, are quickly becoming commonplace. These chapters together argue that we cannot take any approach or theme for granted. Instead, we must look more closely at the ways we can productively complicate these discussions to make lasting, impactful change.

Suzanne Dunn, Jane Bailey, and Yamikani Msosa complicate bystander intervention programs by exploring how an intersectional approach can help these programs better address the needs and experiences of students in a variety of social locations. In their chapter, "Stand by Me: Viewing Bystander Intervention Programming through an Intersectional Lens," the authors highlight and use intersectionality as a frame for discussing seven design and implementation aspects of bystander intervention programming.

In "'Strangers are Unsafe': Institutionalized Rape Culture and the Complexity of Addressing University Women's Safety Concerns," Nicole Jeffrey, Sara Crann, Sandra Erb, and Paula Barata focus on social constructions of sexual violence based on research with students about campus safety concerns. The chapter examines women's experiences and perceptions of safety on one Canadian campus using participatory photography. The authors attend to the complexity and tensions inherent in promoting women's safety on campus to challenge prevailing stereotypes.

"Understanding Students' Intentions to Intervene to Prevent Sexual Violence: A Canadian Study" aims to advance understanding of the factors associated with students' intentions to intervene in situations that could directly or indirectly lead to sexual violence. Here, Mallory Harrigan, Michael R. Woodford, Rebecca Godderis, and Ciann Wilson describe survey data collected at a mid-size Canadian university. They examine the role of demographic characteristics, attitudes, and beliefs related to sexual violence in order to better understand the likelihood of intervention when students witness situations that could lead to sexual violence. The chapter explores students' likelihood to intervene as it relates to gender and other demographic characteristics, personal experiences of sexual violence, participation in anti-violence training, personal beliefs about sexual violence, and perceptions of peer norms relating to sexual violence.

"'Homosociality' in Paradoxes and Erasures in Scholarship on Campus Sexual Assault and Hazing," by KelleyAnne Malinen and Chelsea Tobin, draws on a small thematic analysis comparing Canadian scholarly treatments of hazing on university campuses with

Canadian scholarly treatments of sexual assault on university campuses. The chapter explores how gendered discourses and homosocial ideology shape these two areas of scholarship in contradictory ways.

In the wake of high-profile men being fired for sexual violence, such as Harvey Weinstein, preliminary data from student surveys on sexual violence in universities suggests that students are coming to expect that universities, too, should rapidly dismiss or discipline alleged perpetrators. Shaheen Shariff and Julia Bellehumeur examine universities' legal obligations to address sexual violence in "Privacy and Protection vs Accountability and Transparency: Navigating Sexual Violence Claims in University Contexts." They focus specifically on accusations made in social media, and offer recommendations for the development of guidelines and resources to help university administrators, policy-makers, and legislators.

Problematize

Chapters in this section present different ways to problematize sexual violence. The chapters critique and problematize a number of ways in which we have been addressing campus sexual violence, including policy options and the concept of consent.

Alternative justice forms involve non-criminal justice system processes that respond to crime and harm. Amanda Nelund, in "New Policies, Old Problems? Problematizing University Policies," distinctively frames policy as an alternative justice form and provides a feminist critique of the criminal justice system and of alternative justice. This chapter examines university policy through the lens of alternative justice, using feminist socio-legal research to analyze both the calls for, and critiques of, alternative justice. Nelund argues that although universities had an opportunity to do justice differently through their policies, they are currently replicating many of the shortcomings of both criminal justice and alternative justice forms without mirroring their benefits.

Doris Buss and Diana Majury present another way to problematize sexual violence in their chapter, "Shadow Matters: Campus Sexual Violence and Legal Forms." In their view, university bureaucracies primarily confront sexual violence in the "shadows" of formal complaint processes. Here, "shadow" refers to a less distinct space that is nonetheless very much connected, in multiple ways, to a more visible centre. Drawing on interviews with university administrators and service providers conducted in three Ontario universities, they explore the bureaucracies and the service provision that constitute the primary site of university officials' encounters with sexual violence, and the implications of such an arrangement.

In "Towards Acknowledging the Ambiguities of Sex: Questioning Rape Culture and Consent-Based Approaches to Sexual Assault Prevention," Tuulia Law builds on auto-ethnographical reflections to reconsider rape culture and consent as concepts. Challenging the status of these terms as preferred analytical and activist tools, the chapter then revisits the work of feminist scholars who argue that sexual assault be viewed through a framing of sex as a site of pleasure and danger. In this way, Law reimagines preventive education.

After the Ontario government implemented their bill on campus sexual violence, Marcus A. Sibley and Dawn Moore interviewed survivors and report their findings in "The Silos of Sexual Violence: Understanding the Limits and Barriers to Survivor-Centrism on University Campuses." They explore how university practices are largely uninformed by the experiences of survivors, and instead are guided by dominant "rape myths" surrounding sexual violence. Survivors reported institutional barriers, lack of coordination, and for many, re-victimization by university responses to their complaints. The authors ask: How might we reconfigure the university to account for and support the changing needs of survivors, and what happens when survivors are uninterested in the formal complaint process?

Interrupt

The final chapters each interrupt ongoing conversations on campuses. Those conversations are diverse: they are about faculty/student relationships, student activism, resistance education, the research methods we employ, and care as a political practice.

An important interruption to the conversation about campus sexual violence is to ask the question: What about student-professor relationships? What about faculty? The emphasis of prevention, education, and support efforts are directed toward student-student sexual violence. However, a number of policies govern student-professor relationships in the Canadian post-secondary context. Richard Jochelson, David Ireland, Leon Laidlaw, and Anna Tourtchaninova reviewed a sample of the policies, protocols, and reported tribunal and case decisions to conclude that institutional intervention is complicated not only for students, but also for faculty members. Their chapter,

"Instructor-Student Sexual Misconduct: The Fraught Silences of Liminal Policy Spaces at Canadian Universities," calls for more transparent, concise, and clear policy guidelines on campuses, and proposes doing away with the permissive approach to professor-student relationships that has long governed the academy.

Student activists have been key players in efforts to interrupt campus culture. In "'Calling Out' Campus Sexual Violence: An Analysis of Anti-Rape Student Activism and Media Engagement at McGill University," Ayesha Vemuri uses McGill as a case study to exemplify how student activists' interventions push back against institutional power. Vemuri argues that recent public efforts by students to hold universities accountable are a form of "call out culture" and that these actions can have far-reaching and positive effects.

The chapter "Countering Rape Culture with Resistance Education," by H. Lorraine Radtke, Paula C. Barata, Charlene Y. Senn, Wilfreda E. Thurston, Karen L. Hobden, Ian Newby-Clark, and Misha Eliasziw, focuses on a program that literally interrupts sexual violence: the Enhanced Assess, Acknowledge, and Act program (EAAA). The authors describe a sexual assault resistance education program designed specifically for first-year university women-identified individuals that has been shown to be highly effective in reducing rates of attempted and completed sexual assault. This chapter addresses critics of the program who worry that teaching women to identity and resist risky situations promotes victim-blaming. The authors argue, from a decidedly feminist perspective, that the program is grounded in feminist ethics and provides a means for countering campus rape culture and rape myths.

Lastly, "Telling Stories and Making Sense of Campus Culture" is about more than interventions; it challenges us to interrogate how we understand the problem we are working to change. Diane Crocker outlines the limitations of current efforts to transform campus rape culture and inspires readers to take up the lens of complexity theory by exploring themes that emerged from students' stories. Complex problems, such as rape culture, do not respond well to solutions that assume static, cause-effect relationships.

CONCLUSION

The topic of sexual violence and campus culture is complex and politically charged. We argue that our conversations around sexual violence, and our responses to it, must be similarly complex.

Post-secondary institutions are uniquely positioned to leverage the knowledge and expertise of their faculties to support efforts to address the problem. Academic research in Canada is just beginning to impact the practices, policies, and programs in question. We are optimistic that the field is primed to grow and that the coming decades will see more effective change.

We hope that the book inspires scholars, students, and community groups from many fields and disciplines. While there is a clear connection to women and gender studies and criminology, we aim to engage people working throughout post-secondary institutions, including staff and university administration who are working on this issue in burgeoning offices of Sexual Violence Prevention. Ultimately, this project is not only about building a book, but creating safer communities for us all.

NOTES

1 For information on the restorative justice process used to address this incident, see Llewellyn, Macisaac, and MacKay (2015).

2 Unlike the United States, Canada does not have any mechanism for federal regulation like Title IX. Education policy is the responsibility of provincial governments.

3 More information on this event is available at https://dianecrocker.com/panel-discussion-on-campus-sexual-violence/. Funding for the colloquium was provided by the Social Sciences and Humanities Research Council, Saint Mary's University, MacEwan University, and the Nova Scotia Advisory Council on the Status of Women.

REFERENCES

Anderson, Linda A., and Susan C. Whiston. 2005. "Sexual Assault Education Programs: A Meta-Analytic Examination of their Effectiveness." *Psychology of Women Quarterly* 29: 374–88.

Banyard, Victoria L., Elizabeth G. Plante, and Mary M. Moynihan. 2004. "Bystander Education: Bringing a Broader Community Perspective to Sexual Violence Prevention." *Journal of Community Psychology* 32: 61–79.

Bergeron, Manon, Martine Hébert, Sandrine Ricci, Marie-France Goyer, and Lyne Kurtzman. 2016. *Sexual Violence in a University Setting in Quebec: Main Findings and Recommended Actions. Brief Presented* to the Standing Committee on the Status of Women for Its Study on Violence against Young Women and Girls in Canada. https://www.ourcommons.ca/Content/Committee/421/FEWO/Brief/BR8443144/br-external/BergeronManon-9449558-e.pdf.

Berkowitz, Alan D. 2001. "Critical Elements of Sexual Assault Prevention and Risk Reduction Programs for Men and Women." In *Sexual Assault in Context: Teaching College Men about Gender*, edited by C. Kilmartin, 75–99. Holmes Beach, FL: Psychology Press.

Buss, Doris, Diana Majury, Dawn Moore, George S. Rigakos, and Rashmee Singh. 2016. *Final Report: The Response to Sexual Violence at Ontario University Campuses*. Government of Ontario: Ontario Ministry of Community Safety and Correctional Services, 2013.

CBC. 2015. "School of Secrets." *The Fifth Estate*. https://www.cbc.ca/fifth/episodes/2015-2016/school-of-secrets.

CCI Research. 2019. "Student Voices on Sexual Violence: Summary Report of the Student Voices on Sexual Violence Survey." https://files.ontario.ca/tcu-summary-report-student-voices-on-sexual-violence-survey-en-2019-03.pdf

Choate, Laura Hensley. 2003. "Sexual Assault Prevention Programs for College." *Journal of Counselling Psychology* 6 (2): 166–76.

Davis, Tracy L., and Debora L. Liddell. 2002. "Getting Inside the House: The Effectiveness of a Rape Prevention Program for College Fraternity Men." *Journal of College Student Development* 43: 35–50.

Government of Ontario. 2013. "Developing a Response to Sexual Violence: A Resource Guide for Ontario's Colleges and Universities." http://www.citizenship.gov.on.ca/owd/english/ending-violence/campus_guide.shtml.

Khan, F., Rowe, C.J., and Bidgood, R. 2019. "Courage to Act: Developing a National Framework to Address and Prevent Gender-Based Violence at Post-Secondary Institutions in Canada." Toronto, ON: Possibility Seeds. https://www.couragetoact.ca/.

Llewellyn, Jennifer, Jacob Macisaac, and Melissa MacKay. 2015. "Report from the Restorative Justice Process at the Dalhousie University Faculty of Dentistry." http://www.dal.ca/content/dam/dalhousie/pdf/cultureof respect/RJ2015-Report.pdf.

Lonsway, Kimberly A. 1996. "Preventing Acquaintance Rape through Education: What Do We Know?" *Psychology of Women Quarterly* 20: 229–65.

MacEwan University. 2018 [2015]. "MacEwan University Sexual Violence Policy." https://www.macewan.ca/contribute/groups/public/documents/policy/sexual_violence.pdf.

McGill University. 2019. "IMPACTS: Collaborations to Address Sexual Violence on Campus." https://www.mcgill.ca/definetheline/impacts.

McMahon, Sarah, Judy L. Postmus, and Ruth Anne Koenick. 2011. "Conceptualizing the Engaging Bystander Approach to Sexual Violence Prevention on College Campuses." *Journal of College Student Development* 52 (1): 115–30.

Potter, Sharyn J., Mary M. Moynihan, Jane G. Stapleton, and Victoria L. Banyard. 2009. "Empowering Bystanders to Prevent Campus Violence against Women: A Preliminary Evaluation of a Poster Campaign." *Violence against Women* 15 (1): 106–21.

Quinlan, Elizabeth, Andrea Quinlan, Curtis Fogel, and Gail Taylor. 2017. *Sexual Violence at Canadian Universities: Activism, Institutional Responses, and Strategies for Change.* Waterloo, ON: Wilfrid Laurier Press.

Saint Mary's University. 2019. "Sexual Violence Policy and Procedures." https://smu.ca/webfiles/6-2019_SexualViolencePolicy.pdf.

Student Society of McGill University. 2017. *Our Turn: A National Student-Led Action Plan to End Campus Sexual Violence.* https://ssmu.ca/wp content/uploads/2018/03/our_turn_action_plan_final_english_web2.pdf?x58782.

Task Force. 2015. "Report of the Task Force on Misogyny, Sexism and Homophobia in Dalhousie University Faculty of Dentistry." https://www.dal.ca/cultureofrespect/task-force.html.

PART ONE

Imagine

1

Critical Components of a Survivor-Centred Response to Campus Sexual Violence

Kate Rossiter, Tracy Porteous, and Misha Dhillon

INTRODUCTION

In May 2016, the Ending Violence Association of British Columbia (EVA BC) launched our *Campus Sexual Violence: Guidelines for a Comprehensive Response* (herein referred to as "the guidelines") (Ending Violence Association of BC 2016).[1] We developed this resource to help guide post-secondary institutions' development and implementation of policies, procedures, and programs to prevent and respond to sexual violence, offering our unique perspective as community-based researchers and advocates in the field of gender-based violence.[2] The guidelines were informed by scholarly research, best practices in sexual violence response, and principles of a trauma-informed approach.[3] Although developed in BC for BC universities/colleges, the guidelines are relevant to post-secondary institutions across Canada, and can help them to develop responses that are effective, comprehensive, and survivor-centred.

In this chapter, we emphasize the importance of a campus-wide response to campus sexual violence that prioritizes the needs of survivors, and we outline eight critical components[4] of a survivor-centred and trauma-informed response that has the potential to dramatically improve the well-being of sexual violence survivors (Cleary and Hungerford 2015).

At the time EVA BC launched these guidelines, BC's provincial government announced new legislation, the Sexual Violence and Misconduct Policy Act (Bill 23, 2016). The law requires all public post-secondary institutions in the province to establish a stand-alone sexual violence and misconduct policy. Similar requirements exist in Ontario, under the Sexual Violence and Harassment Action Plan Act (2016). These initiatives follow the lead of the United States, where legislation has been enacted to support responses to and reporting of sexual violence on university/college campuses (see Perkins and Warner 2017). In particular, the American legislation includes Title IX, which prohibits discrimination on the basis of sex in educational institutions that receive funding from the federal government, the Clery Act, which requires post-secondary institutions to record and report crimes on campus, and the Campus Sexual Violence Elimination (Campus save) Act, which extends the Clery Act and requires universities to guarantee survivors' rights and provide campus-wide sexual violence prevention and education (Moylan and Javorka 2020; Sharp, Weaver, and Zvonkovic 2017; Spencer et al. 2017; Strout, Amar, and Astwood 2014).

A SURVIVOR-CENTRED RESPONSE TO CAMPUS SEXUAL VIOLENCE

A survivor-centred response to campus sexual violence prioritizes survivors' needs and rights, rather than those of perpetrators and/or institutions (Our Turn 2017). Survivor-centred approaches are informed by the perspectives of survivors as experts in their own experiences and needs in the aftermath of sexual violence (Gilfus et al. 1999; Richards et al. 2017). The impact of sexual violence varies widely depending on the nature of the incident, the individual survivor, the relationship (if any) between the survivor and the perpetrator, the response of individuals to whom the survivor discloses or reports, and the support the survivor receives following a disclosure or report. An inadequate institutional response (described in the literature as "institutional betrayal") can worsen sexual violence-related trauma, and, for some survivors, may be experienced as worse than the incident of sexual violence itself (Monahan-Kreishman and Ingarfield 2018; Sharp, Weaver, and Zvonkovic 2017; Smith and Freyd 2013).

Survivor-centred responses to campus sexual violence must also be trauma-informed (Sales and Krause 2017). They must incorporate an understanding of the psychological, physiological, social, and financial impacts of sexual violence and trauma. Institutional responses must minimize re-traumatization and support survivors' recovery (Harris and Fallot 2001). A trauma-informed response shifts away from asking "What is *wrong with* this person?" to "What has *happened to* this person?"; and it involves understanding survivors' responses to sexual violence as adaptive attempts to cope with a traumatic experience (BC Centre of Excellence for Women's Health 2013; Klinic Community Health Centre 2013; Royal College of Nursing 2008). A trauma-informed approach also recognizes the potential for sexual violence and trauma to impact survivors' academic performance and progress, as well as career outcomes (Potter et al. 2018).

CRITICAL COMPONENTS
OF A SURVIVOR-CENTRED RESPONSE

Policy and Procedures

A university/college sexual violence policy provides guiding principles, or a framework, that maps out the institution's intention with respect to preventing and responding to sexual violence within the campus community. While some forms of sexual violence may be addressed within existing institutional policies (e.g., student misconduct, discrimination and harassment), developing a stand-alone sexual violence policy is important (METRAC 2014). A stand-alone policy acknowledges the severity of sexual violence and the distinct and varied impacts on survivors, and signals the seriousness of the institution's intentions with respect to preventing and responding to sexual violence. It also recognizes the high risk that young students face and the significant under-reporting of sexual assault, and makes information about support and reporting mechanisms more accessible, both to survivors and to those providing the support.

Policies delineate *why* the institution intends to take action; *who* the policy applies to (e.g., students, staff, faculty, guests/visitors); *what* behaviours are prohibited (e.g., sexual harassment, sexual assault, other sexual offences); and *where* the policy is applicable (e.g., both on and off campus) (White House Task Force to Protect Students from Sexual Assault 2014). Procedures outline *how* a post-secondary institution will respond to incidents of sexual violence that involve campus community members (i.e., clear and transparent step-by-step actions), and articulate *who* is responsible for assisting survivors of sexual violence (e.g., a sexual violence office; specific staff and/or faculty; on- and off-campus sexual assault response services; health and counselling; campus security; law enforcement). Many universities/colleges have chosen to create a dedicated sexual violence response office and/or have identified staff responsible for responding to incidents of sexual violence, as part of a centralized response (Amar et al. 2014).

Survivor-centred policies and procedures should clearly condemn sexual violence, convey belief of and support for survivors, and outline the institution's intention to hold perpetrators accountable for their behaviour and prevent incidents of sexual violence within the campus community (METRAC 2014). The language used in sexual violence policies and procedures should be careful not to reflect commonly held misconceptions about sexual violence, as language fundamentally shapes our ideas about sexual violence, victim-blaming, and perpetrator accountability (Monahan-Kreishman and Ingarfield 2018). To be survivor-centred, policies and procedures must employ trauma-informed language, reinforce survivors' blamelessness, and inform survivors about their rights (Monahan-Kreishman and Ingarfield 2018). Survivors' rights enshrined in such policies may include the right to be treated with dignity and respect; the right to safety and privacy; the right to be informed about available disclosure and reporting options; the right to access advocacy and support services; the right to have their decisions respected; and the right to be informed about any limits to confidentiality and decisions made with respect to their case (Colleges Ontario 2015; Ontario Women's Directorate 2013).

Sexual violence policies should clearly define key terms (e.g., "sexual violence," "sexual harassment," "sexual assault," "sexual misconduct," "consent," "disclosure," "report") (Perkins and Warner 2017). These definitions should avoid using language that might imply mutuality; for example, definitions of sexual assault should avoid words such as "sex" or "intercourse" or "kissing," as these words suggest consensual acts (Coates, Bavelas, and Gibson 1994; Coates and Wade 2004). Instead, definitions should emphasize the lack of consent to any physical contact for a sexual purpose. Similarly, the term "alleged" should be avoided as it conveys doubt about the veracity of survivors' disclosures, contributes to victim-blaming, and perpetuates rape culture (Femifesto and collaborators 2015; Chicago Task Force on Violence Against Girls and Young Women 2012). Finally, post-secondary institutions should consider how using the term "sexual misconduct" as an umbrella term for sexual violence can minimize the egregious nature of sexual violence, and suggest that it is comparable to other forms of non-academic misconduct, such as damage to property or the unauthorized use of university facilities (Weiss and Lasky 2017). A survivor-centred policy should name sexual violence as such, thereby communicating that the administration recognizes it as a serious form of violence and trauma.

In order to be effective, campus sexual violence policies and procedures must avoid a one-size-fits-all approach, and should instead be tailored to the particular contexts of institutions, the communities in which they are located, and their student populations (Perkins and Warner 2017). Campus sexual violence policies and procedures should be reviewed on a regular basis, with changes informed by feedback from members of the campus community – in particular, sexual violence survivors and community-based anti-violence program(s) from the community at large. Universities should update policies and procedures regularly to ensure that they reflect any changes to provincial and federal policy and legislation, evidence-based best practices in sexual violence prevention and response, the departments or persons who have a responsibility to respond, contact information for support services, and the needs of survivors within the campus community based on feedback about their experiences with the policies and procedures.

Disclosing and Reporting

Sexual violence can be extremely traumatic, and therefore difficult to disclose and/or report, particularly within the context of rape culture. In fact, sexual assault is the most under-reported violent crime in Canada[5] (Rotenberg 2017). A survivor-centred approach should be focused first on ensuring that survivors are offered immediate emotional and practical support, information about their options related to medical care and reporting, and supports related to decisions about what to do next. This can help survivors to begin to regain a sense of control over their lives (Richards et al. 2017; Strout, Amar, and Astwood 2014). Universities/colleges should clearly distinguish between *disclosing* (i.e., telling someone about what has happened in order to access support and accommodations), and *reporting* (i.e., making an official or formal report to the authorities, such as police or campus security, thereby initiating a legal or quasi-legal investigative process). Survivors should be able to easily access information (e.g., via university websites[6]) about *all* of the available options for disclosing and reporting, both on and off campus, and about how to access support from a sexual assault response worker or advocate, regardless of which option(s) they choose.

Much can be drawn from research on the barriers to reporting sexual violence to police to better understand the barriers to disclosing to university administrators; however, the campus also offers a unique context that may impact decision-making in this regard (Amar et al. 2014; Spencer et al. 2017). Survivors may choose not to disclose or report for many reasons. They may feel humiliated, embarrassed, or too ashamed to tell anyone what happened (Spencer et al. 2017). They may have already been blamed or fear they will be blamed (Strout et al. 2014). They may fear not being believed or be unsure if what happened constitutes sexual assault (Spencer et al. 2017). Survivors may fear for their own or others' safety or worry about how they will be judged (e.g., by friends, family, members of the campus) (ibid.). In some cases, especially if the survivor was assaulted by someone they know (e.g., an acquaintance or intimate partner), someone who is part of the same close community (e.g., a department or residence), or someone who is in a position of power (e.g., a faculty member or supervisor), they may feel conflicted about the perpetrator getting into trouble (ibid.). They might feel apprehensive due to the possibility of a lack of consequences or inadequate responses from the police, justice system, or university/college administration (Strout et al. 2014). A survivor-centred approach must take into consideration these barriers to disclosing and reporting, recognizing individual and systemic factors that survivors often consider in deciding whether to tell anyone about what happened to them.

Some survivors will want to report to police by making a statement and initiating a criminal investigation. On some campuses, survivors may choose to report to campus security (as well as, or instead of, reporting to police) to alert them to the possibility of a sexual predator within the campus community. As campus sexual violence policies and procedures become more commonplace, survivors are increasingly given the option of submitting a formal complaint to the institution's administration and precipitating an investigation under the institution's sexual violence policy. Although research on reporting sexual violence to campus administrators is still emerging, existing research suggests that very few survivors choose to make formal reports to their institutions (Moylan and Javorka 2020; Spencer et al. 2017; The Student Room 2018).

To be survivor-centred, post-secondary institutions should make every effort to inform survivors about all disclosure and reporting options, and the implications of each option. Universities/colleges should then respect survivors' decisions regarding how they want to proceed (Our Turn 2017). Although public opinion research has found support for mandatory reporting of campus sexual violence (see Mancini et al. 2017), from a survivor-centred perspective, formal reporting to the post-secondary institution should never be mandatory. Instead, reporting should be offered as one of several options available to survivors of sexual violence (Spencer et al. 2017). Policies requiring mandatory reporting (e.g., to the police, campus security, and/or university/college administration) may seem optimal from a public safety perspective, as they appear to promote future violence prevention, increase student safety, and limit institutional liability. However, mandatory reporting processes may have unintended negative consequences (e.g., reducing students' willingness to report), may not improve a survivor's safety, and may lead to further harm (e.g., re-traumatizing survivors) (Moylan and Javorka 2020; Perkins and Warner 2017; Richards et al. 2017; Weiss and Lasky 2017).

Survivors should always have the option of making a disclosure without making a report that would initiate a formal investigation. At the same time, survivors must be informed about available reporting options. Survivors should also be offered support and advocacy services following a disclosure, regardless of whether or not they choose to make a formal report, as research suggests that they may feel better supported to report if they have survivor-centred resources, such as an advocate (Strout et al. 2014).

To address barriers to reporting sexual assault, some jurisdictions have developed innovative solutions to provide survivors with a mechanism to make anonymous reports to police. For example, in British Columbia, adult survivors can make an anonymous Third Party Report (TPR) to police through a community-based victim service agency.[7] A TPR will not instigate a police investigation, but provides police with detailed information about the crime and the perpetrator without the name or contact information of the survivor; it also connects survivors to advocacy and support services. Third Party Reporting was developed as an option of last resort for survivors who would not otherwise provide information to police but who may want to access support and let police know about a sexual predator in order to protect others (Community Coordination for Women's Safety, Ending Violence Association of BC 2014, 2019; Ending Violence Association of BC 2016, 2017).[8]

Similarly, given the low rates of reporting to institutions, universities/colleges in Canada, the United States, and the United Kingdom have considered mechanisms for anonymous reporting to more accurately gauge the incidence of campus sexual violence, to alert institutions to the possible presence of sexual predators within the campus community, and to assist institutions in more quickly and effectively responding to incidents of sexual violence (Monahan-Kreishman and Ingarfield 2018). Anonymous reporting may also facilitate the provision of information about sexual violence response and support services, including health care and forensic medical exams, to survivors who may not receive this information through formal reporting structures.

Ineffective institutional sexual violence policies and reporting mechanisms can make it difficult – even unsafe – for survivors to make a report to university/college administrators. These barriers to disclosing and reporting can contribute to a climate in which repeat sexual assault perpetrators and sexual predators may continue to harm others within the campus community (Amar et al. 2014; Gialopsos 2017). While it is important to ensure due process with every report of sexual violence, given that so few survivors choose to report, institutions also have a critical opportunity and responsibility to take these reports seriously and begin to shift public perceptions that nothing will be done to hold perpetrators accountable (Mancini et al. 2017).

Leadership and Inclusion

Although student activism has been a driving force behind the movement to address campus sexual violence (Krause et al. 2017; Sharp, Weaver, and Zvonkovic 2017), effective institutional responses also require leadership by senior administrators (Monahan-Kreishman and Ingarfield 2018; Universities UK 2016). Administrators need to clearly communicate the institution's commitment to addressing this issue (Lichty, Campbell, and Schuiteman 2008; Ontario Women's Directorate 2013; White House Task Force to Protect Students from Sexual Assault 2014). In doing so, the institution can convey that sexual violence is taken seriously by the administration and will not be tolerated within the campus community, thereby empowering survivors and encouraging faculty and staff to take survivors' needs seriously (Monahan-Kreishman and Ingarfield 2018).

To be truly survivor-centred, sexual violence prevention and response initiatives must be informed by students and survivors (Krause et al. 2017). Survivors who have expressed interest in contributing should be invited to participate in any and all initiatives led by the institution's administration. They should be invited to sit at decision-making tables with the institution's leadership. Special effort should be made to include students representing those groups most impacted by sexual violence (Monahan-Kreishman and Ingarfield 2018; Perkins and Warner 2017). This includes Indigenous students, international students, students with disabilities, LGBT2SQ+[9] students, fraternities and sororities, and students engaged in sex work. Their contributions will help ensure that institutional responses reflect their unique realities and meet their varied needs (Lichty et al. 2008). Administrators should also seek representation from faculty, staff, and those involved in campus housing, athletics, campus security, student government, student services, disability resource centres, Indigenous centres, health and counselling services, and campus and community-based sexual assault centres, given their unique perspectives regarding sexual violence (Strout et al. 2014). Universities must acknowledge that this work may be difficult for survivors, and may require students to take time away from studies and/or other paid and unpaid work (Our Turn 2017). As such, universities should ensure that supports are made available and, whenever possible, compensate students and survivors for their involvement in the development and implementation of sexual violence policies and prevention programs (Our Turn 2017).

Sexual violence policies, procedures, and programs must include survivors of all gender identities while not erasing the gendered nature of sexual violence, and the genders of those who perpetrate this violence and who are targeted by it (Spencer et al. 2017). Men perpetrate approximately 95 per cent of sexual assaults, and the vast majority of sexual assaults are perpetrated against women and girls (Conroy and Cotter 2017). Transgender and gender-diverse (including non-binary) individuals also experience disproportionately high rates of sexual violence, with some sources suggesting that half (50 per cent) of transgender individuals have been sexually abused or assaulted in their lifetime (FORGE 2012; Jauk 2013). While research on sexual violence perpetrated against men is limited and reporting rates are low, some men and boys experience sexual violence, with those who are young, Indigenous, living with disabilities, working in the sex industry, and/or living on the streets or in correctional facilities at higher risk (Du Mont et al. 2013). To be *gender-inclusive* (i.e., inclusive of and responsive to the needs of sexual violence survivors of all gender identities), policies must avoid being *gender-neutral*. Using gender-neutral language suggests *equal risk* of sexual violence across gender identities, which contradicts evidence about who is most impacted by sexual violence (Richards et al. 2017). Using gender-inclusive language, on the other hand, enables us to acknowledge that individuals of any gender identity can experience sexual violence, while recognizing that women and girls, and transgender and gender diverse individuals, face the most risk.

To develop survivor-centred sexual violence policies, procedures, and programs, post-secondary institutions should consult subject matter experts from the gender-based violence response community, such as experienced staff from local sexual assault centres, provincial associations of sexual assault centres, and national associations with a mandate to prevent and respond to gender-based violence (Ontario Women's Directorate 2013; White House Task Force to Protect Students from Sexual Assault 2014). Consultation with anti-violence agencies can help ensure that institutional responses to sexual violence are survivor-centred and trauma-informed, and reflect evidence-based best practice responses to sexual violence.

Privacy, Confidentiality, and Information-Sharing

Given the importance of confidentiality for sexual assault survivors, a survivor-centred and trauma-informed approach to campus sexual violence response requires universities to carefully consider survivors' privacy rights (Elliott et al. 2005; Strout, Amar, and Astwood 2014). Every effort should be made to protect the privacy of any person who discloses sexual violence. Before releasing any information related to incidents of sexual violence, universities should have the survivor's expressed consent and any confidentiality limits embedded in institutional policy must be outlined upon disclosure or as soon as possible after disclosure. Issues of privacy, confidentiality, and information-sharing should be outlined in campus sexual violence procedures. Policies should address when members of the campus community can share information (and when they cannot), what information can be shared and with whom, in what form information can be shared, and when written consent for sharing information is required from the survivor (or when not). University/college administrators are encouraged to consult with subject matter experts and review relevant information-sharing protocols, including those developed to address risk and safety in high-risk domestic violence cases, for guidance.[10]

Privacy rights are not absolute, and universities often grapple with competing rights – those of survivors, perpetrators, and other members of the campus community (Mancini et al. 2017; Strout et al. 2014). There may be times, albeit rare, that a university/college may need to contact police or child welfare authorities as a result of a disclosure: if there are reasonable grounds to believe that an individual is at imminent risk of severe or life threatening self-harm; if an individual is at imminent risk of harming another person; if there is a requirement under provincial legislation to report to child welfare; and/or if there is a requirement to comply with a court order for release of information. Procedures should specify who within a university/college administration has the authority to decide to release information, without the survivor's consent, in such circumstances. A decision to disclose a survivor's information without their consent should only be made in rare circumstances and only information relevant to the health or safety concern in question should be released. The survivor should be kept informed of any decision to release personal information. Post-secondary institutions should consult legal experts who have in-depth knowledge of federal and provincial privacy legislation and sexual violence, as legal obligations vary by province.

In addressing issues related to information-sharing, post-secondary institutions should specify who is responsible for communicating information about incidents of sexual violence both within and outside of the university/college community, and how the confidentiality of survivors will be maintained. For example, in some cases, universities/colleges may decide to alert the campus community about incidents without any details identifying the survivor. Campus safety alerts may not reach everyone within the campus community and may not be effective in preventing future incidents of sexual violence. However, timely campus safety alerts can help ensure that members of the campus community are informed and can take action to protect themselves and other members of the campus community; they also send a message to perpetrators that the institution knows of the incident(s) (Ontario Women's Directorate 2013).

Alerts should be communicated in multiple formats to ensure accessibility for all members of the campus community. They should be carefully worded to avoid any victim-blaming language and to avoid identifying survivors. Where possible, information to be included in safety alerts should be shared with the survivor to ensure accuracy, and alerts should include information about available supports and resources. In all instances, before sharing any information, the immediate safety concerns for the survivor should be canvassed by an advocate with specialized training in risk identification and safety planning related to gender-based violence, and every effort should be made to address these safety concerns.

Survivor Safety

Because the trauma associated with sexual violence can have serious and long-lasting impacts, and because a perpetrator may continue to be on campus while an investigation is underway, institutions should prioritize survivors' safety (Strout et al. 2014). To protect survivors in the immediate aftermath of a report or formal complaint under the institution's sexual violence policy, post-secondary institutions should consider designing and implementing interim provisions to protect survivors while the incident is being investigated. Although not legally enforceable, institutional interim protection provisions may include having a perpetrator move to a different residence; placing limitations on a perpetrator's movement on campus (e.g., restrictions on access to certain buildings); creating an agreement for a perpetrator to have no contact with the survivor or named witnesses/bystanders; and/or reassigning supervision/assessment duties in cases where the perpetrator is the survivor's supervisor or instructor (e.g., graduate research supervisor, lab supervisor, employer). Institutional interim protection provisions should prioritize safety-related needs. Determinations about the specific conditions included in such a provision will necessarily depend on the circumstances of the case and the level of risk to the survivor, which could be illuminated through a process to identify the risks, conducted by a trained first responder with expertise related to gender-based violence.

An institutional interim protection provision is more likely to be adhered to if all concerned parties agree to the provisions; as such, protection provisions should be developed in consultation with the survivor and the perpetrator. However, this process should not require direct contact or communication between the survivor and perpetrator, especially if the survivor does not feel safe engaging with the perpetrator (Our Turn 2017). In all cases, whether a perpetrator agrees to the proposed protection provisions and conditions or not, survivors should be supported to develop a comprehensive safety plan that involves individuals the survivor trusts who can support their safety (e.g., friends, residence staff, advocates) and respond quickly to situations in which their safety is compromised (e.g., campus security).

In some cases, individuals responding to sexual violence reports might benefit from working with police and/or campus security to protect survivors and reduce further risk to members of the campus community. Community-based victim service workers may identify risk indicators, but risk identification processes will generally be enhanced if undertaken in partnership with campus security and/or police. In order to ensure a survivor-centred response, permission should be sought from survivors before consulting with campus security and/or police.

Service Provision and Coordination

One of the most important steps that can be taken as part of a survivor-centred response is ensuring that survivors have timely access to relevant supports. Indeed, although research suggests that survivors may be connected to resources and supports in the process of disclosing and reporting, there may be little coordination among services and responders (Amar et al. 2014; Strout et al. 2014). Any member of a campus community who receives a disclosure of sexual violence should, as soon as possible, offer to connect the survivor with a qualified support person or advocate who has expertise in the area of sexual violence response. A qualified support person or advocate can assist the survivor in dealing with the emotional aftermath of sexual violence, help to identify and address risks and safety needs, and inform the survivor about available options for any next steps (Strout et al. 2014). This step forms part of a coordinated campus response to sexual violence, as an advocate can facilitate access to a wide range of on- and off-campus services from multiple sectors, and support the survivor with whatever options they choose to pursue, while minimizing the number of times the survivor needs to tell their story (ibid.).

Members of the campus community – especially those most likely to respond to disclosures and reports – should be knowledgeable about campus, community, and hospital-based sexual assault response services (Amar et al. 2014). Knowledge about off-campus advocacy and support services will enable first responders to make appropriate referrals and ensure that survivors have access to twenty-four hour supports, especially if campus-based services are only provided during regular office hours. Up-to-date information about hospital-based medical services and Sexual Assault Nurse Examiner (SANE) programs will help to ensure that survivors receive appropriate and timely referrals for health care and forensic medical exams. Referrals to campus- and community-based supports and health services should be provided to survivors regardless of whether they choose to report to the administration or other authorities.

The literature suggests that sexual violence survivors are more likely to use off-campus services than campus-based supports (see Moylan and Javorka 2020). To improve access to specialized services and enhance the coordination of on- and off-campus services, universities / colleges should approach community-based sexual assault response services in their local communities to develop joint protocols for referring survivors to these services (ibid.). Universities / colleges may also consider contracting specialized community-based service providers to deliver sexual assault response services on campus as needed (ibid.). This service delivery model can facilitate access to specialized community-based supports for members of the campus community; eliminate the need for post-secondary institutions to replicate specialized services that are already available in the local community; and strengthen supports so that survivors do not fall through the cracks (ibid.).

Accommodations

In making accommodations to address the varied needs of survivors, every effort should be made to minimize disruption to survivors' studies, employment, and daily routines. Academic and non-academic accommodations should be made for survivors whenever possible, regardless of when they experienced sexual violence (e.g., historical vs recent). What accommodations are beneficial, requested, and / or provided are likely to differ from survivor to survivor. The person(s) and / or department(s) responsible for responding to survivors' requests for accommodations should be clearly identified in campus sexual violence procedures. Survivors should be informed by the institution about the process and timeframe for accommodation requests, and offered support to request accommodations that they feel will increase their safety and support their recovery.

Academic accommodations for survivors who are coping with the impacts of sexual violence while enrolled in a post-secondary institution may include permission to miss class(es) in order to meet with those involved in responding to the incident, to meet with a victim service worker, or to attend counselling appointments (on- or off-campus); assignment extensions or withdrawal from courses without penalty, recognizing the potentially significant impact of sexual violence on a survivor's ability to concentrate and / or process information; and options for completing courses online, if a survivor does not feel safe attending classes in person. Non-academic accommodations may relate to housing, employment, or other forms of financial aid; they may include changing residence or housing, if their accommodation no longer feels safe to them, or being transferred to a different faculty or department, if they have experienced sexual violence within their campus-based workplace. Thoroughly exploring a survivor's unique needs and identifying accommodations to support survivors usually takes time and is better achieved with support.

Although there may be some limitations on the accommodations that a post-secondary institution can provide, universities / colleges are encouraged to be as creative and as flexible as possible within a framework of what could be considered under the control of the institution. For example, a university / college may not refund tuition costs for a student's entire post-secondary program if the survivor withdraws as a result of the impacts of sexual violence; however, it may be able to refund tuition costs for the semester in which the incident occurred or in which the accommodation was requested. Similarly, paying for an international student's flight home to be with family following a sexual assault may be outside of what is possible; however, the institution could provide access to a telephone with long-distance calling for a survivor who could not otherwise afford to speak to family overseas for support. Finally, an institution may not be able to offer unlimited counselling to a survivor, but it may be able to extend the maximum number of counselling sessions available to ensure that a student can continue to access counselling support for the duration of their studies, and even beyond graduation. Any limits to accommodations should be clearly communicated to survivors by university / college administrators, at the earliest possible opportunity, and denial of any requests for accommodation should be communicated in a trauma-informed manner so as not to cause further harm.

Training and Education

Training is a critical component of an effective implementation strategy for sexual violence policies and procedures (Ontario Women's Directorate 2013). Efforts to increase awareness of sexual violence policies and resources are important to facilitate survivors' access to information, including their rights and how to access specialized supports and advocacy. Increasing awareness about policies and options could also increase reporting to the university/college, as students may not be aware of institutional reporting options and mechanisms (Moylan and Javorka 2020; Richards et al. 2017; Spencer et al. 2017). Research also suggests, however, that rape culture itself creates a context where survivors are unlikely to seek support and report sexual violence (Moylan and Javorka 2020; Spencer et al. 2017).

A survivor-centred response to campus sexual violence requires that training and education be made widely available for members of the campus community (Gialopsos 2017; Spencer et al. 2017). Sexual violence prevention initiatives should be delivered campus-wide to reach as many members of the campus community as possible, particularly populations that are at greatest risk of experiencing sexual violence (Gialopsos 2017). Many universities/colleges have implemented consent campaigns in addition to other broad sexual violence prevention programs and initiatives that seek to address rape culture (Monahan-Kreishman and Ingarfield 2018). Other institutions have implemented bystander intervention training programs campus-wide (Amar et al. 2014). Bystander intervention training develops participants' knowledge, skill, and confidence to speak up when they witness gender-based violence, abuse, or hurtful comments and jokes (Public Health England 2016). Bystander programs have been successfully implemented in universities/colleges to address sexual violence, as well as to shift attitudes and social norms about gender-based violence and campus sexual violence (Banyard, Moynihan, and Plante 2007; Palm Reed et al. 2015; Senn et al. 2014). Evidence-based bystander intervention programming can provide members of campus communities with the confidence to speak up and/or take action to address or interrupt sexual violence, thereby contributing to a culture of safety and support (Gialopsos 2017; Gibbons and Evans 2013; Sales and Krause 2017; Universities UK 2016).

The response of a person to whom a survivor of sexual violence discloses can significantly influence how they make sense of, and cope with, what happened to them (see Ullman 2010). Members of campus communities generally receive little, if any, training or education about sexual violence, and many staff and faculty report feeling ill-equipped to respond to disclosures of sexual violence (Ko et al. 2008). Survivor-centred training should therefore be made available to members of the campus community – especially individuals most likely to receive a disclosure, such as student leaders, resident advisors, faculty members, and staff with a responsibility to respond to sexual violence disclosures and reports (Strout, Amar, and Astwood 2014; Moylan and Javorka 2020; Orchowski and Gidycz 2015). Specialized training, tailored to specific members of the campus community, can provide first responders with knowledge about the neurobiological impacts of trauma. This training also teaches the skills needed to offer a trauma-informed, compassionate, and effective response to a disclosure or report of sexual violence (Monahan-Kreishman and Ingarfield 2018; Sales and Krause 2017).

To ensure a survivor-centred approach, all such training and education initiatives to address campus sexual violence should be trauma-informed, intersectional, and developed in collaboration with survivors and/or community-based victim services agencies that support survivors (Krause et al. 2017). Trainers themselves should be experienced in the area of gender-based violence and knowledgeable about evidence-based best practice responses to sexual violence. Additionally, training and education programs should be evaluated and updated regularly to ensure that they reflect the most up-to-date knowledge, research, and best practices, and that they are achieving their stated learning outcomes.

CONCLUSION

A survivor-centred approach provides a solid foundation for preventing and responding to campus sexual violence. In this chapter, we have drawn on research evidence and best practices from the gender-based violence response sector to outline eight critical components of a survivor-centred response to campus sexual violence: (1) the development and implementation of sexual violence policies and procedures; (2) options for disclosing and reporting sexual violence; (3) leadership and inclusion of students and survivors; (4) important considerations related to privacy, confidentiality, and information-sharing; (5) interim protection provisions to support survivor safety; (6) service provision and coordination of on- and off-campus supports; (7) accommodations for survivors; and (8) campus-wide training and education to prevent and respond to sexual violence. By implementing a survivor-centred approach, post-secondary institutions have an opportunity to better support survivors, hold perpetrators accountable, and amplify the efforts of student activists to prevent sexual violence and address rape culture on university campuses.

Recommendations for Future Research

A survivor-centred approach to campus sexual violence is critical; however, we must also recognize that the experiences and needs of survivors vary widely across the campus community. As such, future research on preventing and responding to campus sexual violence must explore the diverse needs of students and survivors, especially those who have been marginalized by intersecting forms of oppression and who face the highest risk of sexual violence. Further research is needed to examine how sexual violence policies are experienced by a wide range of students and survivors, to understand the barriers to disclosing and reporting to university/college administrators, to assess the impacts of various disclosing and reporting options and mechanisms (e.g., mandatory reporting, anonymous reporting) on survivor safety and well-being, and to determine the programs that are most effective in preventing campus sexual violence. Research is also needed to assess the strengths and limitations of various service provision and coordination models to determine the most effective pathways to specialized supports and advocacy for survivors who are members of university/college communities.

Recommendations for Policy

We strongly recommend that universities/colleges work with students and survivors in the development, implementation, and review of stand-alone sexual violence policies and procedures. A survivor-centred approach that honours the experiences of survivors and prioritizes their needs will enhance the overall effectiveness of sexual violence policies, thereby minimizing the negative impacts of sexual violence and supporting survivors' safety and recovery. We recommend that information about sexual violence policies be shared widely throughout the campus community, and that supports be put in place to ensure that survivors who choose to disclose are met with the supports and services that they need and deserve. Resources must be allocated to support the policy implementation process and to ensure that, once such resources are in place, individuals with a responsibility to respond to disclosures and reports have the necessary training and education to do so using a survivor-centred and trauma-informed approach. The ongoing commitment of post-secondary institutions to prevent and respond to campus sexual violence will contribute not only to the well-being of survivors, but also to safer campus communities.

NOTES

1 The guidelines were one of several resources developed as part of the Western Canada Sexual Assault Initiative, funded by Women and Gender Equality Canada and undertaken in partnership with the Alberta Association of Sexual Assault Services (AASAS), Saskatchewan Sexual Assault Services (SSAS), and Klinic Community Services in Manitoba.

2 See Amar, Strout, et al. (2014) for a discussion of the unique insights that campus-based women's centres can offer university administrators, policy-makers, and first responders, based on their unique positioning; see Krause et al. (2017) for a discussion of the unique insights of student activists that can inform research, policy, and programs.

3 The authors acknowledge Gisela Ruebsaat, LL.B., for her legal expertise and contributions to EVA BC's (2016) *Campus Sexual Violence: Guidelines for a Comprehensive Response.*

4 These eight critical components reflect the ten guidelines described in EVA BC's (2016) guidelines; some have been grouped together as an outcome of reflections on our ongoing work with post-secondary institutions across BC.

5 Statistics Canada estimates that only 5 per cent of sexual assaults are reported to police (Conroy and Cotter 2017).

6 Although research suggests that sexual violence policies are regularly posted on university/college websites, information about advocacy and support services, and health and justice options, for sexual assault survivors is often missing from these websites (Moylan and Javorka 2020; Perkins and Warner 2017). Lee and Wong (2017), however, found that most Canadian universities with a sexual assault policy have posted the policy online along with information about support services for survivors.

7 A TPR can also be made through the Alma Mater Society's campus-based Sexual Assault Support Centre (SASC) located at the University of British Columbia, the province's largest post-secondary institution.

8 Third Party Reporting provides police with information about sexual assault perpetration patterns, early identification of trends, and leads on sexual predators. For more information, visit http://endingviolence.org.

9 Lesbian, Gay, Bisexual, Transgender, Two-Spirit, and Queer.

10 See, for example, E V A B C's (2017) *Interagency Case Assessment Teams Best Practices* manual.

REFERENCES

Amar, Angela F., Tania D. Strout, Somatra Simpson, Maria Cardiello, and Sania Beckford. 2014. "Administrators' Perceptions of College Campus Protocols, Response, and Student Prevention Efforts for Sexual Assault." *Violence and Victims* 29 (4): 579.

Banyard, Victoria L., Mary M. Moynihan, and Elizabethe G. Plante. 2007. "Sexual Violence Prevention through Bystander Education: An Experimental Evaluation." *Journal of Community Psychology* 35 (4): 463–81.

B C Centre of Excellence for Women's Health. 2013. *Trauma-Informed Practice Guide.*

Chicago Task Force on Violence against Girls and Young Women. 2012. *Reporting on Rape and Sexual Violence: A Media Toolkit for Local and National Journalists to Better Media Coverage*, edited by Claudia Garcia-Rojas. http://www.chitaskforce.org/wp/wp-content/uploads/2012/10/Chicago-Taskforce-Media-Toolkit.pdf.

Cleary, Michelle, and Catherine Hungerford. 2015. "Trauma-Informed Care and the Research Literature: How Can the Mental Health Nurse Take the Lead to Support Women Who Have Survived Sexual Assault?" *Issues in Mental Health Nursing* 36 (5): 370–8.

Coates, Linda, Janet Beavin Bavelas, and James Gibson. 1994. "Anomalous Language in Sexual Assault Trial Judgments." *Discourse and Society* 5 (2): 189–206.

Coates, Linda, and Allan Wade. 2004. "Telling It Like It Isn't: Obscuring Perpetrator Responsibility for Violent Crime." *Discourse and Society* 15 (5): 499–526.

Colleges Ontario. 2015. *Sexual Assault and Sexual Violence Policy and Protocol Template.* http://campusmentalhealth.ca/wp-content/uploads/2018/03/CO_Sexual-Violence-PP-template_March-2015.pdf.

Community Coordination for Women's Safety, Ending Violence Association of B C. 2014. *Third Party Reporting of Sexual Assault.* http://endingviolence.org/third-party-reporting-sexual-assault/.

– 2015. *Third Party Reporting Guidebook 2.0: Increasing Reporting Options for Sexual Assault Survivors.* http://endingviolence.org/wp-content/uploads/2019/10/TPR-Guidebook-2.0-July-2019.pdf.

Conroy, Shana, and Adam Cotter. 2017. "Self-Reported Sexual Assault in Canada, 2014." *Juristat: Canadian Centre for Justice Statistics*: 1–34. https://www150.statcan.gc.ca/n1/en/pub/85-002-x/2017001/article/14842-eng.pdf?st=dD1hRsRJ.

Du Mont, Janice, Sheila Macdonald, Meghan White, and Linda Turner. 2013. "Male Victims of Adult Sexual Assault: A Descriptive Study of Survivors' Use of Sexual Assault Treatment Services." *Journal of Interpersonal Violence* 28 (13): 2676–94.

Elliott, Denise E., Paula Bjelajac, Roger D. Fallot, Laurie S. Markoff, and Beth Glover Reed. 2005. "Trauma-Informed or Trauma-Denied: Principles and Implementation of Trauma-Informed Services for Women." *Journal of Community Psychology* 33 (4): 461–77.

Ending Violence Association of BC. 2016. *Campus Sexual Violence: Guidelines for a Comprehensive Response.* http://endingviolence.org/wp-content/uploads/2016/05/EVABC_CampusSexualViolence Guidelines_vF.pdf.

– 2017. *Interagency Case Assessment Team Best Practices: Working Together to Reduce the Risk of Domestic Violence.*

Femifesto and Collaborators. 2015. *Use the Right Words: Media Reporting on Sexual Violence in Canada.* https://www.femifesto.ca/wp-content/uploads/2015/12/UseTheRightWords-Single-Dec3.pdf.

FORGE. 2012. *Transgender Rates of Violence: Victim Service Providers' Fact Sheet #6.* http://forge-forward.org/wp-content/docs/FAQ-10-2012-rates-of-violence.pdf.

Gialopsos, Brooke Miller. 2017. "Sexual Violence in Academia: Policy, Theory, and Prevention Considerations." *Journal of School Violence* 16 (2): 141–7.

Gibbons, Roberta E., and Julie Evans. 2013. *The Evaluation of Campus-Based Gender Violence Prevention Programming: What We Know about Program Effectiveness and Implications for Practitioners.* https://vawnet.org/sites/default/files/materials/files/2016-09/AR_EvaluationCampusProgramming.pdf.

Gilfus, Mary E., Susan Fineran, Deborah J. Cohan, Susan A. Jensen, Lisa Hartwick, and Robin Spath. 1999. "Research on Violence against Women: Creating Survivor-Informed Collaborations." *Violence against Women* 5 (10): 1194–212.

Harris, Maxine, and Roger D. Fallot. 2001. *Using Trauma Theory to Design Service Systems.* San Francisco: Jossey-Bass.

Jauk, Daniela. 2013. "Gender Violence Revisited: Lessons from Violent Victimization of Transgender Identified Individuals." *Sexualities* 16 (7): 807–25.

Klinic Community Health Centre. 2013. *Trauma-Informed: The Trauma Toolkit.* 2nd ed. https://trauma-informed.ca/wp-content/uploads/2013/10/Trauma-informed_Toolkit.pdf.

Ko, Susan J., Julian D. Ford, Nancy Kassam-Adams, Steven J. Berkowitz, Charles Wilson, Marleen Wong, Melissa J. Brymer, and Christopher M. Layne. 2008. "Creating Trauma-Informed Systems: Child Welfare, Education, First Responders, Health Care, Juvenile Justice." *Professional Psychology: Research and Practice* 39 (4): 396–404.

Krause, Kathleen H., Stephanie S. Miedema, Rebecca Woofter, and Kathryn M. Yount. 2017. "Feminist Research with Student Activists: Enhancing Campus Sexual Assault Research." *Family Relations* 66 (1): 211–23.

Lee, Chelsey, and Jennifer S. Wong. 2017. "A Safe Place to Learn? Examining Sexual Assault Policies at Canadian Public Universities" *Studies in Higher Education* 44 (3): 432–45.

Lichty, Lauren F., Rebecca Campbell, and Jayne Schuiteman. 2008. "Developing a University-Wide Institutional Response to Sexual Assault and Relationship Violence." *Journal of Prevention and Intervention in the Community* 36 (1–2): 5–22.

Mancini, Christina, Justin T. Pickett, Corey Call, Robyn Diehl McDougle, Sarah Jane Brubaker, and Henry H. Brownstein. 2017. "Sexual Assault in the Ivory Tower: Public Opinion on University Accountability and Mandatory Reporting." *Sexual Abuse* 31 (3): 344–65.

METRAC. 2014. *Sexual Assault Policies on Campus: A Discussion Paper.* http://www.metrac.org/wp-content/uploads/2014/11/final.formatted. campus.discussion.paper_.26sept14.pdf.

Monahan-Kreishman, Mollie and Lisa Ingarfield. 2018. "Creating Campus Communities of Care: Supporting Sexual Violence Survivors." *New Directions for Student Services* 2018 (161): 71–81. https://onlinelibrary. wiley.com/action/doSearch?AllField=Monahan%E2%80%90Kreishman &SeriesKey=15360695.

Moylan, Carrie A., and McKenzie Javorka. 2020. "Widening the Lens: An Ecological Review of Campus Sexual Assault." *Trauma, Violence, and Abuse* 21 (1): 179–92.

Ontario Women's Directorate. 2013. *Developing a Response to Sexual Violence: A Resource Guide for Ontario's Colleges and Universities.* http://www.citizenship.gov.on.ca/owd/english/ending-violence/campus_ guide.shtml.

Orchowski, Lindsay M., and Christine A. Gidycz. 2015. "Psychological Consequences Associated with Positive and Negative Responses to Disclosure of Sexual Assault among College Women: A Prospective Study." *Violence Against Women* 21 (7): 803–23.

Our Turn. 2017. *Our Turn: A National, Student-Led Action Plan to End Campus Sexual Violence.* https://ssmu.ca/wp-content/uploads/2017/10/our_turn_action_plan_final_english_web.pdf?x26516.

Palm Reed, Kathleen M., Denise A. Hines, Jessica L. Armstrong, and Amy Y. Cameron. 2015. "Experimental Evaluation of a Bystander Prevention Program for Sexual Assault and Dating Violence." *Psychology of Violence* 5 (1): 95–102.

Perkins, Wendy, and Jessica Warner. 2017. "Sexual Violence Response and Prevention: Studies of Campus Policies and Practices." *Journal of School Violence* 16 (3): 237–42.

Potter, Sharyn, Rebecca Howard, Sharon Murphy, and Mary M. Moynihan. 2018. "Long-Term Impacts of College Sexual Assaults on Women Survivors' Educational and Career Attainments." *Journal of American College Health* 66 (6): 1–12.

Public Health England. 2016. "A Review of Evidence for Bystander Intervention to Prevent Sexual and Domestic Violence in Universities." Report prepared for Public Health England (Wellington House, London UK). https://assets.publishing.service.gov.uk/government/uploads/system/uploads/attachment_data/file/515634/Evidence_review_bystander_intervention_to_prevent_sexual_and_domestic_violence_in_universities_11April2016.pdf.

Richards, Tara N., Kathryn A. Branch, Ruth E. Fleury-Steiner, and Katherine Kafonek. 2017. "A Feminist Analysis of Campus Sexual Assault Policies: Results from a National Sample." *Family Relations* 66 (1): 104–15.

Rotenberg, Cristine. 2017. "Police-Reported Sexual Assaults in Canada, 2009 to 2014: A Statistical Profile." *Juristat: Canadian Centre for Justice Statistics.* https://www150.statcan.gc.ca/n1/en/pub/85-002-x/2017001/article/54866-eng.pdf?st=jsdQGJqD.

Royal College of Nursing. 2008. *Informed Gender Practice: Mental Health Acute Care that Works for Women.* National Institute for Mental Health in England. https://webarchive.nationalarchives.gov.uk/20110512085546/http://www.nmhdu.org.uk/silo/files/informedgenderpractice.pdf.

Sales, Jessica, and Kathleen Krause. 2017. "Schools Must Include Faculty and Staff in Sexual Violence Prevention Efforts." *Journal of American College Health* 65 (8): 585–7.

Senn, Charlene Y., Misha Eliasziw, Paula C. Barata, Wilfreda E. Thurston, Ian R. Newby-Clark, H. Lorraine Radtke, and Karen L. Hobden. 2014. "Sexual Violence in the Lives of First-Year University Women in Canada: No Improvements in the 21st Century." *BMC Women's Health* 14 (1): 135.

Sharp, Elizabeth A., Shannon E. Weaver, and Anisa Zvonkovic. 2017. "Introduction to the Special Issue: Feminist Framings of Sexual Violence on College Campuses." *Family Relations* 66 (1): 7–16.

Smith, Carly Parnitzke, and Jennifer J. Freyd. 2013. "Dangerous Safe Havens: Institutional Betrayal Exacerbates Sexual Trauma." *Journal of Traumatic Stress* 26 (1): 119–24.

Spencer, Chelsea, Allen Mallory, Michelle Toews, Sandra Stith, and Leila Wood. 2017. "Why Sexual Assault Survivors Do Not Report to Universities: A Feminist Analysis." *Family Relations* 66 (1): 166–79.

Strout, Tania, Angela Frederick Amar, and Krystal Astwood. 2014. "Women's Centre Staff Perceptions of the Campus Climate on Sexual Violence." *Journal of Forensic Nursing* 10 (3): 135–43.

The Student Room. 2018. *Sexual Violence at Universities Statistical Report*. Revolt Sexual Assault. https://revoltsexualassault.com/wp-content/uploads/2018/03/Report-Sexual-Violence-at-University-Revolt-Sexual-Assault-The-Student-Room-March-2018.pdf.

Ullman, Sarah E. 2010. *Talking about Sexual Assault: Society's Response to Survivors*. Washington, DC: American Psychological Association.

Universities UK. 2016. "Changing the Culture: Report of the Universities UK Taskforce Examining Violence against Women, Harassment and Hate Crime Affecting University Students." London: UUK. https://www.universitiesuk.ac.uk/policy-and-analysis/reports/Documents/2016/changing-the-culture.pdf.

Weiss, Karen G., and Nicole V. Lasky. 2017. "Mandatory Reporting of Sexual Misconduct at College: A Critical Perspective." *Journal of School Violence* 16 (3): 259–70.

White House Task Force to Protect Students from Sexual Assault. 2014. *Checklist for Campus Sexual Misconduct Policies*. https://www.justice.gov/archives/ovw/page/file/910271/download.

2

"There Is a Crack in Everything/ That's How the Light Gets In"

Reflections on Selected Arts Interventions Used to Bring Awareness to Sexual Violence at McGill University

Chloe Krystyna Garcia, Mindy R. Carter, Milka Nyariro, Maria Ezcurra, Lori Beavis, and Claudia Mitchell

INTRODUCTION

University campuses are major locations for gendered and sexual violence, which can take different forms, from sexist frosh chants, to catcalling and sexual harassment, to rape (Buchwald, Fletcher, and Roth 2005; Jozkowski 2015). Numerous survivor-activists and news media have drawn attention to the barriers to reporting sexual violence at universities, as this book discusses elsewhere. With mounting pressure to develop new sexual assault policies and to support their students, many post-secondary institutions turn to policy and education reform as potential solutions to the problem of campus-based sexual and gendered violence (Chiose 2016; Quinlan et al. 2017). Yet, finding practical ways to educate faculty, students, staff, parents, and administrators about what "the problem" is, and to best prevent or address issues related to sexual violence once they arise, is a multifaceted issue, sometimes contentious and rife with challenges. Given the documented abilities of the arts to foster new, creative, socio-emotional and socially engaged responses to societal issues (Carter 2017; Low, Carter, Wood, Mitchell, Proietti, and Friedmann 2016), we believe that arts interventions are key players in the fight against rape culture, and merit attention as policy-makers and educators pursue reforms.

We are a new arts-based research team[1] working on a recently obtained seven-year Partnership Grant on sexual violence. Our research situates the arts as a key site for addressing and dismantling rape culture, alongside policy, social media, news media, popular culture, and education. As we engaged with our colleagues from different fields (including legal, media, education, feminist, and dentistry scholars) in conversations about the possibilities of campus-based and cultural reforms, we found ourselves advocating for arts interventions as imaginative, transformative tools (Carter 2015) to address some of the current challenges that universities face regarding raising awareness about sexual violence and dismantling institutional systems that support rape culture.

In this chapter we briefly address how the arts have been used in different areas related to sexual violence, including research, education, therapy, and activism, within a North American context. We highlight four key roles of arts interventions in combatting rape culture and supporting survivors that stand out in the literature and our own experiences: healing, educating, protesting, and community-building. We then turn to practical examples of arts interventions in which we participated or that we organized, and we reflect on their roles in addressing issues of sexual violence in both the university and wider communities. We have chosen to limit our research to examples of arts-based interventions at McGill University because these examples show the range of forms and functions that arts interventions around sexual violence on campuses can take and have taken. Finally, we imagine ways that art can move campus reforms forward. We hope to inspire university leaders interested in dismantling rape culture at their universities to recognize the benefits of sexual violence-related art interventions in empowering survivors, raising awareness about the complexity of sexual and gendered violence, bringing together communities, and drawing attention to potential solutions for change.

Arts-Based Interventions and Sexual Violence

Feminist and activist movements in the twentieth century played a pivotal role in drawing attention to the prevalence and harmful impact of sexual and gendered violence, and expanding legal definitions of rape (Freedman 2013). During this time, art increasingly became a means through which survivors and feminists could speak out against sexual violence. Various artists brought attention to the ways that women experienced violence, sexism, and colonialism. For example, Kathe Kollwitz showed the vulnerability of an assaulted woman in her etching "Raped" (1907), while Yoko Ono's performance "Cut Piece" (1965) depicted the relationship between art and female bodies, as her clothes were cut off by audience members. Anishinaabe performance artist Rebecca Belmore has produced works, such as "Vigil" (2002) and "Fringe" (2008), that examine and respond to the violence that has been perpetuated against Indigenous women in Canada.

Contemporary artists and activists continue to use art to express themselves. Whereas different forms of popular media (e.g., music, movies, and video games) condone and normalize sexual and gendered violence (Ferreday 2015; Phillips 2017), these works of art often emerge as cracks in the system, drawing attention to the personal and social harms of a rape culture. The Ontario Arts Council (2017, para. 2) expresses the importance of art for the community and as means for social change: "Art shapes people's perspectives and opinions. When applied to social justice, artists' works offer a critical perspective that informs, provokes, and holds a mirror to society. Engaging with this kind of art can help equip the public with tools to understand and challenge social injustices, and to imagine a better future."

Arts-based visual and participatory methodologies offer inclusive, emancipatory, and empowering elements to research with vulnerable and disenfranchised groups that have ordinarily been excluded by positivist and elitist research methods (Johnson, Pfister, and Vindrola-Padros 2012; Boog 2003). Some types of arts-based methodologies that have been employed in researching sexual violence and rape cultures include drawing, photography, film, mosaic, collage, dance, drama, painting, music, sculpture, singing, theatre, and writing, among other possibilities. Candice Lys and her colleagues (2016, 2) argue that arts-based methodologies are "rooted in social justice and control over the production and dissemination of knowledge, and have been associated with increases in the feeling of empowerment, especially around sexual health decision-making." The literature shows that these methodologies effectively alter some of the typical power dynamics related to the researched/researcher, and ensure spaces for marginalized populations such as survivors of sexual violence and rape cultures to speak about the issues and then "speak back" (Mitchell, De Lange, and Moletsane 2017a). In many cases, the products of the arts-based methodologies, such as photo exhibitions and video screenings, are accessible to wider audiences, including community groups, community leaders, university administrators, and policy-makers (Mitchell and De Lange 2011). Through visual detail and context, arts-based visual and participatory approaches show why and how the study of one can resonate with the lives of many, mirroring the issues facing a group in a particular community. Arts-based visual and participatory approaches foster reflexivity among participants, just as they do with their audiences (Weber 2014).

The benefits and uses of the arts within research transcend this context as well. Within our work, we use "interventions" as an umbrella term for the ways that activists, survivors, educators, therapists, and other stakeholders in sexual violence use artistic modes of expression – such as theatre, photography, art installations, and more – to support survivors, share experiences, and call attention to rape culture. The next four sections briefly address what we determine to be the key roles that art interventions play in addressing rape culture and supporting survivors. We highlight separately the ways in which art contributes to healing, educating, protesting, and creating stronger and healthier communities; yet we urge readers to keep in mind how the roles of art interventions intersect in many respects.

Art as Healing

In therapeutic interventions, the arts and art therapies involve "the utilization of artistic modalities for the promotion of psychological, physical, and spiritual wellbeing" (Zuch 2015, 4). For survivors, the arts offer non-verbal tools of expression that might enable them to express feelings that they otherwise would not be able to voice (Eisner 1995; Murray, Moore, Stickl, and Crowe 2017). Kazmiervzak (2017) states that "nonverbal modalities are valued in therapy on the premise that some content, such as embodied feelings and unconscious beliefs, can be evoked and better expressed through images than with language alone" (349). Art also enables individuals to tease out and process difficult emotions. Marshall (2014) writes about a student who drew an image symbolizing her rape by her stepfather, and in her process of healing, went on to share her art to ensure that others did not feel alone. Art can sometimes offer cathartic moments as it provides survivors with a space to communicate feelings and share the process of healing with others (Kazmierczak 2017). Moreover, art offers survivors opportunities to focus on self-care, providing the space and tools for survivors to spend time on themselves, work through their trauma, and develop a sense of pride as they create their piece (Murray et al. 2017). For many survivors, their histories of abuse and trauma might have left them feeling vulnerable or like they do not matter, whereas art interventions can "grant them permission to prioritize and value themselves" (194). Finally, through art survivors may reduce feelings of isolation by connecting with others.

Art as Educational

Art is an effective educational tool that can inform both the observer and the artist (Darts 2006; Dewey 2005; Freedman 2013). According to Dewey, the purpose of art is "to break through the conventionalized and routine consciousness" (as cited by Weber 2014, 184). Weber (2014) calls attention to the ways that imagery and performances both reflect the viewpoints of the producers and inspire new interpretations from audiences. Art has the capacity to "draw attention to the importance of the everyday by making it strange or casting it in a new light" (ibid., 9). Notably, artistic interventions offer creative opportunities for individuals affected by sexual violence who may not be given a voice otherwise, such as women, Indigenous and racialized individuals, and LGBTQ communities. As Kazmiervzak (2017) notes, "The push for understanding educational processes, including art education, as emancipatory forces for oppressed, colonized, and marginalized groups and for exploited ecosystems makes art-based programs and interventions more relevant than ever" (341). The expressive and communicative nature of art further provides people with opportunities to explore emotions in an interactive atmosphere. For example, theatre productions can be a form of inspiration for audiences to think about situations and characters whom they would otherwise be unable to imagine. In this way, theatre-based programming is an increasingly popular form of teaching about consent and bystander education (Black, Weisz, Coats, and Patterson 2000; Christensen 2013, 2015; Kress, Shepherd, Anderson, Petuch, Nolan, and Thiemeke 2006; Mitchell and Freitag 2011). Moreover, artistic interventions have been used as means to garner empathy from male audiences and to deepen their understandings of the complex issue of sexual violence against women (Christensen 2015; Walsh 2015).

Art as Protest

Beyond a capacity to heal and educate, art can serve as a medium of protest and resistance, drawing public attention to personal and social problems (Lewis, Marine, and Kenney 2016; Weber 2014). Historically, feminist activists and survivors have used different types of art and platforms, such as public spaces, art galleries, and social media, to draw attention to social inequities and failures of the system. Lewis and Marine (2015, 132–3) write that "contemporary young feminists are not the first to use art, craft, parody, and performance to mock patriarchy and convey their alternative message; there is a history of such activities based on women's traditional arts and crafts that can be woven into our tapestry." Art pieces, installations, and performances are powerful ways to reflect perspectives otherwise ignored by politicians, institutional leaders, and media. For example, in Canada, the works of Indigenous artists such as Rebecca Belmore's "Fringe" (2008) and Christi Belcourt's "Walking with Our Sisters" (2012) have shed light on the country's colonialist and patriarchal histories, which have served to oppress, silence, and control Indigenous women's voices and bodies.

Art activism also means strategically using artistic modes of expression, from visual work to performative pieces, to move communities into action. For instance, Guerrilla Girls Broadband, an activist group that has used street art and posters to protest sexual violence, "use well-crafted humor and intelligence to create positive calls to action that will hopefully make a tough topic more approachable, lower an audience's hostile defenses, drive a salient point and be a cathartic tool for survivors" (Majkut n.d). In many ways, debates around rape culture and university responses have emerged from the art interventions across the US and Canada. To name a few, in 2015, Emma Sulkowitz's performance "Mattress Performance (Carry That Weight)," which symbolized her protest against her university's failure to expel her rapist, brought media attention to the mishandling of sexual assault and rape cases in universities (Gambino 2015). In 2016, a shipping container featuring art pieces by survivors began its journey across Ontario to bring attention to how sexual violence pervades universities and other contexts (Sandals 2016). Referring to the bureaucratic maze of university policy-making and the potential of art in protest and activism, art curator Heather Zises notes, "The role of art in political protest is effective because it attracts public attention in a more democratic way" (Majkut n.d.). Art activism communicates political messages through evocative and meaningful channels that can appeal to wider audiences.

Art to Build Community and Culture

Through education, protest, and healing, the arts can ultimately contribute to the development of stronger communities. Several scholars have reported benefits for artists and their audiences when art was shared with others, such as bringing people together, creating dialogue, inspiring empathy among the public, and empowering artists (Murray et al. 2017; Weber 2014; Zuch 2015). Lewis and her colleagues (2016) write that, for women, "in an environment of everyday sexism, finding a community is reassuring, affirming, and empowering" (11). For survivors of sexual violence, communities where they feel supported and heard are important, particularly when living in a rape culture (Rios 2014). Creating and sharing their art through venues or online can help survivors gain access to, and communicate with, different communities and audiences. The "Monument Quilt" (2013) consists of a powerful example of art as community-building. The art piece now features over 1,000 quilt squares with stories of sexual violence; it will eventually sport a total of 6,000 squares at its final display, spelling out the words "Not Alone" (themonumentquilt.org). By reaching out to wide audiences and calling attention to the ways that today's societies doubt, shame, and ignore survivors of sexual violence, art bears the potential to be culture-changing. The organization in charge of the Monument Quilt have spoken to this effect, suggesting that "the quilt builds a new culture where survivors are publicly supported, rather than publicly shamed" (ibid.). With their wide physical and online reach, art-based campaigns play a crucial role in dismantling harmful rape myths and highlighting the complexity of sexual violence (Branitsky 2015). As popular media continue to misrepresent sexual violence as sexy, art interventions offer important, alternative platforms through which artists can challenge such hegemonic messages and raise public consciousness.

CURRENT CONTEXT

At McGill University, where our Partnership Grant team is located and our research is grounded, the institution has undergone several rounds of policy proposals and recently put into place its final version.[2] As discussed, several arts interventions by activists, student organizations, and service units have taken place concurrent to these processes. Although arts interventions have not garnered the same attention from administrative leaders and media as the policy-making process, we suggest they have had a positive role on campus and within the larger community. These interventions highlighted the need for policy reform and social change, the need for helping survivors, and the need for engaging the community in discussions about sexual violence.[3] The interventions have been either partly or fully focused on creating awareness of sexual violence and/or rape culture on university campuses, in order to resist violence. The interventions vary in form, including visual arts exhibitions, a play, and an arts-based research project. Sub-themes of these projects are "Women and Violence" and "Voice and Remembrance," which serve to categorize these exemplars. In the next few sections, we describe these artworks and address their roles in healing, educating, protesting, and community-building. We later bring these examples together with the literature to propose that university stakeholders seeking to address campus sexual violence consider the potential of arts interventions.

WOMEN AND VIOLENCE

"Seeing How it Works: Participatory Visual Research and Transformation in Addressing Sexual Violence": A Travelling Exhibition

The exhibition "Seeing How it Works: Participatory Visual Research and Transformation in Addressing Sexual Violence"[4] was presented in McGill's Coach House in 2017 as a part of a study called Networks for Change and Well-being: Girl-Led from the Ground Up Policy Making to Address Sexual Violence in Canada and South Africa.[5] The study as a whole focuses on work with Indigenous girls and young women in the two countries in question. The specific project, Girls Leading Change, is located within a university-based field site in South Africa. As described in more detail elsewhere (De Lange, Mitchell, and Moletsane 2015b; Mitchell, De Lange, and Moletsane 2017a; Mitchell, Claudia, DeLange, and Molestane 2017b; De Lange, Mitchell, and Moletsane 2015a; Mitchell and Freitag 2011), this travelling exhibition is based on participatory visual research with fourteen young women, all first-year Education students, at Nelson Mandela University in South Africa. As part of Girls Leading Change, the young women took photographs and created captions to represent the challenges they saw in the residences and in relation to campus security more broadly. They also engaged in Cellphilming (a participatory visual method involving cellphones to produce videos) to explore issues of safety and security. Out of this visual work, the young women also produced policy posters and action briefs. As visually documented in the exhibition, the fourteen young women used these policy posters and action briefs in meetings that they convened with university deans, residence coordinators, and other university administrators. The cellphilms, policy posters, and action briefs acted as tools of activism and policy engagement on addressing sexual violence on campus. While the research team provided material support to the young women in the production of the posters and offered initial assistance in setting up meetings, it was the young women themselves who led the intervention.

In this way, these women gave visibility to the challenges they face on campus in South Africa. For example, they did not feel safe in dark and unlit places on campus. They feared the security guards, the very people who were supposed to offer protection. However, through pictures in the exhibition, they highlighted some of the changes that came about as a result of their meetings with the various administrators noted above. New lighting was added to parts of the campus. The travelling exhibition, which has been shown on universities campuses across South Africa, Sweden, and other parts of Canada (including McGill), offers audiences the opportunity to "see how it [a participatory visual arts-based approach] works," with the focus being on the nature of such an intervention. Through the sharing of this exhibition at McGill University, students, faculty, and staff had the opportunity to view the images and share their comments about this work via written feedback. Thus, the "seeing how it works" exhibition, while begun outside the Canadian context, reflects the potential of art interventions to situate sexual violence as a problem on university communities within a global context. It opens dialogue about not only the potential of art as a tool for protest and education, but as a means to bridge gaps between students and higher administration, by merging administrative and policy work with artistic interventions by young women.

"Sing the Brave Song: This Isn't Over," was described in a review as "a research-based play, written and directed by Alayna Kolodziechuk, that explores some of the lesser known current and historical experiences of Aboriginal peoples in Canada using video montages, residential school and newspaper first-hand accounts, pre-service teacher candidate interviews, and dance" (Carter and Mreiwed 2017). Inspired by the Truth and Reconciliation Commission, "Sing the Brave Song" addresses, among other things, the scale and severity of the violence that Indigenous women and girls in Canada face. It was performed at a McGill campus theatre as a way to foster conversation about the experiences of Aboriginal people in Canada and how education can play a role in shifting some of their realities. A talk-back session after each performance brought up issues related to the sexual violence and rape that some Canadian Aboriginal women have experienced. This play fostered deepened awareness of the experiences of women who had disappeared from locations in Canada that were close to where many of the audience members had lived. As audiences encountered these Indigenous voices and experiences, their reactions spoke to the affective and potentially transformative impacts of they play. Post-performance conversations that began with responses to the play also ignited dialogue led by female students, who expressed not feeling safe in certain places on campus and asked whose responsibility it was/is to change this.

Conversations such as these indicate how arts can provide a space for discussions on campus that may not normally take place. Since this production was a part of a larger research project, the comments were recorded and will be researched, with findings shared with relevant stakeholders. Unexpectedly, the feedback about McGill student experiences on campus has led this research team to seek relevant on-campus avenues to share the findings, such as with the on-campus sexual assault centre.

VOICE AND REMEMBRANCE

"Fire with Water"

The Sexual Assault Centre of the McGill Students' Society[6] (SACOMSS) has been committed for years to creating awareness about gender-based violence, supporting survivors of sexual assault through many initiatives, including the ongoing Sexual Assault Awareness Week. This event hosts workshops, an open library, speakers, and information sessions to raise awareness around sexual assault at McGill and other close communities. It culminates with an annual exhibit and performance evening, called *Fire with Water*. Its purpose is to create a safe space to share experiences and artistic responses to sexual violence, gender-based violence, survivorship, and their intersecting themes. It is a free event and open to everyone, presented at different art galleries in Montreal. The first exhibit was held in 1997, and it has been happening almost annually since then. Several easily identifiable volunteers trained in active listening are always present at the event in case anyone needs support. The presented artwork is varied between mediums, and the performances usually include poets and authors reading their work, as well as musicians performing original compositions. Anyone is free to submit art or to perform (not just McGill students). The event is publicized via social media, posters, and announcements on campus, and there is also an annual zine/program with the artworks and pieces being performed.

The works and the event itself offers audiences spaces and opportunities for dialogue and emotions as they experience the art. However, as one of the organizers has recently commented,[7] the feelings expressed come from a place of catharsis and positivity, and one gets a sense of solidarity between artists and audiences. They noted that artists typically come back year after year. The event offers opportunities for survivors to talk about their experiences, with the artists working through them in their pieces or performances, and also the chance for community healing, as attendees are brought together and become aware that they are not alone.

"Altar for the Day of the Dead: To Honour the Lives of the Missing and Murdered Indigenous Women and Girls in Canada"

To celebrate the Mexican Day of the Dead (Día de Muertos) and to honour the lives of the Missing and Murdered Indigenous Women and Girls in Canada, an altar (*ofrenda*) was installed in McGill's Faculty of Education in the first week of November 2016.[8] The Day of the Dead (Día de Muertos) is a festive and sacred time in Mexico and other Latin American countries. This day, the souls of the dead are welcomed back, joined with the living, and occasion a celebration of life. The altar was created by a group of women artists who wanted to offer this *ofrenda* to the hundreds of Indigenous women and girls who have been murdered in Canada, as well as to the worrying rise of gender-based violence and femicides[9] (the killing of women for

2.1 *Fire with Water* zines

being women) in the Americas and worldwide over the past decades. It was intended to promote awareness of this issue, creating a space for dialogue and bringing the community of McGill together. Once the Dia de los Muertos/Day of the Dead installation was complete, the group of women who made the work and installed the exhibition did a smudge (a cleansing with sage) amongst ourselves. Students, staff, faculty, and the community of McGill at large were invited to

SACOMSS presents

FIRE WITH WATER

The Annual Art Show of the The Sexual Assault Centre of McGill Students' Society

A group exhibition of artwork concerning the themes of **sexual assault** and gender-based violence.

April 2006
Vernissage: Thursday, April 6th
7:00 to 9:00 pm

Café Shaika/Galerie V
5526 Sherbrooke Street West
(24 bus Sherbrooke West from Vendome Metro to Decarie)

2.2 *Fire with Water* zines

collaborate in this initiative by joining the artists to make "punched" paper, *Cempasuchil* flowers, and many more traditional elements for the *ofrenda*, or bringing food or flowers for the women and girls in remembered and honoured in the altar.

The "Altar for the Day of the Dead" provided opportunities for reflection and support to the group of women who made the work and installed the exhibition, and their publics. Moreover, people seemed to

fire with water art exhibit & zine

call for submissions

fire with water is a group exhibition displaying responses and resistance to sexual violence and intersecting themes -- including, but not limited to -- sexuality, gender, race, class, and ability. we invite artistic expressions of any kind: writing, performance, photography, painting, installation, spoken word, and beyond.

to submit, please e-mail **sacomss.firewithwater@gmail.com**
deadline: march 15 2010

organized by the sexual assault centre of mcgill students' society (sacomss.org) helpline : 514-398-8500

2.3 *Fire with Water* zines

be very interested in and sympathetic to their intention to raise awareness and introduce new knowledge and material culture into a space that is so often merely seen as a path that allows people to get from one part of the building to another. The piece fostered conversations about the issue of violence against Indigenous people, including sexual violence, and was a particularly useful tool to educate visitors who were not familiar with this part of North American history.

2.4 *Altar for the Day of the Dead: To Honour the Lives of the Missing and Murdered Indigenous Women and Girls in Canada*

DISCUSSION

The numerous benefits of arts make them excellent tools to prompt social change and reform in the current North American context. As explored within other chapters of this book, Canadian and US post-secondary institutions are undergoing policy and educational reform. In the wake of protests by survivor-activists, among others, over problematic institutional processes and lack of accountability in response to sexual assault and rape cases, several administrative leaders, policy-makers, governments, and scholars are turning to legal frameworks and policy for solutions to sexual violence, through regulations such as the Title IX legislation in the US and recent mandates by Canadian provinces (Sheehy and Gilbert 2015).[10] The responses to university policies and legislation have been varied. Many policy critiques have revolved around the ways survivors and perpetrators are treated through the administration's handling of sexual assault cases (Gerson and Gerson 2016), and some scholars have even debated the extent of the university's role in treating these cases (Shaw 2015).

Moreover, programs and campaigns offering slogans and basic education around consent have been subjected to criticism as well, for
oversimplifying the complex intersections of consent, gender, and
sexuality, and for failing to reflect the realities of today's youth
(Jozkowski 2015; Shaw 2015). Finally, as expressed by Amanda
Nelund in this volume: "although universities had an opportunity to
do justice differently through their policies, they are currently replicating many of the shortcomings of both criminal justice and alternative
justice forms without mirroring their benefits" (223).

In spite of policy reforms evolving over numerous decades within
universities, rape culture in universities is alive and well. We find that
the difficulties universities face in addressing rape culture emerge
largely from their positions as sites of rape culture. Complex structures
of hierarchy and power dynamics, institutional sexism, and misogynist
campus climates make universities problematic sites of sexual and
gendered violence (Jozkowski 2015; Lewis, Marine, and Kenney 2016;
Marshall et al. 2014). This contributes to the difficulties they encounter
in policy and education reform, for even the better survivor-oriented
policies and sex-positive messages spread across campuses will not
reach their full potential unless the very culture and structures of
universities are challenged and changed.

We believe that the persistence of sexual violence in universities in
spite of policy reform suggests that we need to turn to more transformative potential solutions. We feel that in order to move away from
the reproduction of previous inadequate reforms we need to tap into
our collective creativity and imagination. For Greene, in "Releasing
the Imagination" (1995), "Often, imagination can bring the severed
parts together ... can integrate wholes" (38). In artistic interventions,
we find routes to release imagination, to connect with each other, to
take risks and creatively engage in social justice advocacy.

From the literature and examples provided in this chapter, we can
see that for victims of sexual violence and their communities, artistic
modes of expression provide new ways of becoming whole; of learning
about respect, forgiveness, justice, responsibility; and of developing
an openness to growth and change. Works of art, as forms of protest,
play important roles in reminding universities of the ways that they
can improve their treatment of survivors and other vulnerable groups.
We observed from the "Seeing How it Works" project how art raises
awareness and can make change when brought to the attention of
university leaders and communities. Art acts as an effective tool to

break free from the privileging of certain voices within the university, offering spaces where vulnerable and often silenced student populations, such as survivors and Indigenous people, have the opportunity to express themselves. For effective reforms in our campus cultures, these voices need to acknowledged, heard, and brought into conversation. The increased visibility of cultures and their experiences with sexual violence through artistic interventions, such as the "Altar for the Day of the Dead" and "Sing the Brave Song," also provide meaningful opportunities to open the minds of university community members who might otherwise not be aware of the ways that sexual violence affects different populations, and to inform policy-makers at the university of the ways in which some of their students experience rape culture. For example, plays such as "Sing the Brave Song," where we learnt that students felt unsafe in certain parts of campus, can provide new ways of discovering solutions to campus rape culture and to address the fears and concerns of women. The creation of survivor spaces in events like "Fire with Water" also shed light on the value of safe spaces for communities to talk about violence and heal.

In these ways, art has the capacity to move culture in ways that policy cannot – at least not on its own. Yet, in our experience, we find that artistic interventions occupy little space in conversations about campus reform, within the media and amongst university leaders. Many of the artistic interventions discussed within this chapter were spearheaded by survivors, activists, students, and researchers. Moving forward, we suggest that policy-makers and administrative leaders consider the value of artistic interventions when discussing campus reform, to collect stories, concerns, and opinions in creative and transformative ways, and from vulnerable populations who might not feel that they have or can use other platforms to express themselves. While art cannot address the legal barriers encountered within sexual violence policies and reporting processes, we feel that these types of interventions can play an important role in sensitizing the university community – students, faculty, higher administration, and staff – to the experiences of survivors, to the ways that campuses and university rape culture affect members of the community, and to the systemic ways in which universities silence and ignore certain populations. Artistic interventions can help chisel away the structures of power and oppression that divide university communities, in their capacity to bring people together, to garner empathy, to inspire learning through affective modes of expression, and to call for social change in new ways.

RECOMMENDATIONS FOR FUTURE CHANGE

If students come to university to learn, and by default to grow, then can we not acknowledge that there is always the possibility for learning and growth, for shifting behaviour both inside and outside of the classroom? By this logic, the university has the ability to form and shift its very culture, formally and informally. In this chapter, we brought to light the various ways in which art serves to educate about sexual violence, to heal, to call for change and to build communities, in ways that policy reforms cannot. We provided several examples of art interventions at McGill University in order to demonstrate how artistic modes of expressions can play an instrumental role in raising awareness about rape culture and in drawing attention to the ways campus culture can change in other institutions across the country. We noted that current campus reforms to address sexual violence focus on policy, and while this is important, we argued that art needs to be included in conversations around social change. Through art, we may find the "cracks" in the systems exposed, and perceive these as daunting to address – but, as Leonard Cohen reminds us, it is through the cracks that the light shines in. Policy-makers, educators, artists, survivors, and members of the community may face the seemingly insurmountable problems of rape culture and sexual violence on our campuses, but if we work together – with and through art – we can find some hope in this situation, to change this reality.

Moving forward, we call on policy-makers and administrators enacting new anti-sexual violence policies and education reform in post-secondary contexts to consider artistic interventions as channels through which they can learn from survivors in the community, and through which they themselves can raise awareness about sexual violence issues in meaningful, emotional, and constructive ways. We envision the arts complementing policies and anti-sexual violence campaigns, acting as powerful scaffolds for dismantling rape culture on campuses by providing alternative spaces and affective forms of communication to raise awareness about sexual violence, to advocate for change, to support survivors, and ultimately to build a safer and healthier community for all. We also encourage researchers in different settings (community organizations, colleges, universities, TVETS) to consider the benefits of arts interventions for sexual violence-related research. The use of artistic modes for healing, education, community-building, and advocacy offers promise as a participatory channel through which the various stakeholders can learn from one another, work with the difficult emotions that sexual violence evokes, and potentially empower each other, through "making" in safe spaces.

NOTES

1 The co-authors on this chapter are all co-investigators or collaborators on the SSHRC-funded Partnership Grant: Collaborations to Address Sexual Violence on Campus: Social Sciences and Humanities Research Council of Canada Partnership Grant Number: 895-2016-1026, Project Director, Shaheen Shariff, PhD, McGill University.
2 McGill University (2016).
3 For more information, we recommend the chapter by Ayesha Vemuri in this book.
4 McGill University Faculty of Education (2016).
5 Networks for Change and Well-Being: Girl-Led 'From the Ground Up Policy Making to Address Sexual Violence in Canada and South Africa is a six-year Partnership study funded by the Social Sciences and Humanities Research Council of Canada and the International Development Research Centre: http://www.networks4change.ca/.
6 The Sexual Assault Centre of the McGill Students' Society: http://www.sacomss.org/.
7 In an informal conversation.
8 See: https://www.mcgill.ca/education/channels/event/altar-day-dead-honour-lives-missing-and-murdered-indigenous-women-and-girls-canada-263663. This project was led by Maria Ezcurra (McGill Faculty of Education Art Mediator), in collaboration with Lori Beavis (McGill Faculty of Education Artist-in-Residence) and *El Enredo*, a collective of Mexican women artists, including Nuria Carton de Grammont, Carmen Giménez-Cacho, Nancy Guevara, Flavia Hevia, Daniela Ortiz, and Amanda Rius.
9 Iniciativa de Copenhague para Centroamérica y México: http://www.cifcaeu.org/en/our-work/issues/feminicide/.
10 The Title IX legislation aims to reduce gender discrimination, and in recent years, has gained attention for its role in mandating sexual violence policies in American universities. In Canada, no such umbrella policy exists for all universities. Provinces have jurisdiction over educational provinces and university regulations. At this point in time, only Ontario and BC have provincial mandates that require universities to have sexual

violence policies; however, other provinces seem to be following suit, such as Quebec. For more information on US and Canada legislation, see Sheehy and Gilbert (2014).

REFERENCES

Belcourt, Christi. 2012. "Walking with Our Sisters." http://walking withoursisters.ca.

Belmore, Rebecca. 2002. "Vigil." http://canadianart.ca/reviews/ rebecca-belmore/.

– 2008. "Fringe." http://canadianart.ca/reviews/rebecca-belmore/.

Black, Beverly, Arlene Weisz, Suzanne Coats, and Debra Patterson. 2000. "Evaluating a Psychoeducational Sexual Assault Prevention Program Incorporating Theatrical Presentation, Peer Education, and Social Work." *Research on Social Work Practice* 10 (5): 589–606.

Boog, Ben W.M. 2003. "The Emancipatory Character of Action Research, Its History and the Present State of the Art." *Journal of Community and Applied Social Psychology* 13 (6): 426–38.

Branitsky, Alison. 2015. "Art as Activism." *Maryland Coalition against Sexual Assault.* https://www.mcasa.org/newsletters/article/art-as-activism.

Buchwald, Emilie, Pamela R. Fletcher, and Martha Roth. 2005. *Transforming a Rape Culture.* Minneapolis, MN: Milkweed Editions.

Carter, Mindy. 2015. "A Critical, A/R/Tographical Enquiry into the Meaning and Purpose of Performing 'Gallop Apace.'" *Journal of Educational Enquiry* 14 (1): 52–63.

– 2017. "Artful Inquiry and the Unexpected Ethical Turn: Exploring Identity through Creative Engagement with Grades 9–12 Students in Guatemala and Canada." *Art/Research International* 2 (1): 5–19.

Carter, Mindy, and Hala Mreiwed. 2017. "Review of 'Sing the Brave Song: This Isn't Over.'" *Art/Research International* 2 (2): 153–7.

Chiose, Simona. 2016. "Justice on Campus." *Globe and Mail*, 2 April. https://www.theglobeandmail.com/news/national/education/canadian-universities-under-pressure-to-formalize-harassment-assaultpolicies/article29499302/.

Christensen, M.C. 2013. "Using Theater of the Oppressed to Prevent Sexual Violence on College Campuses." *Trauma, Violence, and Abuse* 14 (4): 282–94.

– 2015. "Activating College Men to Prevent Sexual Violence: A Qualitative Investigation." *NASPA Journal about Women in Higher Education* 8 (2): 195–209.

Darts, David. 2006. "Art Education for a Change: Contemporary Issues and the Visual Arts." *Art Education* 59 (5): 6–12.

De Lange, Naydene, Claudia Mitchell, and Relebohile Moletsane. 2015a. "Girl-Led Strategies to Address Campus Safety: Creating Action Briefs for Dialogue with Policy Makers." *Agenda* 29 (3): 118–27.

– 2015b. "Seeing How It Works: A Visual Essay about Critical and Transformative Research in Education." *Perspectives in Education* 33 (4): 151–76.

Dewey, John. 2005. *Art as Experience.* New York: Berkley Publishing Group.

Eisner, Elliot W. 1995. "What Artistically Crafted Research Can Help about Schools." *Education Theory* 45 (1): 1–6.

Ferreday, Debra. 2015. "Game of Thrones, Rape Culture and Feminist Fandom." *Australian Feminist Studies* 30 (83): 21–36.

Freedman, Estelle B. 2013. *Redefining Rape: Sexual Violence in the Era of Suffrage and Segregation.* Cambridge, MA: Harvard University Press.

Gambino, Lauren. 2015. "Columbia University Student Carries Rape Protest Mattress to Graduation." *Guardian*, 19 May.

Gerson, Jacob W., and Jeannie Suk Gerson. 2016. "The Sex Bureaucracy." *Social Science Research Network* ID 2750143.

Greene, Maxine. 1995. *Releasing the Imagination: Essays on Education, the Arts, and Social Change.* San Francisco, CA: Jossey-Bass Publishers.

Johnson, Ginger A., Anne E. Pfister, and Cecilia Vindrola-Padros. 2012. "Drawings, Photos, and Performances: Using Visual Methods with Children." *Visual Anthropology Review* 28 (2): 164–78.

Jozkowski, Kristen N. 2015. "'Yes Means Yes'? Sexual Consent Policy and College Students." *Change: The Magazine of Higher Learning* 47 (2): 16–23.

Kazmierczak, Elzbieta. 2017. "Engaging Communities through an Art Program at a Domestic Violence Shelter." In *Handbook of Research on the Facilitation of Civic Engagement through Community Art*, edited by Leigh Nanney Hersey and Bryna Bobick, 339–76. Hershey, PA: IGI Global.

Kollwitz, Kathe. 1907. "Raped." https://www.metmuseum.org/art/collection/search/367434.

Kress, Victoria E., J. Brad Shepherd, Renee I. Anderson, Aaron J. Petuch, James Michael Nolan, and Darlene Thiemeke. 2006. "Evaluation of the Impact of a Coeducational Sexual Assault Prevention Program on College Students' Rape Myth Attitudes." *Journal of College Counseling* 9 (2): 148–57.

Lewis, Ruth, and Susan B. Marine. 2015. "Weaving a Tapestry, Compassionately: Toward an Understanding of Young Women's Feminisms." *Feminist Formations* 27 (1): 118–40.

Lewis, Ruth, Susan Marine, and Kathryn Kenney. 2016. "'I Get Together with My Friends and Try to Change it.' Young Feminist Students Resist 'Laddism,' 'Rape Culture' and 'Everyday Sexism.'" *Journal of Gender Studies* 27 (1): 56–72. doi:10.1080/09589236.2016.1175925.

Low, B., M. Carter, E. Wood, C. Mitchell, M. Proietti, and D. Friedmann. 2016. "Building an Urban Arts Partnership between School, Community Based Artists and University." *Learning Landscapes* 1 (10): 153–72.

Lys, Candice, Carmen H. Logie, Nancy Macneill, Charlotte Loppie, Lisa V. Dias, Renée Masching, and Dionne Gesink. 2016. "Arts-Based HIV and STI Prevention Intervention with Northern and Indigenous Youth in the Northwest Territories: Study Protocol for a Non-Randomised Cohort Pilot Study." *BMJ Open* 6 (10).

Majkut, Katrina. n.d. "How College Students are Fighting Campus Rape with Art, Humour, And the Guerrilla Girls Broadband." *Bust*. https://bust.com/feminism/16395-how-college-students-are-fighting-campus-rape-with-art-humor-and-the-guerrilla-girls.html .

Marshall, Catherine, Keren Dalyot, and Stephanie Galloway. 2014. "Sexual Harassment in Higher Education: Re-Framing the Puzzle of Its Persistence." *Journal of Policy Practice* 13 (4): 276–99.

Marshall, Laurie. 2014. "Art as Peace Building." *Art Education* 67 (3): 37–43.

McGill University. 2016. "Policy against Sexual Violence." https://www.mcgill.ca/secretariat/files/secretariat/policy_against_sexual_violence.pdf.

McGill University Faculty of Education. 2016. "Exhibition: Seeing How It Works: Participatory Visual Research and Transformation in Addressing Sexual Violence." https://www.mcgill.ca/education/channels/news/exhibition-seeing-how-it-works-participatory-visual-research-and-transformation-addressing-sexual-262859.

Mitchell, Claudia, and Naydene De Lange. 2011. "Community-Based Participatory Video and Social Action in Rural South Africa." *The SAGE Handbook of Visual Research Methods*: 171–85.

Mitchell, C., N. De Lange, and R. Moletsane. 2017a. "Addressing Sexual Violence in South Africa: 'Gender Activism in the Making." In *What Politics? Youth and Political Engagement in Africa*, edited by E. Oinas, H. Onodera and L. Suurpaa, 317–36. Den Haag, Netherlands: Brill.

Mitchell, Claudia, Naydene DeLange, and Relebohile Molestane. 2017b. *Participatory Visual Methodologies: Social Change, Community and*

Policy, edited by Naydene De Lange and Relebohile Moletsane. Los Angeles, CA: SAGE.

Mitchell, Karen S., and Jennifer L. Freitag. 2011. "Forum Theatre for Bystanders: A New Model for Gender Violence Prevention." *Violence against Women* 17 (8): 990–1013.

Murray, Christine E., Kelly Moore Spencer, Jaimie Stickl, and Allison Crowe. 2017. "See the Triumph Healing Arts Workshops for Survivors of Intimate Partner Violence and Sexual Assault." *Journal of Creativity in Mental Health* 12 (2): 192–202.

Ono, Yoko. 1965. *Cut Piece*.

Ontario Arts Council. *Creative Engagement Fund*. 2017.

Phillips, Nickie D. 2017. *Beyond Blurred Lines: Rape Culture in Popular Media*. Lanham, MD: Rowman and Littlefield.

Quinlan, Elizabeth, Andrea Quinlan, Curtis Fogel, and Gail Taylor. 2017. *Sexual Violence at Canadian Universities: Activism, Institutional Responses, and Strategies for Change*. Waterloo, ON: Wilfrid Laurier University Press.

Rios, Carmen. 2014. "Building Supportive Communities: How We Can Make Every Space Safe for Survivors." *Everyday Feminism*. https://everydayfeminism.com/2014/05/supportive-communities/.

Sandals, Leah. 2016. "Sexual Assault: The Roadshow Takes Art and Activism across Ontario." *Canadian Art*. https://canadianart.ca/features/sexual-assault-the-roadshow/.

Shaw, Lori E. 2015. "Title IX, Sexual Assault, and the Issue of Effective Consent: Blurred Lines: When Should Yes Mean No." *Indiana Law Journal* 91: 1363.

Silence Is Violence. n.d. "About: Silence Is Violence." Silence Is Violence. http://www.silenceisviolence.ca/about/.

Silence Is Violence McGill. 2017a. "Watch Nina Statement at a Provincial Round Table on Campus Sexual Assault Here! [Facebook Update]." https://www.facebook.com/SiVMcGill/.

– 2017b. "Here Is Amy's Testimony at the Journee De Reflexion on Prioritizing the Voices of Survivors." https://www.facebook.com/SiVMcGill/.

Sheehy, Elizabeth A., and Daphne Gilbert. 2015. "Responding to Sexual Assault on Campus: What Can Canadian Universities Learn from US Law and Policy?"

themonumentquilt.org. "The Monument Quilt." https://themonumentquilt.org/.

Walsh, Shannon. 2015. "Addressing Sexual Violence and Rape Culture: Issues and Interventions Targeting Boys and Men." *Agenda* 29 (3): 131–41.

Weber, Sandra. 2014. "Arts-Based Self-Study: Documenting the Ripple Effect." *Perspectives in Education* 32 (2): 8–20.

"UNPOPULAR OPINION: I Am a Rape Victim, Not a Survivor." 2016. *XoJane: Women's Lifestyle and Community*, 27 April. http://www.xojane.com/issues/i-am-a-victim-not-a-survivor.

Zuch, Michael Thomas. 2015. "The Effectiveness of Arts in Trauma Intervention." *Vanderbilt Undergraduate Research Journal* 10: 1–15.

3

Alternative Practices and Politics of Care

Women Students' Experiences of Rape Culture and Sexualized Violence on Campus

Marcia Oliver, Rebecca Godderis, and Debra Langan

INTRODUCTION

Recent incidents on university campuses have inspired much public discussion and consternation among university administrators, faculty, staff, and students about the prevalence of, and responses to, rape culture on campus. Of interest in this chapter are the experiences, understandings, and responses of women-identified students[1] to rape culture on Wilfrid Laurier University's Brantford campus (hereafter Laurier Brantford). What becomes clear from our research and broader interactions with students in the last number of years is that students experience rape culture in diverse ways on campus. They also, however, actively engage in what we call "alternative practices and politics of care" that are potentially empowering for women. These practices and politics challenge gendered rape myths, foster solidarity and collective action, and build caring communities as a means of finding ways to exist within institutions that all too often diminish the agency, dignity, safety, and sense of belonging of individuals who identify as women – institutions that fail to meaningfully respond to rape culture and individual experiences of sexualized violence. In what follows, we provide an overview of our research study on rape culture at Laurier Brantford and describe some of the "institutional walls" (Ahmed 2017) that women-identified students often experience in confronting both the formal and informal university structures surrounding gendered and sexual violence on campus (see also Buss and Majury, this volume). We also highlight a number of ways that women-identified students and alumni have responded to these walls, and to rape culture more broadly, by engaging in a range of care practices and politics that are oriented to what Seyla Benhabib calls the standpoint of the "concrete other," or the recognition and validation of one another's specificity; the concreteness of one another's personal experiences, history, needs, and self-descriptions (1987; see also Minaker et al., this volume). These alternative care practices and politics include individual empowerment strategies that challenge dominant norms of femininity and masculinity and offer pragmatic strategies to women to defend themselves (and each other) against male aggression and violence; participating in small group discussions and consciousness-raising practices; and cultivating feminist public spaces on campus, including engaging in online and in-person education and advocacy initiatives and providing material and emotional care and support to survivors of violence.

OUR PROJECT

Our research set out to better understand how university students understand and experience rape culture on Laurier Brantford's campus (with a student population of roughly 3,000). Informed by a critical feminist approach to research that is attuned to researchers' positionality and power hierarchies within the research process (Oakley 2016; Hesse-Biber 2011), we trained three graduate and one undergraduate student research assistants (two cis women and two cis men) to facilitate peer-led focus groups with undergraduate students who self-identify with the same gender category and who were interested in the topic of rape culture.

During a three-month period from February to April 2015, the RAS facilitated eleven same-gendered focus groups (eight groups of self-identified women and three groups of self-identified men), with a total of thirty-six participants in these groups (twenty-seven women and nine men). Regular team meetings informed the direction of the interviews, the coding of the data, and the emergent analyses. To ensure confidentiality, each student chose a pseudonym, and these pseudonyms are used consistently throughout this chapter to identify the different participants who contributed to the focus group discussions. These excerpts comprise one of the primary sources of empirical data used in this analysis, along with various student-led initiatives that transpired after the focus group sessions. We view these initiatives not as the direct outcome of our research project, but as shaped and amplified by the broader political anti-sexual violence climate at Laurier, and other Canadian universities, of which our project is a part.

On Institutional Walls and Rape Culture at Laurier Brantford

Sara Ahmed's powerful analysis of diversity work illustrates the institutional walls that diversity practitioners experience in their work when it comes to transforming the norms of the university as an institution. The concept of the institutional wall is central to our analysis because it symbolizes institutional resistance to meaningful social change and transformation. It denotes how institutional histories of privilege and exclusion become materialized in the present through institutional action that remains inattentive to, and arguably dismissive of, systems of power and inequality within the university, such as cis and trans women's experiences of rape culture and sexualized violence on campus as a systemic social problem. As Ahmed notes (2017, 138), "you come up against what others do not see, and (this is even harder) you come up against what others are often invested in not seeing." Moreover, women-identified students encounter this history in very real, concrete ways as "physical barriers in the present" (ibid., 163), which they quite literally come up against and must navigate in finding ways to be heard and respected and in attempting to enact substantial institutional change. As feminist scholars have long argued, when confronted with the "universal" of the university, the particularities of our being – our gender, race, sexual orientation, class, and abilities – reveal time and again that university spaces are built to accommodate some bodies and ways of knowing more than others (ibid.; Moors 2015; Jenkins 2014; Fotaki 2013; Cannella and Perez 2012; Stockdill and Dancio 2012; Haraway 1988; hooks 1994; Hill Collins 1990; Smith 1987).

Similar to other university satellite campuses emerging across Canada, Laurier Brantford is a provincially driven revitalization project designed to mitigate the lasting effects of the post-industrial economic decline of the 1980s and 1990s. The university campus is integrated into the city's downtown core and consists of formal municipal, commercially zoned, and residential spaces that have been allocated or converted to further university-based projects and priorities, sometimes at the expense of local residents' diverse needs and desires and resulting in "town and gown" tensions. For Laurier Brantford students, and especially those living in residence, university life takes place within a campus that is broadly defined, which includes university-owned spaces and public downtown areas (like the library, restaurants, coffee houses, public square, local bars, and streets). Within this context, women-identified focus group participants described time and time again their everyday encounters with rape culture and sexualized violence, including their intimidation and fear of walking alone (especially at night and in carparks); being subjected to sexual harassment and catcalling while walking to and from class (at all times of day); the unwanted groping of their bodies by men in local downtown bars and nightclubs; constant feelings of doubt or uncertainty about the clothes they wear, the spaces they occupy, or the people they trust; a sense of fatalism or inevitability about experiencing rape culture and sexualized violence; and the continuous advice that they receive about what women ought to be doing to minimize their risk and protect themselves from male violence.[2] As Tina remarks: "It's like if you don't drink too much or if you don't wear this, you're not going to get raped … But if you're wearing improper clothing then you deserve to be raped or don't be surprised if you do get raped. It's like saying, it's, it's like saying, oh we can't really control men … it's okay to always blame the victim." Kay also voices her opposition to this dominant risk-avoidance discourse in describing her experience when she first arrived at Laurier Brantford: "I was handed a rape whistle by the special constables, who told me that it was my responsibility that if I was out at night to protect myself from these people." Annaleshia adds: "And it's like this all the time: instead of teaching women how not to get raped, why aren't we teaching men not to rape? Why isn't that a thing?"

In the context of rape culture and anti-sexual violence work on university campuses, institutional walls seem to be everywhere. For instance, a wall appears when institutions employ dominant risk-avoidance discourses, which, as our students note, have the effects of normalizing sexualized violence as an ever-present possibility for women, rendering invisible the perpetrators of sexual violence, attributing blame to women and making them responsible for the violence that was enacted on them, and serving as a constant reminder that "the right to be safe" is reserved only for women who exercise appropriate caution and follow the rules for prudent (and responsible) behaviour (Lawson and Olle 2006; Stanko 1997; Hall 2004; Gotell 2008).

Institutional walls also appear when official complaints are made, specifically through the university's formal reporting procedures that require women-identified students to provide details about the incident. As our focus group participants describe, if alcohol was consumed, or if they were alone, or if their dress was deemed too revealing, their disclosures to university officials and the reporting process itself too often result in victim-survivors feeling blamed and made responsible for their violation. Shannon comments: "You say that you've been attacked ... and they say, 'Well, look what you were wearing. Look where you were. You shouldn't have been out. Why were you alone? ... Why didn't you take your drink to the bathroom.' Like it's expected of us at this point. And that's kind of what pisses me off ... And I damn well do not want it thrown back in my face if I decide not to take a precaution and something happens – it shouldn't be my responsibility solely." Dimitri shares similar concerns: "Like if I got raped tomorrow and I filed a report, I could almost guarantee: 'What were you wearing?' 'Who were you with?' 'What time were you out?' 'Wow, you were out that late?' 'Why weren't you with anybody?' Maybe restructuring that entire intake process so that the rape victim doesn't feel like she is the one at fault ... Actually, all police officers, all special constables, any sort of Laurier staff who handle this, they should all be ... I don't know, given some training that doesn't condemn the victim."

The institutional walls encountered during the official reporting process have led some students to avoid reporting altogether. For instance, this was Hannah's experience: "The reason that I didn't come forward was because it's scary, having to get authorities involved, having to tell people what happened to you, what situation I stupidly got myself into ... I wasn't comfortable and I didn't think that anything would be done. And even if I did, it would be a long procedure that would just drain me of any fight that I had." Similarly, Jenn recounts a story of her best friend who officially reported her experience of campus-based sexual violence to her university. The humiliation, blame, and devastation that her friend experienced throughout the process led Jenn to reflexively conclude that if her friend had known that "nothing would happen ... that he would get a slap on the hand," then she "wouldn't have come forward in the first place." In their various ways, women-identified students recounted stories with one another of feeling helpless, depleted, and denied justice by the institution, "like there's no way to win" (Hannah). Feeling depleted, as "not having the energy to keep going in the face of what you come up against" (Ahmed 2017), is to come up against an institutional wall.

Beyond the formal complaint processes, more walls emerge in the "spaces of discretion and informality" of university bureaucrats and service providers (see Buss and Majory, this volume), such as when women are discouraged or prevented from filing an official complaint or report. As Ahmed (2017, 139) observes, such discouragement or prevention is achieved by "explicit argument or implicit narratives: if you complain, you will hurt your career ... or if you complain, you will hurt the professor ... or if you complain, you will ruin a center or collective." In the words of one of our research participants, if you complain, "it's going to ruin the rapist's entire life" (Tina).

Women-identified students also report frustration with the university for "not doing enough"; with not knowing where to go to access support (Kay, Jenn, Hannah); and, when do they do access support, being subjected to oppressive support practices that end up disempowering, humiliating, and alienating victim-survivors. The lack of access to sexual violence support services on campus that are guided by survivor-informed principles and executed by trained professionals (see Rossiter et al., this volume) was noted by Jordan, who felt that the seriousness of her circumstances had been minimized when she sought university-based counselling: "I ended up having a situation of harassment. They basically said, 'Oh well, it'll get better. Like just keep pushing through.' And I was like, 'Are you kidding me?'" Taya also recounts her experience with counselling on campus: "So I had PTSD from a sexual assault experience. Then after being beaten up, it was just like everything was kind of mounting. And I went to counselling services and they handed me a wand full of water and sparkles and the counselor made me hold onto it. And she was like, 'Poor [Taya], you must feel so upset. Why aren't you more angry?' And I was just sitting there, being like 'Oh my god. This is humiliating and awful and you're making me hold a rainbow stick. And I don't, like I hate you.'" Her second experience with counselling was no better: "So I was there and I wanted to talk about my experiences with PTSD and rape and stuff and they were kind of like, 'Well, we're not really going to talk about that today. I think it will be a little too heavy.'"

Moreover, for those students (and faculty) that speak out against the pervasiveness of rape culture and sexualized violence on campus, other walls can appear. This is especially the case for many women-, feminist-, and/or survivor- identified activists on campus, who are seen to pose a "problem" by exposing a problem (Ahmed 2017) and whose speech is dismissed as merely sentimental or reactive. As Courtney explains: "this is what societal pressure really is like, you don't want to say something because everyone is going to be like you're overreacting massively"; or, as Shannon describes, "I speak out [against rape culture] and I'm told I'm sensitive" [by her male peers]. Rachel shares a similar experience: "And that makes me really angry too, when it's like, 'Oh it's just feminism.' No it's not. It's a basic human right to be able to say 'no' and to be respected for saying that, and not, you know, just kind of dismissed as 'Oh you're an idiot.'" The dismissal of women's (and of feminist) speech as mere emotion, as "failing the very standards of reason and impartiality that are assumed to form the basis of 'good judgement'" (Ahmed 2014; Young 1994), was also evident in a focus group conversation about a campus-wide need for more explicit conversations about consent. As one participant cautioned, these conversations "should not be held by women's groups because as soon as it's labelled as feminist, it will be dismissed as those crazy feminists are lecturing me. So we need to avoid certain words, [like] feminist, rape culture – those can come later, once everyone gets it" (Kay). Women-identified students generally agreed that efforts to challenge and change deeply engrained hetero-patriarchal norms and practices must be incremental, inclusive, and attentive to broader contextual factors, which, in the context of university structures and life, was thought to require a strategic distancing from feminist discourse to avoid negative student reactions and resistance.

Alternative Politics and Practices of Care

Although our research reveals the diverse ways that women-identified students experience rape culture on campus and the many walls that they confront in navigating the university's formal and informal structures, we also find (and continue to see in our interactions and support of feminist activism on campus) students who self-identify as women participating in alternative practices and politics of care. These practices aim to cultivate caring relations and collectives that are attentive, responsive, and responsible to the needs of particular others (Robinson 2008; Lawson 2009), including oneself. These include self-care and interpersonal care practices, like learning (and teaching) self-defense or participating in small group discussions and consciousness-raising activities; they also include politicized social care practices that are oriented to collective action, like cultivating feminist public spaces on campus for women-identified campus members to gather, disseminate educational materials, organize and advocate for social and institutional change, and provide love and care to survivors of violence.

We are reminded here of Benhabib's "concrete other," which, like the work of other feminist ethic of care scholars, requires us to see "each and every rational being as an individual with a concrete history, identity, and affection-emotional constitution," who is entitled to be treated in ways that confirm and recognize their individuality with "specific needs, talents and capacities" (1987, 87). While some critics have charged care ethics with perpetuating gender essentialisms that reinforce stereotypes of care as feminine or maternal, we follow Robinson in arguing that all people benefit from "an image of care that recognizes responsibility and responsiveness to particular others as positive expressions of both masculinity and femininity" (2011, 136). Moreover, feminist ethic of care scholars challenge the marginalization of care in public and political discourse, and its confinement to private and familial life (Sevenhuijsen 1998; Lawson 2009; Tronto 1989, 1993; Robinson 2008, 2011). Care is instead conceptualized as both a personal and political practice, with the latter raising crucial questions about the organization and workings of our social and political institutions (like the university) (Tronto 1989). As Mountz et al. write in their critique of the academy: "cultivating space to care for ourselves, our colleagues, and our students is, in fact, a political activity when we are situated in institutions that devalue and militate against such relations and practices" (2015, 1239). Below, we adopt a broad definition of care that includes both interpersonal caring practices (of ourselves and others) and a broader social politics of care that aims to transform institutions and relationships in more caring ways, while also "being attentive to the entanglements of power" that shape social relations (Dowler et al. 2014, 338).

In the focus group discussions with women-identified students, a common theme that emerged was the question of what could/should be done to challenge rape culture and sexualized violence on campus. Many participants were explicit in their outright refusal to be passive, subservient, or self-doubting when confronted with rape culture and the possibility of sexual violence. For instance, some women advocated for "protection strategies" so that they were better able to care for and defend themselves and each other from sexualized violence. As Georgia explained, "I started martial arts. I teach self-defense ... I'm not going to rely on others to protect me. I'm going to protect me." Other women stressed the importance of "protecting each other" (Fiona, Rose) from the very possibility of sexual violence, especially in bars when alcohol is consumed. For Jordan, she refuses to leave her friends alone at the bar if they've had too much to drink: "I won't leave ... And some will say, 'just leave her alone, it's no big deal if she wants to be with so-and-so.' But they have no idea where they are or what they're doing." Similarly, Courtney describes her friends as being "super protective of each other" and feeling a deep sense of "personal responsibility" for each other's safety.

In addition, some women-identified students noted making an effort to resist notions of "polite" feminine conduct and speech by naming sexism and calling out rape culture. For instance, Dimitri describes her reaction to sexual harassment and objectification in public spaces: "If I'm walking past [local bar] and I'm being cat-called at, I'm not just going to take it ... I'm going to say something, I'm going to call it out 'cause no, no, you don't get to do that. You don't get to call me babe. You don't get to tell me to come in. You don't get to whistle at me. You don't get to look at my butt. You don't get to ask me where I'm going [or] what I'm doing later. You don't get to call me honey. No ... I don't have to take your crap." This act of naming/calling out is also reflected in Shannon's experience of confronting her male co-workers about an offensive rape joke: "And I sat them down and I was like, 'Listen you can't talk like that ... You can't use that language.' And I painted a picture for them what it is like for a woman to be raped, for a woman to be sexually assaulted ... This is one subject that I know I'm right about. And essentially you can't argue with me when I'm saying, 'Your use of rape language is making me uncomfortable,' and you can't tell me I'm wrong or I'm an idiot for saying it. And so that kind of gives me the confidence then to be like, I'm going to speak out against that ... You can call me a bitch if you want. That's happened." In naming and opposing rape culture and sexualized violence as wrong, many women-identified students expressed a sense of confidence and assurance in their own intelligence and embodied knowledge – despite the varied forms of masculine hostility that would often follow in an effort to re-establish men's power and domination in both physical and discursive space.

The strategies of self-defense and calling out sexist conduct in everyday encounters are commonly found in rape resistance education programs, and are often heavily criticized for offering individualized .

responses to sexualized violence and for enabling men to refuse responsibility for rape (Rich et al. 2010; Stewart 2014). While we are similarly concerned about the ways in which women, and members of many different marginalized groups, are made responsible to prevent rape, we are also reminded of Audre Lorde's much-cited characterization of self-care as "self-preservation" (1988, 131). This serves as a powerful reminder that for some women self-care is literally about survival; it is about managing, coping, and figuring out how to continue to exist within a system that normalizes and trivializes sexualized violence against women and other marginalized individuals. Moreover, the very act of defending oneself or "calling out" sexist conduct can be seen to challenge heteronormative constructions of femininity (as passive, inferior, vulnerable, and, thus, rapeable), which are at the root of "rape culture" and many women's victimization (Henry, Flynn, and Powell 2015, 219; see also Radtke et al., this volume).

A second alternative care practice is found in women-identified students' participation in small group discussions and consciousness-raising practices. As faculty researchers, we were surprised by the extent to which the focus groups themselves became sites for collective support, solidarity, and consciousness-raising among women participants. The students saw these groups as a safe place where they could talk and test out interpretations of day-to-day experiences and ideas about rape culture and sexualized violence. Echoing Powell's finding in her study on the informal justice practices being sought by victim-survivors in online spaces, our students illustrate that the sharing of experiences of sexualized violence with "a community of peers who understand the nature of sexual violence" is empowering for women, particularly in meeting their diverse needs, such as participation, voice, recognition, and validation (Powell 2015a; Powell 2015b; see also Daly 2014; Clark 2010). For instance, Alyssa explains: "I think it's helpful in learning that I'm not the only girl that feels like that. Like I've talked to other roommates about it. But I felt like I was ... isolated ... and that no one else was experiencing this. So like it definitely helped ... in learning that I'm not alone ... I'm learning that it's more common than I thought it was." Other women-identified participants also noted the interpersonal and collective value of the focus groups, specifically for stressing "how important it is to honour everyone's experience and [recognize] that we don't all deal with this the same way" (Taya); "that things need to change" (Kay); and "how frequent [sexualized violence] is in real life, like it's not in our heads" (Jenn,

Suzy). The focus group discussions reveal several "clicking" moments, with participants becoming more aware, both individually and as a collective, of the harmful effects of societal constructions of normative gender relations on both women and men; of gendered and sexist structures on campus that support rape culture; of connections between individual and collective experiences of sexualized violence; and of the need for campus-wide change. In these moments, we see glimpses of Benhabib's "concrete other" and what Dean (1996) calls "affectional solidarity": bonds of mutual care and support that recognize and validate one another's unique histories, needs, capacities, and experiences of sexualized violence. Such consciousness-raising reduces self-blame and isolation, and thus is a politicized act of caring that brings into awareness a structural understanding of sexual violence as a gendered and racialized system of power.

Alternative care practices and politics are also evident in students' call for a women-identified public space on campus. The value of such spaces was discussed amongst participants, but has also been highlighted in broader movements by women on campus. In 2015, a women's centre was (finally) established on Laurier Brantford's campus – the result of women students' labour and organizing, most notably the student-led Women's Safety Action Group (a group formed prior to our research). The centre strives to "provide a woman-positive space and connections to community resources," as well as to "encourage change through action, critical discourse, and personal growth," with the aim of making "every space on the campus safer and supportive" (Laurier Brantford Women's Centre Mission Statement). Moreover, in drafting the centre's mission statement and designing its organizational principles, students considered difficult and complex questions about feminism, representation, and women's intersecting identities, and diverse experiences of oppression and violence. In recognizing that "historically feminism has primarily served the needs of white, heterosexual, cis-gendered, non-intersex, able-bodied women," members committed to a constant questioning of the centre's processes and members' perspectives through "anti-oppressive training, allyship, inclusion of marginalized perspectives, and serving as a venue for disenfranchised voices to be heard" (ibid.). Although there is an appeal to women's commonalities (e.g., concerns and struggles), we see the commitment to a constant questioning and openness to critique as indicative of feminist care ethics, or what Dean calls reflective solidarity: "an expectation that we will responsibly attend to each other"

(1996, 39) in ways that both recognize our individual particularities and differences and attempt to include those who may be excluded from our imagined "we" (ibid., 34).

In many ways, cultivating feminist public spaces on campus for women-identified students is about building an inclusive and caring community and, as such, is a political activity aimed at validating diverse experiences of women and trans students and challenging systemic injustice both within and beyond the university. The need for claiming and cultivating such spaces on campus is also evident in the anti-violence work of a feminist-identified student and alumni collective on campus. Known as Advocates for a Student Culture of Consent (ASCC), this collective engages in a wide range of online and offline initiatives concerning gendered and sexualized violence, including advocacy and education on consent, rape myths, victim-blaming, self-care, and survivor-oriented support. For instance, in response to the reality of rape culture on university campuses and the collective realization that little, if any, formal institutional work was being done at Laurier that provided students with consistent and *continuous* consent education, ASCC designed and launched their online "Consent is Golden" campaign. This campaign seeks to educate and raise awareness about consent by focusing on what consent actually means, what it requires – in all its complexities – and what an affirmative model can look like in practice in both sexual and broader social and colonial contexts.[3]

In addition to defining key norms of consent in fun and colloquial ways, Consent is Golden provides information about local sexual violence support services and offers feminist and survivor-informed education about receiving and responding to a disclosure of sexual violence (such as respecting the survivor-victim's agency in deciding whether or not to report to police or access services). Importantly, the website also clearly explains why many survivor-victims choose not to report their experience of sexual violence, out of very real fears about the possibility of being further subjected to violence and experiencing additional trauma by institutionalized processes (e.g., victim-blaming, lack of control over critical decisions, minimal perpetrator accountability and responsibility, and so on). As Powell (2015b) argues, online communication technologies have become indispensable to challenging rape culture and fostering solidarity among groups of people (see also Powell 2015a; Rentschler 2014; Salter 2013), as well as providing victim-survivors with a mechanism through which their justice needs can be met. Consent is Golden is a just one, albeit important, part of ASCC's labour, which – like all of ASCC's work – can be seen as a political act of caring that recognizes and validates survivor-informed knowledge, distributes resources to foster connections with care providers, disrupts deeply entrenched rape myths and unethical sexual conduct, and provides compassion and support to victim-survivors.[4]

In addition to Consent is Golden, ASCC also hosts community workshops and events on gendered and sexual violence (including consent, dismantling rape myths, disclosure training, self-care, and reproductive and sexual health) and engages in institutional policy advocacy and consultation, specifically concerning Laurier's official Gendered and Sexual Violence Policy and Procedures and recent campus controversies over freedom of expression. The collective publicly speaks out against institutional responses to gendered and sexual violence that routinely silence, devalue, and marginalize survivor's experiences, agency, and justice needs, and it provides substantial material and emotional support to survivors to show love and care. Recent examples of the latter include organizing donation drives for local sexual assault and domestic violence centres and launching a participatory art project, *(Un)Silenced*, that reclaims public space for survivors to tell their own stories, challenge dominant tropes of violence, and find validation and voice in speaking one's truth about violence. Although ASCC does not explicitly speak of a feminist ethics of care, their work on gendered and sexualized violence reflects multiple practices and politics of care that are attentive and responsive to the particularities of others and to the concreteness of one another's identities, experiences, agency, and justice needs.

RECOMMENDATIONS FOR CHANGE

As our students emphasize, the university's formal and informal responses to sexualized violence routinely fail women and victim-survivors, who, time and again, are confronted with various institutionalized walls that often end up trivializing sexualized violence, perpetuating victim-blaming cultural scripts, and marginalizing women's voices, experiences, and needs. As we highlight above, the institutional walls that women students come up against are indicative of problematic practices, gendered assumptions, and a lack of training and knowledge on the part of administrators and service providers, all of which fail to meet the diverse and concrete justice needs of many women who experience sexualized violence (see also Buss and Majury, this volume). In response to what are often experienced as "unjust" and "uncaring" institutional practices and processes, women students seek out and engage in alternative care practices and politics that are oriented toward recognizing and validating women's experiences, histories, needs, and self-understandings, as well as to collective action that aims to challenge and transform institutions and interrelations in more caring and responsive ways. Given the persistent failures of the university to respond to sexualized violence on campus in any meaningful manner for victim-survivors, a feminist ethic and politics of care reveals the urgent need to cultivate more caring academic cultures, policies, processes, and relations concerning sexualized violence on campus.

Recommendations for future research include continuing to document the experiences of students who resist and challenge the many institutional *walls* that they confront in the context of rape culture and sexualized violence on campus, with a particular eye towards how student survivors are navigating newly introduced complaint procedures within universities. It will also be important to use research to help establish the most effective ways to foster a culture of alternative practices and politics of care on campus that recognize and account for the particularities of the "concrete other," while simultaneously conceptualizing care as a politicized resistance strategy that operates on a variety of levels, including individuals, groups, institutions, and society. In conceptualizing future research projects, it is crucial that we remain attentive to and consider how our research designs may, in effect, continue to centre some women's voices and experiences over others, including how our research questions, our methodologies, and our analytical frameworks may uphold whiteness as the norm and may privilege white women's experiences and narratives of sexualized and gendered violence.

Further, in terms of policy, we strongly recommend that institutions increase their efforts to educate and train *all* members of university campuses about the need to challenge rape myths, with a specific emphasis on confronting victim-blaming. The aim of these educational efforts should be reducing, and eventually eliminating, institutional walls related to rape culture and sexualized violence. As part of these efforts, institutional administrators who are creating policies, procedures, and training programs should seek out the knowledge of women-identified students, survivors of sexual violence, and others directly affected by sexual violence in order to ensure that institutional documents and programs are responsive to the needs of communities most directly affected by rape culture and sexualized violence on campus. Finally, institutions should dedicate financial and physical resources on a long-term, ongoing basis to encourage students to create public spaces on campus (physical and online) for peer support and consciousness-raising, thereby reducing isolation and self-blame while also helping to challenge rape culture.

ACKNOWLEDGMENTS

We are most grateful to our research assistants and the student participants in this study who shared their time and insights with us. We are also deeply grateful to the extraordinary labour that feminist-identified students engage in on campus to create a more inclusive and caring culture for women-identified and other marginalized groups. We thank both the members of ASCC and the editors of this collection for their insights and valuable feedback on earlier versions of this chapter. Finally, we extend our thanks to Laurier for providing funding to this study, specifically to the Women's Campus Safety Committee, Diversity and Equity Office; Dean, Faculty of Liberal Arts; Dean, Faculty of Human and Social Sciences; and the Office of the Dean of Students at Laurier Brantford.

NOTES

1 We use "women-identified" and "women" throughout this chapter in an inclusive way to refer to anyone who self-identifies with the gender category "woman," including individuals who identify as transgender, non-binary, gender fluid, and cisgender. Although our research is focused on the experiences of women-identified people, we acknowledge and understand that gendered violence affects people who are not femme or women-identified.

2 It is important to note that these experiences are not restricted to women-identified student's experiences of campus and/or university life; they are also common in their everyday encounters with public spaces more generally.

3 See ASCC's website: https://www.ascconsent.com.

4 Although Laurier (as an institution) often publicly celebrates this campaign as a grassroots, student-led, "made at Laurier" initiative, and frequently disseminates the campaign's website content or Twitter advocacy to students, it is important to stress that this campaign is not formally endorsed by, nor does it belong to, the institution. ASCC has explicitly and purposely maintained distance and autonomy from the university in order to retain control of the campaign messaging.

REFERENCES

Ahmed, Sara. 2014. "Selfcare as Warfare." *Feminist Killjoys*, 25 August.
– 2017. *Living a Feminist Life*. Durham, NC: Duke University Press.
Benhabib, Seyla. 1987. "The Generalized and the Concrete Other: The Kohlberg-Gilligan Controversy and Feminist Theory." In *Feminism as Critique: Essays on the Politics of Gender in Late-Capitalist Society,* edited by S. Benhabib and D. Cornell, 77–95. Cambridge, UK: Polity Press.
Cannella, Gaile S., and Michelle Salazar Perez. 2012. "Emboldened Patriarchy in Higher Education." *Cultural Studies <–> Critical Methodologies* 12 (4): 279–86.
Clark, H. 2010. "'What is the Justice System Willing to Offer?': Understanding Sexual Assault Victim/Survivors' Criminal Justice Needs." *Family Matters* 85: 28–37.
Collins, Patricia Hill. 1990. *Black Feminist Thought: Knowledge, Consciousness, and the Politics of Empowerment*. Boston, UK: Unwin Hyman.
Daly, K. 2014. "Reconceptualizing Sexual Victimization and Justice." In *The International Handbook of Victimology*, edited by S. Benhabib and D. Cornell, 378–96. London: Routledge.
Dean, Jodi. 1996. *Solidarity of Strangers: Feminism after Identity Politics*. Berkeley: University of California Press.
Dowler, L., D. Cuomo, and N. Laliberte. 2014. "Challenging 'The Penn State Way': A Feminist Response to Institutional Violence in Higher Education." *Gender Place and Culture* 21 (3): 387–94.
Fotaki, Marianna. 2013. "No Woman Is Like a Man (in Academia): The Masculine Symbolic Order and the Unwanted Female Body." *Organization Studies* 34 (9): 1251–75.
Gotell, Lise. 2008. "Rethinking Affirmative Consent in Canadian Sexual Assault Law: Neoliberal Sexual Subjects and Risky Women." *Akron Law Review* 41: 865–98.

Hall, Rachel. 2004. "'It Can Happen to You': Rape Prevention in the Age of Risk Management." *Hypatia* 19 (3): 1–18.

Haraway, D. 1988. "Situated Knowledges: The Science Question in Feminism and the Privilege of Partial Perspective." *Feminist Studies* 14 (3): 575–99.

Henry, Nicola, Asher Flynn, and Anastasia Powell. 2015. "The Promise and Paradox of Justice: Rape Justice beyond the Criminal Law." In *Rape Justice: Beyond the Criminal Law*, edited by Anastasia Powell, Nicola Henry, and Asher Flynn, 1–17. New York: Palgrave Macmillan.

Hesse-Biber, Sharlene Nagy. 2011. *Handbook of Feminist Research: Theory and Praxis*. Thousand Oaks, CA: SAGE Publications.

hooks, bell. 1994. *Teaching to Transgress: Education as the Practice of Freedom*. New York: Routledge.

Jenkins, Katharine. 2014. "'That's Not Philosophy': Feminism, Academia and the Double Bind." *Journal of Gender Studies* 23 (3): 1–13.

Lawson, S., and L. Olle. 2006. "Dangerous Drink Spiking Archetypes." *Women against Violence: A Feminist Journal* 18: 46–55.

Lawson, Victoria. 2009. "Instead of Radical Geography, How About Caring Geography?" *Antipode* 41 (1): 210–13.

Lorde, Audre. 1988. *A Burst of Light: Essays*. Ithaca, NY: Fireband Books.

Moors, Marleen. 2015. "Sexism and Gender Issues in Academic Philosophy: Philosophical Practice as a Balancing Act." In *Women in Philosophical Counselling: The Anima of Thought in Action*, edited by Luisa DePaula and Peter Raabe, 233–45. New York: Lexington Books.

Mountz, A., A. Bonds, B. Mansfield, J. Loyd, J. Hyndman, M. Walton-Roberts, R. Basu, et al. 2015. "For Slow Scholarship: Feminist Politics of Resistance through Collective Action in the Neoliberal University." *ACME: An International E-Journal for Critical Geographies* 14 (4): 1235–59.

Oakley, Ann. 2016. "Interviewing Women Again: Power, Time and the Gift." *Sociology* 50 (1): 195–213.

Powell, Anastasia. 2015a. "Seeking Informal Justice Online: Vigilantism, Activism and Resisting a Rape Culture in Cyberspace." In *Rape Justice: Beyond the Criminal Law*, edited by Anastasia Powell, Nicola Henry, and Asher Flynn, 218–37. New York: Palgrave Macmillan.

– 2015b. "Seeking Rape Justice: Formal and Informal Responses to Sexual Violence through Technosocial Counter-Publics." *Theoretical Criminology* 19 (4): 571–88.

Rentschler, C.A. 2014. "Rape Culture and the Feminist Politics of Social Media." *Girlhood Studies: An Interdisciplinary Journal* 7 (1): 65–82.

Rich, Marc D., Ebony A. Utley, Kelly Janke, and Minodora Moldoveanu. 2010. "'I'd Rather Be Doing Something Else:' Male Resistance to Rape Prevention Programs." *The Journal of Men's Studies* 18 (3): 268–88.

Robinson, Fiona. 2008. "The Importance of Care in the Theory and Practice of Human Security." *Journal of International Political Theory* 4 (2): 167–88.

– 2011. "Care Ethics and the Transnationalization of Care: Reflections on Autonomy, Hegemonic Masculinities, and Globalization." In *Feminist Ethics and Social Policy: Towards a New Global Political Economy of Care*, edited by R. Mahon and F. Robinson, 127–44. Vancouver: UBC Press.

Salter, M. 2013. "Justice and Revenge in Online Counter-Publics: Emerging Responses to Sexual Violence in the Age of Social Media." *Crime, Media, Culture: An International Journal,* 9 (3): 225–42.

Sevenhuijsen, Selma. 1998. *Citizenship and the Ethics of Care: Feminist Considerations on Justice, Morality, and Politics.* London and New York: Routledge.

Smith, Dorothy E. 1987. *The Everyday World as Problematic: A Feminist Sociology.* Boston and Toronto: Northeastern University Press.

Stanko, E.A. 1997. "Safety Talk: Conceptualizing Women's Risk Assessment as a 'Technology of the Soul.'" *Theoretical Criminology* 1 (4): 479–99.

Stewart, A.L. 2014. "The Men's Project: A Sexual Assault Prevention Program Targeting College Men." *Psychology of Men and Masculinity* 15 (4): 481–5.

Stockdill, B., and M.Y. Danico, eds. 2012. *Transforming the Ivory Tower: Challenging Racism, Sexism, and Homophobia in the Academy.* Honolulu: University of Hawaii Press.

Tronto, Joan C. 1989. "Women and Caring: What Can Feminists Learn about Morality from Caring?" In *Gender/Body/Knowledge*, edited by Alison Jagger and Susan Bordo, 172–87. New Brunswick, NJ: Rutgers University.

– 1993. *Moral Boundaries: A Political Argument for an Ethic of Care.* New York and London: Routledge.

Young, Iris Marion. 1994. "Comments on Seyla Benhabib, Situating the Self." *New German Critique: An Interdisciplinary Journal of German Studies* 62: 165–72.

4

The Return of the Sex Wars

Contesting Rights and Interests
in Campus Sexual Violence Reform

Daniel Del Gobbo

INTRODUCTION

In December 2014, four female students in the Dalhousie University
Faculty of Dentistry filed complaints under the university's Sexual
Harassment Policy relating to violent and misogynistic comments
posted in a Facebook group by male students in their class (Llewellyn
et al. 2015b). Among other comments, the male students joked about
sedating their female classmates in order to have rough sex with them,
voted in online polls about which of their classmates they wanted to
"hate fuck" and "sport fuck," and suggested a new definition of
"penis" as "the tool used to wean and convert lesbians and virgins
into useful, productive members of society" (Backhouse et al. 2015).
Upon learning that their classmates had found out about the posts,
one of the male students wrote in the group that "lockeroom talk ...
should stay in the locker room," another suggested that the men should
get "rid of the evidence," and another said that "I want to know I can
say whoever I want to HATEFUCK and know some guy isn't going to
go running and tell the girls" (ibid.).

In the end, most of the female students elected to proceed with their
complaints through a consensual dispute resolution process based on
principles of restorative justice instead of the more formal, adjudicative option of an academic discipline hearing.[1] The process ran for
approximately five months. The complainants' rationale for choosing
restorative justice was that a more collaborative approach would

create a safe and confidential environment for participants and other stakeholders to critically reflect on their experiences and find ways to create a healthier culture at the faculty (Llewellyn et al. 2015b). The process culminated in a "Day of Learning" event, in which participating students, facilitators, faculty members, and representatives from more than eighty stakeholder groups engaged in open dialogue about five areas of campus life that needed to be improved (ibid.).[2] Two of the complainants in the case, Amanda Demsey and Jillian Smith, described their experience in the process this way: "restorative justice was a path that we chose for ourselves, and the gains we made individually and as a collective of young professionals will carry on" (Llewellyn et al. 2015a).

The university's response to the case generated a firestorm of controversy among feminist legal theorists, student activists, and academic policy-makers across the country.[3] Some critics argued that the female students were pressured to choose restorative justice in a process that lacked basic fairness and transparency (Hampson 2015). Other critics argued that a more punitive approach than restorative justice was necessary because it would send a stronger message that campus peer sexual violence would not be tolerated at the school (Acorn 2015).[4] Ultimately, four faculty members at the university lodged a formal complaint under the students' code of conduct, requesting that the school commence an adjudicative procedure on a parallel track and suspend the male students on an interim basis in order to protect the safety and well-being of the entire university community (Elliott 2015).[5] According to Jennifer Llewellyn, the law professor who co-facilitated the restorative justice process, Demsey and Smith's decision was enough to render them pariahs in the feminist community despite their self-identifying as feminists who "care[d] deeply about women's issues," who "chose this option to try to do what we felt was best for ourselves as women," yet who "spent our holidays holed up reading article after article about how we had made the wrong choice for women" (Llewellyn et al. 2015a).

The Dalhousie Dentistry case illustrates that the problem of campus peer sexual violence is incredibly thorny. As the media continues to shine a bright light on the problem, feminists have been drawn into a national conversation about how colleges and universities should address it. In response to legislative efforts and sustained political pressure from student activists across the country, nearly every college and university in Canada has now drafted and, in most cases, implemented a stand-alone campus sexual violence policy (Lee and Wong 2017). However, few policy-makers agree about the best way to repair the harm caused by sexual violence and to promote cultural change on campus. The debate is equally contentious in the United States, where critical attention to the issue has intensified since President Obama announced (and President Trump has since rolled back) a bold and aggressive approach to Title IX, a law requiring gender equity in federally funded education programs (Cantalupo 2011; Koss, Wilgus, and Williamsen 2014; Anderson 2016; Gersen and Suk 2016; Collins 2015).[6] The resulting discussions inspired Emily Bazelon to write a feature in the *New York Times Magazine* proclaiming the "Return of the Sex Wars" at American colleges and universities (2015). By "sex wars," Bazelon meant that contrasting views about sexual violence invoked a decades-long debate among feminist legal theorists and activists about the role of law as a tool of sexual governance in intimate relationships (Abrams 1995; Cossman 2018).

Following Bazelon, I would argue that the "return of the sex wars" has spilled across the border. While the role of law is central to many areas of this debate, this chapter focuses on competing feminist legal treatments of one aspect of the Dalhousie Dentistry case: the use of consensual dispute resolution (e.g., negotiation, mediation, and restorative justice) to resolve complaints of campus peer sexual violence in Canada. One of the main sticking points is whether consensual processes should be offered by colleges and universities as an alternative to adjudication at the complainants' request, or whether the gendered power dynamics inherent in these cases mean that consensual processes should be generally unavailable to complainants despite their request.

In my view, feminists on both sides of the return of the sex wars should be able to organize around the idea of a complainant-centred approach to campus sexual violence reform. This requires us to ask complainants what "justice" means to them. For some complainants, "justice" means vindicating their legal *rights* through an adjudicative process that holds offenders accountable to the public in an official way. But for other complainants, "justice" means satisfying their *interests* through a consensual process that takes account of their social, cultural, economic, and legal interests as potentially distinct from their rights, even if that process takes place in a private and more informal setting. In my view, a complainant-centred approach requires us to empower complainants with the choice to pursue adjudicative or consensual options as they wish, so long as every process is administered responsibly by feminist experts in a manner that promotes gender equality on campus.

My argument proceeds in three parts. Part 1 surveys the current legal and regulatory landscape of consensual dispute resolution in Canada, explaining how the law's treatment of consensual processes in the context of campus peer sexual violence is unclear. Part 2 situates this issue in light of historical debates in feminist legal theory about the role of rights- and interests-based approaches to resolving complaints of sexual violence. Part 3 explains why schools should take inspiration from these debates by instituting a "plural process" model that responds to complainants' needs by leveraging the strategic potential of both their rights and their interests. The Dalhousie Dentistry case is used as a critical touchstone throughout.

The Battleground: Consensual Approaches to Campus Peer Sexual Violence

Consensual dispute resolution is an "interests-based" process. Its main objective is to allow two or more disputing parties to resolve their conflicting interests by voluntary agreement, potentially with the assistance of neutral third-party facilitators, legal counsel, or other members of the community who are personally affected by the events. Crucially, the parties' agreement is the product of mutual commitment and compromise, which is reached through a collaborative process rather than imposed by judicial or administrative decree (Menkel-Meadow 1983). The basic rationale is that once freed from the abstract legal categories and cumbersome procedures that characterize the formal law, an interests-based process can get to the heart of the underlying trouble by focusing on building accountability and trust between the parties, which is more likely to assist the parties to generate creative options and design the terms of their own recovery beyond what a court or tribunal might order in the adjudication of rights claims (Menkel-Meadow 1983; Rifkin 1984; Silbey and Sarat 1989).[7]

The place of consensual dispute resolution in the legal and regulatory framework of campus peer sexual violence in Canada is unclear. As of November 2019, four provinces – Ontario, British Columbia, Manitoba, and Quebec – have passed legislation requiring post-secondary institutions to implement stand-alone campus sexual violence policies.[8] Another province, Nova Scotia, has signed two consecutive memoranda of understanding with colleges and universities, with the second memorandum binding through the 2023–24 year, which require post-secondary institutions to create their own policies (Council of Nova Scotia University Presidents 2016; 2019). Other provinces have eschewed formal legal mandates, but encouraged political organizing on this issue in other ways. For example, Alberta's minister of Advanced Education directed colleges and universities in September 2016 to have policies in place by the spring of 2017.[9]

Taken together, these efforts should help to address the problem of campus peer sexual violence by ensuring that public awareness of the issue is heightened, colleges and universities start to develop a coordinated response, and vital services are made available to students. Beyond that, it is difficult to assess their impact because the new laws are thin on specifics about what campus sexual violence policies should actually contain, which has left academic administrators to fill the gap. While several government agencies and advocacy groups have issued optional guidance to schools, it is unclear how the schools' compliance with the laws will be monitored and enforced by the state.[10] This means that colleges and universities have seemingly been granted a wide discretionary berth to handle complaints as they see fit under the laws. As a result, the content of campus sexual violence policies in Canada varies significantly from school to school, particularly as it relates to the use of consensual dispute resolution (Lee and Wong 2017).

To illustrate, Ontario's law provides that policies in that province must describe "the investigation and decision-making processes at the college or university that will take place if an incident or complaint of sexual violence is investigated."[11] The policies must also give "examples of the decisions that may be made and measures that may be imposed after an incident or complaint is investigated."[12] However, the legislation does not say whether these decisions may be reached through a consensual process.[13] This lack of clarity is reflected in the policies themselves, which provide no less than six different approaches with respect to this issue:

1   *Express provision with specifics.* The policy expressly provides
    for consensual dispute resolution as an option for handling
    student complaints, including a detailed description of the
    process and procedural steps. The availability of the process
    may or may not be subject to conditions.[14]

2   *Express provision without specifics.* The policy expressly
    provides for consensual dispute resolution as an option for
    handling student complaints, but without a detailed description
    of the process or procedural steps. The availability of the
    process may or may not be subject to conditions.[15]

3   *Express provision incorporated by reference to another policy
    or procedure.* The policy provides for consensual dispute
    resolution as an option for handling student complaints, but
    only insofar as it is available under other academic protocols.
    In such a case, the other protocol determines the process,
    procedural steps, and any conditions on its use.[16]

4   *Implied provision without specifics.* The policy refers to
    consensual dispute resolution, but only in the context of
    settlement privilege attaching to mediation communications.
    This suggests that a mediation process may be available to
    students, but the policy does not otherwise describe the process,
    procedural steps, or any conditions on its use.[17]

5   *Ambiguous provision.* The policy provides for "other existing
    possibilities" (or similarly vague or ambiguous language) as
    an alternative to the adjudicative process for handling student
    complaints, but without identifying what these other options
    are, their procedural steps, or any conditions on their use.[18]

6   *Absent provision.* The policy does not appear to provide for
    consensual dispute resolution as an option for handling student
    complaints because it is not mentioned anywhere.[19]

It is important to distinguish between what these policies say on their
face and how they are applied in practice. Based on my informal conversations with students, faculty, and administrators, it appears that
many colleges and universities are permitting – and in some cases,
unduly pressuring – complainants to choose consensual dispute resolution despite a lack of clarity around this issue in their policies. More
empirical work is needed to confirm these trends and the reasons for
them because we know relatively little, as of yet, about how schools
are interpreting their statutory mandates and handling complaints
under their policies in a systematic way. It remains an open question
whether consensual dispute resolution should play a role in colleges
and universities' response to campus peer sexual violence, and, if so,
what these processes should look like to ensure that they provide
access to justice for complainants.[20]

Warring Subjects: Rights and Interests
in Feminist Legal Theory

Approaches to consensual dispute resolution are situated within historical debates in feminist legal theory about the relationship between sexual agency and sexual coercion in women's lives. These debates reached their apex in the feminist sex wars from the late 1970s to the early 1990s, which were a series of intellectual entanglements between feminists, queer theorists, and other scholars over the legal regulation of consensual sex in Canada and the United States (Abrams 1995; Cossman 2018). One of the key subjects of the sex wars was the role of the formal law – and specifically, the role of women's rights – in promoting social and cultural change in light of women's sexualized domination by men (Cossman et al. 1997). This issue bore directly on legal and regulatory efforts to define sex that should be permitted or encouraged in society, and sex that should be prohibited as sexual violence by law.

The most influential theory in the sex wars was the radical feminism of Catherine MacKinnon, who theorized that sexual violence is an expression of male dominance that socially determines, rather than arises from, the fact of gender difference between women and men (Mackinnon 1982, 1983). In the return of the sex wars, radical feminist views are reflected by the arguments of many feminists, antiviolence activists, and other critics who primarily frame their political advocacy on the issue of campus peer sexual violence in terms of minoritizing, identity-based conceptions of women's sexual subjectivity, translatable into rights claims, which require the protection of the state (Dubber 1999; Gruber 2006).[21] Following MacKinnon, these critics have championed the use of academic discipline hearings, civil courts, and criminal justice processes to publicly vindicate victims' rights that have been wrongfully infringed (Cantalupo 2012; Halley 2015; Gruber 2015; Coray 2016; Coker 2016).[22] For them, the most effective way to deter male violence and keep victims safe is to punish offenders for the harms they cause, whether in the form of expulsions from school, awards of monetary damages, temporary restraining orders, and criminal charges and convictions in appropriate cases (Coray 2016; Collins 2015).[23]

These critics are particularly concerned that consensual processes can lead to unfair procedures and unjust results that disadvantage women as a group. Annalise Acorn (2015) argues that because the male students in the Dalhousie Dentistry case were "very powerful, very privileged wrongdoers," the expressive value of expelling the male students following an adjudicative process outweighed the value of any compassion for the men that restorative justice is intended to show. Acorn explains that "a traditional process resulting in the expulsion of the students ... would presumably be aimed not at punishing the students but at ensuring standards of good character and good behavior in an elite profession that holds a position of considerable trust" (ibid.).[24] As Anne Kingston put it more bluntly, the restorative justice process at Dalhousie applied "veneers to major cavities," heralding a narrative of culture change on the strength of the male students' apologies and little else. This effectively papered over the rifeness of "rape culture" at the university, which perpetuated the men's conduct in the first place and demanded a more punitive response (Kingston 2015; Côté 2015; Gruber 2015). These arguments reflect the belief that male students will exploit their power advantage in consensual dispute resolution by pressuring female students to agree on settlement terms that advance the men's interests alone, contrary to the public's interest in protecting women's rights under the rule of law (Daly and Stubbs 2006; Kohn 2010; Hopkins 2012; Kaplan 2016).[25]

Radical feminism inspired an unlikely alliance of opposing critics in the sex wars, including sex radical feminists, lesbian and gay rights activists, queer theorists, and libertarians who generally affirmed the role of sexual agency and choice in women's lives, albeit with their own distinct political commitments (Abrams 1995).[26] In the return of the sex wars, these views are reflected by the arguments of a diverse group of feminist and legal process critics whose mission to celebrate the richness and complexity of women's interests and desires cannot be easily enforced by government officials. Specifically, these critics argue that the radical feminist response of "more law" and "more rights" for women has unduly circumscribed the range of political interventions that are necessary to promote gender equality and prevent campus peer sexual violence (Brown and Halley 2002; Gruber 2012; Rittich 2015). These critics believe that a narrow focus on the legal dimension of sexual violence and need for a carceral response has come at the expense of more complex forms of regulatory action that address the social, cultural, and economic aspects of the problem, which may or may not be perfectly translatable into women's rights claims (Bacchi 1998; Whitley and Page 2015; Halley 2015; Collins

2015). While these critics disagree about whether consensual dispute resolution should supplement or supplant the formal system, they generally agree that it should form part of a more holistic strategy that moves away from the "victim-perpetrator" model of individual legal responsibility (Harris 2011; Koss et al. 2014; Kaplan 2016).

These critics explain that while complainants may initially ask for legal relief through findings of liability or guilt, this relief will often be a proxy for the complainants' underlying interests that cannot be achieved by these findings (Rifkin 1984; Menkel-Meadow 1983; Silbey and Sarat 1988; Kohn 2010; Kaplan 2016). To illustrate, Demsey and Smith's main objective in the Dalhousie Dentistry case was to transform the academic culture at their university (Llewellyn et al. 2015a). Had they chosen to proceed with an adjudicative process instead of a consensual one, this would have transferred their decisional power to a tribunal that had limited jurisdiction to award non-legal remedies (Matsuda 2000; Harris 2011). The tribunal's mandate would have precluded it from considering more wide-ranging issues than the content of the Facebook group (Llewellyn et al. 2015b). Its adversarial structure would have discouraged the male students from taking responsibility for their actions and critically reflecting on the harm they caused (Hudson 1998; Harris 2011; Hopkins 2012). Its rules of procedure would have prevented the tribunal from engaging with third parties and outside community members in the healing process (Smith and Martinez 2009; Whitley and Page 2015). Given the limitations of the formal law, the substantive outcome in the case might not have been achieved, or even been possible, had the female students been prevented from exploring their interests in a more flexible and open-textured consensual process (Llewellyn et al. 2015b).

The return of the sex wars reflects an ideological divide over whether adjudicative or consensual processes should take precedence in shaping our strategic response to campus peer sexual violence. On one side, feminists argue that the goals of dispute resolution should prioritize *rights*, focusing on how the law should dismantle the structure of male dominance on behalf of all women at the expense of some women's preference to resolve their complaints otherwise. On the other side, feminists argue that the goals of dispute resolution should prioritize *interests*, focusing on how the law should respect women's individual wants and desires even if and when they replicate gendered power imbalances in society that are the traditional subject of a collective rights claim.[27]

To be clear, I make no pretensions to neutrality in my critical assessment of this ideological divide. I have argued elsewhere that policy-makers should resist radical feminist theories of sexual experience and, by extension, theories of gender and sexuality in legal procedure that have been marshalled in support of unnecessary restrictions on the use of consensual dispute resolution in the name of protecting "all women" over the interests of the parties themselves (Del Gobbo 2019). But this is not to say that policy-makers should impose unnecessary restrictions on the use of adjudicative processes either, which have an important role to play in vindicating women's rights to be free from sexual violence. As we compare these two moments in critical legal thought – the sex wars and the return of the sex wars – how can feminists move beyond our mutual antagonism to come together, as Bazelon says, and leverage the strategic potential of both rights and interests?

Keeping the Peace: A "Complainant-Centred" Approach to Justice

Nearly everyone who works on the issue of campus sexual violence in Canada agrees on one thing: colleges and universities should take a "complainant-centred"[28] approach to resolving complaints of campus peer sexual violence (McGlynn et al. 2012; Randall 2013; Buss et al. 2016; Coker 2016). This term can be confusing.[29] For my purposes here, I am using it to invoke the widely held view among feminist anti-violence workers that schools should "centre" the experience of complainants when deciding on the legal and institutional arrangements that will follow in response to their reports. This is a two-stage inquiry. First, schools should ask complainants what "justice" means to them. Second, schools should work with complainants to determine how the schools can facilitate access to that conception of justice through a dispute resolution process that meets the complainants' unique needs and safeguards against the risk of harm to women and other vulnerable groups. In my view, this represents one way to translate the differences that lie at the heart of the return of the sex wars into a workable model for law and policy reform.

As I have explained above, most radical feminists construct the juridical subjects of sexual violence law, complainants, as possessors of collective rights in a liberal democratic framework (Silbey and Sarat 1988; Halley 2002; Rittich 2015).[30] Focusing on rights as a means of delivering justice is not wrong – at least, not completely. Access to justice, as the term is used in its traditional sense, relates to the basic condition that individuals should be able to access the courts, tribunals, and legal services in civil and criminal proceedings (Bhabha 2007; Farrow 2014).[31] For many complainants, "justice" means feeling validated by an official authority declaring that they are right. It means conveying moral outrage about campus sexual violence as a systemic problem. It means redistributing resources between women and men through the enforcement of formal legal remedies. For these students, the goals of adjudication are almost perfectly aligned with their reasons for reporting in the first place. There is effectively no distinguishing between their rights and interests because their overriding interest is the vindication of their rights by the state, through which they hope to achieve one or more of these legitimate objectives (Kohn 2010; McGlynn, Westmarland, and Godden 2012; Kaplan 2016).

Unfortunately, the formal legal system in Canada has recognized more rights than it is capable of vindicating through adjudicative processes. The problems of mounting judicial backlogs and transaction costs have created significant barriers to legal representation and procedure (Farrow 2014). The barriers may be greatest for members of vulnerable groups, including women, who were historically denied the experience and resources needed to navigate the formal system on equal footing as other groups (Delgado 1999). The situation may be especially dire for complainants of sexual violence (Anderson 2016). Adding to the problems of trial cost and delay, the evidence is clear that for many complainants, the pursuit of civil and criminal justice – with the intense public scrutiny, gendered social media backlash, and widespread disbelief that often come with it – brings further emotional and psychological trauma (McGlynn et al. 2012; Randall 2013; Koss 2014; Buss et al. 2016).

Given this stark reality, one of the driving forces behind current movements to reform campus sexual violence law and policy is the increasing recognition that access to justice is a gender equality issue (Cantalupo 2012; Anderson 2016). Research shows that the high sexual victimization rate of female students and the high non-reporting rate of campus peer sexual violence combine to perpetuate a cycle whereby male students believe that they will not get caught and, if they do, that they will not be held accountable for their actions. Legal and institutional responses to the problem can either feed or break this cycle (Cantalupo 2012). For many feminists, it follows that if colleges and universities adopted formal procedures for handling student complaints, this would help to encourage reporting and streamline campus adjudicative procedures on the front end, while holding perpetrators accountable and preventing future violence on the back end (ibid.; Anderson 2016).[32]

However, the pursuit of gender equality is not adequately captured by the feminist legalism of rights. Access to justice has both a collective and individual dimension, which relates to the more aspirational condition that complainants should be able to access any form of dispute resolution under law, whether rights-based or interests-based, that accords with their individual wants and desires (Bhabha 2007; Rogers et al. 2013; Farrow 2014; Del Gobbo 2019). For many complainants, "justice" means repairing the harm caused by students' actions through healing. It means striving toward reintegration and reconciliation, both on private terms between the parties and on public terms within the community. It means holding students accountable through voluntary measures that prevent future crime. It means transforming relationships with a view to promoting social and cultural change on campus. For many complainants, "justice" means something more than the formal vindication of their rights by the state.[33] It means addressing their legitimate interests through a dispute resolution process that may or may not overlap with the goals of adjudication (Kohn 2010; McGlynn et al. 2012; Koss 2014; Buss et al. 2016; Collins 2015; Coker 2016).

This should not be a controversial idea in feminist legal theory, yet many feminists rarely conceive of complainants' harms as anything other than violations of collective rights that demand the formal legal system to respond. This preference for the rights-based model has meant that other forms of dispute resolution have been sidelined, overlooked, or categorically rejected in some cases of campus sexual violence altogether.[34] This has limited our opportunity to engage in feminist political projects that live outside the public sphere when the evidence is clear that many complaints simply do not require, as a social, cultural, economic, or even legal matter, a rights-based approach to promote gender equality. In many cases, the outcomes that complainants are seeking may only be possible if they choose a private and informal process that permits more open-ended, critical contestation about interests and the community's role in meeting them.

For these reasons, I would argue that a truly complainant-centred approach requires schools to ask students what "justice" means to them and help facilitate access to that conception through a range of dispute resolution processes based on rights and interests. I am calling this the "plural process" model of campus sexual violence reform. To illustrate, Demsey and Smith explained what "justice" meant to them in the Dalhousie Dentistry case:

> [Restorative justice] provided a means to bring all the parties that needed to be present into the conversation, in ways that were safe, so that accountability could be taken and changes could be made. Despite the demand for expulsion that was echoing out across the country, it was never a reasonable option for us. We saw expulsion as the exact opposite of what we wanted. We did not want to see 13 angry men expelled who had learned nothing about why what they wrote was wrong. To us, that was a cop-out. Nor did we want to just forgive and forget. Rather, we were looking for a form of resolution that would allow us to graduate alongside men who held an understanding of the harms they had caused, who had owned these harms, and who could carry with them a sense of responsibility and obligation to do better (Llewellyn et al 2015a).

In principle, this is what a complainant-centred approach to justice looks like. While a more comprehensive review of the issues surrounding the Dalhousie Dentistry case is beyond the scope of this chapter, it appears that the university encouraged Demsey and Smith, at least, to dictate the terms of their own feminist political strategy despite the loudest public voices "echoing out across the country" threatening to drown them out. Naturally, different complainants will have different interests and wish to make different choices – and indeed, some female students opted out of restorative justice in the Dalhousie Dentistry case (Backhouse et al. 2015) – but these feminist contradictions are the strength of "plural process" as a model for reform, not the weakness.[35]

To be clear, my argument is not that consensual dispute resolution can or should be used in every case of campus peer sexual violence. If complainants do not wish to participate at any time, the process should not proceed by its own definition or by law (Archibald 2005; Kohn 2010). If respondents refuse to accept responsibility or respect the accounts, wishes, and proposals of complainants at any time, it may be impossible for the parties to have a constructive discussion and the process may need to be terminated (Hudson 2002; Randall 2013). And if respondents pose an ongoing threat of violence to complainants at any time, it may be impossible to approximate a balance of power between the parties that is required to maintain the integrity of the process and keep complainants safe (Randall 2013).

My argument is that critical approaches to campus sexual violence reform should be contextual to the lived experiences of the parties, which cannot be captured by a single, unified feminist theory of access to justice. This means that complainants should be provided with any form of dispute resolution under law that accords with their personal definition of "justice." Empowering complainants in this way does not mean that feminists should be willfully blind to the reality of gender inequality in society that many rights-based processes are intended to address. Yet acknowledging the reality of gender inequality should not require us to essentialize about women's injury or overdetermine the role of power imbalance in producing the content of women's interests in resolving their disputes otherwise. This tension lies at the heart of the return of the sex wars on campus. Feminists should embrace these contestations by leveraging the strategic potential of both rights and interests.

What might the plural process model look like in practice? Colleges and universities should explicitly provide a range of both adjudicative and consensual options for handling student complaints in their campus sexual violence policies, including the relevant steps in every process, any conditions on their use, the role of third-party facilitators, measures to ensure procedural fairness, as well as the availability of social and community supports for the parties throughout. Both adjudicative and consensual options should be tailored to local conditions on the ground and flexible to changing circumstances between the parties and from case to case. On the front end, this requires schools to screen for power imbalances and risks of harm between the parties to determine the procedural safeguards that are necessary to conduct these options safely and effectively. On the back end, this requires schools to provide loop-back mechanisms in their policies, which allow the parties to move between rights- and interests-based processes as they wish. Both adjudicative and consensual options should be administered responsibly by feminist experts trained in both law and anti-violence work at all times.

More empirical research is needed to confirm how campus sexual violence policies are being interpreted by students and applied by academic administrators so that colleges and universities can integrate more learning from experience into the plural process model. How are rights- and interests-based processes transforming the social, cultural, economic, and legal conditions that have fostered campus peer sexual violence in the past? How might rights- and interests-based processes be operating as tools of sexual governance, for better and for worse? These are still relatively early days in the life of campus sexual violence reform in Canada, but this chapter's recommendations should lead to greater understanding about the role that both rights and interests can play in promoting feminist objectives in the return of the sex wars.

NOTES

1 Here and throughout, I use the term "consensual dispute resolution" to describe a range of interests-based, out-of-court dispute resolution processes that are based on mutual commitment and compromise and could potentially result in settlements. Consensual dispute resolution is a form of "alternative dispute resolution," which is a broader term that can be used to describe any out-of-court process, whether adjudicative or consensual.

2 The five key areas were: (1) *Community Building* ("finding better and more supportive ways to build connections between and among students, faculty, and staff"); (2) *Inclusion and Equality* ("supporting diversity and confronting accepted divisions along lines of gender, race, culture, and religion"); (3) *Professionalism and Ethics* ("adapting a more integrated and principle-based approach to both personal and professional integrity with respect to patient care and safety"); (4) *Curriculum and Program Structure* ("addressing factors within the program and clinic structure that contribute to a competitive and stressful environment"); and (5) *Reporting Processes and Conflict Resolution* ("improving communication and transparency in order to create safer spaces to address and resolve issues"). See Llewellyn, MacIssac, and MacKay 2015.

3 To illustrate the range of reactions to the restorative justice process, the Dalhousie Feminist Legal Association supported the female students' decision, writing in a statement: "If conducted diligently, this process will also unearth the causes and context surrounding the behaviour of these men, thus exposing a deep and systemic culture of misogyny in the dental school that we demand be addressed campus-wide" (Jeffrey 2015). At the

same time, an online petition that Dalhousie University should expel the
male students who participated in the social media group garnered over
50,000 signatures from the public (see https://www.change.org/p/
dalhousie-university-president-dr-richard-florizone-expel-the-students-
who-were-members-and-or-participated-in-the-facebook-group-called-
class-of-dds-2015-gentlemen).

4 Throughout this chapter, I use the term "sexual violence" in a manner that
is intended to be consistent with the Canadian provincial laws mandating
that colleges and universities create sexual violence policies. The term
describes any sexual act or act targeting a person's sexuality, gender identity, or gender expression, whether the act is physical or psychological in
nature, that is committed, threatened, or attempted against a person without the person's consent, and includes sexual assault, sexual harassment,
stalking, indecent exposure, voyeurism, and sexual exploitation. I use the
term campus "peer" sexual violence rather than the more general term
"campus sexual violence" to describe sexual activity between students
that fits the above definition.

5 Ultimately, the complaint was dismissed on the grounds that it was ineligi-
ble for consideration under the students' code of conduct because a professional standards investigation was already underway (Hui 2015).

6 20 USC § 1681(a) (2012) ("No person in the United States shall, on the
basis of sex, be excluded from participation in, be denied the benefits of,
or be subjected to discrimination under any education program or activity
receiving Federal financial assistance"). Sexual harassment that creates
a hostile environment at US colleges and universities is a form of sex
discrimination prohibited by Title IX. See Office for Civil Rights, US
Department of Education 2001). For President Obama's approach, see
US Department of Education (2011) and US Department of Education
(2014). In September 2017, US Secretary of Education Betsy DeVos
announced that the Dear Colleague Letter was being rescinded
(US Department of Education 2017).

7 Some critics may object to my consideration of restorative justice alongside mediation and negotiation here, which are more typically referred to
as "interests-based" consensual dispute resolution processes in the legal
scholarship. Notably, Jennifer Llewellyn's practice of restorative justice
draws on accounts of relational feminist theory, which recognizes that
our understandings about justice are formed through webs of intimate
and broader social, cultural, economic, and professional relationships.
Engaging with these relationships through a restorative justice process is
said to open up new pathways for collective action and opportunities for

closure beyond negotiation and mediation, which may be limited by their focus on individual interests-maximization in a liberal economic model as opposed to relational interests (Llewellyn, Demsey, and Smith 2015). However, I would argue that restorative justice may be properly considered a form of "interests-based" consensual dispute resolution for my purposes in this chapter, to the extent that restorative justice seeks to promote relational interests as distinct from rights in working towards a consensual agreement between the parties.

8 Ministry of Training, Colleges, and Universities Act, RSO 1990, c. M. 19, s. 17 [Ontario Act]; Private Career Colleges Act, RSO 2005, c. 28, s. 32.1; Sexual Violence and Misconduct Policy Act, SBC 2016, c. 23; Advanced Education Administration Act, CCSM c. A6.3, s. 2.2; Private Vocational Institutions Act, CCSM, c. P137, s. 13.1; An Act to Prevent and Fight Sexual Violence in Higher Education Institutions, SQ 2017 c. 32.

9 For more on this topic, see Derworiz (2016).

10 For examples of such guidance, see Ontario Ministry of the Status of Women (2013); British Columbia Ministry of Advanced Education (n.d.); and Government of Manitoba (n.d.).

11 Ontario Act, *supra* note 8, O Reg 131/16, s. 2.(2)5.

12 Ontario Act, *supra* note 8, O Reg 131/16, s. 2.(2)10.

13 Adding to the uncertainty, Ontario's law provides that campus sexual violence policies must give "examples of the measures that may be implemented for the purpose of protecting a person reporting an incident of, or making a complaint about, sexual violence from retaliation and the threat of retaliation." Ontario Act, *supra* note 8, O Reg 131/16, s. 2.(2)2. Here, it would seem that the legislation clearly contemplates that students reporting sexual violence may be vulnerable to reprisals or other forms of abuse. However, the law is unclear about whether these concerns extend to potential abuses of gendered power imbalance between students in consensual processes.

14 See, for example, Ryerson University (2016).

15 See, for example, Brock University (n.d.).

16 See, for example, University of Toronto (2017).

17 See, for example, Carleton University (2016).

18 See, for example, Saint Paul University (2016).

19 See, for example, Nipissing College (2016).

20 Notably, the Human Rights Tribunal of Ontario is also charged with addressing allegations of sexual violence – specifically, sexual harassment and solicitation – and provides mediation services to parties in these cases as mandated by the Ontario Human Rights Code. Presumably, one of the

intents of the legislatures in passing separate laws to address campus sexual violence was to ensure harmony between the different statutory definitions and legal procedures that address the same things, which suggests that the separate laws may be interpreted to permit forms of consensual dispute resolution. See *Human Rights Code*, RSO 1990, c. H. 19, s. 7.

21 Of course, this is not to say that all self-identified "radical feminists" frame their legal and political advocacy in this way. There may be radical feminists who support the use of consensual dispute resolution in cases of campus peer sexual violence.

22 To illustrate, the US Department of Education's Office of Civil Rights prohibited the use of mediation in campus sexual assault cases under the Obama administration. See US Department of Education (2011). Additionally, the Law Society of Upper Canada has an obligation to "facilitate access to justice" and "protect the public interest" under the Law Society Act, RSO 1990, c L 8, s 4.2. See generally Cromwell (2012). See Smith and Freyd (2013), defining "institutional betrayal" as the failure of colleges and universities to prevent sexual violence and respond to sexual assault complaints in an effective and supportive manner.

23 By contrast, Elizabeth Bernstein (2007, 2010) argues that radical feminist agendas that rely on the state's criminal law powers to punish aberrant male sexuality – what she calls "carceral feminism" in the context of prostitution and sex trafficking – are limited in their ability to prevent sexual violence and promote gender equality on account of their narrow focus on individual criminal responsibility.

24 See also Acorn (2005); Archibald (2005).

25 See also Ending Violence Association of BC (2016): "We strongly discourage the use of restorative justice processes, including mediation, in lieu of sanctions in cases of sexual violence, as sexual assault is a power-based crime (that is, a crime where there is an imbalance of power, or an abuse of power by the perpetrator, and the victim/survivor feels powerless to stop it and/or come forward. In these cases, it has been argued that restorative justice processes may be used by perpetrators to manipulate and maintain their power over victims/survivors, and thus the application of these processes to gender-based violence remains controversial." See also METRAC (2014): "The particular dangers of mediation to follow up on campus sexual assault reports have been identified"). For a more general statement of concern about power imbalance in consensual dispute resolution, see Farrow (2014).

26 For complementary accounts in legal scholarship, see Franke (2001); Cossman (2004).

27 For more on rights and interests in the context of consensual dispute resolution, see Macfarlane (2008); Del Gobbo (2019).

28 Some commentators prefer the terms "victim-centred" or "survivor-centred" to describe the same approach, given that many complainants have adopted the terms "victim" or "survivor" to characterize their own experience with campus peer sexual violence. Throughout this piece, I use the term "complainant-centred" as opposed to "victim-centred" or "survivor-centred" to echo the use of the terms "complainant" and "respondent" that appear in the provincial laws as well as most campus sexual violence policies across the country.

29 To be clear, I am not suggesting that a complainant-centred approach requires schools to "decentre" or otherwise breach their duty of procedural fairness to respondents in adjudicative processes, which should be a bedrock principle of any feminist legal strategy that bends toward justice in campus peer sexual violence cases. This bears repeating in light of some US schools' approaches to Title IX enforcement, also called "complainant-centred," "victim-centred," or "survivor-centred," which have been procedurally unfair to respondents (Yoffe 2014; Gertner 2015; see also Bartholet et al.'s 2014 letter to the *Boston Globe*: https://www. bostonglobe.com/opinion/2014/10/14/rethink-harvard-sexual-harassment-policy/HFDDiZN7nU2UwuUuWMnqbM/story.html).

30 I provide a more detailed exposition of the assumptions underpinning the juridical subject of dispute resolution theory elsewhere. See Del Gobbo (2019).

31 Additionally, the Law Society of Upper Canada has an obligation to "facilitate access to justice" and "protect the public interest" under the Law Society Act, RSO 1990, c L 8, s 4.2. See generally Cromwell (2012).

32 See Smith and Freyd (2013), defining "institutional betrayal" as the failure of colleges and universities to prevent sexual violence and respond to sexual assault complaints in an effective and supportive manner.

33 Mandi Gray put it this way after the conviction of Mustafa Ururyar, a fellow PhD student at York University who was charged with sexual assault, was overturned: "People seem to equate higher convictions with a system that works. If the process to get a conviction is so damaging and the rates of appeal for convictions are so high, it is wrong to assume that the system is 'working.' We need to redefine our definition of success – and that may have to be outside of the formal legal system given the burden of evidence is near impossible to prove given the realities of sexual violence and the prevalence of rape myths in Canadian society more generally. I don't equate the conviction in my case as 'justice' – you have to remember we

are still taking about rape and that action done to me cannot be undone –
even if a judge confirms that he believes it to have occurred" (Quinn
2017).

34 These trends are observable elsewhere in the law. Notably, the Nova
Scotia Restorative Justice Program imposed a moratorium on the referral
of all sexual assault cases to the program in April 2000, which remains in
effect today. The moratorium came largely at the urging of feminist advocacy groups (Nelund 2015). Similarly, many US states prohibit the use of
mediation in family law cases involving intimate partner violence
(Goodmark 2012).

35 This idea builds on Carrie Menkel-Meadow's theorization of "process
pluralism" in institutional dispute systems design – namely, that differently situated parties will invariably have different interests in a dispute
or across a range of disputes, and one of the goals of institutional dispute
systems design should be to respond to these interests with a range of procedural options (Menkel-Meadow 2009).

REFERENCES

Abrams, Kathryn. 1995. "Sex Wars Redux: Agency and Coercion in
Feminist Legal Theory." *Columbia Law Review* 95 (2): 304–76.

Acorn, Annalise. 2005. *Compulsory Compassion: A Critique of
Restorative Justice*. Vancouver: UBC Press.

– 2015. "Son Be a Dentist: Restorative Justice and the Dalhousie Dental
School Scandal." *Harvard Negotiation Law Review*, https://www.hnlr.
org/2015/10/son-be-a-dentist-restorative-justice-and-the-dalhousie-
dental-school-scandal-by-annalise-acorn/.

Anderson, Michelle. 2016. "Campus Sexual Assault Adjudication and
Resistance to Reform." *The Yale Law Journal* 125 (7): 1940–2005.

Archibald, Bruce P. 2005. "Why Restorative Justice is Not Compulsory
Compassion: Annalise Acorn's Labour of Love Lost." *Alberta Law
Review* 42 (3): 941–50.

Bacchi, Carol. 1998. "Changing the Sexual Harassment Agenda." In
Gender and Institutions: Welfare, Work and Citizenship, edited by
Moira Gatens and Alison Mackinnon, 75–89. Cambridge: Cambridge
University Press.

Backhouse, Constance, Donald McRae, and Nitya Iyer. 2015. *Report of
the Task Force on Misogyny, Sexism and Homophobia in Dalhousie
University Faculty of Dentistry*. Halifax, NS: Dalhousie University.

Bazelon, Emily. 2015. "The Return of the Sex Wars." *The New York Times Magazine*, 13 September. https://www.nytimes.com/2015/09/13/magazine/the-return-of-the-sex-wars.html.

Bernstein, Elizabeth. 2007. "The Sexual Politics of the 'New Abolitionism.'" *Differences* 18 (3): 128–51.

– 2010. "Militarized Humanitarianism Meets Carceral Feminism: The Politics of Sex, Rights, and Freedom in Contemporary Antitrafficking Campaigns." *Signs* 36 (1): 45–71.

Bhabha, Faisal. 2007. "Institutionalizing Access-to-Justice: Judicial Legislative and Grassroots Dimensions." *Queen's Law Journal* 33 (1): 139–78.

British Columbia Ministry of Advanced Education. n.d. "Preventing and Responding to Sexual Violence and Misconduct at British Columbia Post-Secondary Institutions: A Guide for Developing Policies and Actions." http://www2.gov.bc.ca/assets/gov/education/post-secondary-education/institution-resources-administration/5233_sexual_violence_and_misconduct_policy_guidelines_web.pdf.

Brock University. n.d. "Sexual Assault and Harassment Policy." https://brocku.ca/human-rights/wp-content/uploads/sites/55/Brock-Sexual-Assault-and-Harassment-Policy.pdf.

Brown, Wendy, and Janet Halley. 2002. "Introduction." In *Left Legalism/Left Critique*, edited by Wendy Brown and Janet Halley, 1–38. Durham, NC: Duke University Press.

Buss, Doris, Diana Majury, Dawn Moore, George S. Rigakos, and Rashmee Singh. 2016. *The Response to Sexual Violence at Ontario University Campuses*. Toronto: Ontario Ministry of Community Safety and Correctional Services.

Cantalupo, Nancy Chi. 2011. "Burying Our Heads in the Sand: Lack of Knowledge, Knowledge Avoidance, and the Persistent Problem of Campus Peer Sexual Violence." *Loyola University Chicago Law Journal* 43 (1): 205–66.

– 2012. "Decriminalizing Campus Institutional Responses to Peer Sexual Violence." *Journal of College and University Law* 38 (3): 481–524.

Carleton University. 2016. "Sexual Violence Policy." https://carleton.ca/secretariat/wp-content/uploads/Sexual-Violence-Policy-December-1-2016.pdf.

Coker, Donna. 2016. "Crime Logic, Campus Sexual Assault, and Restorative Justice." *Texas Tech Law Review* 49 (1): 147–210.

Collins, Erin. 2015. "The Criminalization of Title IX." *Ohio State Journal of Criminal Law* 13 (2): 365–96.

Coray, Erica. 2016. "Victim Protection or Revictimization: Should College Disciplinary Boards Handle Sexual Assault Claims." *Boston College Journal of Law and Social Justice* 36 (1): 59–90.

Cossman, Brenda, Shannon Bell, Lise Gotell, and Becki Ross. 1997. *Bad Attitude/s on Trial: Pornography, Feminism, and the Butler Decision.* Toronto: University of Toronto Press.

Cossman, Brenda. 2004. "Sexuality, Queer Theory, and 'Feminism After': Reading and Rereading the Sexual Subject." *McGill Law Journal* 49 (4): 847–76.

– 2019. "#MeToo, Sex Wars 2.0, and the Power of Law." In the *Asian Yearbook of Human Rights and Humanitarian Law*, vol. 3, edited by Javaid Rehman, Ayesha Shahid, and Steve Foster, 18–37 (Leiden: Brill/Nijhoff).

Côté, Isabelle. 2015. "Restorative Justice at Dalhousie is a Depiction of Rape Culture." *Huffington Post Canada*, 18 December. https://www.huffingtonpost.ca/isabelle-cote/restorative-justice-is-a-_b_6347818.html.

Council of Nova Scotia University Presidents. 2016. "Memorandum of Understanding between the Province of Nova Scotia and the Nova Scotia Universities 2015–16, 2017–18 and 2018–19." https://novascotia.ca/lae/pubs/docs/MOU-2015-2019.pdf.

– 2019. "Memorandum of Understanding between the Province of Nova Scotia and the Nova Scotia Universities 2019–2020, 2020–2021, 2021–2022, 2022–2023, and 2023–2024." https://novascotia.ca/lae/Higher Education/documents/MOU-between-the-Province-and-Nova-Scotia-Universities-2019.pdf.

Cromwell, Thomas A. 2012. "Access to Justice: Towards a Collaborative and Strategic Approach." *University of New Brunswick Law Journal* 63 (1): 38-48.

Daly, Kathleen, and Julie Stubbs. 2006. "Feminist Engagement with Restorative Justice." *Theoretical Criminology* 10 (1): 9–28.

Delgado, Richard. 1999. "Goodbye to Hammurabi: Analyzing the Atavistic Appeal of Restorative Justice." *Stanford Law Review* 52 (4): 751–76.

Del Gobbo, Daniel. 2019. "Queer Dispute Resolution." *Cardozo Journal of Conflict Resolution* 20 (2): 283–328.

Derworiz, Collette. 2016. "Alberta Universities and Colleges Expected to Have Sexual Assault Policies in Place Soon: Advanced Education Minister." *Calgary Sun*, 8 September. http://www.calgarysun.com/2016/09/08/alberta-universities-and-colleges-expected-to-have-sexual-assault-policies-in-place-soon-education-minister.

Dubber, Markus Dirk. 1999. "The Victim in American Penal Law: A Systematic Overview." *Buffalo Criminal Law Review* 3 (1): 3–31.

Elliott, Josh. 2015. "Dalhousie Profs Go Public with Complaint Linked to Misogynistic Facebook Posts." *CTV News*, 4 January. https://www.ctvnews.ca/canada/dalhousie-profs-go-public-with-complaint-linked-to-misogynistic-facebook-posts-1.2171828.

Ending Violence Association of BC. 2016. "Campus Sexual Violence: Guidelines for a Comprehensive Response." http://endingviolence.org/wp-content/uploads/2016/05/EVABC_CampusSexualViolence Guidelines_vF.pdf.

Farrow, Trevor C.W. 2014. *Civil Justice, Privatization, and Democracy.* Toronto: University of Toronto Press.

Franke, Katherine M. 2001. "Theorizing Yes: An Essay on Feminism, Law, and Desire." *Columbia Law Review* 101 (1): 181–208.

Gersen, Jacob W., and Jeannie Suk. 2016. "The Sex Bureaucracy." *California Law Review* 104 (4): 881–948.

Gertner, Nancy. 2015. "Sex, Lies and Justice." *The American Prospect*, 12 January. http://prospect.org/article/sex-lies-and-justice.

Goodmark, Leigh. 2012. *A Troubled Marriage: Domestic Violence and the Legal System.* New York: NYU Press.

Government of Manitoba. n.d. "Manitoba Post-Secondary Sexual Violence Policy Guide: Promoting Awareness and Prevention." https://www.edu.gov.mb.ca/docs/sexual_violence/guide.pdf.

Government of Nova Scotia. 2018. "The Nova Scotia Restorative Justice Program." https://novascotia.ca/just/rj/Restorative-Justice-Program.pdf.

Gruber, Aya. 2006. "The Feminist War on Crime." *Iowa Law Review* 92 (3): 741–834.

– 2012. "Neofeminism." *Houston Law Review* 50 (5): 1325–90.

– 2015. "Anti-Rape Culture." *University of Kansas Law Review* 64 (4): 1027–56.

Halley, Janet. 2002. "Sexuality Harassment." In *Left Legalism/Left Critique,* edited by Wendy Brown and Janet Halley, 80–104. Durham, NC: Duke University Press.

– 2015. "Trading the Megaphone for the Gavel in Title IX Enforcement." *Harvard Law Review Forum,* 128: 103–17.

Hampson, Sarah. 2015. "How the Dentistry-School Scandal has Let Loose a Torrent of Anger at Dalhousie." *Globe and Mail,* 6 March. https://www.theglobeandmail.com/news/national/education/how-the-dentistry-school-scandal-has-let-loose-a-torrent-of-anger-at-dalhousie/article23344495/.

Harris, Angela P. 2011. "Heteropatriarchy Kills: Challenging Gender Violence in a Prison Nation." *Washington University Journal of Law and Policy* 37: 13–66.

Hopkins, C. Quince. 2012. "Tempering Idealism with Realism: Using Restorative Justice Processes to Promote Acceptance of Responsibility in Cases of Intimate Partner Violence." *Harvard Journal of Law and Gender* 35 (2): 311–56.

Hudson, Barbara. 1998. "Restorative Justice: The Challenge of Sexual and Racial Violence." *Journal of Law and Society* 25 (2): 237–56.

– 2002. "Restorative Justice and Gendered Violence: Diversion or Effective Justice?" *British Journal of Criminology* 42 (3): 616–34.

Hui, Ann. 2015. "Dalhousie Faculty Disappointed by University's Dismissal of Complaint" *Globe and Mail*, 11 January. https://www.theglobeandmail.com/news/national/dalhousie-faculty-disappointed-by-dismissal-of-complaint/article22405358.

Jeffrey, Davene. 2015. "Dal's Feminist Legal Association Supports Restorative Justice Approach." *Chronicle Herald*, 5 January. http://the chronicleherald.ca/metro/1259821-dal%E2%80%99s-feminist-legal-association-supports-restorative-justice-approach.

Kaplan, Margo. 2016. "Restorative Justice and Campus Sexual Misconduct." *Temple Law Review* 89 (4): 701–46.

Kingston, Anne. 2015. "Report on Dalhousie's Dentistry Scandal Applies Veneers to Major Cavities." *Maclean's*, 25 May. https://www.macleans.ca/education/university/new-report-on-dalhousies-dentistry-scandal-delivers-fresh-veneers-to-major-cavities/.

Kohn, Laurie S. 2010. "What's So Funny about Peace, Love, and Understanding: Restorative Justice as a New Paradigm for Domestic Violence Intervention." *Seton Hall Law Review* 40 (2): 517–96.

Koss, Mary P. 2014. "The RESTORE Program of Restorative Justice for Sex Crimes: Vision, Process, and Outcomes." *Journal of Interpersonal Violence* 29 (9): 1623–60.

Koss, Mary P., Jay K. Wilgus, and Kaaren M. Williamsen. 2014. "Campus Sexual Misconduct: Restorative Justice Approaches to Enhance Compliance with Title IX Guidance." *Trauma, Violence, and Abuse* 15 (3): 242–57.

Lee, Chelsey, and Jennifer S. Wong. 2017. "A Safe Place to Learn? Examining Sexual Assault Policies at Canadian Public Universities." *Studies in Higher Education* 44 (3): 432–45.

Llewellyn, Jennifer, Amanda Demsey, and Jillian Smith. 2015. "An Unfamiliar Story: Restorative Justice and Education: Reflections on

Dalhousie's Facebook Incident 2015." *Our Schools/Our Selves* 25 (1): 43–56.

Llewellyn, Jennifer, Jacob Macisaac, and Melissa MacKay. 2015. "Report from the Restorative Justice Process at the Dalhousie University Faculty of Dentistry." http://www.dal.ca/content/dam/dalhousie/pdf/cultureof respect/RJ2015-Report.pdf.

Macfarlane, Julie. 2008. *The New Lawyer: How Settlement Is Transforming the Practice of Law*. Vancouver: UBC Press.

MacKinnon, Catharine A. 1982. "Feminism, Marxism, Method, and the State: An Agenda for Theory." *Signs* 7 (3): 515–44.

– 1983. "Feminism, Marxism, Method, and the State: Toward Feminist Jurisprudence." *Signs* 8 (4): 635–58.

Matsuda, Mari. 2000. "On Causation." *Columbia Law Review* 100 (8): 2195–220.

McGlynn, Clare, Nicole Westmarland, and Nikki Godden. 2012. "'I Just Wanted Him to Hear Me': Sexual Violence and the Possibilities of Restorative Justice." *Journal of Law and Society* 39 (2): 213–40.

Menkel-Meadow, Carrie. 1983. "Toward Another View of Legal Negotiation: The Structure of Problem Solving." *UCLA Law Review* 31 (4): 754–842.

– 2009. "Are There Systemic Ethics Issues in Dispute Systems Design and What We Should [Not] Do About It: Lessons from International and Domestic Fronts." *Harvard Negotiation Law Review* 14 (1): 195–232.

METRAC. 2014. "Sexual Assault Policies on Campus: A Discussion Paper." http://www.metrac.org/wp-content/uploads/2014/11/final.formatted. campus.discussion.paper_.26sept14.pdf.

Nelund, Amanda. 2015. "Policy Conflict: Women's Groups and Institutionalized Restorative Justice." *Criminal Justice Policy Review* 26 (1): 65–84.

Nipissing College. 2016. "Sexual Violence Prevention, Support, and Response Policy." www.nipissingu.ca/departments/student-development-and-services/nuperspective/Documents/NU_Sexual_Violence_ Prevention_Support_Response_Policy_Dec_13_2016.pdf.

Office for Civil Rights, US Department of Education. 2001. "Revised Sexual Harassment Guidance: Harassment of Students by School Employees, Other Students, or Third Parties." http://www2.ed.gov/ about/offices/list/ocr/docs/shguide.pdf.

Ontario Ministry of the Status of Women. 2013. "Developing a Response to Sexual Violence: A Resource Guide for Ontario's Colleges and

Universities." http://www.women.gov.on.ca/owd/english/ending-violence/ campus_guide.shtml.

Quinn, Faryn. 2017. "Exclusive Interview with Mandi Gray on New Trial for Ururyar." *Nasty Woman Press*, 20 July. https://www.nastywomens press.com/home/2017/7/20/judge-grants-appeal-in-mandi-gray-case.

Randall, Melanie. 2013. "Restorative Justice and Gendered Violence? From Vaguely Hostile Skeptic to Cautious Convert: Why Feminists Should Critically Engage with Restorative Approaches to Law." *Dalhousie Law Journal* 36 (2): 461–500.

Rifkin, Janet. 1984. "Mediation from a Feminist Perspective: Promise and Problems." *Law and Inequality* 2 (1): 21–32.

Rittich, Kerry. 2015. "Out in the World: Multi-Level Governance for Gender Equality." In *Feminisms of Discontent: Global Contestations*, edited by Ashleigh Barnes, 44–70. New Delhi: Oxford University Press.

Rogers, Nancy H., Robert C. Bordone, Frank E.A. Sander, and Craig A. McEwen. 2013. *Designing Systems and Processes for Managing Disputes*. New York: Wolters Kluwer Law and Business.

Ryerson University. 2016. "Sexual Violence Policy." https://www.ryerson. ca/policies/policy-list/sexual-violence-policy/.

Saint Paul University. 2016. *Prevention of Sexual Violence*. https://ustpaul. ca/upload-files/intranet/university_policies_and_regulations/RHR-224_c_-_Prevention_of_Sexual_Violence.pdf.

Silbey, Susan and Austin Sarat. 1989. "Dispute Processing in Law and Legal Scholarship: From Institutional Critique to the Reconstruction of the Juridical Subject." *Denver University Law Review* 66 (3): 437–98.

Smith, Carly Parnitzke, and Jennifer J. Freyd. 2013. "Dangerous Safe Havens: Institutional Betrayal Exacerbates Sexual Trauma." *Journal of Traumatic Stress* 26 (1): 119–24.

Smith, Stephanie, and Janet Martinez. 2009. "An Analytic Framework for Dispute Systems Design." *Harvard Negotiation Law Review* 14 (1): 123–70.

University of Toronto. 2017. "Policy on Sexual Violence and Sexual Harassment." http://www.governingcouncil.lamp4.utoronto.ca/wp-content/uploads/2016/12/p1215-poshsv-2016-2017pol.pdf.

US Department of Education. 2011. "Dear Colleague Letter." 4 April. http://www2.ed.gov/about/offices/list/ocr/letters/colleague-201104.pdf.

– 2014. "Questions and Answers on Title IX and Sexual Violence." 29 April. http://www2.ed.gov/ about/offices/list/ocr/docs/qa-201404-title-ix.pdf.

– 2017. "Dear Colleague Letter." 22 September. https://www2.ed.gov/
about/offices/list/ocr/letters/colleague-title-ix-201709.pdf.
Whitley, Leila, and Tiffany Page. 2015. "Sexism at the Centre: Locating
the Problem of Sexual   Harassment." *New Formations* 86: 34–53.
Yoffe, Emily. 2014. "The College Rape Overcorrection." *Slate*, 7 December.
http://www.slate.com/articles/double_x/doublex/2014/12/college_rape_
campus_sexual_assault_is_a_serious_problem_but_the_efforts.html.

PART TWO

Complicate

5

Stand by Me

Viewing Bystander Intervention Programming through an Intersectional Lens

Suzie Dunn, Jane Bailey, and Yamikani Msosa

INTRODUCTION

As public awareness and institutional concern about sexual violence grow, many post-secondary institutions are developing policies and looking for solutions to address sexual violence and rape culture on campuses. Over the last few years, legislation was introduced in several provinces mandating sexual violence prevention policies for post-secondary institutions (see Nelund and Rossiter, this volume), and these newly developed policies often include commitments to provide sexual violence prevention training to students (University of Ottawa 2016). Many post-secondary institutions have begun implementing bystander intervention programming (BIP)[1] as part of that training. This chapter reviews certain BIP practices and explores how this increasingly popular form of sexual violence prevention programming could be implemented in ways that better reflect the complex needs and realities of diverse student populations by examining BIP through an intersectional lens and making suggestions on ways to incorporate an intersectional lens into sexual violence prevention programming.[2]

BIP has been shown to have some positive results in shifting rape culture on campuses in certain circumstances (Banyard, Moynihan, and Plante 2007; Katz and Moore 2013). For example, Banyard, Moynihan, and Plante's (2007) study showed that a group of predominantly white male and female undergraduate students had decreased rape myth acceptance, increased knowledge of sexual violence, improved bystander attitudes, and increased self-reported bystander behaviours following participation in BIP. However, even with positive results such as those, BIP should not be understood as a monolithic one-size-fits-all "solution" to sexual violence, but rather as part of a multi-prong approach to address prevention training and education. Within universities this programming must be examined critically, adjusted to reflect the complexity of the student population it is being presented to, and supplemented with additional institutional support. BIP programming that focuses primarily on the sexual violence experienced by young, white, heterosexual, cisgender, able-bodied, upper-middle-class women who drink alcohol fails to address the experiences of students who do not fit that mould (Bang, Kerrick, and Wuthrich 2016; Monette 2017; Wooten 2017). As such, advocates have been calling for bystander intervention programming that attends to a multiplicity of student experiences from a wider breadth of social locations, as well as addresses structural systems and interlocking forms of oppression such as misogyny, racism, and transphobia that inform and enable sexual violence (Suchland 2016; Bang, Kerrick, and Wuthrich 2016).

In this chapter, we explore what making a commitment to inter-sectionality might mean in terms of the design and implementation of BIP as part of an institutional response to sexual violence. We do not purport to offer a single blueprint because such an exercise would fly in the face of intersectionality's demand that we recognize the ways in which diverse social locations complicate the experiences of individuals and groups, requiring nuanced and contextually informed responses. Instead, we (1) clarify our approach to intersectionality by drawing on the long-established expertise of intersectionality theorists and practitioners, especially in relation to sexual violence; and (2) draw on these insights to frame suggestions about the ways that adopting an intersectional approach might affect seven specific aspects of the design and implementation of BIP. We conclude with suggestions for further research that could assist institutions that adopt BIP in evaluating its implementation and efficacy from an intersectional perspective, and encourage institutions to consider additional supports to supplement BIP in order to comprehensively address sexual violence.

FROM MARGIN TO CENTRE: INTERSECTIONALITY

History and Definition of Intersectionality

There is a rich global history of feminist activism and scholarship led primarily by black, Indigenous, and other women and trans people of colour demonstrating that the simultaneous experience of social location markers such as gender, race, class, and sexual orientation results in unique forms of oppression that cannot be addressed either by isolating a single marker or by purporting to add up the effects of each (Carastathis 2016). Contributors to this rich history include Sojourner Truth, Ida B. Wells-Barnett, Anna Julia Cooper, Kimberlé Crenshaw, Patricia Hill Collins, Sirma Bilge, Vivian May, and Savitribai Phule, as well as grassroots activist organizations like Somos Hermanas/We Are Sisters and the Combahee River Collective, among others (May 2015; Collins and Bilge 2016).

In her seminal 1989 work, Kimberlé Crenshaw coined the term "intersectionality" to describe this reality (Crenshaw 1989, 139; 1991, 1241). Crenshaw (1991) argued that without a multi-axis analysis, the experiences of those subordinated by various intersecting social categories, such as those of black women, are erased from social justice movements and denied anti-discrimination remedies in the courts. While recognizing that categories such as race and gender are socially constructed and frequently deployed as a tactic to justify discriminatory distinctions, intersectionality theorists also note that social location categorizations can become intertwined with identity in meaningful ways that allow them to be used as positive tools for creating alliances to resist subjugation and building coalitions for achieving social justice (Collins and Bilge 2016; Carastathis 2016).

From Crenshaw's perspective, however, intersectionality "is not primarily about identity" (2016). Instead, it is "about how structures make certain identities the consequence of and the vehicle for vulnerability. So, if you want to know how many intersections matter, you've got to look at the context. What's happening? ... What are the policies, what are the institutional structures that play a role in contributing to the exclusion of some people and not others?" (ibid.).

In 1990 Patricia Hill Collins (1990, 225) described intersectionality in terms of "interlocking systems of oppression" and the "matrix of domination," which work not only to exclude members of subordinated groups, but also to privilege members of dominant groups.

Reflecting this approach, Collins and Sirma Bilge (2016) define intersectionality as:

> a way of understanding and analyzing the complexity in the world, in people, and in human experiences. The events and conditions of social and political life and the self can seldom be understood as shaped by one factor. They are generally shaped by many factors in diverse and mutually influencing ways. When it comes to social inequality, people's lives and the organization of power in a given society are better understood as being shaped not by a single axis of social division, be it race or gender or class, but by many axes that work together and influence each other. Intersectionality as an analytic tool gives people better access to the complexity of the world and of themselves.

Intersectionality's emphasis on the complexity of interactions between factors such as social categories and institutional policies and practices has been central to problematizing essentialism within feminist and anti-racist movements. Yet, no single clear intersectional methodology can be applied to all forms of research or practice. Instead, as Crenshaw has suggested, intersectionality may be taken up as a provisional concept meant to challenge the entrenched ways of understanding ideas such as identity-based discrimination (Carastathis 2016). In this way, intersectionality is an ongoing process that contests dominant mindsets (Carastathis 2016). An intersectional lens can shed light on subjects and experiences that have been overlooked or erased because they do not fit comfortably in entrenched understandings of identity or oppression (May 2015), such as the ways in which state-based racism impact the willingness of Indigenous and racialized women to seek assistance from law enforcement agencies. As such, intersectionality's insights are crucial to developing meaningful responses to sexual violence, which is too often analyzed exclusively through the lens of gender, and/or, by default, from the perspective of those who benefit from matrices of domination.

Framing Potential Experiences of Sexual Violence within BIP on Campuses

We argue that taking an intersectional approach to BIP is essential if institutional responses to sexual violence are going to be meaningful for *entire* post-secondary communities, rather than just specific (and often otherwise privileged) segments of them. Intersectionality provides an important analytical framework for BIP because it highlights the complexities of sexual violence in relation to matrices of oppression such as racism, homophobia, classism, transphobia, and more.

Angela Davis's and Leanne Betasamosake Simpson's intersectional work on sexual violence is particularly instructive for BIP. In *Rape, Racism and the Myth of the Black Rapist* (1981), Davis argued that the second-wave feminist anti-rape movement failed to acknowledge the impact of racism and classism on experiences of sexual violence. Leanne Betasamosake Simpson (2014) understood that sexual violence is not merely a single-axis gendered oppression, but is a tool of "colonialism, settler colonialism and capitalism", along with "white supremacy, rape culture and the real and symbolic attacks on gender, sexual identity and agency."

An intersectional approach benefits BIP programming by addressing the intersectionality of social locations and power structures. The consequences of failing to apply an intersectional lens to BIP design, implementation, and evaluation include overlooking systemic marginalization, perpetuating the shortcomings of previous single-axis analyses of sexual violence, and leaving the sexual violence experiences of some of the most subordinated community members unaddressed.

Taking an intersectional approach to BIP on campuses involves recognizing and naming structural and institutional forces of subordination, and then seeking to dismantle them. These forces include gendered, colonialist, heterosexist, and racist exercises of power, which disproportionately expose women (cis and trans[3]) and gender non-binary people (particularly those who are young, disabled, racialized, Indigenous, and/or members of LGBTQ2S+ communities) to sexual violence at the hands of mainly straight cisgender men.[4] Taking this approach will first mean embracing the complexity of students' social locations, avoiding essentialized versions of who they are, and actively examining whose experiences are neglected or erased in research and programming. Second, BIP should challenge dominant narratives that view sexual violence as only perpetrated against young, white, heterosexual women by male strangers, and challenge the conception of intervention strategies as primarily physical interventions that prevent sexual assault as it is about to occur. This will mean rethinking mainstream narratives about what sexual violence looks like, who is a target or survivor of sexual violence, who is a perpetrator, who is a bystander, and how meaningful interventions can be framed. Finally, BIP should seek to build coalitions against sexual violence across social locations.

BIP DESIGN AND IMPLEMENTATION: INSIGHTS FROM INTERSECTIONALITY

In this section, we explore how taking an intersectional approach might affect seven different aspects of BIP design and implementation. Our intention here is not to specifically critique any existing approaches to BIP, but instead to highlight the difference that taking an intersectional approach might make in BIP. It would be impossible in this limited space to comprehensively address each aspect of BIP that could benefit from an intersectional approach. Therefore we have chosen to focus on seven that figure prominently in the existing literature and/or are particularly edifying in terms of how they illustrate what some of the concrete effects of taking an intersectional approach to BIP might be.

Identifying Patterns of Victimization and Perpetration

In identifying patterns of victimization and perpetration, BIP should avoid single-axis essentialized understandings of who a sexual assault survivor or perpetrator is, such as framing all sexual assault victims as young white women assaulted by young white men they met at a party or bar. BIP should instead explore the complex and diverse social locations of both potential victims and perpetrators. In doing so, it should also specifically identify intersecting structural influences and social location categorizations that make some individuals, such as women, trans, and non-binary students, more vulnerable to sexual violence and others more likely to perpetrate it (May 2015).

If BIP focuses solely on scenarios involving young, white, heterosexual women being physically assaulted at or after drinking excessively at a party or bar, those receiving the training may come to assume that these are the only situations in which sexual violence arises, and/or that they are the only situations in which they ought to intervene. As a result, other acts of victimization at different points on the spectrum of sexual violence, and other experiences of sexual violence that more frequently affect students in less privileged social locations, may go unnoticed and effectively be erased (Wooten 2017). A better intersectional practice of BIP could involve identifying what

Crenshaw (1989) recognized as collective yet divergent experiences, which recognizes that there may be more common experiences shared among a particular group but that no overarching generalizations about that group's experience can be made. As noted by Sara Carrigan Wooten (2017), failure to recognize divergent experiences in sexual violence programming can work to reinforce systems of privilege that perpetually marginalize the understandings and experiences of sexual violence of members of groups most vulnerable to it.

First and foremost, students and frontline administrators of sexual violence training must come together to share information about current trends on university campuses that would speak to students' lived experiences in a nuanced way. This can be conducted via informal or formal methods, but, either way, it should include detailed and sustained consultation with students from diverse social locations before, during, and after the provision of sexual violence training.

A BIP training session itself could incorporate a multiplicity of experiences and / or be tailored to address the specific needs and experiences of particular audiences, which allows for an intersectional approach suited for that particular group of students. Attempts to use neutralized language in an effort to be inclusive of all people by addressing no one in particular – for example, by not centring the gender, sexual orientation, or race of the individuals involved in the scenario (without further discussion of the assumptions made about those individuals) – can, in fact, undermine identifying patterns of victimization and perpetration of sexual violence by burying social location categorizations and power structures that influence perpetration and victimization (Wooten 2017). Wooten suggests that the imagining of a so-called generic student experience that is not influenced by cultural, social, or historical factors merely embodies the experiences of the privileged white student (Wooten 2017). Value-neutral language erases the various lived experiences of students impacted by factors such as sexism, colonialism, racism, and transphobia, as the default "neutral" language reverts to scenarios that prioritize the experiences and intervention strategies that are meaningful to survivors who are white, heteronormative, able-bodied, and cisgender women (Bang, Kerrick, and Wuthrich 2016). Moreover, it risks erasing systems of privilege, such as patriarchy and white supremacy, that are arguably reflected in the fact that men represent the overwhelming majority of perpetrators of sexual violence (Conroy and Cotter 2017; Wooten 2017). Where neutral language is used and no opportunity is given for recognition and discussion of systems of oppression, it can also undermine BIP's capacity to address the need for structural interventions and change.

In any event, patterns remain that are central to better understanding social structures and categorizations that inform sexual violence, and these should be shared with students. For example, sexual violence is a gendered phenomenon where cisgender men are overwhelmingly the most common perpetrators (Conroy and Cotter 2014). Women (cis and trans) are the most common targets of sexual violence in general and on campuses specifically (Gunraj 2014; DeKeseredy 2011). However, other social locations are irreducibly enmeshed with gendered experiences that contribute to sexual violence, disproportionately leaving students who are gender non-conforming (Coulter and Rankin 2017; Association of American Universities 2015), Indigenous (Native Women's Association of Canada 2018), LGBTQ2S+, racialized, immigrant, and disabled at a higher risk of sexual violence while attending Canadian post-secondary institutions (Gunraj 2014; Canadian Federation of Students 2015). These realities should be addressed during BIP.

Structural Critiques

Because intersectional practice is grounded in seeking social justice through individual *and* structural change (Collins and Bilge 2016), BIP that is committed to an intersectional approach must go beyond individual intervention strategies. We suggest that training related to individual strategies for intervening in particular incidents of sexual violence should be fully contextualized with information and discussion about institutional and societal structures that contribute to sexual violence on and off campuses, along with strategies for intervening in those structures (ibid.). This could, for example, include discussing scenarios from several points along the continuum of sexual violence, as well as discussing harassing online behaviours that signal tolerance for transphobic, sexist, racist, homophobic, and other oppressive behaviours.

Further, post-secondary institutions need to look inward at the systemic factors that contribute to sexual violence by, within, and against members of their student body, such as the normalization of rape culture, rather than just focus on individual interventions. As Sarah McMahon (2015, 473) states, "although the bystander approach is often framed as a community level intervention, most of the programming and research has actually focused largely on the individual level of change, with an emphasis on addressing personal attitudes, beliefs and behaviors." Personal changes and individual feelings of responsibility are certainly important factors in preventing sexual violence. However, BIP that also helps students to identify opportunities to challenge and change institutional systems that inculcate an atmosphere that sanctions, tolerates, or even ignores sexual violence can also assist in addressing the interlocking systems of power whose existence is a key insight from intersectional theory and practice (Bowes-Sperry and O'Leary-Kelly 2005; Fuchs 2016). This could include discussing whether an institution provides effective reporting systems, clear and cohesive sexual violence policies, and meaningful support for those situated in vulnerable social locations who experience sexual violence.

It can be challenging to develop systems that meet the needs of survivors with intersecting social experiences (INCITE! 2016, 208). However, institutions can begin by acknowledging the historic and current neglect of the sexual violence perpetrated against racialized, Indigenous, and disabled women and LGBTQ2S+ students. This acknowledgment can be made, in part, by seeking guidance to provide meaningful services for survivors of sexual violence from all communities, and by providing services using an anti-oppression framework (Ryerson University 2016, part V (1); Ristock and Timbang 2005). These steps are key factors in preventing sexual violence (Ristock and Timbang 2005) because they communicate to sexual violence survivors from all social locations that they will not be blamed for the violence perpetrated against them or denied services to address their situation (Banyard 2015). This may in turn lead to improved reporting and opportunities for dealing with perpetrators in ways that minimize the risk of reoffending.

Intervention Strategies

Where BIP approaches sexual violence as a spectrum, it becomes possible to imagine opportunities to intervene *before* physical violence occurs, including through acts that challenge rape culture itself (Banyard 2015). An intersectional approach can challenge the dominant narrative of what meaningful intervention looks like in two ways. First, as discussed above, it can integrate discussion and recognition of the need for institutional and social structural interventions, as well as address patterns that leave certain groups more vulnerable to sexual violence and others more likely to perpetrate it. Second, BIP can be designed to ensure recognition and discussion of how social location influences the ways in which any particular bystander can intervene *safely* (Bowes-Sperry and O'Leary-Kelly 2005).

Adriane Bang et al. argue that forms of BIP that do not engage with the experiences relevant to particular communities on campuses may falsely presume that there is a general consensus of ideas about sexual violence, including when individuals may be at risk of sexual violence, what is considered harmful sexual behaviour, when it is meaningful to intervene, and what strategies are most helpful when intervening (Bang, Kerrick, and Wuthrich 2016). Whereas, in reality, sexual violence is interpreted differently in different communities, calling for different forms of intervention relevant to that community (INCITE! 2009). Research has shown that bystander training tailored for specific communities has proven beneficial (McMahon 2015; Moynihan et al. 2011). However, some mainstream programs have been criticized by authors such as Wooten (2017) for neglecting to bring to light the experiences of students from a broad range of social locations. Recognizing a breadth of students' social locations is important not only in relation to targets and perpetrators of sexual violence, but also to bystanders.

For example, bystanders from communities that are more frequently and intensely surveilled and who face institutionalized discrimination and sexual victimization at the hands of white men and authority figures, such as black (Wooten 2017), Indigenous (Human Rights Watch 2013), or gender non-binary (Bang, Kerrick, and Wuthrich 2016) communities, have legitimate reasons to fear intervening in situations involving white men, or in ways that may lead to the involvement of authorities (INCITE! 2016). Further, members of these communities are more likely to have experienced state interventions that were in themselves violent and where reporting did not stop the violence perpetrated against them (ibid.). As such, even when sexual violence is being perpetrated by a member of their own community, survivors and bystanders from those communities may prefer intervention strategies that avoid criminalizing their communities out of concern for perpetuating stereotypes about violence within their community (Wooten 2017) or perpetuating discriminatory treatment by the criminal justice system (Bang, Kerrick, and Wuthrich 2016).

LGBTQ2S+ survivors of sexual violence may have unique concerns about individual interventions, including the risk of discrimination from students and staff, and in some cases the loss of friends, family, and jobs, if their sexual orientation is revealed to particular groups or individuals (Potter, Fountain, and Stapleton 2012). Since the population of LGBTQ2S+ students may be smaller on a campus, it can be difficult for survivors to address sexual violence within their communities without risking being isolated from their unique social groups. This is particularly challenging for students who have been rejected by their families or previous social groups because of their sexual or gender identity or expression (ibid.).

Social locations (Banyard 2015) can also differentially affect bystanders' ability to *safely* intervene in sexual violence (McMahon and Banyard 2012) since students experiencing intersecting social locations that result in lower social status may place themselves at considerable risk when intervening in sexual violence (de la Cretaz 2017). This causes a troubling conflict for these students. While BIP places an expectation on students to intervene in sexual violence, students may correctly feel that it is not safe for them to intervene due to their social location. For example, members of racialized, LGBTQ2S+, and Indigenous communities who are more at risk of physical violence may rightly hesitate to intervene in sexual violence involving a straight white male perpetrator. At the same time, they may feel pressured into acting in a way that could place them in danger. BIP that aims to address intersectionality would therefore address the complexity of responsibility and the personal well-being of interveners, as well as offer possibilities for structural interventions and for identifying less intrusive opportunities to intervene earlier, before a situation escalates into physical violence.

Audience

When implementing BIP, post-secondary institutions should have a clear understanding of who their audience is. Without conscious planning around this issue, institutions may default to framing their audience as a monolithic group of white, able-bodied, heterosexual, upper-middle class young people (Wooten 2017), even though the actual composition of student bodies is typically much more complex (McGill University 2009). Committing to addressing the intra- and inter-group differences among students in a non-hierarchal manner is key to an intersectional approach (Carastathis 2016). It can also strengthen anti-violence movements (INCITE! 2016) by identifying spaces for coalition and solidarity within complicated matrices of social locations (May 2015; Collins and Bilge 2016).

Post-secondary institutions should clearly understand the demographics within their student population and seek out knowledge of sexual violence experiences and interventions from students from a multiplicity of social locations – especially those, such as transgender students, who are systemically vulnerable and face disproportionate levels of sexual violence, even though members of those communities may only represent a small fraction of the overall student population. Unfortunately, detailed demographics for Canadian post-secondary institutions are difficult to locate; many post-secondary institutions do not collect data on various relevant demographics, such as race (McDonald and Ward 2017). However, some institutions have gathered this data, illuminating the actual composition of their students. A 2009 survey of students at McGill University determined that a significant percentage of students were members of a visible minority group (37 per cent), LGBTQ++ (9 per cent), or were international students (19 per cent) (McGill University 2009). These statistics demonstrate the problem with developing policies based on an implicit or explicit assumption of a single *type* of student or a single student experience. The reality is that student bodies are complex and no single definition of a student can capture the plethora of experiences of the actual student body.[5]

We suggest that sexual violence programs at post-secondary institutions should aim to actively generate visibility for a multiplicity of experiences of sexual violence relevant to their student body and subsections within it, rather than rely on a single standardized BIP aimed at a homogenous, and, by default, white population (Bang, Kerrick, and Wuthich 2016). This may require the development of specific BIP for various student populations within each institution.

Studies on BIP aimed at specific groups, such as sorority students (Moynihan et al. 2011, 712) and intercollegiate athletes (Moynihan et al. 2010, 197), showed improvements in these students' attitudes about sexual violence and greater intentions to intervene in sexual violence following BIP training developed specifically for their group. Bystander interventions that are developed within the community and put members of that community in leadership roles are more likely to meet the needs of groups with intersecting and diverse experiences, and may better address the simultaneously marginalized and privileged positions of that student group (Bang, Kerrick, and Wuthich 2016). Assumptions should not be made about the social locations of particular student groups, such as assuming that all male athletes are cisgender or heterosexual. Efforts must be made to understand and address the actual composition of the group receiving the training. Program developers can look to BIP training by groups such as Draw the Line (n.d), which have collaborated with various communities to develop community-specific bystander intervention material, including programming developed in collaboration with Indigenous populations.

Due to the complexity of the student population, BIP will often be offered to groups with diverse audience members, even when presenting to smaller groups. When presenting to mixed audiences of students, facilitators should use BIP as an opportunity to build coalitions among students not only by recognizing the multiplicity of experiences among students, but also by seeking to build solidarity among students to end sexual violence (Collins and Bilge 2016). As noted by Elizabeth "Betita" Martinez, learning about and sharing experiences with violence, while respecting and validating varying experiences and historical relationships with violence, can assist in alliance building across difference (INCITE! 2016).

Bystander Bias

Part of addressing the structural issues discussed in the previous sections, such as institutionalized racism, sexism, and homophobia, is discussing how these forces impact bystanders' willingness to intervene – not just for reasons of personal safety, but also due to their own implicit biases. BIP that examines the intersecting structures that influence bystanders' intent to intervene can better achieve intersectionality's goals of naming and dismantling individual and systemic forces that increase oppression (Collins and Bilge 2016). Further, BIP that specifically addresses the structural complexity of sexual violence risks can assist in making visible the experience of particular groups of survivors, and potentially reduce their vulnerability, while increasing the likelihood that they will receive support from others once they have been alerted to their experiences (Crenshaw 1991).

Research indicates that the social location of the target of sexual violence affects whether a bystander will intervene. For example, Lynn

Bowes-Sperry and Anne M. O'Leary-Kelly's (2005) research shows that bystanders are more likely to help targets of sexual harassment with whom they share social identity categorizations, such as race, gender, or area of employment. David Byers (2013, 255) argues that homophobia and transphobia may cause bystanders to either deny the harm of homophobic sexualized bullying of LGBTQ2S+ targets in order to avoid acknowledging their own bias, or to elect not to intervene out of fear of being labelled homosexual themselves. In a study by Katz et al., women students showed less intention to intervene in a potential sexual assault if both the perpetrator and target were male and presumed gay, when compared to a similar situation involving a heteronormative pairing with a female as a potential target of sexual violence (Katz, Colbert, and Colangelo 2015, 274). Differences in bystander intervention intentions were noted in studies focused on race as well. In several studies, white individuals were statistically less likely to identify a situation as an emergency or have an intention to intervene if the person at risk was black (Saucier, Miller, and Doucet 2005; Katz, Merrilees, et al. 2017). Katz has also suggested that this kind of bias could apply when those with less social status or privilege are targeted (ibid.).

These examples demonstrate the urgency of addressing underlying prejudice and discrimination, and in particular, of making students from privileged communities aware of their own biases when deciding whether to intervene in sexual violence. Without a critical analysis that addresses this underlying power dynamic and seeks to identify and dismantle structural forms of sexism, racism, homophobia, and other categorizations used as bases for discrimination, individuals with diverse social locations outside of white, heteronormative, and otherwise privileged groups seem less likely to benefit from BIP.

Selection and Training of Facilitators

According to Vivian May (2015, 35), an intersectional approach requires "unmasking knowledge claims purported to be neutral and universal ... it raises questions about who has been perceived to be an authoritative knower, whose claims have been heard, which forms of knowledge have received recognition ... and who has had access to the means of knowledge production and training." By actively selecting facilitators from a wide variety of social locations, this approach shifts who is traditionally recognized as a knowledge bearer, and what knowledge is considered legitimate, away from where it has been traditionally centred to embrace the complexity of various understandings. BIP grounded in intersectionality should commit to seeking out knowledge bearers affected by various social locations, both to utilize those bearers' positional expertise, and to shift audiences' perceptions of who is an authority in understanding sexual violence prevention.

When training facilitators to present BIP to the larger student population, facilitators from communities inside and outside of white heteronormative communities should be selected to facilitate the workshops. Post-secondary institutions can benefit from engaging with various student community groups to understand who is actually represented within their student body and how those students experience sexual violence (Wooten and Mitchell 2016). Intentionally selecting students from multiple communities and various social locations as leaders legitimizes the experiences of students from diverse social locations, and can shift understandings of sexual violence and alert potential bystanders to less recognized forms of sexual violence (Wooten and Mitchell 2017).

Where possible, facilitators providing training for specific communities – such as students in particular programs, older students, athletic teams, LGBTQ2S+ groups, or international students – should come from within those communities (Bang, Kerrick, and Wuthrich 2016). Those facilitating BIP often have a great deal of power to select and develop the scenarios they determine to be relevant to the group sessions (Cares et al. 2015; Coker et al. 2016). Leaders from specific communities will have intimate knowledge of the nuances of community expectations and what language and scenarios can be most effective in communicating the bystander message to those specific groups (Bang, Kerrick, and Wuthrich 2016). There must be opportunities to present various student perspectives and scenarios related to sexual violence.

However, merely training facilitators from a broad range of communities will not necessarily ensure against discriminatory programming. Facilitators must have an understanding of their own implicit biases and knowledge gaps, as well as potential biases and gaps in the knowledge of participants. An intersectional approach focuses on structural blank spots in understandings of sexual violence, and places where willful ignorance about sexual violence exists (May 2015). Seeking out facilitators from a variety of student communities can potentially offset some of these biases, but as all individuals will have some knowledge gaps, direct training on implicit bias and sexual violence is recommended regardless of who is facilitating the workshops.

Empirical Data Collection on BIP

An intersectional approach for studying BIP at post-secondary institutions requires a commitment to establishing new narratives of sexual violence experiences involving post-secondary students, and making space for those students who are not traditionally viewed as statistically significant (May 2015). To understand a diversity of narratives, an intersectional approach would call for research that goes beyond data sets that fit smoothly into dominant understandings. An intersectional approach purposely examines the interstices between dominant logics and identities, actively seeking out what lies at the edges, what claims to be well understood but isn't, and what exists outside of common understanding (May 2015; Crenshaw 2005).

Some empirical evaluations of BIP at post-secondary institutions have demonstrated initial positive results, such as a reduction in sexual violence perpetration (Coker et al. 2016; Casey and Ohler 2011), reduced acceptance of rape myths, and increased self-reported bystander interventions (Banyard, Moynihan, and Plante 2007; Katz and Moore 2013). However, the impact of these programs is sometimes evaluated using a predominantly young, white, heteronormative student population (Coker et al. 2016; Bennett, Banyard, and Garnhart 2014). Even where demographic information on factors like race was collected, studies did not always specifically analyze and discuss data specific to racialized groups (Brown, Banyard, and Moynihan 2014). When the positive effects of the program on students affected by diverse social locations – including those who represent a smaller portion of the student body but experience disproportionately high levels of sexual violence – have not been disaggregated to test the effectiveness of BIP on those groups, their experiences with BIP can be neglected or buried in the research results.

In order to better understand a wider variety of student experiences and the impact of BIP on those populations, academics and post-secondary institutions should evaluate sexual violence involving their students and the impacts of their program using disaggregated data (Bang, Kerrick, and Wuthrich 2016), particularly among smaller populations who are disproportionately vulnerable to sexual violence. Information gleaned from these studies should be used to identify gaps and improve programming (ibid.). Without accurate data on sexual violence against their students and the actual impact of the programming aimed at preventing it, post-secondary institutions will be unable to meaningfully address this issue.

CONCLUSION

Intersectionality provides a framework for offering BIP that better addresses the needs and realities of students from a multiplicity of social locations, rather than primarily serving the interests of students from privileged communities. Post-secondary institutions committed to addressing sexual violence through BIP informed by intersectionality will need to conduct research to better understand the diverse social locations occupied by the members of their student bodies and provide programming that addresses these needs. In this way, intersectionality steers BIP away from presumed homogeneity and the use of neutral language that risks defaulting to a cisgender, white, heterosexual standard. Addressing this underlying complexity creates the opportunity to prevent rendering more vulnerable those who are already vulnerable. BIP informed by intersectionality ensures discussion of the needs and realities specific to students affected by varying social locations and addresses the biases affecting others' willingness to intervene in violence against members of groups more likely to be victimized. It also ensures recognition of the expertise and knowledge of individuals from varying social locations through their consultation and their inclusion as facilitators in the process.

BIP with an intersectional approach also addresses systemic issues. In the context of sexual violence, socially constructed locations are reflected in gendered patterns that disproportionately expose women (cis and trans) to sexual violence that is disproportionately committed by cis men. Intersectionally informed BIP also allows for nuanced conversations of sexual violence experienced by men, particularly gay, trans, and bisexual men. Further, power structures informed by racism, colonialism, transphobia, homophobia, and ableism affect survivors' experiences in ways that cannot be separated from their experience of gender. These intersecting experiences of social categories add complexity to understanding the risk and impact of sexual violence, the availability of assistance, and the willingness of bystanders to intervene. Taking an intersectional approach to BIP would encourage not only laying those structures bare, but also expanding the notion of "intervention" beyond reactions to individual instances of sexual violence, so that it includes developing self-awareness of bias, coalition building, and systemic change.

Intersectionality theory and practice undoubtedly raise complexities for designing and implementing BIP, but the insights and opportunities they yield, in particular in relation to understanding the structural underpinnings of sexual violence and expanding the community of students who stand to benefit from them, are both practically and morally impossible to ignore.

Recommendations for Future Research

We have identified three areas of further research that could aid in realizing intersectionality's benefits in BIP. First, our review of the current literature on BIP indicates a lack of research in which data are disaggregated in order to evaluate the impact and effect of BIP on student bodies at various social locations. The experiences of smaller student populations who experience disproportionate levels of sexual violence, such as transgender or Indigenous students, are often neglected. These experiences must be taken into consideration in future studies to ensure that the programming being provided is useful and relevant to those groups, and that their experiences are not erased. Second, academic attention should be paid to those institutions that are providing BIP using an intersectional lens, assessing the effectiveness of their programming and highlighting diverse and unique approaches to BIP. By examining a variety of programming styles, institutions can identify ways to alter their programming to take better account of the experiences of subordinated groups. Third, research must be conducted on what other forms of institutional support are required to supplement sexual violence intervention programming like BIP. Even with an intersectional approach, BIP and individual actions cannot serve as the sole solutions to sexual violence. Structural and systemic change is needed. A better understanding of what other supports and programming are needed to fully address sexual violence and rape culture on campus will help institutions provide a robust and supportive space to improve the safety, autonomy, and well-being of their student population.

Recommendations for Policy

We have identified three policy changes that could aid in realizing intersectionality's benefits in BIP. First, we recommend that post-secondary institutions acknowledge the historic and current neglect of the violence perpetrated against racialized, Indigenous, and disabled women, and LGBTQ2S+ students, in their policies. This includes seeking guidance from those groups on how to provide meaningful services for survivors of sexual violence from all communities, gaining knowledge about these communities' experiences with sexual violence, and using an anti-oppressive framework in their sexual violence prevention policies and services. Second, as part of their sexual violence prevention policies, institutions should commit to collecting and publishing disaggregated data about student demographics, including disaggregated data on sexual violence reporting by their student population (concerning both perpetrator and survivor demographics, where possible), and the effectiveness of their sexual violence programming and services across a breadth of social locations. Third, both governmental and academic institutional actors should invest in community-developed anti-oppression programming aimed at addressing underlying systems of discrimination that work to disproportionately expose women (cis and trans) and gender non-binary people (especially those who are young, disabled, racialized, Indigenous, and/or members of LGBTQ2S+ communities) to sexual violence at the hands of mainly straight cisgender men.

NOTES

1 In this chapter, we use the term "bystander intervention programming" in a general sense to refer to programs that aim to create a community sense of responsibility of and for sexual violence. BIP can and does take a variety of forms from institution to institution, although many post-secondary institutions that offer BIP use variations of popular programs such as *Bringing in the Bystander* and the *Green Dot*. BIP, as it is currently practised, often involves educating community members about sexual violence and encouraging bystanders to intervene to address it (Kingkade 2016; Banyard et al. 2007).

2 We have specifically chosen to focus on student populations only in this chapter as we believe that unique considerations may apply to faculty, staff, and other groups receiving BIP that require specific attention and further research.

3 We have adopted the definition transgender/trans as the encompassing term for many gender identities of people who do not identify or

exclusively identify with the sex assigned at birth. The term "transgender" is not indicative of gender expression, sexual orientation, hormonal makeup, physical anatomy, or how one is perceived in daily life (Trans-Student Educational Resources n.d.).

4 The Sexual Assault Centre of Hamilton reports that one in three women and one in six men will experience sexual violence in their lifetime, while 80 per cent of disabled women will be sexually abused in their lifetime, rates of victimization are five times higher for women under age thirty-five, and one in five members of the LGBTQ++ community experienced sexual/physical violence in an intimate relationship, with bisexual women reporting this type of violence most frequently, followed by gay men, lesbian women, and bisexual males. In 99 per cent of sexual assaults the perpetrator is male (Sexual Assault Centre 2015).

5 This complexity should be explicitly recognized in institutional sexual violence policies. See for example Ryerson University's policy (Ryerson University 2016).

REFERENCES

Association of American Universities. 2015. "AAU Climate Survey on Sexual Assault and Sexual Misconduct (2015)." https://www.aau.edu/key-issues/aau-climate-survey-sexual-assault-and-sexual-misconduct-2015.

Bang, Adriane, Annie Kerrick, and Christian K. Wuthrich. 2016. "Examining Bystander Intervention in the Wake of #BlackLivesMatter and #TransLivesMatter." *Preventing Sexual Violence on Campus: Challenging Traditional Approaches through Program Innovation*: 65–80.

Banyard, Victoria L. 2015. *Toward the Next Generation of Bystander Prevention of Sexual and Relationship Violence: Action Coils to Engage Communities*. Durham, NH: Springer.

Banyard, Victoria L., Mary M. Moynihan, and Elizabethe G. Plante. 2007. "Sexual Violence Prevention through Bystander Education: An Experimental Evaluation." *Journal of Community Psychology* 35 (4): 463–81.

Bennett, Sidney, Victoria L. Banyard, and Lydia Garnhart. 2014. "To Act or Not to Act, That Is the Question? Barriers and Facilitators of Bystander Intervention." *Journal of Interpersonal Violence* 29 (3): 476–96.

Betasamosake Simpson, Leanne. 2014. "Not Murdered and Not Missing: Rebelling against Colonial Gender Violence." *Indigenous Nationhood*

Movement: Nations Rising [blog], 5 March. https://www.leannesimpson.
ca/writings/not-murdered-not-missing-rebelling-against-colonial-
gender-violence.

Bowes-Sperry, Lynn, and Anne M. O'Leary-Kelly. 2005. "To Act or Not
to Act: The Dilemma Faced by Sexual Harassment Observers." *The
Academy of Management Review* 30 (2): 288–306.

Brown, Amy L., Victoria L. Banyard, and Mary M. Moynihan. 2014.
"College Students as Helpful Bystanders against Sexual Violence."
Psychology of Women Quarterly 38 (3): 350–62.

Byers, David S. 2013. *"Do They See Nothing Wrong with This?":
Bullying, Bystander Complicity, and the Role of Homophobic Bias in
the Tyler Clementi Case*. Vol. 94. Los Angeles, CA: Sage Publications.

Canadian Federation of Students. 2015. *Sexual Violence on Campus*.
Accessed 22 August 2017.

Carastathis, Anna. 2016. *Intersectionality: Origins, Contestations,
Horizons*. Lincoln: University of Nebraska Press.

Cares, Alison C., Victoria L. Banyard, Mary M. Moynihan, Linda M.
Williams, Sharyn J. Potter, and Jane G. Stapleton. 2015. "Changing
Attitudes about Being a Bystander to Violence: Translating an In-Person
Sexual Violence Prevention Program to a New Campus." *Violence
against Women* 21 (2): 165–87.

Casey, Erin A., and Kristin Ohler. 2011. "Being a Positive Bystander:
Male Antiviolence Allies' Experiences of 'Stepping Up.'" *Journal of
Interpersonal Violence* 27 (1): 62–83.

Coker, Ann L., Heather M. Bush, Bonnie S. Fisher, Suzanne C. Swan,
Corrine M. Williams, Emily R. Clear, and Sarah DeGue. 2016. "Multi-
College Bystander Intervention Evaluation for Violence Prevention."
American Journal of Preventive Medicine 50 (3): 295–302.

Collins, Patricia Hill. 1990. *Black Feminist Thought: Knowledge,
Consciousness, and the Politics of Empowerment*. London, UK: Unwin
Hyman.

Collins, Patricia Hill, and Silma Bilge. 2016. *Intersectionality*. Malden,
MA, and Cambridge, UK: Polity Press.

Conroy, Shana, and Adam Cotter. 2017. "Self-Reported Sexual Assault in
Canada, 2014." *Juristat: Canadian Centre for Justice Statistics*: 34.

Coulter, R.W.S., and S.R. Rankin. 2017. "College Sexual Assault and
Campus Climate for Sexual- and Gender-Minority Undergraduate
Students." (2017) *Journal of Interpersonal Violence*. 1-16.

Crenshaw, Kimberlé. 1989. "Demarginalizing the Intersection of Race and
Sex: A Black Feminist Critique of Antidiscrimination Doctrine, Feminist

Theory and Antiracist Politics." *University of Chicago Legal Forum*: 139.

– 1991. "Mapping the Margins: Intersectionality, Identity Politics, and Violence against Women of Color." *Stanford Law Review* 42 (6), 1241–99.

– 2005. *Mapping the Margins: Intersectionality, Identity Politics, and Violence against Women of Color.* Pearson Education New Zealand.

– 2016. "On Intersectionality." Keynote Address wow, 2016." https://www.youtube.com/watch?v=-DW4HLgYPlA.

Davis, Angela Y. 1981. "Rape, Racism and the Myth of the Black Rapist." In *Women, Race and Class*, edited by Angela Davis, 173–291. New York: Random House.

de la Cretaz, Britini. 2017. "Rethinking Bystander Intervention." *Safe Hub Collective*. http://safehubcollective.org/post/105275458151/rethinking-bystander-intervention.

DeKeseredy, Walter S. 2011. *Violence against Women: Myths, Facts, Controversies.* Toronto, on: University of Toronto Press.

Draw the Line. 2018. "What Is Draw the Line?" http://www.draw-the-line.ca/about.html.

Fuchs, Jacki. 2016. "Let's Stop Blaming Passive Bystanders – and Start Holding the Actual Predators Accountable." *Huffington Post*. https://www.huffingtonpost.com/jackie-fuchs/lets-stop-blaming-passive-bystanders-_b_7785482.html.

Gunraj, Andrea. 2014. *Sexual Assault Policies on Campus.* metrac. Toronto, on.

Human Rights Watch. 2013. *Those Who Take Us Away: Abusive Policing and Failures in Protection of Indigenous Women and Girls in Northern British Columbia, Canada.* Human Rights Watch.

incite! "Dangerous Intersections.," last modified 2009, accessed 13 March 2018. https://incite-national.org/dangerous-intersections/.

– 2016. *Color of Violence: The incite! Anthology.* Durham, nc: Duke University Press.

Katz, J., S. Colbert, and L. Colangelo. 2015. "Effects of Group Status and Victim Sex on Female Bystanders' Responses to a Potential Party Rape." *Violence and Victims* 30 (2): 265–78.

Katz, Jennifer, Christine Merrilees, Jill C. Hoxmeier, and Marisa Motisi. 2017. "White Female Bystanders' Responses to a Black Woman at Risk for Incapacitated Sexual Assault." *Psychology of Women Quarterly* 41 (2): 273–85.

Katz, Jennifer, and Jessica Moore. 2013. "Bystander Education Training for Campus Sexual Assault Prevention: An Initial Meta-Analysis." *Violence and Victims* 28 (6): 1054–67.

Kingkade, Tyler. 2016. "This Is Why Every College Is Talking about Bystander Intervention." *Huffington Post*. https://www.huffingtonpost. ca/entry/colleges-bystander-intervention_us_56abc134e4b0010e80ea 021d.

May, Vivian M. 2015. *Pursuing Intersectionality, Unsettling Dominant Imaginaries*. New York: Routledge.

McDonald, Jeremy, and Lori Ward. 2017. "Why So Many Canadian Universities Know So Little about Their Own Racial Diversity." CBC *News*. https://www.cbc.ca/news/canada/race-canadian-universities-1.4030537.

McGill University. 2009. *Student Demographic Survey: Final Report*. Montreal: McGill University.

McMahon, Sarah. 2015. "Call for Research on Bystander Intervention to Prevent Sexual Violence: The Role of Campus Environments." *American Journal of Community Psychology* 55 (3-4): 472–89.

McMahon, Sarah, and Victoria L. Banyard. 2012. "When Can I Help? A Conceptual Framework for the Prevention of Sexual Violence through Bystander Intervention." *Trauma, Violence and Abuse* (13) 1: 3–14.

Mobilizing the Bystander. 2017. Directed by Ronald Monette. YouTube.

Moynihan, Mary M., Victoria L. Banyard, Julie S. Arnold, Robert P. Eckstein, and Jane G. Stapleton. 2010. "Engaging Intercollegiate Athletes in Preventing and Intervening in Sexual and Intimate Partner Violence." *Journal of American College Health* 59 (3): 197–204.

– 2011. "Sisterhood May Be Powerful for Reducing Sexual and Intimate Partner Violence: An Evaluation of the Bringing in the Bystander In-Person Program with Sorority Members." *Violence against Women* 17 (6): 703–19.

Native Women's Association of Canada. 2018. *Fact Sheet: Violence against Aboriginal Women*. Ottawa, ON.

Potter, S.J., K. Fountain, and J.G. Stapleton. 2012. "Addressing Sexual and Relationship Violence in the LGBT Community Using a Bystander Framework." *Harvard Review of Psychiatry* 20 (4): 201–8.

Ristock, Janice, and Norma Timbang. 2005. "Relationship Violence in Lesbian/Gay/Bisexual/Transgender/Queer [LGBTQ] Communities." *Violence against Women Online Resources*.

Ryerson University. 2016. *Sexual Violence Policy.* https://www.ryerson.ca/policies/policy-list/sexual-violence-policy/.

Saucier, Donald A., Carol T. Miller, and Nicole Doucet. 2005. "Differences in Helping Whites and Blacks: A Meta-Analysis." *Personality and Social Psychology Review: An Official Journal of the Society for Personality and Social Psychology* 9 (1): 2-16.

Suchland, Jennifer. 2016. "4 (Intersectional!) Ways to Stop Campus Rape Culture." *Ms. Magazine Blog.* https://msmagazine.com/2016/03/25/4-intersectional-ways-to-stop-campus-sexual-assault/.

Trans-Student Educational Resources. n.d. "LGBTQ+ Definitions." http://www.transstudent.org/definitions/.

University of Ottawa. 2016. *Policy 67b Prevention of Sexual Violence,* s 4.9.

Wooten, Sara Carrigan. 2017. "Revealing a Hidden Curriculum of Black Women's Erasure in Sexual Violence Prevention Policy." *Gender and Education* 29 (3): 405–17.

Wooten, Sara Carrigan, and Roland W. Mitchell. 2016. *Preventing Sexual Violence on Campus: Challenging Traditional Approaches through Program Innovation.* New York: Routledge.

6

"Strangers Are Unsafe"

Institutionalized Rape Culture and the Complexity of Addressing University Women's Safety Concerns

Nicole K. Jeffrey, Sara E. Crann, Sandra R. Erb, and Paula C. Barata

INTRODUCTION

Sexual assault is a primary safety concern for women (Ferraro 1996, 686–7; Lane and Gover et al. 2009, 187). This fear of sexual assault is not unfounded: over 550,000 women reported being sexually assaulted in Canada in 2014, and – unlike all other crimes, which have decreased – this number has remained relatively stable over the past two decades (Perreault 2015). Young Canadians are particularly likely to be sexually victimized (Brennan and Taylor-Butts 2008, 12–13). Among post-secondary students, women in their first and second year are at the highest risk (Humphrey and White 2000, 422; Kimble et al. 2008, 335–6). Recent legislation in Ontario has mandated the development of stand-alone sexual assault policies to address sexual assault on university campuses (Legislative Assembly of Ontario 2016). Criticism and debate have ensued regarding responsibility for addressing safety issues and the presence of rape culture in the university community (Vemuri, this volume).

In light of the increased attention to sexual assault on university campuses, we examined women's experiences and perceptions of safety on one Canadian campus. We situate our analysis within a broader discussion of the Canadian university context and institutional efforts to adequately address sexual assault. Throughout this chapter, we also discuss an overarching tension in both our analysis and in promoting women's safety on campus more generally; that is, the tension between (1) taking seriously women's voices and safety concerns (which, as our results demonstrate, often rely on stereotypical social constructions of sexual assault), and (2) challenging stereotypical social constructions of sexual assault and institutionalized rape culture.

The Social Construction of Sexual Assault and Institutionalized Rape Culture

Previous research suggests that women are more fearful of sexual assault: at night compared to during the day (Fisher and Sloan 2003, 646; Fisher et al. 1995); in public compared to private spaces (Starkweather 2007, 362–5); and by a stranger compared to by someone they know (Hickman and Muehlenhard 1997, 537; Wilcox et al. 2006, 361). These concerns do not match where and from whom women are most at risk – a paradox previously noted (e.g., Pain 1997, 306) but rarely critically examined in the literature. Moreover, little research has specifically examined how these fears relate to the social construction of sexual assault or how university characteristics such as infrastructure, policies, and programs may influence women's safety concerns on campus, particularly as contemporary university campuses are connected with broader rape culture (discussed in detail below).

Rape myths, rape scripts, and sexual scripts are all part of the social construction of sexual assault (Burt 1998). Such narratives and assumptions appear normal and natural, with the function of maintaining a patriarchal power structure. Rape myths are prejudicial or stereotyped beliefs about rape, rape victims, and rapists that serve to deny and justify male sexual violence (Bohner et al. 2013, 19; Burt 1998). Rape scripts are "individuals' notions of what a typical rape entails" (Littleton 2011, 794) and tend to match the stereotypical rape scenario (Littleton et al. 2009, 801–2; Ryan 1988, 242–3): "a rape by a stranger who uses a weapon – an assault done at night, outside (in a dark alley), with a lot of violence, resistance by the victim, and hence severe wounds and signs of struggle" (Burt 1998, 130). Importantly, however, this script does not correspond to the reality of most rapes or sexual assaults, which most often are perpetrated by men known to women, do not involve physical force or injury, and occur in private indoor spaces (Abbey et al. 2001, 793–9; Brennan and Taylor-Butts

2008, 13–14; Smith et al. 2017, 23). Sexual assaults that do not fit the stereotypical rape script (i.e., the majority of sexual assaults) often become invisible.

Finally, sexual scripts are notions of how women and men should behave in normative romantic or sexual interactions (Simon and Gagnon 1986, 104–11), and many of their elements are supportive of sexual assault. Traditional sexual scripts depict men as more sexually assertive, more commonly initiating sexual activity, and unable to control their sexual behaviour (Dworkin and O'Sullivan 2005, 153; Ryan 2011, 779; Simon and Gagnon 1986, 104–11). These scripts also underlie rape myths that function to exonerate perpetrators (Bohner and Eyssel et al. 2013, 19; Ryan 2011, 777–9).

While rape myths, rape scripts, and sexual scripts exist at the individual level, they are socially and culturally determined and embedded (e.g., in laws, media, religion; see Edwards et al. 2011, 763–9; Ryan 2011, 779). Universities are part of this broader sociocultural context and institutionalize rape culture; that is, they facilitate sexual assault and stereotypical social constructions of sexual assault through policies, resources, and infrastructure focused on stranger sexual assault and individualized causes of sexual assault (e.g., alcohol consumption). Moreover, universities may actually have a stake in perpetuating rape culture and stereotypical social constructions of sexual assault. Universities are increasingly operated like businesses and are motivated to maintain a favourable public image to ensure economic interests (e.g., preserving enrolment numbers; Gregory 2012, 76; Smeltzer and Hearn 2015, 353). These motivations have influenced campus policies and practices that (1) "make individuals the ultimate agents of their own safety," (2) discourage victims from reporting campus sexual assault, and (3) focus on stranger danger and suggest that threats of violence come from outside the university (Gray and Pin 2017, 96–9; Gregory 2012, 72). In these ways, universities can effectively maintain their public image as "safe and reputable" institutions while circumventing their own responsibility for sexual assault (Gregory 2012, 76). It is within this context that we situate our analysis of nine woman-identified Canadian university students' subjective experiences and perceptions of safety through the lens of the social construction of sexual assault. We aim to highlight the sheer strength and embeddedness of dominant social constructions of sexual assault in our participants' safety concerns, as well as the effects of these concerns on participants' academic and social lives.

Situating Ourselves and Our University Campus

The authors of this chapter occupy distinct and overlapping social positions. We are all women, Western, and middle class. At the time of writing, two of us were psychology graduate students and two had PhDs. We identify with various sexual orientations and ethnoracial identities (though all have light-skin privilege). We are all feminist researchers influenced by various academic and theoretical backgrounds and perspectives (e.g., clinical psychology, social psychology, critical feminism, participatory research, poststructuralism). As such, during this research we were concerned with understanding and taking seriously participants' safety concerns while challenging rape culture (goals which often conflicted in this project, as we will discuss).

Our research comes from a mid-sized university in Southwestern Ontario with a student population that predominantly occupies positions of race and class privilege. In addition to an institutional sexual assault policy, the university has a number of sexual assault resources (e.g., an institutional website) and annual sexual assault and consent-based campaigns and programs available to students. For example, there were several programs held on campus for first-year students in the academic year when our research took place, including sexual assault information sessions for residence students and the "Can I Kiss You?" program by Mike Domitrz, which was mandatory for all first-year students (Domitrz 2019).

METHOD

We used participatory photography (sometimes termed PhotoVoice) to examine participants' subjective experiences and perceptions of safety on campus during the Winter 2015 semester. Participatory photography is a participatory action research (PAR) strategy that allows participants to represent and share their lives, expertise, and knowledge through photography (Wang 1999, 185–9; Wang and Burris 1997, 369). PAR aims to understand and improve social systems by making positive change within them. It is a collective, self-reflective method in which participants act as researchers themselves and can become empowered in the process (Baum et al. 2006, 854–5). This method allows people to: (1) record and reflect on aspects of their daily lives; (2) promote critical dialogue and knowledge about personal and community issues through group discussion; and (3) use photography to catalogue social issues to reach policy-makers. We chose this method because we wanted to go beyond gaining a better understanding of women's safety concerns – we wanted to use women's voices and the visual power of photos to help foster positive change on our campus. However, this endeavour became complicated by our process and results. In particular, uncritically using our participants' voices and safety concerns would have meant reproducing problematic rape myths and rape and sexual scripts, and promoting potentially less effective safety policies and practices.

Participants

Our study sample included nine first-year woman-identified university students. Although two did not continue their participation after the first workshop, we include them here because we used some data from the first workshop in our analysis. Although there is variability in sample size across participatory photography studies, a sample size under ten is not uncommon (see Catalani and Minkler 2010, 439). All nine participants were eighteen years old and lived in campus student residences. One participant identified as lesbian, one as bisexual, three as heterosexual, and the remaining four were unreported. Four identified as White/European, two as Black/African/Caribbean, two as South Asian, and one as "other." Five were single, three were in a serious relationship, and one was casually dating. We use pseudonyms for participant names throughout this chapter.

Procedure

We adapted our methodological procedure from Wang and colleagues' PhotoVoice practices (Wang 1999, 187–9; Wang and Burris 1997, 378–80). Participants first attended a two-hour workshop where we introduced the method of participatory photography and the goals of the project, and stimulated engagement with the topic through individual and group brainstorming about what made them feel safe and unsafe on campus. Over the course of the following week, participants took approximately fifteen photos each of people, places, and things that make women feel (un)safe on campus, or that could convey how safety influences women's activity on campus. We collected a total of eighty-one photos from the seven participants who attended the second workshop.

We held the second, three-hour workshop two weeks after the first. The purpose was to review and reflect on the photos as a group and to collaboratively develop overarching themes and discuss how the results could be disseminated. First, participants selected three of their photos from the hard copies we provided and wrote a brief description of each. Next, participants took turns in an open and dynamic process of sharing their photos and experiences. We encouraged participants to engage in discussion and critical thinking by considering different perspectives and whether their safety concerns matched their actual risk. Importantly, however, we tried to balance this with our goal of understanding women's safety concerns independent of the researchers' influence and the potential ethical concerns of adding to women's fears. The facilitators helped link the photos and themes within the broader goal of the research, and the group then further developed and refined the themes that had been identified. We also discussed possible dissemination efforts and later encouraged participants by email to engage in this process; however, only two women ultimately participated by providing feedback on a zine (a homemade magazine-style publication) that was created based on our research findings.

Data Analysis

To address our goal of developing a practically and materially grounded understanding of participants' campus safety concerns, we began with a semantic thematic analysis (Braun and Clarke 2006, 84–5). This involved reading the transcripts as straightforward reflections of participants' subjective perceptions. Using the coding and organizing principles of thematic analysis, five members of the research team developed an initial set of content themes regarding participants' safety concerns. These were: (1) men and strangers; (2) alcohol and drugs; (3) darkness and isolation; (4) ineffective and unreliable resources; and (5) an unfavourable campus climate for women.

In line with the values and goals of PAR, we believe that the ways in which women experience and perceive the world are important to highlight, particularly to the extent that they influence women's behaviour and how they take up space in the world. Notably, however, most of our participants' safety concerns reflected dominant, stereotypical social constructions of sexual assault. This created a challenge for us as feminist researchers because the impetus for our project was to use this research to facilitate effective change on campus. We were

surprised not by the existence of these stereotypical social constructions of sexual assault among our participants, but rather by their
strength (even in the face of our efforts to promote critical thinking),
and we did not want to reproduce them or broader institutionalized
rape culture. Thus, in an effort to theorize the institutional and socio-
cultural conditions that might have enabled participants' accounts,
the first two authors further analyzed the data for more latent meaning
(i.e., underlying ideas, assumptions, and ideologies). Accordingly, we
adopted a critical feminist perspective to examine the ways in which
women's safety concerns interacted with and reproduced social constructions of sexual assault, how these concerns impacted participants'
lives on campus, and the potential implications for addressing women's
safety on contemporary Canadian university campuses.

UNDERSTANDING WOMEN'S CAMPUS SAFETY
CONCERNS AND FEAR OF SEXUAL ASSAULT

Our analysis focuses on how our participants' notions of sexual assault
and campus safety concerns reflected sociocultural constructions of
sexual assault – what it looks like and what causes it. We are not suggesting here that women's safety concerns are trivial or unwarranted,
nor are we conflating *feeling* unsafe with *being* unsafe. Rather, our
analysis demonstrates how stereotypical social constructions of sexual
assault shape women's safety concerns and necessitates grappling with
the tension between recognizing and challenging these concerns in
order to fully address women's safety on campus.

What Sexual Assault Looks Like: The Power
of the Stereotypical Rape Script

One manifestation of the broader social construction of sexual assault
was a dominant, stereotypical definition of rape among participants.
The notion that sexual assault involves a violent nighttime attack by
a stranger was deeply embedded in participants' safety concerns on
campus. The fears that participants expressed were almost exclusively
related to men, strangers, and being alone outside at night. While these
safety concerns have been well documented in the literature, our data
depict not only the presence, but the *extent* to which participants'
understandings of safety on campus were rooted in the representations
of a stereotypical rape. In addition to their discussions noted below,

6.1 "This photo ... is a representation of my fear about walking alone at night. The shadowy man figure staring out of the picture is symbolic of the constant paranoia I feel at night. Is someone following me? Am I safe?" – Audrey

participants' photos also illustrated these patterns: roughly 70 per cent (n = 56) of the photos reflected safety concerns related to men, strangers, darkness, or isolation (see figures 6.1 and 6.2 for examples).

Drawing on the stereotypical rape script that implicates strangers as the main perpetrators of sexual assault (Burt 1998), participants' campus safety concerns were centred around male strangers. When they did acknowledge women's fear of known men, it was usually reserved for women who have men in their lives who are "scary" or

6.2 "In this tunnel, whether it is night or day, when I walk through it, I get shivers down my spine. The echoes of my footsteps almost make it seem as if there is someone bigger, stronger following me. Tunnels like this are the stereotypical place where you, as a woman, would expect yourself to become prey. Dark isolated corners, a staircase that leads up to something or someone you cannot see, the possibility of getting trapped when both entrances are blocked. It is another area where a girl dreads to walk through alone." – Lucy

"threatening," such as women with abusive intimate partners. Perceived risk was also reserved mainly for certain *atypical* men. When they discussed the potential for sexual assault in the home, the comments seemed to imply that sexual assault is still perpetrated by strangers (e.g., "balcony rapists").

Further drawing on the stereotypical rape script, participants reported that being alone outside at night made them feel unsafe. For example, Audrey explained that many women experience "paranoia and fear ... when they are walking at night" and that this fear is always in the back of women's minds. Participants pointed to such concerns as isolated areas on campus – including parking lots and pedestrian tunnels – where they felt afraid or "very vulnerable," especially at night, as well as a lack of accessible well-lit buildings. In contrast, they expressed that being with friends or around other people at night (unless it was only one man "lurking around") is where they felt safe. Underlying this appears to be an assumption that no one would attempt to harm them with others around, or that, "if anything came up, [they could] ask for help" and bystanders would step in. Thus, women's reported feelings of safety in any given situation were contingent on the degree to which their encounter reflected a stereotypical rape scenario.

Participants' protective strategies also suggested a strongly held fear or concern associated with the stereotypical rape scenario. These strategies often involved their attempts to avoid being alone outside at night. Participants commonly reported practices like being alert at night; taking faster, better-lit, and more populated walking routes; avoiding taking classes or going to the library at night; and taking a taxi or bus instead of walking at night (even for short distances across campus). Notably, these strategies parallel the safety resources available on campus, which are intentionally made visible by the university: night walking services, outdoor lighting, and outdoor emergency call posts. Participants identified these resources as elements of the campus infrastructure that helped them to feel safer. What was conspicuously missing from these discussions was any reference to activities associated with acquaintances, such as only inviting a romantic or sexual partner over if other roommates are home. It is possible that the participatory photography method contributed to these results (i.e., participants may have taken pictures of *visible* safety concerns and resources); however, their discussions further highlight how strongly such concerns were held.

While the mismatch between women's knowledge about general risks and their fear and perceptions of personal risk is well documented (e.g., Ferraro 1996, 686–7; Fisher and Sloan 2003, 646; Pain 1997, 306), we wish to highlight the extent to which participants' understandings of what sexual assault looks like were rooted in these stereotyped accounts of sexual assault. To illustrate, despite prompts from the facilitators to consider acquaintance risk in general and despite participants' own real-life experiences with acquaintance risk, participants continually returned to stereotypical rape scripts. For example, in response to a prompt from the facilitator reminding participants that women are more likely to be sexually assaulted by someone they know, Audrey confirmed that she was aware of this risk; however, her own photos and fears shared throughout the workshops were still steeped in stereotypical rape scripts. Similarly, while participants pointed to specific sources of misinformation that position women as being unsafe when they are alone at night, such as messages from parents and the media, their reported *feelings* of fear and danger remained. Finally, despite participants recounting several real-life stories of acquaintance-perpetrated violence and no stories of personally known stranger-perpetrated sexual assault, their safety concerns were still overwhelmingly centred on strangers outside at night and the belief that bystanders would step in to help.

What Causes Sexual Assault:
The Power of Rape Myths and Sexual Scripts

Participants' discussions of their safety concerns were also replete with stereotyped explanations about the causes of sexual assault. Their discussions suggested that they believed sexual assault to be caused by men's sexual urges, alcohol, and women's behaviour and clothing. Discussed in detail below, each of these "causes" reflect common rape myths that blame the victim, suggest that only certain types of women are sexually assaulted, and exonerate the perpetrator (Bohner et al. 2013, 19). To illustrate, within a single story, Lucy suggested that alcohol causes sexual assault, that women's behaviour elicits sexual assault, and that men cannot control themselves when drunk or when women provoke or attract them:

> sometimes it's not really the man's fault ... you know how they say like they have two heads ... when that other head takes over like they can't ... Especially when at the party I went to, there were two girls on the bed dancing like they were really drunk ... like taking their shirts off and I mean sometimes like they do provoke it and they – it isn't their fault entirely because they are drunk as well but if they know that they... are doing this when they are drunk and if they know they will regret it afterwards.

Lucy's account offers a powerful example of how women's understandings of sexual assault are influenced by (1) rape myths that exonerate perpetrators (i.e., sexual assault happens when a man's sex drive gets out of control; Bohner al. 2013, 19), and (2) traditional sexual scripts that depict men as biologically driven to be sexually assertive (e.g., Ryan 2011, 779; Simon and Gagnon 1986, 104–11). Lucy linked the idea that men have "two heads" to their intoxication, implying that men have an irrational and uncontrollable side that "takes over" when intoxicated. Her reference to the women dancing provocatively also suggests that this second "head" is related to sexual urges that cannot be controlled once a man is provoked.

Participants' discussions and photos often reflected a culture of heavy alcohol consumption on campus (e.g., see figure 6.3). Concerns with alcohol were mainly related to men, described by participants as sometimes misbehaving or acting rowdy, aggressive, or possessive when intoxicated. Participants' protective strategies also often reflected these concerns, including avoiding parties and groups of people who were drinking. Feeling unsafe around intoxicated men included male friends and acquaintances, though not more so than strangers. Several participants also spoke about women's own alcohol consumption putting them in danger, therefore making them partly to blame if sexually assaulted while drunk – either because they are less coherent and attentive, or because their behaviour provokes it.

Importantly, participants often described the presence of alcohol – rather than people's specific behaviour when intoxicated – as inevitably leading to situations getting out of hand. In this way, they shifted responsibility from the person's behaviour to the alcohol itself (see also description of figure 6.3): "I had a friend this year who got raped because she was really drunk and the guy was really drunk and it was just a mess and everyone else is really drunk and everyone left her with him and … things like that happen when people are really drunk" (Lily). While there is evidence that sexual assault often involves alcohol consumption by both the perpetrator and victim (Abbey and McAuslan et al. 2001, 794), rape myths about alcohol do more than point to alcohol as a risk factor; they act to shift blame from the perpetrator to the alcohol itself or to women's behaviour when intoxicated. Moreover, in the university context, focus on alcohol allows the issue to remain individualized. In this way, universities can distance themselves from cases of sexual assault where alcohol is involved. Rather than addressing the broader issue of rape culture, university policy can shift the problem to individuals' alcohol consumption in campus residences. Our participants explained that the university punished individual students who were caught drinking too much or in residence common areas (for example, by having them attend a seminar or create a poster about responsible drinking).

Participants also implicitly described other aspects of women's behaviour as eliciting sexual assault. This was mainly illustrated in

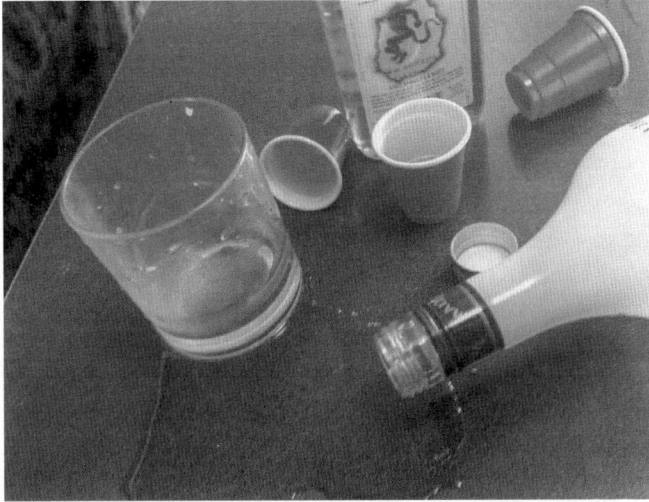

6.3 "This photo ... represents how the consumption of alcohol could easily get out of hand and things can escalate very quickly. This is very important because this is when women are most taken advantage of." – Rabina

participants' protective strategies such as dressing more conservatively, limiting their own alcohol consumption, and locking their residence doors. These strategies imply, at the least, that women hold some of the responsibility for preventing sexual assault and, at the most, that women are to blame if they do not engage in these strategies and are then sexually assaulted. Thus, participants' understandings of sexual assault emphasized personal responsibility for making oneself a target with respect to lifestyle choices (e.g., being intoxicated) and self-presentation (e.g., wearing provocative clothing) (Fileborn 2016, 112; Madriz 1997, 88; Snedker 2012, 86–93).

As occurred in discussions about what sexual assault looks like, constructions of the causes of sexual assault were so deeply engrained in some participants' understandings of sexual assault that they continually defaulted to them, despite challenges from the facilitators and other participants to consider alternative explanations. For example, following a discussion of alcohol consumption, women's behaviour, and victim-blaming spurred by Lucy's party story described above, Audrey introduced her staged photo of someone's hand over a woman's mouth (see figure 6.4) and explained that women are often blamed for sexual assault and that this can prevent women from reporting sexual assault or speaking out about women's issues. Despite these arguments, Jillian responded: "I just totally agree with everything that's been said like, so much. But again ... I totally feel it's you know, really it is both sides." Even participants who challenged stereotypical constructions about sexual assault in some ways (e.g., questioned women's responsibility in provoking sexual assault) still promoted them in other ways (e.g., alcohol as causing sexual assault, strangers as likely perpetrators of sexual assault).

DISCUSSION

Our findings highlight the strength of stereotypical social constructions of sexual assault in shaping women's safety concerns, even in the face of contradictory knowledge and experiences. Previous research has shown that men and women continue to endorse rape myths, hold erroneous rape scripts, and adhere to traditional sexual scripts (Hayes et al. 2016, 1546; Littleton et al. 2009, 800–2; Masters et al. 2013, 418–19), and our results support recent contentions that rape myths and scripts have evolved to be subtler and more covert (McMahon and Farmer 2011, 71–2). For example, while most of our participants did not directly blame women, they did suggest that women sometimes put themselves in undesirable situations and that, in some cases, men should not be held entirely accountable for sexual assault (ibid., 71–5). Our findings provide further evidence that fear of sexual assault continues to restrict women's activities and use of public and academic spaces (e.g., Fisher and Sloan 2003, 651; Hickman and Muehlenhard 1997, 537–41; Valentine 1989, 389). In addition, rape scripts and fear of sexual assault continue to perpetuate largely ineffective protective strategies and lead to false assumptions about safety in private spaces (Hickman and Muehlenhard 1997, 537–41; Turchik and Probst et al. 2010, 81–2; Valentine 1989, 385).

Many of the resources that currently exist on university campuses, including our own, effectively promote, or at least fail to challenge, notions of "stranger danger," including night walking services and emergency call posts. Other examples from our own university include safety bulletins that tend to only report sexual assault by strangers who are not part of the university community and smartphone applications that promote safety only in stereotypically unsafe situations. Most campus resources also suggest that individuals are responsible

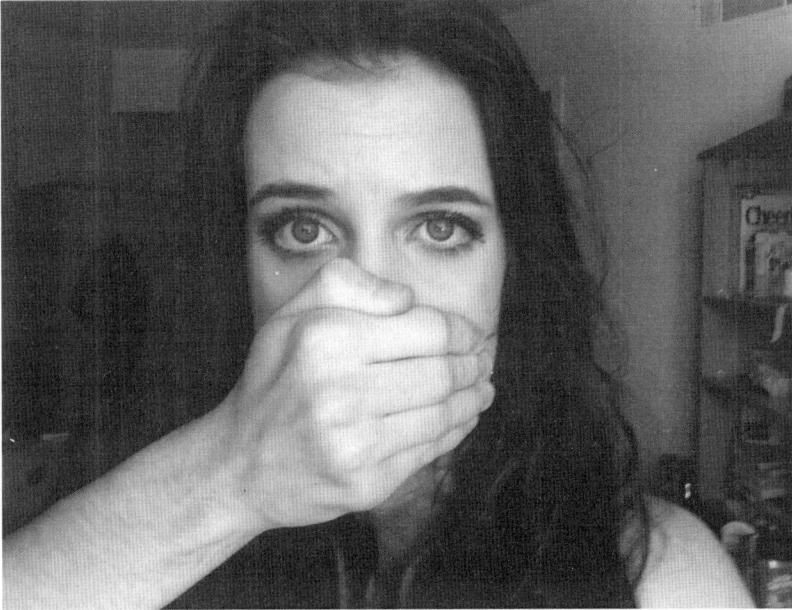

6.4 "[This photo is] a representation of the silencing many women may feel on campus ... the inability to speak out about injustices in fear of ridicule ... [including] fear to speak out about being sexually assaulted, or the fear to voice 'feminist' opinions ... It is also representative of the stigma associated with women who do speak out, which works to keep us quiet ..." – Audrey

for preventing sexual assault. These messages and resources perpetuate stereotypical constructions of sexual assault, and thereby uphold and institutionalize rape culture. They also allow universities to point to these interventions as evidence of their commitment to addressing sexual assault – indeed, our participants highlighted these resources as doing just that – while simultaneously distancing universities from the broader institutional and sociocultural issues that contribute to rape culture in the first place.

As previously mentioned, universities might also gain from promoting individualizing and "stranger danger" messages that allow them to distance themselves from sexual assault cases and to appear safe. To this end, the promotion of stereotypical constructions of sexual assault allows universities to effectively manage parent and student concerns by obscuring acquaintance/student sexual assault and the university's own responsibility in preventing it (because it is an *individual* problem). While the work of student activist-survivors has been instrumental in holding universities responsible for creating policies and procedures to adequately address sexual assault on campuses, the ensuing institutional response seems to be continually motivated by the need to preserve the university's reputation rather than a true commitment to supporting women and victims (Vemuri, this volume).

As we have stressed throughout this chapter, there is a tension between taking seriously women's safety concerns and challenging stereotypical social constructions of sexual assault and institutionalized rape culture. Thus, how to best address women's safety on campus is not straightforward. On the one hand, we do not wish to discount or trivialize women's perceptions of safety. Our participants appreciated and felt safer with resources such as night walking services and outdoor lighting. Such efforts might, therefore, be important for helping women feel freer to go about their academic and social lives, and for showing at least some women that their concerns are taken seriously. Upon personal reflection, we, as women who study sexual assault, also admitted to holding some of the same fears as our participants. And it is important to acknowledge that the scenarios in which participants felt unsafe do pose *some* risk for women and warrant attention.

On the other hand, campus interventions that focus more on stranger assault are unlikely to keep women safe from most sexual assault scenarios (and, indeed, have not shown reduced rates of sexual assault on university campuses; Cass 2007, 361). They are also complicit in promoting notions of "stranger danger" and other rape scripts and myths on campus, especially because they are often the most visible resources available. Like rape myths and scripts themselves, these resources might hinder women's recognition of risk cues in contexts outside of the stereotypical rape script, create an "illusion of invulnerability," and, ultimately, prevent women (and universities) from engaging in more effective protective strategies (Bohner et al. 2013, 31; Turchik et al. 2010, 81–2). Importantly, while "stranger danger" resources did help our participants to feel safer in some ways, they did not eliminate the fear of being attacked by strangers on campus. Moreover, university administration does not appear to give equal attention to the breadth of women's safety concerns. Participants spoke about the overconsumption of alcohol as a safety concern related to sexual assault, but there were no visible institutional remedies that addressed it as such. Instead, it was treated as an individual problem or a broad nuisance related to university life that is not linked to women's safety, sexual assault, or rape culture. This valuing of certain safety concerns (e.g., fear of walking alone at night) over others, and the treatment of sexual assault and alcohol as separate issues, simultaneously reinforces stereotypical constructions of sexual assault and absolves universities from addressing acquaintance sexual assault (and from being held responsible when it does occur). Nevertheless, in deconstructing stereotypical myths and scripts about sexual assault and fostering acquaintance risk awareness, there is also a risk that women will become fearful of men they know, which would also hinder their freedom.

Our collective goal has been to help bring attention to women's ongoing safety concerns and the ways in which they impact women's psychological, social, and academic success, and to facilitate improvements to campus safety. In collaboration with a fine arts student, our research team created a zine to share key results from our project. The zine brings to life our participants' safety concerns by following the story of a fictional young woman's concerns about safety while she leaves for a party on campus. The story is created through participant quotes and photos and highlights the unjustness of those concerns (i.e., few men feel afraid on campus), but also works to shift risk awareness to acquaintances (i.e., unacknowledged safety concerns at campus parties (Jeffrey and Crann 2016). It also provides community resources and ways to work towards improving women's safety on and beyond our campus.

Despite our best efforts to include our participants in this knowledge mobilization effort, most were not interested in being involved. We speculate that this was because they did not feel invested in the topic of the study. This lack of investment is telling: our participants conceptualized sexual assault and women's safety in the same narrow and stereotypical ways that the university portrays them; thus, for the most part, participants were not outraged at the university's lack of (effective) response. Nevertheless, we took the "action" piece of this study seriously and worked hard to share the zine widely at campus events, organizations, and public spaces (e.g., bulletin boards); at national academic conferences; and at undergraduate guest lectures at several local universities.

Our findings highlight the tension involved in representing women's lives and voices when those voices contradict feminist interpretations of oppression. Feminist researchers have previously discussed this challenge (Andrews 2002; Kitzinger and Wilkinson 1997; Lewis 2007). While privileging participants' interpretations can be "dangerous in enforcing dominant constructions" that they may reproduce, privileging researchers' interpretations risks discrediting women's voices and reproducing power relations between researchers (positioned as experts) and participants (Kitzinger and Wilkinson 1997, 573; Lewis 2007, 274). The latter would be particularly counter to the goals of PAR. Throughout this research process, we had countless discussions in which we grappled with the incongruities between participants' fears and the reality of acquaintance rape. This chapter and our zine highlight this tension, and both are attempts to disrupt rape culture (and universities' role therein) while still doing justice to our participants' and other women's fears and concerns.

Recommendations for Future Research and Policy

While our feminist PAR women's safety project resulted in several "action" outputs (such as the zine and invited talks on campus) in spite of limited participant interest in these activities, future PAR research on women's safety might consider deeper integration of the action components into recruitment and data collection processes. Similarly, recruiting participants who are passionate about women's safety and committed to creating positive change on campus may result in greater collective interest in the action components. Future research on women's safety should also aim to recruit larger and more diverse samples with respect to ethnoracial background, sexual orientation, and age to improve representativeness.

What is ultimately required to improve women's safety on and off campus is a complete dismantling of the sociocultural, political, and institutional conditions that enable sexual assault and rape culture. As discussed above, university policies and practices often enable sexual assault and rape culture, and, thus, they could play an important role in dismantling rape culture. In light of the tension involved in valuing women's safety concerns without promoting stereotypical and often inaccurate ideas about sexual assault, universities must work to promote women's *feelings* of safety while simultaneously critically deconstructing rape culture. The development of alternative campus resources congruent with this goal might include: male-focused messages around campus that focus on consent or that disrupt hetero-normative depictions of men's sexuality as aggressive and as taking precedence over women's; smartphone apps that allow women to seek peer support or interruption (e.g., from residence assistants) when they feel unsafe at residence parties or in their dorm rooms; and programs that equip women with accurate knowledge about risk and effective resistance strategies and provide alternative understandings about the nature and causes of sexual assault. Although equipping women with these new understandings is difficult (as our study demonstrated), targeted resistance programs are theorized to undermine rape culture (Radtke et al., this volume) and have demonstrated success in reducing the incidence of rape (Senn et al. 2015, 2332–4). University policy-makers might also consider how to address heavy alcohol consumption on campus and its link to acquaintance sexual assault – while being careful not to victim blame, or to shift responsibility from perpetrators to alcohol itself, or to position the issue and its solution as individual matters instead of institutional ones. While it can be difficult to imagine what alternative resources could even look like given the pervasiveness of rape culture, our study showed that it is an increasingly important endeavour and these examples are only a starting point. Ultimately, universities must acknowledge the role of (institutionalized) rape culture in efforts to address sexual assault on campuses.

REFERENCES

Abbey, Antonia, Pam McAuslan, Tina Zawacki, Monique A. Clinton, and Philip O. Buck. 2001. "Attitudinal, Experiential, and Situational Predictors of Sexual Assault Perpetration." *Journal of Interpersonal Violence* 16 (8): 784–807.

Andrews, Molly. 2002. "Feminist Research with Non-Feminist and Anti-Feminist Women: Meeting the Challenge." *Feminism and Psychology* 12 (1): 55–77.

Baum, Fran, Colin MacDougall, and Danielle Smith. 2006. "Participatory Action Research." *Journal of Epidemiology and Community Health* 60: 854–7.

Bohner, Gerd, Friederike Eyssel, Afroditi Pina, Frank Siebler, and G. Tendayi Viki. 2013. "Rape Myth Acceptance: Cognitive, Affective and Behavioural Effects of Beliefs that Blame the Victim and Exonerate the

Perpetrator." In *Rape: Challenging Contemporary Thinking*, edited by M. Horvath and J. Brown, 17–45. New York: Routledge.

Braun, Virginia, and Victoria Clarke. 2006. "Using Thematic Analysis in Psychology." *Qualitative Research in Psychology* 3 (2): 77–101.

Brennan, Shannon, and Andrea Taylor-Butts. 2008. *Sexual Assault in Canada: 2004 and 2007.* Catalogue no. 85F0033M, no. 19. Ottawa, ON: Statistics Canada, Canadian Centre for Justice Statistics. http://www.statcan.gc.ca/pub/85f0033m/85f0033m2008019-eng.pdf.

Burt, Martha R. 1998. "Rape Myths." In *Confronting Rape and Sexual Assault*, edited by M. Oden and J. Clay-Warner, 129–44. Lanham, MD: Scholarly Resources.

Cass, Amy I. 2007. "Routine Activities and Sexual Assault: An Analysis of Individual- and School-Level Factors." *Violence and Victims* 22 (3): 350–66.

Catalani, Caricia, and Meredith Minkler. 2010. "Photovoice: A Review of the Literature in Health and Public Health." *Health Education and Behavior* 37 (3): 424–51.

Domitrz, Mike. 2019. "Mike Domitrz and the 'Can I Kiss You?' Program for Students." *The Centre for Respect.* https://www.centerforrespect.com/universities/keynote-speaking/.

Dworkin, Shari L., and Lucia O'Sullivan. 2005. "Actual versus Desired Initiation Patterns among a Sample of College Men: Tapping Disjunctions within Traditional Male Sexual Scripts." *The Journal of Sex Research* 42 (2): 150–8.

Edwards, Katie M., Jessica A. Turchik, Christina M. Dardis, Nicole Reynolds, and Christine A. Gidycz. 2011. "Rape Myths: History, Individual and Institutional-Level Presence, and Implications for Change." *Sex Roles* 65 (11–12): 761–73.

Ferraro, Kenneth F. 1996. "Women's Fear of Victimization: Shadow of Sexual Assault?" *Social Forces* 75 (2): 667–90.

Fileborn, Bianca. 2016. "Doing Gender, Doing Safety? Young Adults' Production of Safety on a Night Out." *Gender, Place and Culture* 23 (8): 1107–20.

Fisher, Bonnie S., and John J. Sloan. 2003. "Unraveling the Fear of Victimization among College Women: Is the 'Shadow of Sexual Assault Hypothesis' Supported?" *Justice Quarterly* 20 (3): 633–59.

Fisher, Bonnie S., John J. Sloan, and D.L. Wilkins. 1995. "Fear and Perceived Risk of Victimization in an Urban University Setting." In *Campus Crime: Legal, Social, and Policy Perspectives*, edited by B.S. Fisher and J.J. Sloan, 179–209. Springfield, IL: Charles C. Thomas.

Gray, Mandi, and Laura Pin. 2017. "'I Would Like It If Some of Our Tuition Went to Providing Pepper Spray for Students': University Branding, Securitization and Campus Sexual Assault at a Canadian University." *The Annual Review of Interdisciplinary Justice Research 6. Centre for Interdisciplinary Justice Studies.*

Gregory, Julie. 2012. "University Branding via Securitization." *Canadian Journal of Cultural Studies* 28: 65–86.

Hayes, Rebecca M., Rebecca L. Abbott, and Savannah Cook. 2016. "It's Her Fault: Student Acceptance of Rape Myths on Two College Campuses." *Violence against Women* 22 (13): 1540–55.

Hickman, Susan E., and Charlene L. Muehlenhard. 1997. "College Women's Fears and Precautionary Behaviors Relating to Acquaintance Rape and Stranger Rape." *Psychology of Women Quarterly* 21 (4): 527–47.

Humphrey, John A., and Jacquelyn W. White. 2000. "Women's Vulnerability to Sexual Assault from Adolescence to Young Adulthood." *Journal of Adolescent Health* 27 (6): 419–24.

Jeffrey, N.K., and S.E. Crann on behalf of the Research Facility for Women's Health and Wellbeing, University of Guelph (Ellard-Gray, A., K.M. McLean, S.R. Erb, and P.C. Barata). 2016. "The Participatory Photography and Women's Safety Research and Knowledge Mobilization Toolkit." https://womensafetyresearch.wixsite.com/photovoicetoolkit/women-s-safety-zine.

Kimble, Matthew, Andrada D. Neacsiu, William F. Flack, and Jessica Horner. 2008. "Risk of Unwanted Sex for College Women: Evidence for a Red Zone." *Journal of American College Health* 57 (3): 331–7.

Kitzinger, Celia, and Sue Wilkinson. 1997. "Validating Women's Experience? Dilemmas in Feminist Research." *Feminism and Psychology* 7 (4): 566–74.

Lane, Jodi, Angela R. Gover, and Sara Dahod. 2009. "Fear of Violent Crime among Men and Women on Campus: The Impact of Perceived Risk and Fear of Sexual Assault." *Violence and Victims* 24 (2): 172–92.

Legislative Assembly of Ontario. 2016. Bill 132: Sexual Violence and Harassment Action Plan Act (Supporting Survivors and Challenging Sexual Violence and Harassment). http://www.ontla.on.ca/web/bills/bills_detail.do?locale=en&BillID=3535.

Lewis, Lydia. 2007. "Epistemic Authority and the Gender Lens." *The Sociological Review* 55 (2): 273–92.

Littleton, Heather. 2011. "Rape Myths and Beyond: A Commentary on Edwards and Colleagues." *Sex Roles* 65 (11–12): 792–7.

Littleton, Heather, Holly Tabernik, Erika J. Canales, and Tamika Backstrom. 2009. "Risky Situation or Harmless Fun? A Qualitative Examination of College Women's Bad Hook-up and Rape Scripts." *Sex Roles* 60 (11–12): 793–804.

Madriz, Esther. 1997. *Nothing Bad Happens to Good Girls: Fear of Crime in Women's Lives*. Berkeley: University of California Press.

Masters, N. Tatiana, Erin Casey, Elizabeth A. Wells, and Diane M. Morrison. 2013. "Sexual Scripts among Young Heterosexually Active Men and Women: Continuity and Change." *Journal of Sex Research* 50 (5): 409–20.

McMahon, Sarah, and Lawrence Farmer. 2011. "An Updated Measure for Assessing Subtle Rape Myths." *Social Work Research* 35 (2): 71–81.

Pain, R. 1997. "Whither Women's Fear? Perceptions of Sexual Violence in Public and Private Space." *International Review of Victimology* 4 (4): 297–312.

Perreault, Samuel. 2015. "Criminal Victimization in Canada, 2014." *Juristat*, Statistics Canada Report no. 85-002-X.

Ryan, Kathryn M. 1988. "Rape and Seduction Scripts." *Psychology of Women Quarterly* 12 (2): 237–45.

– 2011. "The Relationship between Rape Myths and Sexual Scripts: The Social Construction of Rape." *Sex Roles* 65 (11–12): 774–82.

Senn, Charlene Y., Misha Eliasziw, Paula C. Barata, Wilfreda E. Thurston, Ian R. Newby-Clark, Lorraine Radtke, and Karen Hobden. 2015. "Efficacy of a Sexual Assault Resistance Program for University Women." *New England Journal of Medicine* 372 (24): 2326–35.

Simon, William, and John H. Gagnon. 1986. "Sexual Scripts: Permanence and Change." *Archives of Sexual Behavior* 15 (2): 97–120.

Smeltzer, Sandra, and Alison Hearn. 2015. "Student Rights in an Age of Austerity? 'Security,' Freedom of Expression and the Neoliberal University." *Social Movement Studies* 14 (3): 352–8.

Smith, Sharon G., Jieru Chen, Kathleen C. Basile, Leah K. Gilbert, Melissa T. Merrick, Nimesh Patel, Margie Walling, and Anurag Jain. 2017. *The National Intimate Partner and Sexual Violence Survey (NISVS): 2010–2012 State Report*. Atlanta, GA: National Center for Injury Prevention and Control, Centers for Disease Control and Prevention.

Snedker, Karen A. 2012. "Explaining the Gender Gap in Fear of Crime: Assessments of Risk and Vulnerability among New York City Residents." *Feminist Criminology* 7 (2): 75–111.

Starkweather, Sarah. 2007. "Gender, Perceptions of Safety and Strategic Responses among Ohio University Students." *Gender, Place and Culture* 14 (3): 355–70.

Turchik, Jessica A., Danielle R. Probst, Clinton R. Irvin, Minna Chau, and Christine A. Gidycz. 2010. "Prediction of Sexual Assault Experiences in College Women Based on Rape Scripts: A Prospective Analysis." *Journal of Consulting and Clinical Psychology* 77 (2): 361–6.

Valentine, Gill. 1989. "The Geography of Women's Fear." *Area* 21 (4): 385–90.

Wang, Caroline C. 1999. "Photovoice: A Participatory Action Research Strategy Applied to Women's Health." *Journal of Women's Health* 8 (2): 185–92.

Wang, Caroline, and Mary Ann Burris. 1997. "Photovoice: Concept, Methodology, and Use for Participatory Needs Assessment." *Health Education and Behavior* 24 (3): 369–87.

Wilcox, Pamela, Carol E. Jordan, and Adam J. Pritchard. 2006. "Fear of Acquaintance versus Stranger Rape as a 'Master Status': Toward Refinement of the 'Shadow' of Sexual Assault." *Violence and Victims* 21 (3): 355–70.

7

Understanding Students' Intentions to Intervene to Prevent Sexual Violence

A Canadian Study

Mallory Harrigan, Michael R. Woodford, Rebecca Godderis, and Ciann L. Wilson

INTRODUCTION

Contemporary approaches to addressing sexual violence on university and college campuses (and beyond) call for addressing rape culture, and demanding accountability among the entire community to create a climate where sexual violence is not tolerated (Banyard, Plante, and Moynihan 2004). These approaches focus on all community members, not just women as potential targets of violence and/or men as potential perpetrators (ibid.). Individuals' willingness to intervene as prosocial bystanders is key to a safe climate. Prosocial bystanders intervene to prevent or stop an assault, challenge sexist comments, and/or support survivors (McMahon, Postmus, and Koenick 2011).[1]

To promote prosocial actions and concomitant campus norms, many schools offer bystander training programs. Though these programs are growing in popularity, theoretical and applied research on bystander intervention on campus is still in its development. Furthermore, bystander intervention research has focused on American colleges, with few studies on Canadian campuses (Senn and Forrest 2016; DeKeserdy, Schwartz, and Alvi 2000). In this study, we provide evidence to inform bystander training programs, as well as other efforts to promote a culture of prosocial bystanderhood. We examine university students' intentions to intervene in hypothetical cases of sexual violence on campus. Specifically, we explore students' likelihood to intervene depending on gender and other demographic characteristics; personal experiences of sexual violence; participation in anti-violence training; personal beliefs held about sexual violence; and perceptions about peer norms relating to sexual violence.

For the purpose of this chapter we define sexual violence broadly, to include physical violence as well as heteropatriarchical speech and behaviours that encourage or justify sexual victimization. This includes sexually degrading remarks and victim-blaming rhetoric. As McMahon et al. (2011) argue, elements of rape culture exist on a continuum of social acceptability, with rape and physical violence considered unacceptable while other rape culture elements, such as misogynistic comments, are tolerated or even celebrated. Using this definition, we argue that campuses should aim to create a climate where all speech and actions that perpetuate rape culture are challenged rather than focusing only on those that cause physical threats. Below we outline existing literature related to our key variables, describe our methods and study results, and discuss the implications of our findings, including practical recommendations.

Gender

Sexual violence is a gendered phenomenon, with women reporting significantly higher rates of violence than men (Benoit et al. 2015). Further, as Edwards et al. (2011) argue, commonly accepted beliefs that excuse or minimize sexual violence are rooted in sexist beliefs that assume fundamental differences between men and women. These include beliefs that characterize women as being likely to lie about their sexual experiences, or as being unable to explicitly express their sexual agency and thus "ask for it" indirectly, or as secretly enjoying rape. These myths require women to monitor their behaviours in ways that significantly impact their lives. For example, many women avoid walking alone at night, limit their drinking, and monitor how they look and what they say to avoid being viewed as promiscuous. These beliefs and actions severely limit women's freedom. Moreover, trans individuals face constant surveillance and risk violence because they do not conform to social expectations related to the gender binary (Perry and Dyck 2014).

Gender also appears to play a major role in student's likelihood to intervene as a bystander. Women, on average, intervene more often than men to address sexual violence (Brown, Banyard, and Moynihan 2014). The reasons for this are not fully understood; however, some studies indicate that sexist attitudes and social pressures from male peer groups pose major barriers to intervening for many male students. Women may not feel these pressures to the same an extent (Fabiano et al. 2003). The gendered nature of experiences and social pressures related to sexual violence led us, in this study, to compare female and male students'[2] intentions to intervene. Due to the small number of trans-identified students who took the survey, we were not able to include them in our multivariable regression analysis. However, we include trans students in the descriptive and bivariate findings.

Intersecting Identities

While gender has been studied for its association with bystander behaviours, other important demographic characteristics, such as race (Brown, Banyard, and Moynihan 2014), Indigenous ancestry, and sexual orientation have been largely unexplored. As intersectionality scholars have argued (Crenshaw 1989; Harris and Linder 2017), focusing too narrowly on gender oversimplifies sexual violence (and bystander intervention). Without explicit efforts to address intersectional elements, the experiences and bystander intentions of the most dominant groups on campuses – white heterosexual students – are assumed to apply to all students.

Race, sexual orientation, and other elements of a person's social location complicate judgements of who can and cannot be understood as a legitimate victim of sexual violence (Bang, Kerrick, and Wuthrich 2016). Donovan (2007) found that male students perceive black women as more promiscuous and as "wanting rape" more than white women. Katz et al. (2017) found that white women reported being less likely to help a black woman at risk of sexual assault than another white woman in the same situation. The potential victim's sexual orientation may also impact judgements of whether a situation is intervention-worthy. Basow and Thompson (2012) found that domestic violence service providers view violence as less severe when it occurs in a same-sex relationship compared to when it occurs in a heterosexual relationship.

Additionally, to contextualize decisions to intervene, we must consider that many students belonging to marginalized groups feel unsafe on university campuses. In their examination of the LGBT inclusivity of bystander programs, Potter, Fountain, and Stapleton (2012) emphasize that many LGBT students feel unwelcome at school, and have been victimized or alienated by other students or university staff. Instances of racism are also extremely common on North American campuses (Currie et al. 2012). Smith, Allen, and Danley (2007) describe how racist microaggressions create "racial battle fatigue" among black college men. Currie et al. (2012) apply this concept to document Indigenous students' experiences at a Canadian university who face subtle and overt discrimination from other students and campus staff.

Research suggests that members of marginalized groups may have a heightened awareness of sexual violence. Worthen and Wallace (2017) found this when comparing LGB and heterosexual students. Awareness and desire for positive change may motivate students in marginalized groups to take action. However, concern for personal safety may create barriers for these students to intervene, due to the apprehension that they themselves could be vulnerable to violence if they get involved. Furthermore, marginalized students including women and trans people have less confidence that school officials would handle sexual assault reports appropriately compared to their peers (ibid.), which may lower their likelihood to intervene.

In this study, we explore intersecting identities among male and female students by examining how race, Indigenous ancestry, and sexual orientation relate to bystander behaviours among female and male students. We also include students' level of study in our analysis (i.e., undergraduate/graduate). Because researchers have not examined the relationship between these factors and students' intentions to intervene, we do not offer specific hypotheses, but take an exploratory approach. Alongside demographic variables, we include students' personal experiences, attitudes, and perceptions of peer norms related to bystander intervention. We discuss these below.

Experiential Variables: Survivorship and Participation in Training

In our analysis, we have included sexual violence survivorship and participation in anti-violence training as experiential variables that may impact students' likelihood to intervene. To our knowledge, no research has explored the relationship between surviving sexual violence and bystander intervention. Given that sexual violence survivors make up a significant proportion of the student body, we believe that including sexual violence survivorship in our analysis may be helpful in understanding the campus climate of bystanderhood. Research to date has shown some support for the effectiveness of bystander training. In a meta-analysis of studies evaluating the effectiveness of campus bystander training programs, Katz and Moore (2013) found moderate support that training can lead to higher bystander efficacy and higher intent to intervene, and modest evidence that training can lead to less rape myth acceptance and more actual intervening behaviours.

Personal Attitudes and Rape Myth Acceptance

Rape myth acceptance is closely tied to rape culture. Rape myths include beliefs about rape and sexual violence that partially or fully blame the targets of violence for their victimization. Rape myths support a narrow and stereotypical idea about which behaviours and incidents constitute "legitimate" sexual violence worthy of intervention by a bystander. As Hockett et al. (2016) argue, so-called legitimate incidents require that the targeted person not be intoxicated, have no prior relationship with the perpetrator, have experienced obvious distress, have immediately reported the crime, and have clear, blatant evidence of the assault. Other scholars (Bang, Kerrick, and Wuthrich 2016; Worthen and Wallace 2017) add that the target's race, sexual orientation, and ability level also influence what is judged legitimate. Studies have found that those who endorse rape myths or believe that some victims are more worthy of intervention than others are less likely to intervene (Banyard and Moynihan 2011; McMahon 2010; Burn 2009).

Past literature has established that gender affects rape myth acceptance. Two meta-analyses have found that men report higher rape myth acceptance than women (Suarez and Gadalla 2010; Hockett et al. 2016). Given these findings, we hypothesize a negative association between rape myth acceptance and students' intentions to intervene when witnessing a range of acts of sexual violence, and that the association will be greater among male than female students.

Peer Norms

Beyond individuals' attitudes, peer or group norms are gaining attention for their role in encouraging or discouraging prosocial bystander behaviours. Studies have found that individuals who perceive their peers as being more likely to intervene are more likely to intervene themselves (Brown, Banyard, and Moynihan 2014; Banyard and Moynihan 2011). The impact of peer norms appears to be especially strong for male students (Brown, Banyard, and Moynihan 2014) and thus men have been the focus of much of the research and programming in this area. Two studies (Brown and Messman-Moore 2010; Fabiano et al. 2003) have found that college men's perception of their male peers' attitudes and likelihood to intervene were more strongly related to their likelihood to intervene than the men's own personal attitudes about sexual violence. Based on these studies, we hypothesize a positive relationship between pro-intervention peer norms and students' intentions to intervene, and that the association will be greater for males than females.

METHOD

The research presented in this chapter comes from a survey conducted at Wilfrid Laurier University, a mid-sized university in Southern Ontario. We extracted data for this analysis from an anonymous campus safety survey conducted online with students in 2016. An external organization, the Education Advisory Board, developed and administered the survey, which is designed to allow post-secondary institutions to assess students' experiences of sexual violence (including verbal and physical violence, harassment, and abuse within romantic relationships), as well as their personal attitudes and perceptions of the campus climate concerning sexual violence. All students registered during the Winter 2016 semester were invited to participate in the survey. The survey asked students to report their likelihood to intervene in a variety of scenarios that represented potential sexual violence situations that students could encounter on campus. The use of hypothetical situations that mirror real-life cases is common in bystander research (Gini et al. 2008; Dessel, Goodman, and Woodford 2017), given the usefulness of such scenarios in examining sensitive topics (Hughes and Huby 2012). The survey items that we use in our analysis include questions about demographics, sexual violence experiences, rape myth acceptance, and perceptions of peers' likelihood to intervene. We describe the study measures in more detail in table 7.1.

RESULTS

In total, 3,141 students participated in the survey (response rate 18 per cent). After data cleaning, the final sample includes 2,021 respondents

Table 7.1
Study measures

Variable	Description	Theoretical range*	Cronbach's Alpha
Personal intentions to intervene	8-item scale assessing students' likelihood of intervening in various situations of sexual violence; 1 = not likely at all, 4 = very likely (see table 7.3 for items)	1–4	.79
Peer's intentions to intervene	8-item scale assessing students' perceptions of their peers' likelihood of intervening in various situations of sexual violence; the situations of sexual violence are the same as those in the "Personal intentions to intervene" scale; 1 = not likely at all, 4 = very likely	1–4	.87
Rape myth acceptance	10-item scale assessing students' endorsement of common rape myths. Items address myths related to survivors' truthfulness, survivors being partially to blame, and holding perpetrators accountable; 1 = strongly disagree, 4 = strongly agree	1–4	.87
Sexual violence in current academic year	Single question asking about experiences of sexual violence during the current academic year (since September 2015); sexual violence was defined broadly, including attempted and completed incidents of unwanted sexual touching, oral sex, and sexual penetration; response options: yes, no, and unsure. Due to the very small number of "unsure" responses, we combined "unsure" responses with "yes" responses, theorizing that students would only select "unsure" if they had experienced some form of sexual aggression, even if they were unsure whether it could be labelled sexual violence.		
Sexual violence prior to studies	Single question asking about experiencing unwanted sexual contact prior to going to university; response options: yes, no, and unsure. As per the previous variable, we combined "unsure" and "yes" responses.		
Sexual violence training in current academic year	Single question asking if students received training during the academic year related to sexual violence, such as on the definition of sexual violence and reporting procedures; response options: yes, no, and do not recall. Very few respondents selected "do not recall," therefore we recoded those responses as "no."		

Gender identity	6 response categories provided, including "male," "female," 3 non-binary options and other. We combined the non-binary options into trans.
Race	12 categories provided, including other. Due to sample sizes we dichotomized race into white/student of colour.
Indigenous ancestry	Dichotomous question asking about Aboriginal ancestry (First Nations, Metis, Inuit). Though the survey used the term "Aboriginal" we use "Indigenous" in our reporting, as this is the preferred terminology in Canada.
Sexual orientation	7 response categories provided, including other. Due to sample sizes, we dichotomized sexual orientation into heterosexual/LGBQ+.
Level of study	Response categories ranged from first year student to graduate or professional student. We dichotomized this variable into undergraduate and graduate for the analysis.

* Higher scores indicate greater intentions/acceptance of myths.

(12 per cent of Laurier students). Compared to the general university population, female students are overrepresented in the sample, representing 73 per cent of respondents. Trans students comprise 1 per cent of the sample, students of colour comprise 26 per cent, Indigenous students comprise 4 per cent, and LGBQ+ students comprise 12 per cent. Comparative institutional data is unavailable for these demographic variables. Fourteen per cent of students had experienced sexual violence in the current academic year and 29 per cent had experienced sexual violence prior to attending university. For those questions, sexual violence was defined as someone having or attempting to have unwanted sexual contact with the student.

Table 7.2 shows that, based on average scores, students reported being likely to intervene, with scores being significantly higher among females compared to males. Trans students' likelihood to intervene was the highest among the three groups. This difference was not significant, though the difference between trans and male students' likelihood to intervene was nearly significant ($p = .051$). Collectively, students perceived their peers to be fairly likely to intervene in sexual violence, and no significant differences were observed between the three groups. Overall, students indicated disagreeing with most rape myths. However, males reported significantly higher rape myth acceptance than both trans and female students, while scores were statistically similar between female and trans students.

Continuum of Violence and Intentions to Intervene

Table 7.3 shows that for the full sample, intentions to intervene were highest for items relating to helping someone who is at risk of sexual violence or who had experienced sexual violence. Scores were lower for items relating to holding perpetrators of sexual violence accountable, and lowest for confronting sexism that is not directly related to physical violence. On five of the eight items, female students reported significantly higher intentions to intervene than male students. Trans students were more likely than both males and females to intervene in instances of commonplace sexism, and reported being more likely to intervene by challenging victim-blaming statements compared to male students.

Intentions to Intervene among Female and Male Students

To understand the factors associated with students' intentions to intervene, we ran two four-step linear regression models. Linear

Table 7.2
Descriptive statistics; full sample and by gender

	Full sample	Female sample	Male sample	Trans sample	
CATEGORICAL VARIABLES	n (%)	n (%)	n (%)	n (%)	x^2
Race					4.92
White	1,493 (73.9)	1,149 (74.6)	320 (70.6)	24 (85.7)	
Student of colour	528 (26.1)	391 (25.4)	133 (29.4)	4 (14.3)	
Indigenous ancestry					3.80
No	1,937 (95.8)	1,470 (95.5)	441(97.4)	26 (92.9)	
Yes	84 (4.2)	70 (4.5)	12 (2.6)	2 (7.1)	
Sexual orientation					164.56***
Heterosexual	1,780 (88.1)	1,363 (88.5)	414 (91.4)	3 (10.7)	
LGBQ+	241 (11.9)	177 (11.5)	39 (8.6)	25 (89.3)	
Level of study					2.91
Undergraduate	1,831 (90.6)	1,394 (90.5)	415 (91.6)	23 (82.1)	
Graduate	189 (9.4)	146 (9.5)	38 (8.4)	5 (17.9)	
Sexual violence in current academic year					39.42***
No	1,748 (86.5)	1,293 (84.0)	432 (95.4)	23 (82.1)	
Yes/unsure	273 (13.5)	247 (16.0)	21 (4.6)	5 (17.9)	
Sexual violence prior to studies					121.50***
No	1,444 (71.4)	1,016 (66.0)	415 (91.6)	13 (46.4)	
Yes/unsure	577 (28.6)	524 (34.0)	38 (8.4)	15 (53.6)	
Sexual violence training in current academic year					1.92
No	1,261 (62.4)	966 (62.7)	281 (62.0)	14 (50)	
Yes	760 (37.6)	574 (37.3)	172 (38.0)	14 (50)	
CONTINUOUS VARIABLES[i]	M (SD)	M (SD)	M (SD)	M (SD)	F
Personal intentions to intervene in sexual violence [ii]	3.24 (0.45)	3.27 (0.42)	3.11 (0.50)	3.33 (0.45)	24.00***
Peer norms regarding intentions to intervene in sexual violence	2.84 (0.55)	2.83 (0.55)	2.90 (0.52)	2.75 (0.66)	NS
Rape myth acceptance [iii]	1.68 (0.51)	1.59 (0.47)	1.96 (0.53)	1.44 (0.55)	105.00***

i   Theoretical range for all variables 1–4. Higher scores indicate greater intentions to intervene or greater endorsement of rape myths.

ii Games-Howell post hoc test revealed a significant difference between males and females.

iii Games-Howell post hoc test revealed significant differences between males and females, and between males and trans people.

* $p < .05$. ** $p < .05$. *** $p < .001$, NS = not significant.

Table 7.3
Mean scores for likelihood to intervene scale; full sample and by gender

SCALE ITEM	Full sample M (SD)	Female sample M (SD)	Male sample M (SD)	Trans sample M (SD)	ANOVA F	Games-Howell post hoc test (m = male, f = female, t = trans)		
						m x f	t x m	t x f
Express my discomfort if someone makes a sexual joke about a person's body.	2.78 (.79)	2.84 (.78)	2.55 (.80)	3.25 (.64)	28.98***	***	***	**
Express my discomfort if someone says that sexual assault victims are to blame for being assaulted.	3.49 (.71)	3.56 (.66)	3.21 (.81)	3.68 (.61)	45.60***	***	**	NS
Talk to a friend who I suspect is in a sexually abusive relationship.	3.28 (.65)	3.30 (.63)	3.22 (.71)	3.32 (.55)	NS	—	—	—
Ask someone who looks very upset at a party if they are OK or need help.	3.23 (.70)	3.27 (.68)	3.09 (.77)	3.32 (.72)	11.97***	***	NS	NS
Confront a friend who tells me that they had sex with someone who was passed out or didn't give consent.	3.42 (.71)	3.45 (.69)	3.32 (.74)	3.39 (.83)	5.85**	**	NS	NS
Tell a campus authority about information I have that might help in a sexual violence case even if pressured by my peers to stay silent.	3.06 (.77)	3.06 (.77)	3.08 (.78)	3.04 (.88)	NS	—	—	—
Report a friend who committed sexual violence.	2.94 (.77)	2.96 (.77)	2.91 (.79)	3.00 (.78)	NS	—	—	—
Help a friend report an incident of sexual violence or abuse.	3.71 (.52)	3.77 (.47)	3.53 (.60)	3.61 (.68)	39.50***	***	NS	NS

* $p < .05$. ** $p < .05$. *** $p < .001$, NS = not significant

regression allows us to explore the degree to which various independent variables predict an outcome, which in this case is the likelihood that a student would intervene. We ran separate analyses for male and female students. In both cases, we first examined demographic characteristics (race, Indigenous ancestry, sexual orientation, and level of study), and then sequentially added personal experiences (training, experiences of sexual violence during the school year, experiences of sexual violence prior to beginning university), rape myth acceptance, and finally perception of peers' intentions to intervene to address sexual violence.[3]

Entering variables sequentially allows us to examine the contribution made by a given variable or set of variables in predicting the outcome, while controlling for all of the variables entered at previous stages. By entering the variables as we have, we are able to assess how much impact peer norms have on intentions to intervene, above and beyond the effect of the variables that were entered at previous stages (demographic characteristics, personal experiences, and rape myth acceptance). See table 7.4 for regression results.

Female students. In the model addressing only demographics, both L G B Q + students and graduate students tended to report higher intentions to intervene compared to their peers. When adding student experiences, sexual orientation was no longer statistically significant. In this model we found higher intentions among those who experienced sexual violence prior to university as well as those who participated in training in the current academic year, and we found lower intentions among those who experienced sexual violence in the current academic year. In the next model, we found that rape myth acceptance was negatively associated with students' intentions to intervene. With the exception of level of study, all other variables significant in the previous model remained so. In the final model, students who reported higher perceptions of peer norms tended to report higher intentions to intervene. Except for training, all other variables remained statistically significant. In this model, peer norms emerged as the strongest predictor of intentions to intervene (β = .30), followed by rape myth acceptance (β = -.22).

Male students. When only including demographics, intentions to intervene were significantly higher among graduate students compared to undergraduate students. In the next model, none of the experiential variables were statistically significant, but level of study remained significant. In the third model, we found that students who were more

Table 7.4
Multivariable linear regressions predicting male and female students' intentions to intervene in sexual violence

	Model 1			Model 2			Model 3			Model 4		
	B	SEB	β	B	SEB	β	B	SEB	β	B	SEB	β
Female (N = 1539)												
Race (ref. white)	.00	.03	.00	.00	.02	.00	.03	.02	.03	.03	.02	.03
Indigenous ancestry	.09	.05	.04	.06	.05	.03	.08	.05	.04	.08	.09	.04
Sexual orientation (ref. heterosexual)	.07	.03	.05*	.05	.03	.03	.01	.03	.01	.04	.02	.03
Level of study (ref. undergraduate)	.10	.04	.07**	.09	.04	.06*	.06	.04	.04	.02	.05	.02
Sexual violence in current academic year				-.07	.03	-.06*	-.07	.03	-.06**	-.01	.03	-.01
Sexual violence prior to studies				.11	.02	.13***	.11	.02	.12***	.12	.02	.14***
Sexual violence training in current academic year				.07	.02	.08***	.07	.02	.08***	.04	.02	.05
Rape myth acceptance							-.21	.02	-.23***	-.20	.02	-.22***
Peers' intentions to intervene										.23	.15	.30***
Adj. R^2	.01			.04			.09			.17		
F for R^2 change	3.99***			12.91***			84.87***			156.37***		
Male (N = 452)												
Race (ref. white)	.00	.05	.00	.00	.05	.00	.04	.05	.03	.05	.04	.05
Indigenous ancestry	.24	.15	.08	.25	.15	.08	.27	.14	.09	.19	.13	.06
Sexual orientation (ref. heterosexual)	.14	.08	.08	.13	.08	.07	.10	.08	.06	.14	.07	.08
Level of study (ref. undergraduate)	.28	.08	.16***	.29	.09	.16***	.19	.08	.10*	.11	.07	.06

	B	SE	β	B	SE	β	B	SE	β
Sexual violence in current academic year	-.03	.11	-.01	.01	.11	.01	.10	.10	.04
Sexual violence prior to studies	-.02	.09	-.01	-.04	.08	-.02	-.10	.07	-.06
Sexual violence training in current academic year	.04	.05	.04	.06	.05	.06	.02	.04	.02
Rape myth acceptance				-.28	.04	-.30***	-26.00	.04	-.28***
Peers' intentions to intervene							.42	.04	.44***
Adj. R^2	.04	0.26		.12			.31		
F for R^2 change	4.01***			41.58***			119.57***		

Note: Ref. = reference group category
* $p < .05$. ** $p < .01$. *** $p < .001$

accepting of rape myths also expressed fewer intentions to intervene, and graduate students continued to be more willing to intervene than undergraduates. The final model found that students who perceived high pro-intervention peer norms tended to express greater personal intentions to intervene. Rape myths continued to be statistically significant, while level of study lost significance. Likelihood to intervene was most strongly predicted by peer norms (β = .44), followed by rape myth acceptance (β = -.28).

DISCUSSION

Intentions to Intervene across the Continuum of Violence

We found that students, regardless of gender, reported lower personal intentions to intervene when overhearing a sexist remark or comments that reflect rape myths, compared to situations in which a threat of bodily violence is more obvious. It may not be surprising that students do not think they would intervene in instances of commonplace sexism because these instances are often not coded as "sexual violence," or as contributing to a culture where rape is more likely to occur. In comparison, students appear to think they would feel an increased sense of urgency if an incident involved an immediate threat of physical harm. Such scenarios align more closely with typical representations of violence in society. These disparities in intentions to intervene may indicate that students lack understanding regarding the continuum of violence, and thus too commonly dismiss incidents of "commonplace" sexism or expressions of rape myths as not being harmful. Our regression findings support this possibility because we found that higher rape myth acceptance predicted decreased intention to intervene as a bystander. While these findings are helpful in understanding the situations when students are most likely to intervene, the scale is overly simplistic as it ignores variables such as the race, sexual orientation, and gender expression of the targeted person. As research shows that these factors impact judgements of who is considered a legitimate victim (Bang, Kerrick, and Wuthrich 2016), readers should be mindful that these factors also influence intervention decisions.

Gender and Intentions to Intervene

Consistent with earlier research (Brown, Banyard, and Moynihan 2014), we found significantly higher overall intentions to intervene among female students than their male peers, and trans students reported higher intentions than both other groups, but the differences were not statistically significant. In terms of male students' versus female students' intentions, Carlson's (2008) qualitative research sheds light on the possible reason for this difference. Her findings showed that "appearing weak" poses a major barrier to intervening when men observe that someone is in need of help. That is, men believe that showing sensitivity and compassion are feminine characteristics, and they fear facing significant social consequences, including ridicule and homophobia (in the form of having their heterosexuality questioned), if they displayed these qualities. Carlson argues that men's constant self-monitoring in relation to the norms of masculinity constitutes a major component of rape culture.

Given that women and trans students face more sexual violence than men, individuals who identify with these groups may have an increased awareness of the problem and feel greater motivation to address it. Moreover, their experiences may explain why we found significantly lower rape myth acceptance among female and trans students than males. However, while students who have personally experienced sexual violence may be particularly compelled to take action, personal safety concerns may deter some students from intervening, as may be the case for students who experienced sexual violence in the current year.

Though the literature supports examining bystander intentions by separating students by gender, as we have done, we acknowledge that the approach assumes a gender binary and so does not capture the fluid nature of gender. Furthermore, when considering the gender differences that we identify in our analyses, it is vital to recognize that experiences of womanhood and manhood are not universal, but rather are shaped by other intersections in identity. Thus, we caution readers to interpret the results from this study within a framework that allows for a nuanced understanding of different experiences within gender categories.

Rape Myth Acceptance and Peer Norms

The findings supported our hypotheses. For both female and male students, those who endorsed rape myths tended to report significantly lower intentions to intervene. This result was found when controlling for demographic and experiential variables, as well as when perceptions of peers' intentions were included. This provides evidence that an individual's attitudes about rape are a major component of intentions to intervene, and thus efforts need to focus on challenging rape myths in order to encourage a prosocial bystander culture. Hockett et al. (2016) suggest that rape myths can be challenged by programming that educates students about the nuanced contexts in which rape often occurs, as opposed to "stranger in the night" stereotypes that rape myths support. We found that the association between rape myth acceptance and intentions was stronger among male students compared to female students, which is consistent with past literature (Banyard and Moynihan 2011; McMahon 2010; Burn 2009). Therefore programming aimed at challenging rape myths among male students may be particularly beneficial.

In terms of peer norms, among both groups, they played a greater role than rape myths in explaining students' intentions to intervene. We found that students with a higher sense that their peers would intervene were more likely to think that they themselves would intervene, and this association was especially strong for male students. These findings indicate that social pressures may have more influence on students' decisions of whether or not to intervene than the attitudes that they individually hold. Therefore, while it is certainly important to challenge individual attitudes, it is also important to encourage students to express to their peers that they do not tolerate sexual violence and are willing to intervene.

Given that peer norms are especially salient among male students, programs specifically designed for male students may be helpful. Fabiano et al. (2003) suggest amplifying the voices of men who oppose sexual violence. For example, men's groups can provide opportunities for men to talk with peers about sexual violence, challenge constructions of masculinity (a major component of rape culture), and decrease men's misconceptions about the attitudes held by their peers. Such programs may encourage men to become better allies to women.[4]

Additionally, institutions might consider implementing programming to leverage the high level of motivation that many students (of all genders) feel to address sexual violence. This can be done through programming to encourage highly motivated students to act as champions for creating a culture where sexual violence is not tolerated (Banyard, Moynihan, and Crossman 2009). These approaches may help to change campus culture, as our findings indicate that a positive campus culture may be self-perpetuating, with students becoming more likely to intervene when they perceive that their peers will do the same.

Given that our findings showed that graduate students are particularly likely to intervene, they might be targeted as potential allies.

Sexual Orientation, Race, Indigenous Ancestry

Race and Indigenous ancestry did not emerge as significant predictors of students' intentions to intervene in our study. The insignificance of our findings could be because we combined racialized students into one group due to small sample sizes of many minoritized students. Therefore we could not detect differences between racial groups. To avoid conflating the experiences of students of colour and to understand the role of racism in bystander decisions, research with larger racially diverse samples in needed.

Sexual orientation predicted likelihood to intervene only among female students, with higher bystander intentions among sexual minority females compared to heterosexual females. It is likely that our sample of sexual minority males was too small to detect statistical significance. Interestingly, the discrepancy within female students lost its significance once experiential variables, including receiving antiviolence training, were added in. This finding is encouraging, as it suggests that LGBQ+ female students are not inherently more likely to intervene than their peers, but that other students may be equally likely to intervene if their attitudes about rape and perceptions of peer and gender norms are challenged.

Graduate students in both gender groups reported higher intentions to intervene when demographic and experiential variables were included in the analysis. Level of study (undergraduate/graduate) continued to be significant for males when adjusting for rape myth acceptance, but was no longer significant when peer norms were included. This suggests that undergraduate students could be equally likely to intervene if their attitudes and perceptions of their peers' willingness to intervene were challenged.

Turning to the experiential variables (sexual violence training and sexual violence experiences before coming to university and in the current school year), important differences emerged across the two samples. None of these variables significantly predicted intention to intervene scores among male students (possibly due to the small number of male students reporting experiences of sexual violence). In contrast, each was significant among female students, even when controlling for rape myth acceptance. Females who experienced sexual violence in the current academic year reported *lower* intentions to intervene, whereas those who had experienced violence before attending university and those who participated in sexual violence training expressed higher intentions to intervene. Female students who have recently experienced sexual violence may be hesitant to intervene because of immediate safety concerns or a heightened sense of vulnerability. Sexual violence is a profoundly distressing experience (Carey et al. 2018), and self-blame is common among survivors (Donde 2015). Furthermore, survivors who did not receive adequate support from peers or an academic institution after experiencing sexual violence may feel powerless to intervene. Encouragingly, the association between survivorship and intentions to intervene lost significance when peer norms were added in, suggesting that survivors who feel that peers are supportive may be more comfortable intervening.

RECOMMENDATIONS

Recommendations for Future Research

More research is needed to better understand the reasons why people choose to intervene or not. This includes why peer norms are so highly influential on individuals' likelihood to intervene, such as concerns of safety among individuals who perceive their peers as being unwilling to intervene. It also includes characteristics of the potential victim, and situational variables. In particular, research is needed to examine why students are less willing to intervene when they witness sexism or the reinforcement of rape myths in order to better understand bystander behaviour in relation to the full continuum of sexual violence.

Future research should deliberately seek to capture intersectional experiences by making efforts to reach racialized, Indigenous and LGBTQ+ students on campuses. This will likely involve specific efforts to recruit minoritized students or undertake coordinated efforts across multiple institutions in order to draw large enough samples for statistical analysis.

Recommendations for Policy

There are several ways that insights from this research can be incorporated into the development of programs on campus. Policy-makers can support the development of programming to address rape myths and other misconceptions that students of all genders harbour relating to rape and sexual violence (including stereotypes about women), as well as factors such as racism that influence judgements about who is considered an intervention-worthy victim and who is not. Programs can also educate students about the continuum of violence, including connections between commonplace sexism and physical manifestations of violence, and prioritize addressing everyday forms of sexual violence to encourage a culture of bystander intervention in which the full continuum of violence is challenged.

Given that peer norms are so influential on students' willingness to intervene, programs should encourage dialogue between students about their willingness to intervene in order to challenge the assumption that one's peers are unlikely to intervene. Research presented in this chapter shows a high level of motivation that many students feel to address sexual violence. Programs can leverage this motivation by developing programming in which students can act as champions for an anti-violence culture.

Those developing programs should be mindful that many students who are the most compelled to address sexual violence are themselves survivors of violence. When designing programming it is important to consider the needs of sexual violence survivors, by directly asking how programming can be made more accessible and what should be incorporated to increase their sense of safety when intervening within a rape-supportive climate. These programs should also be explicitly intersectional, including providing information and encouraging discussion about the ways in which various forms of marginalization affect rates of victimization and impact individuals' intentions to intervene.

CONCLUSION

Given urgent calls to address rape culture and promote community accountability for creating university campuses in which violence is not tolerated, and the critical role that prosocial bystander intervention can play in realizing this outcome, our findings help advance a more nuanced understanding of students' intentions to intervene when witnessing sexual violence. Ultimately, we hope that our findings will inform on-the-ground efforts to create and strengthen a climate of bystander intervention.

NOTES

1 All of these actions are considered "prevention." Primary prevention is defined as taking action to prevent an assault before it happens, secondary prevention aims to minimize harm while an assault is occurring, and tertiary prevention includes efforts to minimize harm after an assault has occurred (McMahon et al. 2011).

2 In our introduction and review of literature, we use the language of "man/woman" to denote the socially constructed nature of gender, and because this is the language most often used in the existing literature; however, in reporting our results we use language of "male/female," in keeping with the terminology used in the survey. The survey question about gender was worded in such a way that it is possible that some trans students selected "male" or "female" rather than specifying trans; therefore we do not want to make an assumption and label male- and female-identified students as cisgender here.

3 Intentions to intervene and rape myth-acceptance are both non-normally distributed. However, the assumption of homoscedasticity is satisfied and the sample size is large, so we determined that the skew in these variables would not pose a threat to the validity of findings. Collinearity values were all well within acceptable levels.

4 Some communities already run these programs. For example, there is one such program in Kitchener called Male Allies (Male Allies, n.d).

REFERENCES

Bang, Adriane, Annie Kerrick, and Christian K. Wuthrich. 2016. "Examining Bystander Intervention in the Wake of #BlackLivesMatter and #TransLivesMatter." In *Preventing Sexual Violence on Campus: Challenging Traditional Approaches through Program Innovation,* edited by Sara Carrigan Wooten and Roland W. Mitchell, 65–80. New York: Routledge.

Banyard, Victoria L., and Mary M. Moynihan. 2011. "Variation in Bystander Behavior Related to Sexual and Intimate Partner Violence Prevention: Correlates in a Sample of College Students." *Psychology of Violence* 1 (4): 287–301.

Banyard, Victoria L., Mary M. Moynihan, and Maria T. Crossman. 2009. "Reducing Sexual Violence on Campus: The Role of Student Leaders as Empowered Bystanders." *Journal of College Student Development* 50 (4): 446–57.

Banyard, Victoria L., Elizabethe G. Plante, and Mary M. Moynihan. 2004. "Bystander Education: Bringing a Broader Community Perspective to Sexual Violence Prevention." *Journal of Community Psychology* 32 (1): 61–79.

Basow, Susan A., and Janelle Thompson. 2012. "Service Providers' Reactions to Intimate Partner Violence as a Function of Victim Sexual Orientation and Type of Abuse." *Journal of Interpersonal Violence* 27 (7): 1225–1.

Benoit, Cecilia, Leah Shumka, Rachel Phillips, Mary Clare Kennedy, and Lynne M.C. Belle-Isle. 2015. *Issue Brief: Sexual Violence against Women in Canada.* Ottawa, ON: Status of Women Canada.

Brown, Amy L., Victoria L. Banyard, and Mary M. Moynihan. 2014. "College Students as Helpful Bystanders against Sexual Violence: Gender, Race, and Year in College Moderate the Impact of Perceived Peer Norms." *Psychology of Women Quarterly* 38 (3): 350–62.

Brown, Amy L., and Terri L. Messman-Moore. 2010. "Personal and Perceived Peer Attitudes Supporting Sexual Aggression as Predictors of Male College Students' Willingness to Intervene against Sexual Aggression." *Journal of Interpersonal Violence* 25 (3): 503–17.

Burn, Shawn Meghan. 2009. "A Situational Model of Sexual Assault Prevention through Bystander Intervention." *Sex Roles* 60 (11–12): 779–92.

Carey, Kate B., Alyssa L. Norris, Sarah E. Durney, Robyn L. Shepardson, and Michael P. Carey. 2018. "Mental Health Consequences of Sexual Assault among First-Year College Women." *Journal of American College Health* 66 (6): 480–86.

Carlson, Melanie. 2008. "I'd Rather Go Along and Be Considered a Man: Masculinity and Bystander Intervention." *The Journal of Men's Studies* 16 (1): 3–17.

Crenshaw, Kimberlé. 1989. "Demarginalizing the Intersection of Race and Sex: A Black Feminist Critique of an Antidiscrimination Doctrine, Feminist Theory and Antiracist Politics." *University of Chicago Legal Forum* 8 (1): 139–67.

Currie, Cheryl L., T.C. Wild, Donald P. Schopflocher, Lory Laing, and Paul Veugelers. 2012. "Racial Discrimination Experienced by Aboriginal University Students in Canada." *The Canadian Journal of Psychiatry* 57 (10): 617–25.

DeKeseredy, Walter S., Martin D. Schwartz, and Shahid Alvi. 2000. "The Role of Profeminist Men in Dealing with Woman Abuse on the Canadian College Campus." *Violence against Women* 6 (9): 918–35.

Dessel, Adrienne B., Kevin D. Goodman, and Michael R. Woodford. 2017. "LGBT Discrimination on Campus and Heterosexual Bystanders: Understanding Intentions to Intervene." *Journal of Diversity in Higher Education* 10 (2): 101–16.

Donde, Sapana D. 2015. "College Women's Attributions of Blame for Experiences of Sexual Assault." *Journal of Interpersonal Violence* 32 (22): 3520–38.

Donovan, Roxanne A. 2007. "To Blame or not to Blame." *Journal of Interpersonal Violence* 22 (6): 722–36.

Edwards, Katie, Jessica Turchik, Christina Dardis, Nicole Reynolds, and Christine Gidycz. 2011. "Rape Myths: History, Individual and Institutional-Level Presence, and Implications for Change." *Sex Roles* 65 (11): 761–73.

Fabiano, Patricia M., H. Wesley Perkins, Alan Berkowitz, Jeff Linkenbach, and Christopher Stark. 2003. "Engaging Men as Social Justice Allies in Ending Violence against Women: Evidence for a Social Norms Approach." *Journal of American College Health* 52 (3): 105–12.

Gini, Gianluca, Tiziana Pozzoli, Francesco Borghi, and Lara Franzoni. 2008. "The Role of Bystanders in Students' Perception of Bullying and Sense of Safety." *Journal of School Psychology* 46 (6): 617–38.

Harris, Jessica C., and Chris Linder, 2017. *Intersections of Identity and Sexual Violence on Campus: Centering Minoritized Students' Experiences*. Sterling, VA: Stylus Publishing.

Hockett, Jericho M., Sara J. Smith, Cathleen D. Klausing, and Donald A. Saucier. 2016. "Rape Myth Consistency and Gender Differences in Perceiving Rape Victims." *Violence against Women* 22 (2): 139–67.

Hughes, Rhidian, and Meg Huby. 2012. "The Construction and Interpretation of Vignettes in Social Research." *Social Work and Social Sciences Review* 11 (1): 36–51.

Katz, Jennifer, Christine Merrilees, Jill C. Hoxmeier, and Marisa Motisi. 2017. "White Female Bystanders' Responses to a Black Woman at Risk for Incapacitated Sexual Assault." *Psychology of Women Quarterly* 41 (2): 273–85.

Katz, Jennifer, and Jessica Moore. 2013. "Bystander Education Training for Campus Sexual Assault Prevention: An Initial Meta-Analysis." *Violence and Victims* 28 (6): 1054–67.

"Male Allies." n.d. Accessed February 2018. https://maleallies.org/.

McMahon, Sarah. 2010. "Rape Myth Beliefs and Bystander Attitudes among Incoming College Students." *Journal of American College Health* 59 (1): 3–11.

McMahon, Sarah, Judy L. Postmus, and Ruth Anne Koenick. 2011. "Conceptualizing the Engaging Bystander Approach to Sexual Violence Prevention on College Campuses." *Journal of College Student Development* 52 (1): 115–30.

Perry, Barbara, and D. Ryan Dyck. 2014. "I Don't Know Where It Is Safe": Trans Women's Experiences of Violence." *Critical Criminology* 22 (1): 49–63.

Potter, S.J., K. Fountain, and J.G. Stapleton. 2012. "Addressing Sexual and Relationship Violence in the LGBT Community Using a Bystander Framework." *Harvard Review of Psychiatry* 20 (4): 201–8.

Senn, Charlene Y., and Anne Forrest. 2016. "And Then One Night When I Went to Class…": The Impact of Sexual Assault Bystander Intervention Workshops Incorporated in Academic Courses." *Psychology of Violence* 6 (4): 607–18.

Smith, William A., Walter R. Allen, and Lynette L. Danley. 2007. "Assume the Position … You Fit the Description." *American Behavioral Scientist* 51 (4): 551–78.

Suarez, Eliana, and Tahany M. Gadalla. 2010. "Stop Blaming the Victim: A Meta-Analysis on Rape Myths." *Journal of Interpersonal Violence* 25 (11): 2010–35.

Worthen, Meredith G.F., and Samantha A. Wallace. 2017. "Intersectionality and Perceptions about Sexual Assault Education and Reporting on College Campuses." *Family Relations* 66 (1): 180–96.

8

"Homosociality" in Paradoxes and Erasures in Scholarship on Campus Sexual Assault and Hazing

KelleyAnne Malinen and Chelsea Tobin

INTRODUCTION

A student once jovially recounted to Malinen's Gender and Society class what could not be categorized as anything other than a sexual assault carried out by veteran members of his football team on rookie members. Against concerns expressed by another class member, the student insisted that this exercise had been good for team cohesion, had been entirely heterosexual, and that the rookies in question could have said "no." This incident left us wondering about the construction of gender, sexuality, and violence in popular and scholarly understandings of sexual assault versus hazing. We began to ask ourselves questions about these constructions particularly with respect to university-aged students, because this was the context in which the matter had presented itself, and because we knew that both sexual violence and hazing are strongly associated with post-secondary environments.

An early foray into the thought process that emerged from this classroom exchange, the present chapter offers a small thematic analysis comparing Canadian scholarly treatments of hazing on university campuses with Canadian scholarly treatments of sexual assault on university campuses. Our results provide preliminary exploration of how gendered ideology and discourses shape these areas of scholarship. Our analysis revealed the following: (1) Male survivors of sexual violence were recognized only within hazing-focused articles (and often as hazees rather than sexual assault victims) – sexual assault-focused articles made no reference either to male victims or to hazing as a potential context for sexual assault. (2) Forms of trauma sustained by victims/survivors of hazing were regularly enumerated in hazing articles but generally absent from sexual assault articles. (3) While homophobia was sometimes addressed in hazing-focused articles, it was not addressed in sexual assault-focused articles. Furthermore, neither literature referred directly to LGBTQ survivors.

We will argue that the paradox of our first observation and the omissions displayed by our second and third observations all exemplify homosocial ideology. We begin by unpacking "homosociality" before detailing our study and findings. Finally, we conclude by offering suggestions for future research and for policy.

HOMOSOCIALITY AND MAN-TO-WOMAN SEXUAL ASSAULT

Many gender and sexuality scholars focus on relationships between masculinity and femininity and/or between men and women as the basis of gender inequities (a few of the countless examples include Butler 1990, 1993, 2004; Cahill 2001, 2010; Beauvoir 1949; Greer 1970, 1999; MacKinnon 2016). In contrast, researchers who have taken up the concept of male homosociality suggest that the lives of many men, including their relationships to women, are largely organized by man-man bonds (Flood 2008, 341; Sedgwick 1985). In the case of these latter researchers, gender-based inequities including violence are understood as caused by the relationships between men instead of by the relationships between men and women. We take up the insights of these homosociality researchers to interrogate the gaps we have identified in scholarship on hazing and sexual assault in Canadian universities.

The concept of homosociality can be applied to people of any shared gender, and to relationships that are horizontal or hierarchical in structure (Hammarén and Johansson 2014). Here, we use "homosociality" in the tradition of Sedgwick to explore the most socially problematic form of homosociality, namely, hierarchical relationships between men. As we will explain, the problem with these relationships has to do with their connections to sexual and other forms of violence, homophobia, and misogyny.

Sedgwick draws a causal path from "homosexual panic" to misogyny. As Hammarén and Johansson (2014, 4) put it, her "definition of homosociality is characterized by a triangular structure in which men have bonds with other men and women serve as the conduits through which these bonds are expressed. However, this triangle may portray as rivalry what is actually an attraction between men. The argument … that there is an underlying continuum between different kinds of male homosocial desires opens up a potential arena for research on the fragile boundaries and lines between different masculinities and hetero-/homosexuality." This fragility means that heteronormative, hierarchical male bonding is vulnerable to homosexual panic, in which the men involved react to the often unconscious fear of homosocial commitments slipping into homosexual ones. This panic would not be produced by closeness between men in a queer-positive social context. But, in homophobic conditions, a reaction to homosexual panic can be an intense objectification of women.

Women are positioned exclusively as hetero-patriarchal sex objects within the male homosocial triangle. Heterosexual sexual activity (1) is a means for achieving male power and prestige; (2) positions women as different from and beneath men by treating women as sex objects and not as people; and (3) ostensibly demonstrates the heterosexuality of men whose primary commitments are in fact to one another. For heterosexual activity to serve these functions, it requires an audience of men who can confer power within the homosocial group. Flood's (2008) research demonstrates that such groups regulate the primacy of relationships between men by imposing a paradoxical view of heterosexuality in which men who are deemed overly committed to female partners are accused of being homosexual.

Male homosocial hierarchies rely "on group cohesion, male domination, and woman-distancing rituals" (Lenskyj 2004, 91). Such rituals may include attending strip clubs, watching pornography, or exchanging nude pictures of women. Some of the young Australian men whom Flood interviewed (2008) shared that during sexual encounters with women, they particularly enjoyed thinking about how impressed other men would be were they in attendance. Indeed, young men often recount their (sometimes embellished) sexual encounters to friends. In so doing, they vie for position in masculine hierarchies, solidify man-man bonds, and provide mutual reassurance of the heterosexuality of the group. Flood (ibid., 350) recounts an exchange with one participant in his study:

Asked what makes a 'good mate,' Tim laughs at length at the response he perceives as hilarious: 'I don't know, what, the other guy on the other end of a pig on a spit!' He explains that 'pig on a spit' is a type of sexual act in which a woman on her hands and knees performs oral sex on one man while having intercourse with another man from behind. She is the 'pig' on their penile 'spits.' Thus, in this scenario, the woman's body literally is the medium through which the two men are connected to each other.

In the same study, Tim elaborates on games played by "the boys" during which women are sexually humiliated for "men's collective amusement." In one, called "Rodeo," a man brings a woman to a hotel room "and begins to have sex with her. He ties her to the bed with her stockings, on her hands and knees. Then, he calls out to the hiding men, the lights are switched on, and he jumps on her back, trying to hold on for as long as he can while she struggles" (ibid., 351).

As Flood argues, sexual violence perpetrated against women contributes to male bonding, and vice versa: men's sexual violence against women can be understood as homosocial (Boswell and Spade 1996; Flood 2008, 340), whether it takes the form of a gang rape during which perpetrators perform for one another, street harassment inflicted for the benefit of male compatriots, or violence before an imagined audience. Were it not for relationships and competitions between men, there would be little to motivate these deplorable behaviours.

A focus on this form of homosociality in theorizing sexual violence does not contravene the feminist truism that man-to-woman sexual violence reproduces objectification of women. Rather, the concept of homosociality helps us to understand how and why women and girls are sexually objectified. Under conditions of homophobia, men must not appear to feel passionately for one another, even when homosocial relationships contain such passions. Women are not part of these relationships as people, but only as objects that allow male homosocial commitments to escape the feminizing spectre of homosexuality. Another way of seeing this dynamic is that "the sexual objectification of women facilitates self-conceptualization as positively male by distancing the self from all that is associated with being female" (Bird 1996, 123). In this manner, homosociality links homophobia with the subjugation of women.

The problematics of hierarchical male homosociality as they bear on the issue of sexual violence are particularly relevant for campus communities, where men's athletic groups and fraternities are concentrated. Sometimes referred to as "fratriarchies," these organizations share a homosocial structure: "they bring men together, they keep men together, and they put women down" (Loy cited in Lenskyj 2004, 87–8). Furthermore, university men are at an age when many are more vulnerable to homosocial pressures than they will likely be later in life. On the cusp of the coveted social construction of "manhood," they are in many cases deeply uncertain of whether this is a category they will adequately attain. Therefore, young men in universities face a great deal of pressure to live up to social standards of masculinity (Edwards and Jones 2007). For example, the documentary film *Liberated: The New Sexual Revolution* (Nolot 2017) includes interviews with young men deeply involved in Spring Break hook-up culture, and yet who recall being pressured into their first heterosexual encounters by male friends. In this way, the film shows that university men may succeed in attaining homosocial ideals of masculinity, not least through dehumanization of young women, with regret and under duress.

HOMOSOCIALITY AND HAZING

To say that men's hazing practices are hierarchically homosocial seems both more and less obvious than to say that man-to-woman sexual violence is homosocial. On the one hand, men's hazing practices take place directly between men, making the male-male character of the hazer-hazee relationship immediately obvious. On the other hand, hazing practices appear to lower hazee status through processes referred to in the hazing literature as denigration or humiliation, which commonly occur through the perpetration of "sadistic sexual acts" (Lenskyj 2004, 83). As Lenskyj asks, "how is it that men's sexual victimization of other men proves their *heterosexual* superiority, and not their *homosexual* interests?" (ibid., 92).

One answer lies in the reconstruction of masculine hierarchy, and the value placed in that hierarchy by those who aspire to upward mobility within it. The logic of sexual assault as hazing can be differentiated from the logic of sexual assault in other contexts by the fact that being hazed is seen as a step on the path to the coveted status of veteran, and therefore being a hazer. Temporarily forcing men in homosocial environments to take on the feminized role of sexual victim maintains a pecking order in which real men dominate feminized people, reinforcing the interest in attaining the "real man" status reserved for veterans and achieved by fidelity to the group (Kirby and Wintrup 2002). In these ways, even in its most sexually violent form, hazing adheres to male homosocial logic. For all of this, it is no less the case that hazees can and do suffer trauma as a consequence of sexual assault experiences or other forms of violence inflicted under the guise of hazing.

Our initial goal was to narrow the sample by selecting only those articles that would focus on the contexts of university athletics and/or Greek letter organizations. However, whereas many publications from the United States fit these parameters, Canadian articles that did so proved far less common. No doubt this lacuna is partly a consequence of the fact that our smaller population translates into a smaller population of scholars. Furthermore, the dearth of Canadian articles about sexual assault or hazing in the context of Greek letter organizations is at least partially attributable to the less pronounced presence of Greek letter organizations on our side of the border. In Canada as compared to the United States, these student groups are less popular and less visible because housed off campus.

The dearth of Canadian scholarship in these areas illustrates the importance of the current volume. Interestingly, it was more difficult to find qualifying Canadian research about campus sexual assault than it was to find Canadian research about hazing. In the end, we included three articles on sexual assault that addressed neither the Greek letter context nor the athletic context. We compared six pieces of scholarship focused on hazing in Canadian university sport (Fogel 2013; Hamilton et al. 2016; Johnson 2011; Kirby and Wintrup 2002; Lenskyj 2004; Massey and Massey 2017) with six pieces of scholarship focused on sexual assault in Canadian universities, three of which were focused on university but not sport or Greek letter contexts (Moore and Valverde 2000; Quinlan, Clarke, and Horsley 2009; Senn, Gee, and Thake 2011; Fogel 2017; Haiven 2017; DeKeseredy, Schwartz, and Alvi 2000).

Of each article, we asked the following questions: Is gender and/or sexuality part of the analysis? Is the violence in question problematized? Is the violence framed as having negative or traumatic effects? Is violence framed as having potential benefits? Our final question was included because some researchers believe, like Malinen's student who initiated my interest in this area, that hazing enhances team cohesion (e.g., Keating et al. 2005). We also looked at whether hazing-focused texts mentioned sexual violence, and whether sexual violence-focused texts mentioned hazing. Finally, Bagh and Tobin noted any further patterns observed among texts during their analyses.

Close reading by Malinen of three patterns that emerged for Bagh and Tobin suggest the appropriateness of using homosociality as an analytic framework.[1] In other words, not only does this framework provide a tool for understanding the recalcitrant problem of sexual violence on campus, as argued by Flood (2008) and others, it also helps us to understand the paradoxes and erasures that emerged from the articles we read, as described below.

FINDINGS

Pattern 1

Within the literature we examined, "hazing-focused" sometimes referred to sexual assault as a form of hazing, and sometimes referred to female hazees, but sexual assault-focused articles made no reference to hazing, and no reference to male survivors.

The exceptions to each pattern appear in Fogel's 2017 chapter "Precarious Masculinity and Rape Culture in Canadian University Sport."

To the extent that each pattern maintains, it preserves the homosexual/heterosexual divide that is foundational to Euro-Canadian and Euro-American homosociality. On one hand, popular and academic traditions understand sexual assault as a form of violence that feminizes/objectifies the victim, thereby masculinizing the perpetrator. This is true whether the understanding is misogynistic (i.e., women *are and should be* mere objects for men's gratification) or feminist (i.e., women *have been positioned as* mere objects for men's gratification, and this problem must be rectified). To reiterate, this dualism is consistent with the triangular structure of homosociality in which women are objectified and inserted between men to provide the conduit for relationships between men while fending off the spectre of homosexuality.

On the other hand, hazing is widely understood as a form of violence that ultimately masculinizes the victim. For example, in exploring sexual violence in hazing, Kirby and Wintrup (2002, 52) note, "If hazing exists, rookies are the targets of such practices. Rookies who successfully pass through hazing are accepted into the 'team family' and become part of the tradition or legacy." One might extrapolate that the more violent the hazing, the more manly the man who has survived it. While hazing-focused articles frequently include sexual assault among forms of hazing rituals, their authors categorically have chosen hazing rather than sexual assault as the overarching frame of analysis, presenting the sexual assaults as hazings first and foremost.

As a result, men who live through incidents that read for all intents and purposes as gang rapes are still not seen as sexual assault survivors. Identification of these men as such would compromise the masculinity of these survivors/hazees as well as the masculine structural integrity of the homosocial hierarchies to which they belong. This taxonomy bridges scholarship, popular media, and institutional reports. Fogel's (2013) hazing-focused text begins by citing McGill University: "After a thorough investigation, officials at McGill released a statement that described the initiation ritual involving 'nudity, degrading positions and behaviours, gagging, touching in inappropriate manners with a broomstick, as well as verbal and physical intimidation of rookies by a large portion of the team.'" Why view this incident, again with the exception of Fogel's 2017 chapter, as a "hazing" rather than a gang rape? Part of the answer may be that this taxonomy functions to protect the masculine status of the hazing victim against the more permanent humiliation associated with sexual assault victimization, through its association with victimization.

While men are rarely identified as sexual assault survivors in our literature, except under the umbrella category of hazing, women are sometimes identified as hazing survivors in the articles where hazing is the focus. This inclusion of women hazees poses less of a threat to homosocial structures than one might imagine. Euro-Canadian and Euro-American societies appear to accept women and girls performing masculine activities more easily than men and boys performing feminine activities, a fact that underlines the cultural valuing of masculinity. Inversely, researchers have found that young adults responding to descriptions of gender-conforming and gender-nonconforming children rated both "the typical girl and the 'mama's boy' ... more likeable and competent than the typical boy, [yet] would encourage 'mama's boys' to behave more like typical boys" (Coyle, Fulcher, and Trübutschek 2016, 1836). The authors concluded that because masculinity is culturally valued, "the behaviours of nonconforming boys are seen as problematic" (ibid.; see also D'Augelli, Grossman, and Starks 2006). This is not to suggest that sexualized hazings were seen in any literature to render women hazees more masculine and therefore more powerful as individuals – only that the linking of hazing and masculinization may not pose a barrier to the discussion of women hazees in the same way that the linking of sexual violence and feminization seems to impede discussion of male sexual assault victimization/survival.

Indeed, research about sexual victimization of men and boys – some of which has been produced, but without focus on the post-secondary arena – routinely refers to the additional shame men and boys experience as a consequence of the feminization that is culturally understood as inherent to sexual assault (e.g., Dorais 2002; Gear 2007; Knowles 1999; Pino and Meier 1999). The implication can be that men suffer more from sexual assault victimization than women, because men also have their masculinity to lose. On the other hand, if we see male athletes and frat boys as sexual assault victims/survivors rather than as hazees, we would be pushed toward the recognition of all men as permeable and prone to feminization, and perhaps to question the putative heterosexuality of their perpetrators.

Pattern 2

Rarely were negative impacts on victims/survivors mentioned in the sexual assault-focused articles. The negative impacts on hazing victims, however, were frequently detailed. For example: "The impact of hazing is notable as there have been cases of death, burns, cold exposure, acute alcohol intoxication, blood loss, blunt trauma, and sexual abuse reported in the media and documented through empirical study … Beyond the physical ramifications of hazing, psychological consequences include suicide ideation, loneliness, embarrassment, depression, and post-traumatic stress disorder [citations omitted]" (Hamilton et al. 2016, 256).

While sexual assault victims/survivors experience a range physical and psychological traumas, as a matter of course, literature on campus sexual assault does not enumerate these impacts. We were surprised by this result, as we began with the expectation that victimhood was more culturally acceptable for women and would therefore be more readily recognized. We also expected that researchers of campus-based sexual violence would be largely motivated by concern over harm to student survivors, and that this concern would be expressed in written reports. There are a few possible underlying beliefs that could explain this lack of recognition regarding the harms of sexual violence on university campuses: (1) the belief that the negative effects of sexual violence on women are too obvious to require unpacking; (2) the belief that men's suffering is culturally invisible and must therefore be spelled out; (3) the belief that men's suffering is more important than women's suffering; or (4) the belief that men suffer more from hazing than women do from sexual violence.

This fourth idea appears to animate a term coined by Brackenridge and Kirby (cited in Kirby and Wintrup 2002, 63), "The Stage of Imminent Achievement," when athletes are particularly at risk for hazing. At this time, "the athlete has the most to lose from dropping out as she or he has invested the most in terms of time, effort and dedication and has the most to gain from remaining." This notion closely mirrors the kind of discourse commonly applied in popular culture when men who are university students and often athletes perpetrate sexual violence. When former Stanford swimmer Brock Turner was sentenced to six months in jail, the judge, Aaron Persky, explained, "I think you have to take the whole picture in terms of what impact imprisonment has on a specific individual's life. And ... the character letters that have been submitted do show a huge collateral consequence for Mr. Turner based on the conviction" (2016).

The concept of the Stage of Imminent Achievement, exemplified by Persky's comments in the Brock Turner case, is interrelated with the homosocial maintenance of focus on men's experiences, and its concomitant neglect of women as people with interests. This focus is evidenced when we worry about the impacts of sexual assault conviction on promising young perpetrators. It is also evidenced by Pattern 2 identified by our study, whereby researchers pay little attention to the negative effects of sexual assault on survivors (typically women in the reviewed articles), and much attention to the negative effects of hazing on hazees (typically men in the reviewed articles). Homosociality positions women as objects between men, who therefore face no risk of losing anything by being objectified.

Consider that, whereas a defining question in an instance of hazing is whether the victim has been harmed and humiliated, defining questions in an instance of sexual assault are whether or not the victim "liked" it, was "looking" for it, or "asked" for it. In contrast, when we invoke the term "hazing," even where sexual abuse is a "physical ramification" (Hamilton et al. 2016, 256), we do not find bright young male victims facing interrogation about their sexual fantasies, desires, or histories, or about whether they might have sent mixed messages by going to that initiation party and acting as if they were having a good time. Someone might say that the hazee "took it like a man," others might say that he was "harmed by the humiliation," but it is unlikely that anyone will suggest he was "turned on." Again, fore-grounding the concept of hazing over sexual assault protects hazees from the feminization of sexual assault.

Scholars often emphasize "humiliation" and "degradation" as nega-tive impacts of hazing. In fact, one commonly cited definition of hazing includes both humiliation and degradation: hazing is "any activity expected of someone joining a group that humiliates, degrades, abuses or endangers, regardless of the person's willingness to participate" (Hoover 1999, cited in Johnson 2011, 200). It is no accident that these humiliations take normatively feminizing forms, from dressing "like women" to anal penetration. As Lenskyj (2004, 87–8) argues: "In a more progressive social context, taking the female role in terms of dress or behaviour might not be seen as sexual degradation, but rather as an act of playfulness, or an ironic challenge to gender boundaries. However, a key component of male initiation is distancing from and domination over women ... and therefore enforced cross-dressing clearly constitutes sexual degradation in the context of male sport subcultures."

The culturally unpalatable feminization of students valued for their masculinity may generate among researchers a fascination with the harms of hazing accompanied by a failure to consider including hazees in sexual assault research and policy.

Pattern 3

Given that LGBTQ people are disproportionately targets of sexual violence in Canada and the United States (Walters et al. 2013; Xavier et al. 2007; Bauer and Scheim 2016), it is curious and troubling that queer identities are erased by texts about sexual assault on campus and about hazing on campus. Hate crimes inflicted against LGBTQ people in Canada are shown to be more violent than hate crimes against any other Canadian population (Allen 2015), and yet LGBTQ survivors are absent in these literatures.

Meanwhile, the erasure of LGBTQ university students from analyses of hazing becomes especially worrisome when viewed through the framework of homosociality. As argued above, homosociality involves foreclosure of the very homosexuality that might appear to coexist logically with man-to-man commitments and passions. The homoso-ciality of hazing implies that those hazers might be particularly threatened by, and therefore violent toward, hazees who are read as queer. Indeed, Lenskyj (2004, 88) describes the homosocial dynamic of the "fratriarchy" as characterized by disproportionate involvement in "gay-bashings" among other forms of violence. For example, in the United States, many observers have suggested that the 2012 hazing-related murder of Florida A&M drum major Robert Champion was largely motivated by his sexual orientation. Our analyses of campus-based sexual assault and hazing should be alert to the experiences of LGBTQ students.

CONCLUSION

We do not imagine that authors of any of the texts we have examined intend to operate through homosocial lenses. On the contrary, these authors are clearly motivated to critique and counteract gender-based forms of oppression. However, academic and other understandings of both sexual assault and hazing emerge from a social context so pervaded with gendered and misogynist ideologies that these ideologies can subtly frame even politically forward texts. In particular: (1) Hazing-focused articles in our sample sometimes referred to sexual assault as a form of hazing, and sometimes referred to female hazees, but sexual assault-focused articles made no reference to hazing, and no reference to male victims. (2) Diverse traumas sustained by hazing victims were regularly enumerated with a particular focus on "humiliation" and "degradation," while articles on sexual assault included no such information. Finally, (3) Queer identities are virtually absent from all articles. To understand these patterns, we have drawn on the interventions of thinkers like Flood and Sedgwick who link misogyny and homophobia through homosociality to the prevalence and meaning of sexual assault and hazing practices. We suggest that researchers ought to be cautious of the ways in which their work reproduces these patterns, and with them, homosocial discourse and ideology.

DIRECTIONS FOR FUTURE RESEARCH
AND POLICY RECOMMENDATIONS

We have discussed the tight relationship between male homosociality and fratriarchies such as athletic teams and fraternities, contexts in which there are high rates of hazing practices and of sexual assault perpetration. While these fratriarchal contexts are clearly problematic, they will continue to be a part of North American culture in the foreseeable future. Therefore it is important that future research uncover ways to prevent the emergence of gendered violence from fratriachal contexts in contemporary Canada.

We suggest that scholars and service providers working in this area of sexual violence should broaden their attention to include hazing-related sexual assault, which seems most commonly to take a man-to-man form. Homosocial initiation contexts should be analyzed as situations that pose important challenges to young men's capacities to consent, and appropriate sexual violence prevention measures should be put in place.

Some might object that by including these young men (who are in many cases strongly identified with a misogynistic version of hetero-sexuality) among sexual assault victims/survivors, we would risk evacuating gender-based analysis from sexual violence research. While it remains crucial to reserve safe spaces for people who identify as women, transgender, or queer, erasure of feminist concerns is by no means a necessary conclusion of the inclusion of male hazing victims in sexual assault research and prevention. In fact, critical theorizations of homosociality can provide a thoroughly queer and feminist framework that is better articulated in tandem with the introduction of fratriarchal violence than through its exclusion.[2] If the maintenance of male homosocial ideology – that fragile and fearful investment in hetero-patriarchy – is conducive to violent hazing, sexual violence, and homophobic attacks, then it is incumbent upon us to break that ideology down when and where we can. Framing fratriarchal violence as sexual assault when appropriate may help to corrode the boundaries that homosociality endeavours to erect between women and men. Furthermore, pointing out the man-to-man commitments and passions that animate sexual violence against women may challenge the notion that sexually assaulting women proves heterosexual orientation.

In conclusion, if Sedgwick argues correctly in her seminal text *Between Men: English Literature and Male Homosocial Desire* (1985) that homosociality is the glue sustaining Anglo-European patriarchy, sexual violence research and anti-violence practice will be strengthened by analyzing and dismantling the homosocial triangle wherein women are objectified and inserted between men in order to heterosexualize male-male passions.

NOTES

1 Thanks to Ardath Whynacht and El Jones for conversations that helped make connections between literatures.
2 Malinen (2013a, 2013b, 2014, and 2018) elaborates on how feminist and queer concerns can be synthesized in anti-sexual violence work.

REFERENCES

Allen, Mary. 2015. "Police-Reported Hate Crime in Canada, 2013." *Juristat: Canadian Centre for Justice Statistics*, catalogue no. 85-002-X. 1–29.

Bauer, Greta, and Ayden Scheim. 2016. *Transgender People in Ontario, Canada: Statistics from the Trans PULSE Project to Inform Human Rights Policy.* London, ON: Western University.

Beauvoir, Simone de. 1949. *Le Deuxième Sexe.* 2 vols. Paris: Gallimard.

Bird, Sharon R. 1996. "Welcome to the Men's Club: Homosociality and the Maintenance of Hegemonic Masculinity." *Gender and Society* 10 (2): 120–32.

Boswell, A. Ayres, and Joan Z. Spade. 1996. "Fraternities and Collegiate Rape Culture: Why Are Some Fraternities More Dangerous Places for Women?" *Gender and Society* 10 (2): 133–47.

Butler, Judith. 1990. *Gender Trouble: Feminism and the Subversion of Gender.* New York: Routledge.

– 1993. *Bodies that Matter: On the Discursive Limits of "Sex."* New York: Routledge.

– 2004. *Undoing Gender.* New York: Routledge.

Cahill, Ann J. 2001. *Rethinking Rape.* Ithaca, NY: Cornell University Press.

– 2010. *Overcoming Objectification: A Carnal Ethics.* New York: Routledge.

Coyle, Emily, Megan Fulcher, and Darinka Trübutschek. 2016. "Sissies, Mama's Boys, and Tomboys: Is Children's Gender Nonconformity More Acceptable when Nonconforming Traits are Positive?" *Archives of Sexual Behavior* 45 (7): 1827–38.

D'Augelli, Anthony, R., Arnold H. Grossman, and Michael T. Starks. 2006. "Childhood Gender Atypicality, Victimization, and PTSD among Lesbian, Gay, and Bisexual Youth." *Journal of Interpersonal Violence* 21 (11): 1462–82.

DeKeseredy, Walter S., Martin D. Schwartz, and Shahid Alvi. 2000. "The Role of Profeminist Men in Dealing with Woman Abuse on the Canadian College Campus." *Violence against Women* 6 (9): 918–35.

Dorais, Michel. 2002. *Don't Tell: The Sexual Abuse of Boys*. Montreal, QC: McGill-Queen's University Press.

Edwards, Keith E., and Susan R. Jones. 2007. "'Putting My Man Face On': A Grounded Theory of College Men's Gender Identity Development." *Journal of College Student Development* 50 (2): 210–28.

Flood, Michael. 2008. "Men, Sex, and Homosociality: How Bonds between Men Shape their Sexual Relations with Women." *Men and Masculinities* 10 (3): 339–59.

Fogel, Curtis. 2013. "Hazing in the Aftermath of McGill's 'Mr. Broomstick.'" In *Game-Day Gangsters: Crime and Deviance in Canadian Football*. Edmonton, AB: Athabasca University Press.

– 2017. "Precarious Masculinity and Rape Culture in Canadian University Sport." In *Sexual Violence at Canadian Universities*, edited by Elizabeth Quinlan, Andrea Quinlan, Curtis Fogel, and Gail Taylor, 139–58. Waterloo, ON: Wilfrid Laurier Press.

Gear, Sasha. 2007. "Behind the Bars of Masculinity: Male Rape and Homophobia in and about South African Men's Prisons." *Sexualities* 10 (2): 209–27.

Greer, Germaine. 1970. "The Female Eunuch." London, UK: MacGibbon and Kee.

– 1999. *The Whole Woman*. London, UK, and New York: Doubleday.

Haiven, Judy. 2017. "The Rape Chant at Saint Mary's University: The Convergence of Alcohol, Business, and Sport Cultures." In *Sexual Violence at Canadian Universities: Activism, Institutional Responses, and Strategies for Change*, edited by Elizabeth Quinlan, Andrea Quinlan, Curtis Fogel, and Gail Taylor, 93–116. Waterloo, ON: Wilfrid Laurier University Press.

Hamilton, Ryan, David Scott, Diane LaChapelle, and Lucia O'Sullivan. 2016. "Applying Social Cognitive Theory to Predict Hazing Perpetration in University Athletics." *Journal of Sport Behavior* 39 (3): 255–77.

Hammarén, Nils, and Thomas Johansson. 2014. "Homosociality: In between Power and Intimacy." *Sage Open* 4 (1): 1–11.

Johnson, Jay. 2011. "Through the Liminal: A Comparative Analysis of Communitas and Rites of Passage in Sport Hazing and Initiations." *Canadian Journal of Sociology* 36 (3): 199–227.

Keating, Caroline F., Jason Pomerantz, Stacy D. Pommer, Samantha J.H. Ritt, Lauren M. Miller, and Julie McCormick. 2005. "Going to College and Unpacking Hazing: A Functional Approach to Decrypting Initiation Practices among Undergraduates." *Group Dynamics: Theory, Research, and Practice* 9 (2): 104–26.

Kirby, Sandra L., and Glen Wintrup. 2002. "Running the Gauntlet: An Examination of Initiation/Hazing and Sexual Abuse in Sport." *Journal of Sexual Aggression* 8 (2): 49–68.

Knowles, Gordon James. 1999. "Male Prison Rape: A Search for Causation and Prevention." *The Howard Journal of Criminal Justice* 38 (3): 267–82.

Lenskyj, Helen. 2004. "What's Sex Got to Do with It? Analysing the Sex Violence Agenda in Sport Hazing Practices." In *Making the Team: Inside the World of Sport Initiations and Hazing*, edited by Jay Johnson and Margery Homan, 83–96. Toronto, ON: Canadian Scholar's Press.

MacKinnon, Catharine A. 2016. *Sex Equality*. 3rd ed. Minnesota: Foundation Press New York.

Massey, Kyle D., and Jennifer Massey. 2017. "It Happens, Just Not to Me: Hazing on a Canadian University Campus." *Journal of College and Character* 18 (1): 46–63.

Moore, Dawn, and Mariana Valverde. 2000. "Maidens at Risk: 'Date Rape Drugs' and the Formation of Hybrid Risk Knowledges." *Economy and Society* 29 (4): 514–31.

Liberated: The New Sexual Revolution. 2017. Directed by B. Nolot. Magic Lantern Pictures.

Persky, Aaron. 2016. "Stanford Sexual Assault: Read the Full Text of the Judge's Controversial Decision." *Guardian*, 14 June. https://www.the guardian.com/us-news/2016/jun/14/stanford-sexual-assault-read-sentence-judge-aaron-persky.

Pino, Nathan, and Robert Meier. 1999. "Gender Differences in Rape Reporting." *Sex Roles* 40 (11): 979–90.

Quinlan, Elizabeth, Allyson Clarke, and Joanne Horsley. 2009. "From Outrage to Action: Countering the Institutional Response to Sexualized Violence on University Campuses." *Canadian Woman Studies* 28 (1): 46–55.

Sedgwick, Eve Kosofsky. 1985. *Between Men: English Literature and Male Homosocial Desire*. New York: Columbia University Press.

Senn, Charlene Y., Stephanie S. Gee, and Jennifer Thake. 2011. "Emancipatory Sexuality Education and Sexual Assault Resistance: Does the Former Enhance the Latter?" *Psychology of Women Quarterly* 35 (1): 72–91.

Walters, Mikel L., Jieru Chen, and Matthew J. Breiding. 2013. "The National Intimate Partner and Sexual Violence Survey (NISVS): 2010

Findings on Victimization by Sexual Orientation." Atlanta, GA: National Center for Injury Prevention and Control, Centers for Disease Control and Prevention.

Xavier, Jessica, Julie A. Honnold, and Judith B. Bradford. 2007. *The Health, Health-Related Needs and Life Course Experiences of Transgender Virginians*. Richmond, VA: Virginia Department of Health.

9

Privacy and Protection
vs Accountability and Transparency

Navigating Sexual Violence Claims
in University Contexts

Shaheen Shariff, Julia Bellehumeur, and Bethany Friesen

LEGAL RESPONSIBILITIES OF UNIVERSITIES

Canadian students expect their universities to be responsible for protecting them from sexual violence. Preliminary data from student surveys on sexual violence in Canadian universities suggests a highly evolved student expectation that universities react in the same way as private industry, by rapidly dismissing or disciplining alleged perpetrators (Student Society of McGill University 2017). Many have improved policies and practices. Nonetheless, the expectation to be protected from sexual violence on campus is both important and reasonable. It is a right protected under the Canadian Charter of Rights and Freedoms.[1] Furthermore, university employees may be classified as agents of the state, subjecting their actions to review under the Charter.[2] The law is unsettled around judicial review of decisions made by authorities within the university, but there is clear legal authority for judicial review of any decision made by university administrative tribunals.[3]

Our paper begins with a discussion of universities' legal obligations to respond to sexual violence and then explores how privacy legislation presents a significant challenge as university administrators attempt to meet their legal and social obligations. Post-secondary institutions can put policies and procedures in place to respond to allegations of sexual violence by university employees. However, the handling of such complaints is qualified as private information, pursuant to provincial privacy legislation and relevant case law.

Scholarship on sexual violence in universities indicates that a power imbalance is one of the most enduring and concerning aspects for students, relating to university responses to sexual violence by professors or supervisors (Garcia and Vemuri 2017). This raises important questions about how universities can best protect vulnerable students from coercive sexual harassment when instructors, faculty members, and other university employees are protected by provincial privacy laws.

There are some cases where claimants' rights were upheld and properly addressed, such as *University McGill v Margolis* (1994) and the arbitration case *Okanagan University College v Okanagan University College Faculty Assn.* (1997). In these cases, the disciplinary measures taken against respondent professors were upheld in an administrative court.[4] Some cases that do not make it to court nonetheless receive proper handling by universities. However, decisions made by university administrators as to investigation and disciplinary processes in cases of sexual violence involving university employees are rarely made public. Decisions are generally made behind closed doors as universities attempt to navigate a balance between protection of privacy under provincial legislation (Brohman 2018b), and protection of the students they are meant to serve. Students and the public are often left with the sometimes erroneous impression that universities prioritize the rights of professors over those of student survivors. In the wake of #MeToo, as powerful celebrities and high-level executives in private industry have lost careers based on allegations of sexual harassment, the discrepancy has been noticed.

Our paper explores these dilemmas by reviewing the relevant legislation and case law. We seek to illustrate the competing tensions between justice for survivors, due process and privacy for the accused, and the liability incurred by the university in sharing protected information.

LEGAL OBLIGATIONS OF UNIVERSITIES RELATED TO PRIVACY LEGISLATION

University settings subject students to relationships of trust in which power imbalances are inherent. These relationships are important for student learning and development. Although in most cases these are adult relationships, the validity of consent when such relationships become romantic or sexual is subject to much debate (Seiff 2018). The particular intimacy of working and learning together in close proximity results in increased vulnerability for students. Specifically, it is the precariousness of students retaining their employment or graduate status, receiving fair marks, and renewing student visas (in the case of international students) that blurs the lines of consent, in ways that are largely unparalleled in peer-to-peer relationships (Hutcheson and Lewington 2017).

Despite a lack of legal clarity on the issue of consent in student-professor relationships in university settings, Canadian case law and statutory law supports student expectations that they should be protected from sexual violence committed in a university context. Universities can be held liable for sexual violence committed by their employees against students. There is an obligation arising out of human rights codes for universities to respond to harassment or discrimination against members of the general public in the provision of their services.[5] In the case of *University of British Columbia v Berg* (1993), for example, it was clarified that services provided by universities are services ordinarily offered to the public, and that the obligation to protect students from harassment and discrimination applies to universities.[6] The case of *Janzen v Platy Enterprise Ltd* (1989) specified that sexual harassment constitutes discrimination on the basis of sex,[7] and the case of *Canada (Treasury Board) v Robichaud* (1987) established that employers are liable for the acts of their employees when it comes to sexual harassment in the workplace. *Robichaud* also stated that it is not necessary to prove intention for liability in sexual harassment.[8] It was ruled that even if a worker is sexually harassed by a co-worker outside of the institution, if they must work with the same co-worker within the workplace, there is an obligation on the institution not only to remedy the situation at hand, but to engage in constant re-education of its employees to ensure that they do not contribute to a discriminatory workplace.

The case law further emphasizes that students in universities should be protected from discrimination so that their learning is not hindered. In *North Vancouver School District No. 44 v Jubran* (2005), the BC Human Rights Tribunal was supported by the BC Court of Appeal in finding that schools (and by extension universities) are obliged to create an environment "free from discrimination that is conducive to learning."[9] Similarly, in the landmark case of *R. v Ross* (1996), the Supreme Court of Canada held that if an instructor or teacher makes discriminatory statements outside of the classroom context but students have to face him or her in class, it creates a "poisoned learning environment" for the students who are being discriminated against.[10] This case is relevant by extension to universities, emphasizing their obligation to ensure a positive environment that is free of discrimination.

The case of *Mahmoudi v Dutton* (1999) is an example of Canadian human rights tribunals supporting the notion that students must be protected from sexual violence committed by university faculty. In this human rights claim, an undergraduate student was awarded $4,000 by the BC Human Rights Tribunal to compensate for sexual assault by her professor, Don Dutton, who invited her to his home to study and whom she assumed would give her a reference for graduate school.[11] The reference was not provided. Although it is unclear whether Mahmoudi was an international student, this case highlights the power imbalance and precarious situation of students (especially students from visible minorities or international students), and the blurred line of consent when students rely on professors. The tribunal recognized this imbalance in awarding Mahmoudi the funds. The circumstances surrounding this case highlight the need for protection of students from sexualized environments created by established academics. More specifically, it underscores the power differential and vulnerability of students in supervisory relationships.

In light of their human rights obligations, universities across the country have been working hard to put in place sexual violence, harassment, and discrimination policies to protect students (Rubineau and Jaswal 2017, 20). However, these policies often conflict with privacy legislation, in particular when claimants demand information on how their complaint was handled. Universities must balance their obligations with regard to providing services free from discrimination and harassment with their privacy obligations under provincial legislation. Even though public universities are subsidized by the federal government, they are administered by provinces.[12] Provincial legislatures have approached the issue of protecting private information through two different tracks that follow but do not mirror the federal legislative structure: (1) privacy legislation, and (2) personal information protection legislation.[13]

Although both tracks address similar issues, privacy legislation tends to cover the personal information-handling practices of federal or provincial government departments and agencies, while personal information protection legislation tends to cover the personal information-handling practices of private sector businesses.[14] Alberta, Quebec, and British Columbia have personal information protection legislation that has been deemed "substantially similar" to the federal private sector laws (PIPEDA) and to each other.[15] Each province and territory in Canada has a commissioner or ombudsperson responsible for overseeing provincial and territorial privacy legislation.[16]

Provinces differ in which type of legislation applies to universities. In Ontario, for example, universities are not covered by the provincial Freedom of Information and Protection of Privacy Act (FIPPA),[17] while in British Columbia, FIPPA legislation does apply.[18]

Some provinces, such as Alberta and British Columbia, have passed privacy laws that apply to employee information. Since professors are employees of the university, this applies to them. As noted above, most public universities across Canada are governed by a web of privacy laws that restrict the sharing of formal complaints against faculty members. Consider for example, Quebec's Act Concerning Access to Documents Held by Public Bodies and the Protection of Personal Information (the "Quebec Privacy Act").[19] Regardless of the universities' jurisdiction, they are prevented from efficiently and effectively handling cases of sexual violence committed by their employees because they must balance the public's right to access information with the rights of members of the university community to privacy of personal information.

In Quebec, universities are also governed by the Quebec Charter of Rights and Freedoms (the "Quebec Charter"), and the Civil Code of Quebec (the "CCQ"). According to these laws, everyone has the right to access information held by universities, subject to some exceptions.[20] Exceptions may include the release of confidential information, or the release of an individual's personal information when doing so may injure a third party. Confidential information includes personal information such as information in any document which allows a person to be identified, including their image, likeness, or voice.[21] Quebec laws protect every person's right to respect of his name, reputation, and privacy.[22] Universities must therefore treat personal information as confidential and not disclose it, even where there is an "access to information" request.[23]

Exceptions to the disclosure of confidential personal information require consent from the individual whose information is to be disclosed. Under the Quebec Privacy Act, personal information can only be released without consent "in order to prevent an act of violence, including suicide, where there is reasonable cause to believe there is a serious risk of death, or serious bodily injury such as any physical or psychological injury that is significantly detrimental to the physical integrity or the health or well-being of a person or an identifiable group of persons."[24] Finally, a university may release personal information without the consent of the person concerned if that information is necessary for the carrying out of a collective agreement, order, directive, or regulation establishing conditions of employment.[25] The result is that universities do not disclose information about sexual violence investigations, and they do not disclose the disciplinary records of their students and employees because these are considered personal and confidential information.

In the common law jurisdiction of Ontario, universities are primarily governed by the provincial legislation Freedom of Information and Protection of Privacy Act (FIPPA).[26] This act defines personal information broadly as information about an identifiable individual, including a multiplicity of factors such as employment history.[27] Similar to Quebec, this act also provides for a right to access information under the control of an institution such as a university, subject to exceptions. The primary exception relevant to sexual violence on campus is the release of personal information, and the release of records about labour relations or employment-related matters in which the institution has an interest.[28]

There have been many references made in the Ontario courts about the application of FIPPA and the balancing of the right to access information and the right to privacy. In *Ryerson University (Re)*, Ryerson University was responding to a request for all the formal complaints of sexual harassment filed with them during a specified time frame.[29] The university sought to withhold information by invoking the exemption for personal information as well as the labour relations and the employment-related matters exceptions. The court noted that "all responsive records concern formal sexual harassment complaints against persons who are in an employment relationship with the University. Tenured faculty are employees of the University. They are subject to provisions of a collective agreement and are in the employ of the University."[30] Therefore, the court concluded, the records could be protected from access to information requests under the FIPPA regulations and the university was entitled to withhold them.

The findings in the decision did not require an elaboration on the exemptions under personal information and solicitor-client privilege because all matters were dealt with under the labour relations and the employment-related matters exception. Other references concerning requests made to universities under FIPPA do, however, elaborate upon the exemption for personal information. For example, in *University of Ottawa (Re)*, it is stated that "to qualify as personal information, the information must be about the individual in a personal capacity. As a general rule, information associated with an individual in a professional, official or business capacity will not be considered to be 'about' the individual ... However, even if information relates to an individual in a professional, official or business capacity, it may still qualify as personal information if the information reveals something of a personal nature about the individual."[31]

Our goal in highlighting these statutes and cases is to illustrate the deep extent to which personal information within the university context, especially the unionized environments, is protected. The FIPPA in Ontario in sections 65 (6–7) specifically refers to a unionized environment. This exacerbates the dilemmas for universities in balancing claimants' demands for information on how the disciplinary process or claim was dealt with, and the reluctance to communicate this information to survivors because of the potential risk of lawsuits from (1) alleged perpetrators and (2) the provincial governments for breach of privacy laws.

The widely publicized case of a University of British Columbia (UBC) professor who was reported to have been suspended and then fired by the university in 2006 following allegations of sexual violence brought against him by a student (Lederman 2017) highlights the deep tensions created by the legal landscape of incompatible human rights laws and privacy obligations held by universities. The findings of an internal investigative report by a retired judge presumably led to a decision to dismiss the employee. However, there is no way to access the complete findings of the investigation or the reasons for his dismissal, because the university has not made it available to the public (and may never do so). The university is bound by law to protect the professor's privacy rights under provincial privacy legislation.[32] The possibility of damages resulting from defamation lawsuits further incentivize universities to err on the side of caution when dealing with those in their employ accused of sexual violence. Policies may push for reduction and transparency around sexual violence, but policies are not law, and law creates a high threshold for survivors to meet before they can publicly access and identify information about their abusers.

A lesser known case, also from UBC, further illustrates these issues.[33] A student made a sexual harassment and sexual assault complaint against a faculty member. UBC investigated the complaint, and the applicant subsequently requested the resulting investigation report. UBC disclosed portions of the report to the applicant and withheld the rest on the basis that disclosure would be an unreasonable invasion of the personal privacy of third parties within the meaning of FIPPA. The adjudicator from the Office of the Information and Privacy Commissioner of British Columbia discussed other similar situations and found that if UBC divulged the information it would be an unreasonable invasion of privacy. The adjudicator relied on the fact that the report did not conclude that the faculty member was guilty or not. The report said the faculty member engaged in inappropriate conduct, but the adjudicator thought that the student would be able to damage the faculty member's reputation significantly more with the full report, despite the report not concluding one way or the other.

The arbitrator in the UBC case implied that if the report *had* found that the faculty member committed these acts, then there would be less of a need to protect the faculty member's privacy. Since the university's report did not conclude either way, the privacy protection fell in favour of the accused faculty member. If we assume that serious claims of sexual violence are always accompanied by evidence, and tribunals involved in their adjudication hear them fairly, then we can agree with this adjudicator's decision. However, if serious claims are being dismissed by universities, and tribunals are excluding those experiencing and surviving sexual violence, then privacy rulings do not seem to be an effective remedial tool for survivors.

DISCUSSION

Universities in particular face the challenges and complexities of this dilemma, but educational institutions are not alone. There is a strong public outcry calling for justice for survivors of sexual violence, as illustrated by the recent appointment of Justice Brett Kavanaugh to the US Supreme Court. It has been argued that the #MeToo movement encouraged several women, especially Professor Christine Blasey Ford, to come forward with claims of sexual violence by Kavanaugh. The extent to which the FBI inquiry and the testimonies by Dr Ford and Judge Kavanaugh invaded the privacy and character assessment of both parties was at issue. In this case, the politics of partisanship won out, resulting in the lifetime judicial appointment of a justice with the perceived potential to impede women's rights, especially in the realm of sexual violence, and particularly in cases of abortions needed as a result of rape (Dockterman 2018). Moreover, Kavanaugh's nomination has impacted the reputation of the high court as an impartial decision-making body (Barnes and Gaskin 2018).

There is a particular outcry for justice in cases where a significant power imbalance is involved, and this includes the military, police forces, parliament, and private corporations. Nonetheless, there are opposing concerns that our public institutions should not be persuaded by "extreme" movements. We need to ensure that all alleged perpetrators are provided with due process, and that all survivors are heard, supported, and treated fairly. Procedural fairness should apply effectively and expeditiously to all parties concerned. Universities find themselves caught between the need to ensure privacy and the need to ensure due process. When this happens, neither the supporters of the survivors, nor those who support alleged perpetrators, can be satisfied with the universities' handling of cases. This is because the key information that would demonstrate that both parties received due process is shielded by privacy laws.

This lack of transparency enables some to argue that universities would rather protect perpetrators, especially tenured professors, than survivors of sexual violence (Student Society of McGill University 2018). The current state of privacy law has resulted in significant frustration among university administrators who find their hands tied by privacy legislation, the tenets of due process, and procedural fairness (Brohman 2018a). These laws not only affect disciplinary procedures, but preclude the timely and accurate communication of the outcomes of internal university investigations to survivors (Lederman 2018). Universities as well as participants and parties to these conflicts often find themselves in a lose-lose situation.

A contentious issue underlies recent debates around sexual violence: in a democratic society that recognizes systemic and historical inadequacies of the legal system in protecting survivors of sexual violence, how can we also ensure that the pendulum does not swing too far and deprive alleged perpetrators of due process and procedural fairness? The #MeToo activism has been highly effective and extremely important in raising awareness and clarifying the boundaries of institutionally normalized sexual violence. However, we cannot overlook the increase in concerns that alleged perpetrators, who can lose their careers, marriages, and reputations, ought to have access to due process. The courts have, in the past, been the venue where the evidence for such accusations was investigated, analyzed, and addressed within the law. But the criminal courts were never created to protect survivors from sexual violence, and so have had trouble adapting to adequately accomplish that feat (MacFarlane 1993). Following the #MeToo movement in particular, many people have been in search of other means to achieve justice, and have turned to the courts of public opinion. However, the courts of public opinion are not regulated, nor are they reliable. The #MeToo movement has helped to raise awareness of a need for better systems of justice for survivors of sexual violence, but the movement itself cannot be the ultimate venue for that justice.

RECOMMENDATIONS AND IMPLICATIONS

Canadian universities taking steps to meet new legislative requirements to improve sexual violence policies should keep in mind some of the following recommendations. (1) In order to improve public confidence in the university's administration, it would be beneficial to release the number of cases of sexual violence reported and addressed and the annual number of disciplinary actions, suspensions, dismissals, and so on to students. (2) A sexual violence policy, sexual violence resource office, and a central, easily accessible source for intake of reports and disclosures should be available. (3) An independent investigator with no ties to any faculty should also be appointed to oversee intake of cases and distribution of cases to the best-suited bodies within the university. (4) Cohesive and collaborative efforts, sensitivity workshops, bystander workshops, and consent workshops are all essential in this process. (5) Committees should be set up to examine the boundaries of intimate relationships between faculty and students/staff and supervisors, and to develop guidelines for those in powerful positions over others. (6) A code of conduct and general limits of imposed inti-mate relationships would be helpful, though there will be difficulties such as those outlined by Jochelson et al. in this volume.

Ultimately, the concerns of survivors should be respected without capitulating on the due process and procedural fairness rights of alleged perpetrators. Common among student complaints about their universities are that there are few clear points of entry for reporting and/or disclosing sexual violence incidents. Instead, there is a "referral loop" that sends complainants from one department or disciplinary office to another – hence the need for a clear, centralized system of reporting, process clarification, and training on due process and the requirements of procedural fairness. According to Karen Busby (2018), the issues are complex and should not be oversimplified by those speaking for the institution, survivors, or alleged perpetrators. She cites the need for clear definitions of the terms "procedural fairness" and "due process" to be understood by all parties involved.

It is important to remember that sexual violence does not occur in a vacuum. As Garcia and Vemuri (2017) and Shariff (2017) have highlighted elsewhere, policies and procedures will not in and of themselves reduce or prevent sexual violence. While the challenges seem insurmountable, they can be approached as opportunities to integrate dialogue about these issues within every aspect of curricu-lum and school life, addressing intersecting barriers of oppression involving sexism, misogyny, homophobia, ableism, ageism, and racism. It is important to remember that some members of our uni-versity communities, whether they are students, professors, staff, or administrators, may experience intersecting forms of these deeply embedded and normalized forms of discrimination within our uni-versities – both online and offline. Universities should incorporate a consciousness about these issues in professional programs such as medicine and dentistry that are recruiting higher numbers of women. Ultimately, it will take sustained, collaborative, multidisciplinary work to address sexual violence in universities, and a rethinking of the bureaucratic laws and confusing legal tests that prevent universi-ties from delivering expeditious but fair responses to sexual violence in their communities.

Due process is essential for the benefit of both the accused and the survivor. Transparency and predictability are key elements of due process. Universities and the Canadian courts will need to take the appropriate measures within their systems to navigate free expression, privacy, protection, safety, equality, and regulation in order to achieve a more realistic balance of the rights of students, staff, professors, and administrators. Communicating these challenges with students and survivors would be a first step in developing trust within university communities. Conducting climate studies of perceptions and experiences with sexual violence with input from active advocacy groups across the university, with staff and faculty representation, would provide evidence-based information to administrators as they navigate this difficult terrain.

CONCLUSION

Unless the privacy, accountability, and transparency constraints are thoughtfully resolved, survivors and their advocates will legitimately continue their mistrust of university administrations and the justice system; and university policies will continue to be perceived as window dressing developed to protect the reputations of those institutions and their tenured staff.

Because of the difficulties in balancing the university's human rights and privacy obligations, trust in university administrations is eroded, and the court of public opinion has the potential of taking over. In a world where the truth has been branded as "fake" and where divisive lies and bullying are presented as officially sanctioned truth and "policy," we would argue that the courts of public opinion cannot be left to decide on sanctions for alleged perpetrators. We accept that, to date, the law has been an inadequate tool to protect students from sexual violence and that there is a need for non-arbitrary and evidence-based systems both within universities and in the courts to address sexual violence fairly and effectively. This requires consistent, reliable, and predictable policies, procedures, and practices that allow for due process for survivors and alleged perpetrators.

NOTES

1 Schedule B. Canadian Constitution, Charter of Rights and Freedoms, 1982.
2 *Doré v Barreau du Québec*, [2012] 1 SCR 395 [*Doré*]; *Loyola High School v Quebec* (Attorney General), [2015] 1 SCR 613.

3 *Doré.*

4 *Re Okanagan University College v Okanagan University College Faculty Association,* [1996] 64 LAC (4th) 416; *University McGill v Margolis* (1994) CanLII 2191 (QC SAT).

5 Canadian Human Rights Act, RSC 1985 c H-6, s 14(1)(1); Charter of Human Rights and Freedoms, CQLR 1975 C-12, s 12 [Quebec Charter]; Human Rights Code, RSO 1990 c H-19, ss 1-26.

6 *University of British Columbia v Berg,* [1993] 2 SCR 353 [*Berg*].

7 *Janzen v Platy Enterprises Ltd,* [1989] 1 SCR 1252 [*Janzen*].

8 *Canada (Treasury Board) v Robichaud,* [1987] 2 SCR 84 [*Robichaud*].

9 *North Vancouver School District No. 44 v Jubran,* [2005] BCCA 201 [*Jubran*].

10 *Ross v New Brunswick School District No. 15,* [1996] 1 SCR 825 [*Ross*].

11 *Mahmoodi v Dutton,* 1999 BCHRT 56 [*Mahmoodi*].

12 Constitution Act, 1982, s 93, being Schedule B to the Canada Act 1982 (UK), 1982, c 11.

13 Office of the Privacy Commissioner of Canada (2019a).

14 Office of the Privacy Commissioner of Canada (2019b).

15 Office of the Privacy Commissioner of Canada (2018).

16 Office of the Privacy Commissioner of Canada (2017).

17 *York University v York University Faculty Association,* [2007] CanLII 50108 (ON LA) at para 6.

18 *University of British Columbia (Re),* [2014] BCIPC 12.

19 Act Respecting Access to Documents Held by Public Bodies and the Protection of Personal Information, CQLR c A-2.1 [Quebec Privacy Act].

20 Quebec Privacy Act, *supra* note 19, s 9; Quebec Charter, *supra* note 5, s 44; Civil Code of Quebec, art 39 [CCQ].

21 Quebec Privacy Act, *supra* note 93, s 54; CCQ, *supra* note 94, art 36(5).

22 CCQ, *supra* note 94, arts 3, 35; Quebec Charter, *supra* note 79, s 5.

23 Quebec Charter, *supra* note 79, s 9; Quebec Privacy Act, *supra* note 93, s 53.

24 Quebec Privacy Act, *supra* note 93, s 59.1.

25 Ibid., ss 53(2), 55, 57, 59(1), 67.1.

26 Freedom of Information and Protection of Privacy Act, RSO 1990 c F-31 [*FIPPA*]. ·

27 Ibid., s 2(1).

28 Ibid., s 49.

29 *Ryerson University (Re),* 2007 CanLII 54657 (ON IPC).

30 Ibid.

31 *University of Ottawa (Re),* 2011 CanLII 7189 (ON IPC).

32 British Columbia Privacy Act, [RSBC 1996] Ch.373.
33 *University of British Columbia (Re)*, 2014 BCIPC 12.

REFERENCES

Legislation
Act Respecting Access to Documents Held by Public Bodies and the
    Protection of Personal Information, CQLR c A-2.1.
Canadian Human Rights Act, RSC 1985 c H-6.
Charter of Human Rights and Freedoms, CQLR 1975 c C-12.
Civil Code of Quebec, SQ 1991 c 64.
Constitution Act, 1982, being Schedule B to the Canada Act 1982 (UK),
    1982, c 11.
Freedom of Information and Protection of Privacy Act, RSO 1990 c F-31.
Human Rights Code, RSO 1990 c H-19.

Jurisprudence
Canada (Treasury Board) v Robichaud, [1987] 2 SCR 84.
Doré v Barreau du Québec, [2012] 1 SCR 395
Janzen v Platy Enterprises Ltd, [1989] 1 SCR 1252.
Loyola High School v Quebec (Attorney General), [2015] 1 SCR 613.
Mahmoodi v Dutton, 1999 BCHRT 56.
North Vancouver School District No. 44 v Jubran, 2005 BCCA 201.
*Re Okanagan University College v Okanagan University College Faculty
    Association*, [1996] 64 LAC (4th) 416; *University McGill v Margolis*
    (1994) CanLII 2191 (QC SAT).
Ross v New Brunswick School District No. 15, [1996] 1 SCR 825.
Ryerson University (Re), 2007 CanLII 54657 (ON IPC).
University of British Columbia (Re), 2014 BCIPC 12.
University of British Columbia v Berg, [1993] 2 SCR 353.
University of Ottawa (Re), 2011 CanLII 7189 (ON IPC).
York University v York University Faculty Association, 2007 CanLII
    50108 (ON LA).

Secondary Materials
Barnes, Robert, and Emily Gaskin. 2018. "More Americans Disapprove
    of Kavanaugh's Confirmation than Support It, New Poll Shows."
    Washington Post, 12 October. https://www.washingtonpost.com/politics/
    more-americans-disapprove-of-kavanaughs-confirmation-than-support-
    it-new-poll-shows/2018/10/12/18dbf872-cd93-11e8-a3e6-44daa3d35ede_
    story.html.

Brohman, Erin. 2018a. "Hands of Universities Are Tied by Privacy Laws Preventing Disclosure of Sexual Misconduct by Staff: Prof." *CBC News*, 29 August. https://www.cbc.ca/news/canada/manitoba/u-manitoba-privacy-laws-sexual-misconduct-accusations-1.4802517.

– 2018b. "U of M Students Renew Call for Mandatory Consent Training for Faculty." *CBC News*, 22 August. https://www.cbc.ca/news/canada/manitoba/university-manitoba-consent-culture-harding-1.4794146.

Busby, Karen. 2018. "Can a Complaints-Based Process Provide Complainants with the Outcomes They Seek?" Unpublished presentation, 30 May. Canadian Symposium on Sexual Violence sponsored by ESSIMU and IMPACTS.

Dockterman, Eliana. 2018. "The Battle over Brett Kavanaugh Has Ended but the Pain His Hearing Caused Has Not." *Time*, 11 October. http://time.com/5413109/brett-kavanaugh-supreme-court-survivors-trigger-ptsd/.

Downard, Peter A. 2018. *Law of Libel in Canada*. 4th ed. Toronto, ON: LexisNexis Canada.

Hutcheson, Shannon, and Sarah Lewington. 2017. "Navigating the Labyrinth: Policy Barriers to International Students' Reporting of Sexual Assault in Canada and the United States." *Education and Law Journal*, 27 (1).

Garcia, C., and A. Vemuri. 2017. "Theorizing 'Rape Culture': How Law, Policy and Education Can Support and End Sexual Violence." *Education and Law Journal* 27 (1): 1–17.

Larsen, Karin. 2018. "Fired UBC Prof Suing Woman Who Accused Him of Sexual Assault." *CBC News*, 29 October. https://www.cbc.ca/news/canada/british-columbia/fired-ubc-prof-suing-woman-who-accused-him-of-sexual-assault-1.4882591.

Leavitt, Sarah. 2019. "McGill Launches New Mandatory Online Course on Sexual Violence and Consent." *CBC News*, 22 August. https://www.cbc.ca/news/canada/manitoba/university-manitoba-consent-culture-harding-1.4794146.

Lederman, Marsha. 2016. "Under a Cloud: How UBC's Steven Galloway Affaire has Haunted a Campus and Changed Lives." *Globe and Mail*, 28 October. https://www.theglobeandmail.com/news/british-columbia/ubc-and-the-steven-galloway-affair/article32562653/.

– 2018. "Main Galloway Complainant Urges University Policy Change." *Globe and Mail*, 28 August. www.theglobeandmail.com/canada/british-columbia/article-main-galloway-complainant-urges-university-policy-change.

MacFarlane, Bruce A. 1992. "Historical Development of the Offence of Rape." In *100 Years of the Criminal Code in Canada: Essays*

Commemorating the Centenary of the Criminal Code in Canada, edited by Josiah Wood and Richard C.C. Peck. Ottawa: Canadian Bar Association.

Office of the Privacy Commisioner of Canada. 2017. "Provincial and Territorial Privacy Laws and Oversight." https://www.priv.gc.ca/en/about-the-opc/what-we-do/provincial-and-territorial-collaboration/provincial-and-territorial-privacy-laws-and-oversight.

– 2018. "Summary of Privacy Laws in Canada." https://www.priv.gc.ca/en/privacy-topics/privacy-laws-in-canada/02_05_d_15/#heading-0-0-3.

– 2019a. "Protecting and Promoting Privacy Rights." https://www.priv.gc.ca/en/.

– 2019b. "Privacy Laws in Canada." https://www.priv.gc.ca/en/privacy-topics/privacy-laws-in-canada/.

Rubineau, Brian, and Nazampal Jaswal. 2017. "Response Is Not Prevention: Management Insights for Reducing Campus Sexual Assault." *Education and Law Journal* 27 (1).

Seiff, Joanne. 2018 "U of Manitoba's 'Sorry' Isn't Good Enough When It Comes to Harassment, Assault On Campus." *CBC News*, 16 September. https://www.cbc.ca/news/canada/manitoba/opinion-seiff-u-manitoba-harassment-assault-apology-1.4825554.

Shariff, S. 2017. "Navigating the Minefield of Sexual Violence Policy in Expanding 'University Contexts.'" *Education and Law Journal* 27 (1): 39–58.

Student Society of McGill University. 2017. *Our Turn: A National, Student-Led Action Plan to End Campus Sexual Violence.* www.ssmu.ca/wp-content/uploads/2017/10/our_turn_action_plan_final_english_web.pdf?x26516.

– 2018. "Open Letter Re: Complaints Against Professors." https://ssmu.ca/blog/2018/04/ssmu-statement-open-letter-regarding-complaints-against-professors/.

Todd, Douglas. 2016. "Don Dutton: Controversy Ensues when Science Butts Heads with Liberal Ideology." *Vancouver Sun*, 11 July. www.vancouversun.com/opinion/columnists/douglas-todd-controversy-ensues-when-science-butts-heads-with-liberal-ideology.

PART THREE

Problematize

10

New Policies, Old Problems?
Problematizing University Policies

Amanda Nelund

INTRODUCTION

The past several years in Canada have seen high-profile media events, student activism, and for some institutions provincial legislation, all focused on sexual violence on campus. In response, universities have been actively developing institutional policy. In this chapter, I argue that university policies have become an alternative justice form. They provide non-criminal justice system processes to respond to sexual assault and sexual violence more generally. I examine university policy as a form of alternative justice, using feminist socio-legal research that both calls for and critiques alternative justice. In what follows, I discuss the feminist critique of the criminal justice system and of one specific form of alternative justice, restorative justice. I use these critiques to analyze forty-three policies from across Canada.[1] I argue that although universities had an opportunity to do justice differently through their policies, they are currently replicating many of the shortcomings of both criminal justice and alternative justice forms without mirroring their benefits.

Criminal Justice Response

It took decades of struggle by the women's movement to push the criminal justice system to address sexual violence, inclusive here of sexual assault and intimate partner violence (see Sheehy 1999 for an overview of this history). Prior to this activism, male violence against women was often treated as a domestic dispute, a private matter for the couple to resolve on their own. This attitude, along with related sexist ideologies, was embedded in legislation that excluded marital rape from being prosecuted. In 1983 a set of feminist-inspired changes created the new offence of sexual assault and eliminated the marital exclusion. The increased attention gave some women the option to invoke the criminal justice system when they experienced various forms of sexual violence. The new law provided one more tool that women could use in their fight to keep themselves safe. It also demonstrated that the state took violence against women seriously.

Although many had originally pushed for greater justice system involvement, feminist advocates and scholars have criticized the criminal legal response to sexual violence, and other forms of gendered violence, for re-victimizing survivors and not believing their complaints (see for example the various contributors to Sheehy 2012). Sexual assault has one of the lowest police reported rates of any crime, with only 5 per cent of sexual assaults reported to police (Perreault 2015). Researchers have documented some of the many reasons why women do not report to police, including the fact that they know their assailant and may not perceive the harm as serious enough to report (Perreault 2015). Another reason is the often skeptical and sometimes hostile response from police. That skepticism is reflected in the rates at which police unfound – that is, determine that no crime actually took place – reports of sexual assault compared to physical assault. In 2000 research showed that police unfound 16 per cent of sexual assault reports compared to 9 per cent of other assaults (Roberts et al. 2009). A recent piece of investigative journalism examined data from 2010–14 and showed that nationally 19 per cent of sexual assaults reports are unfounded by police, compared to 11 per cent of physical assaults (Doolittle 2017). The court process, for those cases that advance to it, also presents challenges for survivors. Having to relive the traumatic event or act of violence, coupled with the skepticism, victim-blaming, racialized discourses, and adversarial nature of the process, all contribute to many women reporting that the court process is worse than the original offence (Craig 2018; Dylan et al. 2008; Regehr et al. 2008).

Feminist scholarship has documented the persistence of myths in our justice system. The Ideal Victim of sexual assault is "a responsible, security conscious, crime preventing subject who acts to minimize her own sexual risk" (Gotell 2008, 879). She should be able to show physical, or increasingly digital, proof of her struggle against the assailant (Larcombe 2002). In Canada, the Ideal Victim is prudent and responsible, and she is also shaped by larger inequalities of race, class, ability, and others. When survivors cannot present themselves as someone who "fits" this ideal type, their harm is at risk of being disqualified (Randall 2010; Craig 2018).

Feminist attempts to reform the criminal justice system illustrate the unintended consequences of new laws and policies. For example, in the late 1980s, various jurisdictions implemented mandatory arrest to combat the police tendency to encourage couples to work out their own problems when called to the scene of intimate partner violence. These policies stated that police must arrest the aggressor upon arrival to a scene. As a result, rates of women being arrested for domestic violence went up, as police often simply arrest both people so as to not run the risk of violating the policy (Johnson and Dawson 2011). Racialized women have suffered even more under this policy (Pratt 1995). In addition, no-drop prosecution policies forced Crown prosecutors to pursue cases even when the woman did not want to testify or did not want to go through with the prosecution. Researchers have found that these policies have had no effect on recidivism and some feminists have been critical of the ways in which these policies disempower women by removing their ability to make choices about their lives (Johnson and Dawson 2011).

These and other reforms promoted by feminist scholars and researchers have, in many cases unwittingly, helped to strengthen and expand "law and order" politics and carceral institutions. Indeed, Kristen Bumiller (2008, 15) argues that "the feminist alliance with the state has produced something far more significant than unintended consequences – a joining of forces with a neoliberal project of social control." She argues that feminist analyses of sexual and gendered violence that call for increased or differing use of the criminal justice system align nicely with neoliberal themes and governance strategies (Bumiller 2008). This has led to a variety of negative consequences, such as the hyper-criminalization of men (especially racialized and poor men), and the individualizing of responses to gendered crime in the form of medical or psychological assistance (to the detriment of addressing systemic oppression).

Restorative Justice and Sexual Violence

This context has led some feminists to study, and sometimes call for, alternative justice forms, particularly restorative justice (RJ). Restorative justice focuses on relationships. It is animated by various theories, including Braithwaite's (1989) theory of reintegrative shaming and communitarian theories of justice (see, e.g., Christie's 1977 work on returning conflict to communities). What Llewellyn (2012) calls a relational theory of justice lies at the base of most restorative justice. Crime is seen as a violation of relationships and restorative responses must engage stakeholders to restore or repair the harm that has been done. RJ is practised through several forms, including victim offender mediation, family group conferencing, circles, and truth and reconciliation commissions. These processes differ in terms of the number and scope of participants, the amount of focus on mediation, and counselling versus dialogue or testimony. They all share an ideal commitment to the active participation of all affected parties, engaged dialogue, and efforts to address each harm and the relationships involved in their specificity (Woolford and Nelund 2019).

As a response to sexual violence, RJ has the potential to centre the victim, her voice, and her needs. Participation and empowerment, especially for victims, constitute strong themes in restorative justice. Giving women the opportunity to narrate their own story returns their power to them and can assist in their healing and ability to move forward (McGlynn, Westmarland, and Godden 2012). In one of the few programs designed specifically to use RJ in cases of sexual violence, the RESTORE program, Koss found that survivor victims were satisfied with the preparation they received, the face-to-face meeting with the person who committed the violence, the redress plan, and how RESTORE handled their case; all would recommend the process to others (Koss 2014). These findings align with other restorative justice evaluations that consistently show high levels of victim satisfaction (Sherman and Strang 2007).

Most restorative justice theories and practices encourage including both the victim's and offender's communities, such as their friends, families, and representative members of the wider community. Presser and Gaarder (2004, 410) highlight the strengths of including community, as "communities provide support *and* enforcement; both are deemed necessary to stop the violence and to repair the harms caused by it." Pranis (2002) argues that the community is better equipped than the criminal justice system to deal specifically with women who have been in relationships of repeated and entrenched violence. While the courts consider each incident of violence as a discrete event, community members can see the relationship in its totality.

The community-focused feature of restorative justice aligns with feminist analyses of violence against women as a social and public problem, rather than an individual and privatized one. Feminists argue that effective violence prevention efforts need to challenge and change social norms. Challenging the social norms that minimize, rationalize, or legitimize the pervasiveness of gendered violence can and should be part of the community's role in a restorative justice approach to crimes such as sexual assault. This work should help create new and egalitarian social norms. Restorative justice's ability to challenge and clarify the normative underpinnings of crime is present in the dialogue focus of restorative justice (Hudson 2006; Coker 2002).

While many feminist scholars see enough benefits to advocate for a restorative approach, others have concerns that lead them to advance more cautious recommendations. Safety is an important consideration; however, this can be addressed with careful program design (Koss 2014; Presser and Gaarder 2004). Two more substantive criticisms are less easily resolved: first, that RJ has the potential to re-privatize gender-based violence, and second, that using restorative justice does not send a strong enough message condemning sexual violence. On the first point, Stubbs (2002) challenges restorative justice advocates' desire to return conflicts to the community. She reminds us that the criminal justice system has not "stolen" the conflict when it comes to sexual violence. Indeed, the state has too often denied the existence of sexual violence. The worry is that RJ takes a matter of public concern – a crime, an equality issue – and turns it back into a private dispute between individuals (Cameron 2006). The second point relate to concerns that using RJ in cases of gendered violence will decriminalize it. This critique focuses on punishment and the expressive role of punishment. Barbara Hudson worries that using restorative justice in response to sexual violence will send the message that it is not serious enough to warrant the full application of the criminal justice system (Hudson 1998). As a result, victims may feel that restorative justice offers second-class justice and sends a message that sexual violence is not a "real" crime.

With the crime of sexual assault in particular – due to our long history, and many contemporary examples, of denying and minimizing it – vindication of the harm is vitally important for any justice response. However, as Daly (2002, 63) reminds us, "law's vindication, especially its more harsh manifestation such as prison, is visited on the more marginal members of society and especially on its male marginal members." Neither Daly nor Hudson offer any solutions to this dilemma. Nonetheless, it is one that any justice response to sexual violence, including policy, must grapple with.

Responding to Sexual Violence on Campus

All forty-three policies included in this study prohibit sexual violence and provide an institutional response to a policy violation. Mount Allison's policy is an example: "Sexual Violence in unacceptable and will not be tolerated. Mount Allison University has a legal obligation to provide a working and learning environment that is free from sexual violence. Where there is reason to believe that sexual violence has taken place, action will be taken."[2] While all of the policies prohibit something, the precise labels given to the action vary; nine limit themselves to sexual assault, three refer to sexual misconduct, and the remainder target sexual violence more broadly defined. Definitions vary but policies generally capture the range of behaviour outlined in Laurentian University's policy: "This includes, but is not limited to, sexual assault, sexual harassment, stalking, indecent exposure, voyeurism, degrading sexual imagery, distribution of sexual images or video without consent, cyber harassment and cyber stalking."[3]

The policies state a variety of goals. The most common include providing support for survivors, promoting a safe campus environment, engaging in education efforts, and, importantly for this analysis, holding those who commit sexual violence accountable. York University's preamble encapsulates these very clearly: "York University affirms its ongoing commitment to foster a climate where sexual assault and its impact are understood, survivors are supported, and those who commit incidents of sexual assaults are held accountable."[4] Many policies reassure the reader that choosing to report to the institution neither precludes or obligates reporting to police.

The overall procedure for investigating and adjudicating a report of sexual violence is similar across institutions. Once a formal report is made, it usually goes to a response team. The response teams themselves are often diverse groups. Concordia's Sexual Assault Response Team has a larger composition than most, but encompasses the variety of roles that other institutions include as well:

In addition the Sexual Assault Resource Centre Coordinator, the team may include a representative from:
  Security
  Health Services
  Office of Rights and Responsibilities
  Dean of Students

Department Chair or Program Director
HR representative
Residence Director
University Secretariat
The Access Centre for Students with Disabilities
Or any of their designates.[5]

The team looks at the report and decides whether, if true, the behaviour described would be a violation of the policy. If they determine in the affirmative, the file is given to an investigator for follow-up. For some institutions, the team makes a finding based solely on the report. Others hold a meeting at which both the complainant and respondent can make written or oral submissions and the team can ask questions or invite witnesses to attend.

Once the investigation is complete a final report is generally compiled. A decision is reached about whether there has been a violation of the policy, and what, if any, disciplinary actions will be taken. Very few policies specify what discipline may be given in response to violating the policy. Carleton University's policy is one exception:

> The following list provides examples of consequences and measures and is not meant to be exhaustive nor necessarily represent a progression of consequences or measures:
> - A letter of apology,
> - Attendance at educational sessions on the impact of sexual violence,
> - Attendance at coaching sessions to improve communication or conflict resolution skills,
> - Restricted or prohibited access to University campuses and/or services;
> - For employees discipline up to and including termination;
> - For students discipline up to and including suspension or ban from the university.[6]

One complication for universities creating specific policies about sexual violence is that they do not exist in a policy vacuum. As a consequence, sixteen of these stand-alone policies do not lay out a distinct process for reporting sexual violence. While some noted that a process was under development, it is more common that the reader of the policy is directed to report an incidence of sexual violence as a violation of other policies and to file a complaint under one of them, including student codes of conduct, collective agreements, and workplace harassment policies. The policies that do lay out a distinct process almost always mention these other, related, policies.

The institutions vary regarding whom they will share that final information with. The draft version of the Thompson Rivers University policy clearly sets out the information-sharing, and, uniquely, states some findings will be shared with the complainant:

- Legal Counsel will provide a copy of the Investigator's Report to the President and to the Respondent.
- The President will send a letter to the Sexual Violence Prevention and Response manager, who will deliver this letter to the Complainant (the "Outcome Letter") which will contain the following:
  a. those findings that would constitute personal information of the Complainant;
  b. whether or not a breach of the policy was found to have occurred; and
  c. if disclosure of any sanction imposed is necessary for reasons of safety, the sanction imposed against the Respondent.[7]

The University of Ottawa has the only policy stating that both the respondent and the complainant will receive the full investigation report. Most of the policies cite confidentiality requirements and note that survivors will be told only whether or not a breach of policy was found, not any details of the report or the disciplinary action taken.

Comparing Policy to Other Justice Responses

These policies constitute a sign, from the university rather than the state, that they recognize sexual violence and take it seriously. The identification of the problem of sexual violence and the condemnation of it from post-secondary institutions is a strength of the policies and procedures being put in place. This is a step in the long and continuing push by feminist advocates to make sexual violence a public issue and to change norms around the acceptability of this violence. Just as feminist advocates had to fight for our legal system to address this sexual assault, so too have advocates had to put pressure on universities to include these explicit condemnations in their policy apparatus.

The policies also create one more option for survivors to seek redress and resources; indeed, much of the pressure for their creation came from survivors.

The procedure for most resembles court more than restorative justice. As an example, Mount Saint Vincent University uses criminal justice language: "when a student denies or does not accept responsibility for having committed a sexual assault, the report of sexual assault shall proceed as a complaint through the *formal judicial process* under the Student Non-Academic Discipline Policy."[8] It is common for a policy to mention its responsibility to provide due process, to operate under principles of natural justice, or "to fulfil its duty to be fair" (UBC Policy). The UBC policy continues: "as part of this duty, UBC must test and weigh the evidence provided by all parties involved, in order to make its findings based on a balance of probabilities."[9] Here we see the replication of the types of process that the criminal court system engages in. We know that part of the "testing" and "weighing" of evidence in criminal law is scathing cross-examination of survivors, often framed to draw and rely on victim-blaming cultural scripts (Craig 2018). This could be replicated in those policies that include a hearing, and in the interview part of the investigation for all of the policies. University processes are set up to conduct investigations and present evidence, without some of the protections that victims have in the court process, such as rape shield provisions.[10]

None of the policies provide opportunities for active participation, dialogue, or community-engaged norm clarification. The procedures therefore fail to include the primary benefits of RJ that feminist scholars have identified. Most policies state that survivors have a choice in how, if at all, their case will be processed. But that only extends to which process they trigger; that is, criminal, university-level, or none. Survivors can stop engaging with the investigative process, but most policies (thirty-two of forty-three) explicitly identify the university's right to proceed even when the survivor does not want to. The processes also limit the involvement of affected parties. Survivor and respondent participation mirrors the criminal justice system and therefore fails to be the type of participation that feminists value in RJ. Where stakeholders do participate, they do not engage with each other. The opportunity in RJ for realizing personal and social change comes from empathy building and relationship repair through dialogue. The university policies reviewed offer nothing that would contribute to these outcomes.

The benefits provided by restorative justice are largely unrealized in these policies, while the one strength of the criminal justice approach is replicated. Unfortunately, this small strength, the symbolic power of the university condemning sexual violence, is overwhelmed by the reproduction of the weaknesses of both the criminal and restorative responses. Although the policies in most cases express a desire to be sensitive to survivors, there is the real potential for the process to re-victimize those who have experienced sexual violence. Many policies direct survivor victims to campus security services to file a formal report. While we may hope that security services receive sexual violence training, there is no reason to believe that they will somehow be better than police, attorneys, and judges at filtering out cultural myths and scripts around sexual violence, survivors, and perpetrators. They will remain, for many students, the first points of contact, and there is the potential for the same re-victimization that survivors experience with police.

There was no consistent obligation written into the policies that investigation team members undergo training around sexual violence. There is also no guarantee that they will approach this issue in a way that centres survivors' voices and experiences. This is especially true because of the lack of dialogue in the process. These team members will not be in a conference or circle with the survivor and other stakeholders.[11]

Many policies replicate how the criminal justice system pursues investigations. University response teams and investigators can decide that there has been no breach – they can, essentially, "unfound" a complaint. The policies contain no guidelines around how to assess the complaint and no commitments to training that might include unpacking cultural scripts around sexuality, class, race, and other factors.

A clause contained by many of the policies, but not all, relates to false statements and accusations: "Any person who knowingly makes a false statement of accusation in connection with an investigation under this policy will be in violation of this policy and is subject to disciplinary action. False statements include statements that omit a material fact, as well as statements that the speaker/writer knows to be untrue. False accusations include accusations that are not based on material fact or honesty."[12] This clause allows the myths that survivors lie and that women are not to be trusted to be embedded in the policy and by extension in the procedure. This may allow personnel involved to feel comfortable doubting complainants. It also sends a direct message to survivors that even though the institution recognizes such harms in the abstract, they are skeptical when it comes to particular instances.

In addition to replicating the weaknesses of the criminal justice system, there is very clearly a risk that the policies also replicate the weaknesses of restorative justice. In responding to sexual violence by engaging only the university, there is a danger of re-privatizing the crime. Two features create cause for concern. The first is confidentiality. Because of universities' other legal and statutory responsibilities (such as those outlined by Shariff and Bellehumeur in this volume), as well as a stated desire to protect survivors, they almost universally reiterate the confidentiality rights of survivors and respondents: "The university will protect the confidentiality of individuals and events under investigation to the extent possible, except where disclosure is required by law. The details and particulars of any case reported or under investigation will not be disclosed or discussed with any individuals or parties other than those deemed necessary for investigation or adjudication purposes, or as required by law."[13] Particularly when members start using this process in lieu of criminal law, we go from cases being adjudicated in open court, with some publicly available decisions, to private proceedings. The situation changes from a matter of public concern to a private dispute between individuals adjudicated by quasi-public institutions. The public is deprived of any details about the case, such as information on how it was handled and any disciplinary response. This often extends to the complainant being kept in the dark as well. This application of confidentiality deprives the complainant of some key pieces of information about the resolution of her case, in addition to re-privatizing this type of harm.

The university's commitment to confidentiality is often made the burden of the participants. In nine of the policies, survivors are encouraged to not discuss their case publicly. Here, the Carleton policy sets out its non-disclosure clause: "To ensure procedural fairness while a formal complaint process is underway, the Complainant, the Respondent and others who may have knowledge of the matter, including a support person, must maintain confidentiality in accordance with this Policy and not make public statements (for example: media, public and/or social media statements) that may jeopardize the proper handling of the matter. The confidentiality obligations do not prevent a person from seeking counselling, treatment, support services or from speaking to friends and family."[14] Lakehead goes one step further by stating "the public accusation of sexual misconduct without engaging appropriate procedures for adjudication of the complaint is a violation of community standards, privacy and due process."[15] Public discussion is central to addressing sexual violence in a broad-based, systemic way. Feminists are beginning to examine the role of social media in particular in creating counter-publics that challenge sexual violence and support survivors (Powell 2015). By prioritizing confidentiality and non-disclosure, university policies contribute to the privatization of sexual violence and remove some key tools in the fight against it.

The second criticism of RJ, that it may decriminalize or trivialize sexual violence, is realized in complex ways in the policies. By their very creation the policies decriminalize a number of actions that are criminal offences, including sexual assault and criminal harassment. We place sexual violence in a non-criminal context when we create and encourage the use of institutional policy and procedure rather than criminal law. This, by itself, is not necessarily a problem. Feminists are increasingly looking for non-criminal, non-carceral ways to respond to sexual violence (see for example the contributors to Powell and Henry 2015). However, by making it a matter of institutional policy, in many ways, we equate it with other university policy. Sexual violence becomes one more student conduct issue, alongside plagiarism and dormitory noise complaints. This is formalized in the language that some of the policies use, referring not to sexual violence but to sexual *misconduct*. Indeed, in the policies that direct the reader to other policies, this harm is not equated with other types of harm; instead it is fully subsumed into non-academic misconduct or collective agreement disputes.

Despite this seeming trivialization, it seems clear that the policies' main intent was to communicate the seriousness of this harm. There was no practical purpose in adding the policies; the reason so many policies direct the reader to pre-existing ones is because this behaviour was already prohibited under those older policies. Most of the policies state that they have been created in order for the institution to publicly condemn sexual violence, as expressed in McMaster's policy: "The purpose of this Policy is to: a) articulate McMaster University's commitment to preventing and addressing Sexual Violence."[16] Stand-alone sexual violence policies are now necessary for institutions to communicate their disapproval. Because they have been legislated in some provinces and encouraged in others, it is now jarring, and indeed communicative in itself, for an institution not to have one. In their presence and purpose, the policies attempt to send the message that universities care about sexual violence.

The ability for the policies and their response to send this message is complicated further when we consider the potential outcomes of the process. The sanctions available to universities cannot communicate the wrongness of this act in a way that survivors or feminists will be satisfied with. At the low end of the range of sanctions described by a few of the policies are actions that do not communicate the seriousness of this harm. Things like writing a letter of apology or attending an educational session obviously do not fulfil the symbolic censure that survivors and feminists are often looking for, especially for forms of violence like sexual assault. It is hard to imagine that many people would feel that the gravity and harm of sexual violence is fully acknowledged by forcing a perpetrator to attend coaching sessions to improve their communication skills. Because these do not communicate our disapproval of sexual violence, they end up sending the opposite message: that this act is trivial and we do not mind all that much if it happens in our communities. But these are the sanctions available to universities. This is not a failure of execution; it is a failure of form. In responding to sexual violence with institutional level policy, our desire to communicate the seriousness of this harm, to highlight our campuses' commitment to this issue, has left us with a mechanism that communicates our lack of commitment.

This should not be misconstrued as support for our criminal process. Indeed, the criminal justice system often fails to censure these types of violence as well. The impact of that can be immense: as our primary institution for communicating disapproval, its failure to do so sends a loud message. In addition, the messages sent by the justice system are, as noted above, saturated with colonial, racist, and other oppressive discourses. One of the key issues with sexual violence, however, is that the dominant societal discourse does not communicate our disapproval well. These policies have chosen sanctions, or punishments, as a key way to communicate that disapproval. They did not have to do so; they could have chosen a restorative justice-style dialogue process, which, through dialogue and a focus on problem-solving, has the potential to denounce violence. But because the institutions made the decision to retain traditional disciplinary processes with sanctions as the outcome, they need then to use strong punishments in order to fulfill that expressive function. Those crafting new justice processes need to think carefully about the expressive function of the response. Gotell (2015, 67), while clearly acknowledging the uneven impacts of law reform, argues that "the absolute rejection of criminalization strategies would only intensify the silence around sexual violence as a systemic problem, re-privatising sexual assault and risking the return of impunity for acts of sexual violence." While I do not think this is inevitably true, the ways that these stand-alone sexual violence policies have been written contribute to the worries that Gotell raises. To point to concerns about punishment and validation is not simply to reproduce carceral feminist logics, as argued by Del Gobbo in this volume. Instead, it is necessary to raise these points to complexly think through what it means to respond to crimes of sexual violence.

RECOMMENDATIONS FOR POLICY AND RESEARCH

The implications of this analysis for policy are clear but not simple. Post-secondary institutions must strive to eliminate the harms of the criminal justice system that they are replicating. As of now, policies offer survivors an alternative to reporting to police, and then the process has many of the same re-victimizing tendencies. In order to try to mitigate the latter, policies should mandate that investigators and others who will be part of the process – that is, members of the response teams – receive ongoing training on working with victims of violence. Universities also need to think carefully about how they may be able to share information with survivors, respondents, and the community at large. Allowing stakeholders to access some details about the investigation and outcomes can help survivors feel more confident in the process. It can allow transparency, and hopefully guard against the influence of cultural myths and stereotypes on investigations. While universities clearly have a multitude of legal obligations, as pointed out in this volume by Sharrif et al. and Jochleson et al., the need for sharing information and allowing public information and discussion should be a strong consideration when balancing those obligations.

I offer these conclusions tentatively in light of what Buss and Majury, and Oliver et al., have shown elsewhere in this volume: many survivors are not going to access these policies. This, combined with the uneven impacts of law reform, means that I do not think policy should be the main site of energy or change-making. Further, there is a bigger question to explore around whether or not universities should be fulfilling this type of punishment and control function. Do we think it should be within the purview of post-secondary institutions to be offering a criminal justice system-lite response? Greater emphasis could be placed, both in policy and in broader university efforts, on those aspects of response that align more closely with the work of universities: education and support. My focus here – because it is generally the focus of the policies themselves – has been on the investigative and disciplinary provisions of the policies. A real strength of them, however, may be the goals articulated in relation to education, awareness, and survivor support. Future research should look at how these are being put into practice, as these are the areas that could make a real difference in preventing sexual violence. Building on education and support may allow us to construct new and genuine alternative justice forms.

Policy has come into being at Canadian universities because of pressure from a variety of stakeholders. Survivors have been vocal about institutional failure. Much of the campaigning for policy has come from students, faculty, and staff working from a feminist understanding of sexual violence, and many policies echo a feminist analysis.[17] For example, the University of Victoria's draft policy is one of many with an intersectional analysis: "Sexualized violence does not exist or operate in isolation. Acts of sexual violence can also be acts of colonial violence, racism, sexism, ableism, ageism, classism, homophobia, transphobia, queer antagonism, trans antagonism, and/or any other form of discrimination. Hence, university strategies to address sexualized violence must be linked to broader equity and anti-discrimination initiatives and goals."[18]

Bringing decades of feminist socio-legal research and reform to bear on this response should inspire us to approach the issue of sexual violence on campus with what Lofton (2004) calls cautious urgency. This phrase is meant to alert us to two important facets of this issue. One is that because of the harm that people are suffering, we must bring a sense of urgency to our work. Sexual violence is a traumatic experience for survivors and impacts women's equality more generally. Sexual violence is a destructive gendering and gendered practice. However, we must at the same time move cautiously, with the knowledge that change, even well intentioned, is sometimes worse in its consequence than the status quo (ibid.). Unintended consequences are clearly evident in feminist efforts to reform the criminal justice system's response to gendered crimes (Minaker and Snider 2006; Moore 2008).

It behooves us not to replicate those errors in our rush to address sexual violence on post-secondary campuses.

NOTES

1 I limited the sample to university policies, although other types of post-secondary institutions, such as colleges and technical institutions, are also crafting and implementing policy. I searched for publicly available policy or draft policy on all Canadian university websites from May 2016 to August 2017. This search garnered forty-three policies. The policies were then coded through a process of open coding. The initial themes were compared to criminal justice themes and restorative justice ones. In the time between data collection and publication some of the policies have been revised. Throughout this chapter I link to policies that contain the same as was studied here. In the event the policy has been substantially revised I cite the version I collected but do not link to it.

2 Mount Allison University Sexual Violence Prevention and Response Policy: https://www.mta.ca/Community/Governance_and_admin/Policies_and_procedures/Section_1000/Policy_1006/Policy_1006/.

3 Laurentian University Prevention and Response to Sexual Violence: https://laurentian.ca/policies-accountability/sexual-violence.

4 York University Sexual Assault Awareness, Prevention, and Response Policy (approved February 2015 version).

5 Concordia University Policy regarding Sexual Violence (approved May 2016 version).

6 Carleton University Sexual Violence Policy: https://carleton.ca/secretariat/wp-content/uploads/Sexual-Violence-Policy.pdf.

7 Thompson Rivers University Sexual Violence Policy Draft (January 2017 version).

8 Mount Saint Vincent Policy against Sexual Assault (June 2015 version, italics added).

9 Proposed University of British Columbia Sexual Assault Policy, 131.

10 My thanks to Mandi Gray for reminding me of this point.

11 Instead, the unidirectional power relationship of team to survivor or team to respondent replicates the relationships in the justice system.

12 University of Regina Sexual Assault and Violence Policy (September 2015 version).

13 University of Saskatchewan Sexual Assault Prevention Policy: https://policies.usask.ca/policies/health-safety-and-environment/ Sexual%20Assault%20Prevention%20.php#Policy.

14 Carleton University Sexual Violence Policy: https://carleton.ca/secretariat/ wp-content/uploads/Sexual-Violence-Policy.pdf

15 Lakehead University Sexual Misconduct Policy and Protocol: Dealing with Sexual Harassment, Sexual Stalking and Sexual Assault (June 2014 version).

16 McMaster University Sexual Violence Policy: https://www.mcmaster.ca/ vpacademic/Sexual_Violence_Docs/Sexual_Violence_Policy_effec-Jan_1,2017.pdf.

17 That said, there are only two policies that I have found (the draft policy of Thompson Rivers University and that of the University of Toronto) that explicitly acknowledge the central feminist claim that "sexual violence is overwhelmingly committed against women." UNB notes that the "majority of complaints in cases of sexual assault are female and the majority of respondents are male." This, however, is a slightly different claim.

18 University of Victoria Sexualized Violence Prevention and Response Policy: https://www.uvic.ca/universitysecretary/assets/docs/policies/ GV0245.pdf.

REFERENCES

Bumiller, Kristin. 2009. *In an Abusive State: How Neoliberalism Appropriated the Feminist Movement against Sexual Violence.* Durham, NC: Duke University Press.

Cameron, Angela. 2006. "Stopping the Violence: Canadian Feminist Debates on Restorative Justice and Intimate Violence." *Theoretical Criminology* 10 (1): 49–66.

Christie, Nils. 1977. "Conflicts as Property." *British Journal of Criminology, Delinquency and Deviant Social Behaviour* 17 (1): 1–15. doi:10.1093/ oxfordjournals.bjc.a046783.

Coker, Donna. 2002. "Transformative Justice: Anti-Subordination Processes in Cases of Domestic Violence." In *Restorative Justice and Family Violence,* edited by H. Strang and J. Braithewaite, 128–52. Cambridge: Cambridge University Press.

Daly, Kathleen. 2002. "Sexual Assault and Restorative Justice." In *Restorative Justice and Family Violence,* edited by H. Strang and J. Braithwaite, 62–88. Cambridge: Cambridge University Press.

Doolittle, Robyn. 2017. "Unfounded: Why Police Dismiss 1 in 5 Sexual Assault Claims as Baseless." *Globe and Mail*, February 3.

Dylan, Arielle, Cheryl Regehr, and Ramona Alaggia. 2008. "And Justice for All? Aboriginal Victims of Sexual Violence." *Violence against Women* 14 (6): 678–96.

Gotell, Lise. 2008. "Rethinking Affirmative Consent in Canadian Sexual Assault Law: Neoliberal Sexual Subjects and Risky Women." *Akron Law Review* 41 (4): 865–98.

– 2015. "Reassessing the Place of Criminal Law Reform in the Struggle against Sexual Violence." In *Rape Justice: Beyond the Criminal Law*, edited by A. Powell, Nicola Henry, and Asher Flynn, 53–71. Houndmills, UK and New York, NY: Palgrave Macmillan.

Hudson, Barbara. 1998. "Restorative Justice: The Challenge of Sexual and Racial Violence." *Journal of Law and Society* 25 (2): 237–56.

– 2006. "Beyond White Man's Justice: Race, Gender and Justice in Late Modernity." *Theoretical Criminology* 10 (1): 29–47.

Johnson, Holly L., and Myrna Dawson. 2011. *Violence against Women in Canada: Research and Policy Perspectives*. Don Mills, ON: Oxford University Press Canada.

Koss, Mary P. 2014. "The RESTORE Program of Restorative Justice for Sex Crimes: Vision, Process, and Outcomes." *Journal of Interpersonal Violence* 29 (9): 1623–60.

Larcombe, Wendy. 2002. "The 'Ideal' Victim v Successful Rape Complainants: Not What You Might Expect." *Feminist Legal Studies* 10 (2): 131–48.

Llewellyn, Jennifer. 2012. "Restorative Justice: Thinking Relationally about Justice." In *Being Relational: Reflections on Relational Theory and Health Law and Policy*, edited by Jocelyn Downie and Jennifer Llewellyn, 89–108. Vancouver: UBC Press.

Lofton, Bonnie Price. 2004. "Does Restorative Justice Challenge Systemic Injustices?" In *Critical Issues in Restorative Justice*, edited by Howard Zehr and Barb Toews, 381–9. Monsey, NY and Devon, UK: Criminal Justice Press.

McGlynn, Clare, Nicole Westmarland, and Nikki Godden. 2012. "'I Just Wanted Him to Hear Me': Sexual Violence and the Possibilities of Restorative Justice." *Journal of Law and Society* 39 (2): 213–40.

Minaker, Joanne, and Laureen Snider. 2006. "Husband Abuse: Equality with a Vengeance?" *Canadian Journal of Criminology and Criminal Justice* 48 (5): 753–80. doi:10.3138/cjccj.48.5.753.

Moore, Dawn. 2008. "Feminist Criminology: Gain, Loss and Backlash."
    Sociology Compass 2 (1): 48–61. doi:10.1111/j.1751-9020.2007.00052.x.
Perreault, Samuel. 2015. *Criminal Victimization in Canada: 2014*.
    Statistics Canada.
Powell, Anastasia. 2015. "Seeking Informal Justice Online: Vigilantism,
    Activism and Resisting a Rape Culture in Cyberspace." In *Rape Justice:
    Beyond the Criminal Law*, edited by Anastasia Powell, Nicola Henry
    and Asher Flynn, 218–37. New York: Palgrave Macmillan.
Powell, Anastasia, Nicola Henry, and Asher Flynn, eds. 2015. *Rape Justice:
    Beyond the Criminal Law*. Houndmills, UK, and New York: Palgrave
    Macmillan.
Pranis, Kay. 2002. "Restorative Values and Confronting Family Violence."
    In *Restorative Justice and Family Violence*, edited by H. Strang and J.
    Braithwaite, 23–41. Cambridge: Cambridge University Press.
Pratt, Anna. 1995. "New Immigrant and Refugee Battered Women: The
    Intersection of Immigration and Criminal Justice Policy." In *Wife
    Assault and the Canadian Criminal Justice System: Issues and Policies*,
    edited by M. Valverde, L. MacLeod, and K. Johnson, 84–103. Toronto,
    ON: Centre of Criminology, University of Toronto.
Presser, Lois, and Emily Gaarder. 2004. "Can Restorative Justice Reduce
    Battering? Some Preliminary Considerations." *Social Justice* vol. 27,
    no. 1 (79): 175–95.
Randall, Melanie. 2010. "Sexual Assault Law, Credibility, and 'Ideal
    Victims': Consent, Resistance, and Victim Blaming." *Canadian Journal
    of Women and the Law* 22 (2): 397–433.
Regehr, Cheryl, Ramona Alaggia, Liz Lambert, and Michael Saini. 2008.
    "Victims of Sexual Violence in the Canadian Criminal Courts." *Victims
    and Offenders* 3 (1): 99–113.
Roberts, Julian, Holly Johnson, and Michelle Grossman. 2009. "Trends in
    Crimes of Sexual Aggression in Canada: An Analysis of Police Reported
    and Victimization Statistics." In *A Guided Reader to Research in
    Comparative Criminology/Criminal Justice*, edited by John Winterdyke,
    Philip Reichel, and Harry Dammer. Bochum, Germany: Universitätsverlag
    Brockmeyer.
Sheehy, Elizabeth A. 1999. "Legal Responses to Violence against Women
    in Canada." *Canadian Women Studies*, 19 (1–2): 62–73.
– 2012. *Sexual Assault in Canada: Law, Legal Practice and Women's
    Activism*. Ottawa, ON: University of Ottawa Press/Les Presses de
    l'Université d'Ottawa.

Sherman, Lawrence W., and Heather Strang. 2007. *Restorative Justice: The Evidence*. London, UK: The Smith Institute.

Stubbs, Julie. 2002. "Domestic Violence and Women's Safety: Feminist Challenges to Restorative Justice." In *Restorative Justice and Family Violence*, edited by H. Strang and J. Braithwaite, 42–61. Cambridge: Cambridge University Press.

Woolford, Andrew John, and Amanda Nelund. 2019. *The Politics of Restorative Justice: A Critical Introduction*. 2nd ed. Halifax, NS: Fernwood Publishing.

11

Shadow Matters

Campus Sexual Violence and Legal Forms

Doris Buss and Diana Majury

INTRODUCTION

On 8 March 2016, Ontario passed Bill 132 (Government of Ontario 2016), requiring each of the province's universities and colleges to formalize their sexual violence policies and institutional processes. Clear and formalized systems for sexual violence complaints within universities and colleges are certainly needed. At the time Bill 132 was introduced, many of Ontario's universities either had no explicit policy for making or pursuing a sexual violence complaint, or the policies in place were dated, confusing, or inadequate (Gunraj 2014). While the government's initiative and the conversations it has provoked about sexual assault and university cultures should be applauded, we argue that the resulting focus on instituting formal complaint processes is predicated upon and perpetuates misunderstandings about campus sexual violence, as well as misconceptions concerning the formal and informal university responses to campus sexual violence. Our argument is founded upon research commissioned by the Ministry of Community Safety and Correctional Services (Ontario) for a study on sexual assault reporting on Ontario campuses (Buss et al. 2016).[1] The results from that study, and the over fifty interviews we completed with university administrators and service providers at three institutions,[2] revealed the complex, varied circumstances in which disclosure and reporting take place (or don't), and the equally varied understandings and values assigned to reporting and disclosure by our interviewees.

Our research revealed that universities most commonly confront and "address" sexual violence through what are seen as "informal" responses – academic accommodations (changing courses or adjusting program requirements), residence room reassignment, counselling, and sometimes "cautioning" perpetrators. While these measures may seem inadequate and unresponsive to the serious problem of campus sexual violence, our research suggests that these "informal" approaches are often preferred by survivors. The majority of survivors chose to turn to service providers, rather than accessing more formalized reporting processes that include complaints or disclosures that generate formal records. Our findings are consistent with the generally low reporting rates for sexual violence in other contexts, and were foreshadowed by the government of Ontario's own 2013 Resource Guide for Ontario Colleges and Universities, which notes: "The vast majority of survivors do not formally report to authorities and many do not even disclose to someone they trust. A campus environment in which individuals feel comfortable coming forward helps ensure they receive the assistance they need and supports the institution in its efforts to identify and deal with perpetrators" (Government of Ontario 2013).

In this statement, non-reporting and non-disclosure of campus sexual violence are positioned as a problem to be rectified through policies and interventions aimed at fostering disclosure, increasing formal reporting (both by survivors and institutions who must report on their own conduct and statistics), and, it is hoped, "dealing with" perpetrators. The government anticipates that formal policies will lead to better services and justice, and will have a performative effect, signalling official condemnation of sexual violence, deterring would-be perpetrators, and providing clarity and redress to victims. It is assumed that, in the shadow of strong and clear policies and protocols, people and systems will behave better: "Formal policies and response protocols can play a critical role in creating an environment where everyone on campus knows that sexual violence is unacceptable, victims receive the services they need, and perpetrators are held accountable" (Government of Ontario 2013).

While we agree with these goals, we are troubled by the hierarchized binary constructed between the "informal" array of campus contexts where "non-reporting/non-disclosure" are said to take place, and formalized policies understood as a corrective that will have beneficial effects. This binary perpetuates a conceptual framing that brackets off, however unintentionally, the systemic nature and complexity of sexual violence and the range of university responses to disclosures. It invokes an idea of the "informal" realm of university responses (where "non-reporting" takes place) as unsatisfactory, opaque, and failing victims, against which a formal system is imbued with corresponding qualities of transparency, effectiveness, and justice, despite the overwhelming evidence that formal systems reflect a myriad of similar failings. The formal/informal binary, further, places the burden of exposing and addressing campus sexual violence on the victims and survivors of the violence. While reporting policies and services may be critically important for some survivors, they are limited vehicles for addressing the systemic issues that underlie campus rape culture and the full range of sexual violence and coercion spawned by that culture.

In this chapter, we use the metaphor of the shadow to describe and unpack the arena of informality and discretion in which university bureaucrats and service providers encounter, and endeavour to address, sexual violence disclosures, and to challenge the binary often invoked to characterize "reporting" and "non-reporting" of sexual violence on university campuses.[3]

SITUATING THE SHADOWS

Around the time that the Ontario government introduced Bill 132, a number of news articles[4] and university reports emerged[5] about sexual violence on Canadian university campuses that, collectively, depict a culture of secrecy and obfuscation in university administration. Accounts of sexual violence claimants being compelled by university administrators to sign non-disclosure agreements when coming forward to report abuse, or universities failing to collect, or report on, incidences of sexual violence on campus gave the clear impression that university administrators were either ignoring the problem or discouraging and derailing sexual violence complaints.

These and other reports offer a compelling picture of universities acting primarily to protect their reputations by keeping sexual violence reports out of the spotlight. There is plenty of evidence – in the spate of incidents on Canadian university campuses and in our research – to suggest that some Canadian university administrators may indeed prefer to minimize sexual violence reports to preserve institutional reputations. But our research found that this depiction of universities is not always or entirely accurate. University responses are far from uniform, both internally and across universities. As large institutions, university responses are often uncoordinated and disjointed; much depends on which university processes are engaged and at what time. Nonetheless, it is important to pay attention to the narrative depicting university administrators as preferring to draw a protective curtain around campus sexual violence reports, not only because it is at least partly accurate, but also because it functions to rationalize a governmental and university response to campus sexual violence that prioritizes formal reporting and public forms of accountability, such as regular reporting of statistics.

The metaphor of the "shadow" is helpful in understanding the ways that universities respond to sexual violence disclosures, and in exploring the dominant understandings of the weaknesses in and the need for formal complaint processes. The shadow metaphor operates in multiple, possibly conflicting ways – as obscuring, as diminishing, as deflecting, as misleading. In the above representation of universities as hiding or obscuring sexual violence complaints, there is an implicit conjuring of sexual violence as taking place in the shadows of university institutional structures, and of university institutions trying to keep sexual violence in the shadows and out of public attention. Informal responses – counselling, supports, disclosures – may be seen as necessary but are also seen as complicit in hiding the phenomenon of campus sexual violence. "Shadows" in this sense are ominous and threatening; there is something larger looming in the shadows that we cannot know for certain until it is brought into the full light of day. For some of the administrators and service providers we interviewed, informal disclosures and responses to campus sexual violence were seen in this negative light; a "shady" behind-the-scenes response that was second-best to formal reports that would handle campus sexual violence with full transparency and high visibility.

For other research participants, the sense that something was happening in the shadows of formal university processes meant that the phenomenon, and the informal institutional responses, were definitionally *in*substantial, a "side show" to the more important, formal processes of reporting. A smaller subset of participants downplayed campus sexual violence altogether, depicting it as a passing shadow, smaller and less significant than the "real" of most students' experience.

In invoking the metaphor of the "shadow," we are simultaneously playing with and against the prevailing use of the shadow metaphor in relation to law – that is, the notion of "negotiating in the shadow of the law." The concept is generally traced back to Mnookin and

Kornhauser, whose 1979 article argued that divorce settlements, negotiated outside the courtroom, are nonetheless framed and informed by the law (Mnookin and Kornhauser 1979, 950–97). While in concrete terms formal law only played the role of giving legal validation to the parties' negotiated agreements, it provided the "framework" by which the parties understood and negotiated their "rights and responsibilities." Hence, even while people negotiate "outside" of the formal law (the courtroom, for example), law nonetheless provides the "principal norm by which people define their troubles and formulate their claims" (Jacob 1992, 565). In the context of campus sexual violence, this approach to law and its shadow would translate to "the law" (or the formal reporting process) framing and directing sexual violence policies which in turn would frame and direct sexual behaviours on campuses, including informal responses to violence disclosures. In its most basic articulation this sense of "shadow" assumes that the law/policy will significantly affect campus attitudes and behaviours, a view reflected in the government's expectation that formal policies and reporting mechanisms will play a critical performative role in denouncing and eliminating campus sexual violence, as reflected in the quote from the Ontario government's Resource Guide above (Government of Ontario 2013).

Other scholars provide additional insights on forms of law and legality that unfold in the "shadow" of law (i.e., outside of, but in relation to, formal legal processes), as well as insights into how people operate "in the shadow" of law. Scholars examining the social dimensions of law demonstrate that law is not (just) a received framework that shapes action. Expectations, understandings, and beliefs about law comprise some of the "conceptual categories and schema that help construct, compose, communicate and interpret social relations" (Silbey 2005, 327). Decisions about "dispute behaviour" are informed by our conceptions of law and "the legal," and shape law as part of "a reciprocal process in which the meanings given by individuals to their world become patterned, stabilized, and objectified" (ibid.). That is, law and legality are "made" in everyday life, not just in formal legal venues (or processes). While new, more legalistic reporting mechanisms are being designed and implemented for universities, these are unfolding within and alongside cultures and social schema about sexual violence and university reporting systems. As these mechanisms are implemented and potentially deployed, they will be shaped by these social relations and meaning systems.

Individual approaches to formal legal options are also shaped by social norms and relationships. Sally Engle Merry's landmark study of working-class plaintiffs found that norms associated with or derived from social relationships played a more critical role for these plaintiffs in understanding their claims and determining if and how to proceed with them than did formal legal rules (Merry 1990). The question that Merry's research raises for us is whether the current focus on sexual violence policies and reporting procedures reflects an assumed responding-in-the-shadow-of-the-policy perspective that downplays or ignores the important social norms and relationship factors that influence responses to sexual violence and provide the cultural context within which campus sexual violence is normalized.

An additional consideration of law and its "shadows" comes from Kristen Bumiller (1987), who argues that the model of legal protection underpinning contemporary antidiscrimination policies makes inaccurate assumptions about the protected class and places the onus of recognition and action upon them, ignoring the needs and realities of their day to day lives. She concludes: "Though antidiscrimination law may have produced positive social change, legal strategies put unacceptable burdens on disadvantaged groups with little promise of success. The gap between the symbolic life of the law and the ineffectiveness of the law in action imposes a cost borne by the intended beneficiaries of civil rights policies. The inability of civil rights strategies to fulfill their promise appears to have left many who experience discrimination on uncertain ground between public and private action where they are without faith in themselves or the law" (439).

For Bumiller, the shadow cast by law is neither the normative guiding framework that shapes how individuals act outside of (but in relation to) law, nor is it one among many competing norms that guide people's actions and responses; rather, law's shadow is an illusory ideal that burdens and disempowers the victims and impedes meaningful engagement with the issues.

There are three implications from these rich accounts of law and legality in everyday life that we wish to draw out. The first is that "informal" dimensions of university responses to sexual violence disclosures, as well as participant understandings of the roles and impact of these processes, are partly constituted by the shadows cast from the more formalized system. However, the reverse is equally true – the design of formalized responses is predicated in part on a construct of the shadow and presumptions about what happens in the shadows. Individuals invoke ideas about law in their own behaviours and sense-making about the place of law in resolving problems or disputes, and law takes shape in and through those articulations. We need to pay close attention to the ways in which university responses themselves invoke constructs of the formal and informal and how this serves to validate certain forms of sexual violence, and certain forms of legal response, as the "real" that matters – implicitly invalidating as equally serious other forms of sexual violence and other forms of responses.

Second, this "shadow" world of accommodations and service delivery is also a site of legality, where expectations about law play an important role, but in interaction with other systems, relationships, and social structures (such as gender and sexuality) by which individuals make sense of their experiences and their available options. The everyday formulations of meanings and decisions about law and legality are shaped by cultural norms and social relations. Merry's research invites attention to the impact that individual systems of campus relationships, operating in the context of campus culture, may have on the choices that victims/survivors make in dealing with the sexual violence they have experienced, and on the ways in which administrators and service providers understand and respond to those choices.

Third, the introduction and translation of "formal" processes within university settings will take shape against understandings of "informal" responses to sexual violence, and the appropriateness of each as a response. Behind the perceived dichotomy between an effective formal system of reporting and an ineffective, shadowy, informal world of "soft" responses is an assumption that the lack of credible formal policies and reporting mechanisms is what deters women from coming forward to report their experiences of sexual violence. However, Bumiller's analysis suggests that the introduction of formal policies may impose inappropriate burdens on individual survivors while failing to address even their basic needs. At the same time, the policies may create unrealistic expectations that will not be met, demoralizing rather than empowering victims/survivors and further widening the gap that makes campus sexual violence invisible. The uncertain ground created by the shadow of the law that Bumiller describes may be an accurate description of where many survivors of campus sexual violence find themselves. In the following discussion, we explore how administrators and service providers defined their work of responding to student disclosures (and non-disclosures) about sexual violence drawing on these three clusters of interpretive meanings. These are: the often problematic ways in which ideas and understandings of "law" are taken up and defined by university personnel; the operation of other normative frames and social contexts that shape (and trouble) the ways in which sexual violence disclosures are made and received; and the potential impact of the burdens, expectations, and assumptions that accompany the reporting regime.

A TRICK OF THE LIGHT: "VICTIM CENTRED" AND THE CONSTITUTION OF LEGAL MEANING

The administrators and service providers we interviewed stated overwhelmingly that their largely informalized responses to sexual violence are driven by the express wishes of the survivor/victim. Being "victim centred" was represented in a range of (contradictory) ways – as a compunction, as a limitation, and/or as a value (Buss et al. 2016).[6] But we came to see that the repeated allusions to "victim centredness" as structuring administrative or service responses served to mask a range of interpretive decisions, for both survivors and university personnel. These decisions were informed by conceptions of law (mostly criminal law) and legality that reflected deeply gendered understandings (and myths) of sexual violence. Disclosures and experiences of sexual violence are evaluated by administrators and service providers, as well as by victims and survivors, based on their understandings both of criminal law and how it functions, and of "sexual assault" as a legal category and how it delimits "wrongful" behaviour. Rather than providing a strong, victim-centred anti-violence norm that would "creat[e] an environment where everyone on campus knows that sexual violence is unacceptable" (Government of Ontario 2013), law provides a narrow understanding of sexual violence that minimizes anything but the most overt forms of sexual violence, hence discouraging many victims from coming forward.

THE SHADOW OF CRIMINAL LAW

Cultural understandings of the powerful impact of criminal law cast a strong shadow over university sexual policies and procedures. Many interviewees described survivors as reluctant to make a formal complaint, citing fears that their or the assailants' careers would be harmed. "They [survivors] don't want to ruin their [own] lives," one interviewee told us. They don't want to "get the guy in trouble" or "ruin his career," others said. Some expressed both concerns. "Even before Jian Ghomeshi, people didn't want to go through that [a formal complaint]; they are busy, they want to get back to studying; they decide they will emotionally deal with it later; and they also say they don't want to ruin his life with a criminal record," summarized one administrator.

While these concerns were relayed to us by university personnel, we can infer that survivors are likewise envisioning a complaint process similar to a criminal trial in which the victim's behaviour would be in question and the potential penalties for the assailant would be significant. Given that at the time of our research the university processes in place were little used and largely unknown to many, including administrators, it is striking that there was such a clear sense by so many people that the process would be "hard." It was evident that the perceived harshness of the criminal justice system guided decision-making in these non-criminal processes.

Administrators and service providers, in turn, implicitly and explicitly framed their own roles akin to the "trier of fact" in a court of law, expressing deep concern about balance between the two parties; fairness in receiving and assessing evidence; and viewing events in terms of legalistic evidentiary thresholds. Concerns about "fairness," while certainly understandable, seemed to have a meaning that was informed by a criminal process standard. In the words of one administrator: "The person against whom allegations are made hasn't had their day in court. At the moment, being fair to one side is being grotesquely unfair to the other." The spectre of false allegations and unfounded rumours loomed large for some of our interviewees, echoing the large numbers of sexual assault claims rejected as unfounded by police forces across Canada[7] and the undermining of victim credibility in the court room.

In describing how they assess sexual violence claims, administrators and service providers frequently invoked legal terminology – such as presumption of innocence, credibility, evidence, the accused – and used those concepts to distinguish the seriousness, even the actuality, of the sexual violence. One administrator advised us: "I don't like saying accused – that is the right term for extremely violent cases but in other cases where there are complicated cases, to say accused is very hard."

Some of the people we interviewed explicitly raised the concern that decision-makers dealing with sexual violence issues are trying to follow criminal law procedures without the training to do so: "[They] are making very legalistic decisions and distinctions, weighing evidence, effectively running trials and do not have the training to do this." Similarly, "without education or training on this, we are replicating the criminal justice system." Other administrators were less reflective about their assumed role as trier of fact, making decisions about levels of severity and requirements for evidence that are clearly inscribed by a legalistic frame. One administrator provided an account that we summarize (changing some facts for confidentiality) as an example:

> A female student came forward to report that she had been sexually assaulted by a male student with whom she was working. Both students were known to the administrator. The administrator's course of action in such a case was to hear from both the complainant and respondent, to weigh the evidence and then reach a decision. The administrator heard from the respondent that the sexual activities were consensual and that the complainant was 'out to get him.' While the administrator determined that 'something' had indeed happened, he felt that there was insufficient evidence to have the perpetrator removed from campus, as the complainant had asked. 'I don't have tonnes of evidence, and I don't have tonnes of experience. But my first concern was with her.' The result was that the male student had some limits placed on his movements and volunteer activities on campus.

Even though he understood himself to be operating from the premise that his "first concern" was with the victim/claimant, the administrator ultimately decided against the female student's request for more security (further limitations on the male student's movements) because he perceived that the situation did not warrant it; he assessed her complaint as not serious enough. The administrator's reference to "tonnes of evidence" reflects the premise from which he was actually operating, confirmed later in the interview when he went on to explain what would be done in cases with "clear" evidence: "If there is someone with a clear complaint and camera footage of the guy going into her room ... we're pretty strong in this area and willing to remove him from (residence)."

Drawing distinctions between types of violence and levels of severity is inevitable. As sexual violence unfolds along a continuum shaped by gender norms, different types of violence will present as involving varying degrees of severity. The important point is the basis – the latent beliefs and assumptions – on which administrators are making distinctions between clear and less clear, serious and less serious. Presumptions of what constitutes "clear" rape (such as stranger rape with videotape evidence in the above example) have an impact on decisions made about the remedies for the survivor, even when her story is believed, as in the case summarized above.

DEFINING AND CATEGORIZING SEXUAL ASSAULT

The shadow of the law is also imprinted in the delineations of what constitutes "sexual assault" for administrators and service providers (and likely also for victims and survivors). The Ghomeshi trial and decision[8] were frequently referenced, explicitly and implicitly, standing as a marker of how the "law" responds to sexual violence reports. In the words of one interviewee: "The law has directed survivors of sexual violence to see the violence as a flaw in them. They think sexual violence against them has more to do with them. Look at how cross examination of them [unfolds] in court."

Our interviewees categorized sexual violence on campus according to a set of cultural norms or expectations about real or "serious" sexual violence. These actors tended to conjure archetypal conceptions of campus sexual violence, and also of sexuality. Familiar myths and stereotypes of sexual assault and sexuality inherited from the criminal law system (and its representations) influenced meanings and frames within which conceptions of sexual assault and hierarchies of seriousness and believability were indexed. Sexual assault trials are contexts in which rape culture myths and stereotypes are reinforced and imbued with authority.[9] These legally endorsed myths and stereotypes are fundamental components of the normative framework of sexual assault law. They are woven into the individual understandings of sex and sexual violence that inform student relations and through which administrators and service providers assess the disclosures of sexual violence. Shaped by these myths and stereotypes, terms like "sexual violence," "rape," and "date rape" carry sets of meanings within the university context that frame the intelligibility of certain forms of campus sexual violence. They are important in understanding not just how administrators or service providers make sense of the accounts of sexual violence they encounter, but also how students present and make sense of experiences of sexual violence.

Understandings of sexual violence among interviewees in our study clustered around the archetypes of "stranger rape," "date rape," and "party rape." Stranger rape (an innocent victim and a "crazed" perpetrator unknown to the victim) continues to function, legally and culturally, as the "real rape"[10] against which other allegations of sexual violence are assessed. The more that sexual violence aligns with the stereotype of stranger rape, the more likely it is to be understood as sexual violence. "Date rape" is often understood as the result of mismatched expectations, as "her" leading "him" on, or as post-sex "regret." Our interviewees made references to "mixed signals," "a consensual relationship gone bad," women "changing their minds," "muddy consent," students "stumbling around with sexual feelings," and the allegation itself as a "prank." A number of interviewees understood campus sexual violence as either "party rape" or "date rape" or both. Implicit or explicit degrees of seriousness flowed from these categorizations, implying some degree of responsibility on the part of both (or all) students involved – for not making their intentions clearer, for drinking too much, for "taking advantage" of another person's drunkenness. And, for these two "types" of sexual violence, solutions in the form of "consent education" were understood as pivotal. Repeatedly we were referred to the online short video, "Consent; It's Simple as Tea," as a paradigm-shifting response to campus sexual violence.[11]

These sexual assault categories – stranger rape, party rape, date rape – operate in the university setting as particular "cultural categories" (Merry 2006, 978) that are given meaning in this milieu. In our research, these categories were most visibly in operation in indexing hierarchies of "assault" between "clear" and "serious" sexual violence, and "less clear" and "less serious" incidents. That is, these categories were influential in helping administrators to "make sense" of the phenomenon of campus sexual assault. Disclosures of sexual violence that did not line up with stereotypical understandings of these cultural categories tended to be minimized by administrators and/or were seen as requiring only a limited response, on the grounds that these incidents were "not clear" or not supported by enough evidence to be definitively labelled as sexual violence. Claims that they are acting in ways that are "victim-centric" further masked the administrators' role in sorting and minimizing the sexual violence encounters disclosed to them.

In this context, consent – a concept imported from the legal arena – has become the sharp dividing line between sex and sexual assault, a line that frequently created confusion. Survivors were not always convinced that what they had experienced was sexual assault and/or that they were not somehow to blame. Our interviewees heard from survivors: "it was my fault"; "I was drinking"; "I lead him on"; "he's a nice guy." These kinds of comments were a concern for a number of service providers who saw survivors' downplaying of their experience as evidence of the normalization of some forms of sexual violence. "People are agreeing to sex because of pressure. They are not sure if they wanted sex and they aren't sure they actually consented." And yet, consent was the primary focus of attention both in assessing a disclosure and in the prevention education programs provided on campuses.

THE RELATIONAL CONTEXTS
OF CAMPUS SEXUAL VIOLENCE

Our interviewees depicted a complicated web of interactions that framed sexual violence and its disclosures. Our interview data points to universities as a complex site of sexual experimentation, gendered expectations of sexual liberty, and abusive interpersonal relationships that are not fully captured by notions of sexual violence defined in terms of non-consent or "mismatched expectations." While our research did not directly explore different kinds of sexual activities, the examples provided to us indicated that the array of sexualized harms that are "dealt with" informally may be substantially different from what is made visible through formalized policy processes. Cultures of sexual experimentation and social relations may play a bigger role in the survivor's decision-making about coming forward than is commonly realized. Will she be seen as a sexual prude if she complains? Is she responsible because she initially agreed to experimental sexual activity? Several service providers underscored the important, and sometimes problematic, role of friends in shaping whether or not a woman discloses or seeks help. Just as university personnel and survivors reflect a range of myths and assumptions about sexual violence and the reporting process, the "friends" of survivors also hold these views. We heard several examples of "friends" discouraging women from coming forward because a complaint would get the assailant in trouble, or because the process would be hard, or because her reputation would be sullied.

Sexual experimentation also underscored the limits of university responses and educational programming on "consent." As one interviewee explained, forms of sexual experimentation are much more diverse than what university administrators – who are usually significantly older than the average student – envision. We were told that the tools and responses that universities use in relation to sexual assault are outdated and ineffective for current forms of sexual experimentation. One interview subject said of the sexual education tool being used at her university, "Single and Sexy was good 10–15 years ago ... we need to be having a 2016 conversation."

The normative framework of the law posits a victim of sexual violence as clearly identifiable and as clearly – but not too aggressively[12] – pursuing the perpetrator through the legal mechanisms available to her. A "clear dividing line" between consensual sex and sexual violence is itself problematic while simultaneously becoming idealized as the means of identifying and addressing sexual violence, building up the kinds of expectations of justice and remedy that Bumiller warns will inevitably disappoint and disempower. The social relationships and social norms of campus culture, sometimes consistent with the norms of the legal framework and sometimes in conflict with them, inform those deliberations, individually and collectively. Victims who come forward with an allegation but do not want to pursue a formal complaint are often considered unreliable and treated with suspicion. The relational factors that might inform such a decision are not considered relevant in the legal framework.

CONCLUSION

In this chapter, we have urged a closer examination of the ways in which current approaches to reforming university sexual violence policies and services are predicated upon assumed divisions and normative orderings of a formalized array of responses (understood in terms of reporting and complaints), and informal (understood as ad hoc) responses. The formalized responses tend to be seen as clear and fair and as bringing the violence to light; the informal responses are viewed as hidden, partial, and ripe for abuse. The shadow metaphor conjures a number of different meanings – from nefarious and obscure, to authentic and revelatory – with which to (re)consider informal approaches. By thinking through the range of practices, offices, and cultures that might be associated (and overlooked) within the "shadow" world of informality, we have sought to offer a more complex picture of what goes on in the informal practices and services offered at universities.

Shadow, as metaphor, also requires attention to its counterpoint, the "real" object: in this case, the formalized system of reporting and complaint. Just as the "shadow" world has many different components, actors and norms, so too do the formalized systems within universities. Our concern is that the current focus – by policy-makers, administrators, and activists working on violence against women – is too heavily weighted toward formal policies. While we accept that formal policies have a role to play in responding to campus sexual violence, our concerns are threefold. First, we fear that formal processes are taking on a quality and character defined through their deemed opposition to an informal realm that is itself caricatured. Second, we are concerned that formal responses (complaints, hearings) will be seen as the ideal in ways that reinforce narrow, formulaic views of sexual violence, understood as lack of consent, with a clear perpetrator and victim. Third, the formal focus, and its failure to address more complex forms and experiences of sexual violence, will not expose systemic conditions of violence and abuse, and their gendered underpinnings.

In addition, the focus on formal sexual violence policies on university campuses places an intolerable and unrealistic burden on individual victims/survivors. It is a burden that some administrators and service providers put on them explicitly. But the job of making campuses safer – less violent and less inhospitable for women – cannot be assigned to the individual survivors, especially not at their most vulnerable time. As Bumiller (2011) has argued, placing the onus of recognition and action on the disadvantaged group means that they bear the cost of (in our context) eliminating sexual violence or of failure to do so, at the expense of not having the needs and realities of their day-to-day lives addressed.

It is a major question whether clearer, stronger, more comprehensive policies will prove effective for the individual victims who choose to pursue them. It seems likely that, for the foreseeable future, most victims will continue to choose not to pursue a formal complaint. We do not want to see victims pressured to report or blamed for ongoing violence. The current emphasis on a survivor-centric approach – that is, the survivor leading the decision-making and others respecting her choices – may foster a sense that it is the survivors' fault if the new policies do not lead to the anticipated climate shift. We noted in our report that "the emphasis placed on survivors to lead the process legitimates university responses that are minimalist and individualistic" (Buss et al. 2016).

Finally, we need to recognize that the extensive array of informal responses is itself a normative context in which meanings of campus sexual violence are constituted in and through gendered legal and social structures. As with the formal systems of complaint or records, informal systems are contradictory and highly circumscribed, riddled with sexism and misogyny, shored up by myth and stereotype. Nonetheless, they are an arena that is, and likely will continue to be, a primary context in which survivors try to make sense of their experience, decide, bargain, contest, exert control, and reframe their recourse. The shadows matter.

RESEARCH AND POLICY IMPLICATIONS

One of the most clear implications of our research and analysis is the need to pay much greater attention to the systemic institutional and cultural practices and beliefs that foster or mask campus sexual violence. Research into effective methods to shift these entrenched patterns should be a priority. Education/prevention programs need to be updated to address current sexual practices. Campus policies should be designed as an alternative to the criminal law, leaving survivors free to pursue a criminal charge if they so wish. Internal processes to address sexual violence complaints should not be modelled on criminal law processes or import criminal law presumptions and definitions, and the option of a restorative justice process should be available. Informal processes and support systems for survivors need to be recognized as at least as important as formal complaint mechanisms. These informal responses require innovative programming, well-trained staff, and adequate resources.

The report submitted to the Ontario Ministry of Community Safety and Correctional Services that was based in part on the research discussed in this chapter offered a series of eighteen recommendations, grouped under these headings: focus, training, prevention and education, health and continuing services, research, anonymous reporting, oversight, dedicated sexual violence co-ordinator, and restorative justice. The following three recommendations relate most directly to the issues raised in this chapter:

Focus: The government and university focus for action on sexual violence on university campuses should move beyond the development of better reporting and policy environments in order to concentrate more on service provision, informal remedies, and the prevention of sexual violence, in accordance with the needs and wishes of the majority of survivors of sexual violence on our campuses.

Research: Research should be commissioned on the specific issues and impacts relating to racialization and racism, indigeneity, sexual identity, gender identity, disability, and intimate partner violence, and the impact they have on sexual violence on university campuses.

Research: On-site research – for example, program evaluation and impact studies – should be integrated into the delivery of educational programming and training. Given that we really do not know what works in reducing sexual violence and shifting rape culture, innovation and research should be a central component of the provincial strategy on sexual violence on campuses.

NOTES

1 This paper is based only on the field research with university administrators and service providers conducted by Doris Buss and Diana Majury.
2 Carleton University, Lakehead University, and University of Waterloo. This paper only draws from the interviews and focus groups with administrators and service delivery personnel that were conducted by the authors between February and May 2016. The full study also included interviews and focus groups with survivors (mostly students), campus security, and local police forces.
3 While we want to push beyond or beneath the binary, we are acutely aware that in focusing on the binary we are inevitably, at least to some extent, reinforcing that which we critique. The concept of the shadow that we found so helpful in stimulating our thinking is itself, at least to some extent, based on a binary.
4 See, for example, Laychuck (2016) and Sawa and Ward (2016).
5 See, for example, Harrison et al. (2015); Sexual Assault Centre of Hamilton and Area and YWCA Hamilton (2014); Lalonde (2014); Oliver,

Langan, and Godderis (2015); Saint Francis Xavier University (2014); Saint Mary's University (2013); University of Toronto (2014); Concordia University (2015); Dalhousie University (2015); University of Ottawa (2015); Ryerson University (2015); and University of Alberta (2016).

6 These different iterations are discussed more fully in the complete report.

7 This long-standing issue was the subject of a twenty-month investigation (Doolittle 2017).

8 *R v Ghomeshi* (2016) ONCJ 155 (CanLII).

9 See for example the essays in Sheehy (2012).

10 For the original exploration of this concept, see Estrich (1987) and Kahn et al. (1994).

11 The brief stick-figure video draws an analogy between sexual consent and accepting (or declining) an offered cup of tea – e.g., an unconscious person does not want tea, so don't pour tea down their throat. There are numerous critiques of the tea video. See for example King (2015) and Young (2015).

12 Victims who are seen as aggressively pursuing a perpetrator, particularly one who is known to them, risk being seen as vindictive or vengeful, as the stereotyped "woman scorned."

REFERENCES

Bumiller, K. 1987. "Victims in the Shadow of the Law: A Critique of the Model of Legal Protection." *Signs Journal of Women in Culture and Society* 12 (3): 421–39.

Buss, Doris, Diana Majury, Dawn Moore, George S. Rigakos, and Rashmee Singh. 2016. *The Response to Sexual Violence at Ontario University Campuses.* Ottawa, Ontario: Ministry of Community Safety and Correctional Services.

Concordia University. 2015. "Report of the Sexual Assault Policy Working Group." http://www.concordia.ca/content/dam/concordia/now/docs/ FINAL-en-report-sexual-assault-policy-review-working-group-august-2015.pdf.

Doolittle, Robyn. 2017. "Why Police Dismiss 1 in 5 Sexual Assault Claims as Baseless." *Globe and Mail.* https://www.theglobeandmail.com/news/ investigations/unfounded-sexual-assault-canada-main/article33891309/.

Estrich, Susan. 1987. *Real Rape.* Cambridge, MA, and London, UK: Harvard University Press.

Dalhousie University. 2015. "Report on the Task Force of Misogyny, Sexism and Homophobia in Dalhousie University Faculty of Dentistry."

https://cdn.dal.ca/content/dam/dalhousie/pdf/cultureofrespect/
DalhousieDentistry TaskForceReport-June2015.pdf.

Government of Ontario. 2013. "Developing a Response to Sexual
Violence: A Resource Guide for Ontario's Colleges and Universities."

– 2016. Bill 132: Sexual Violence and Harassment Action Plan Act
(Supporting Survivors and Challenging Sexual Violence). https://www.
ola.org/en/legislative-business/bills/parliament-41/session-1/bill-132.

Gunraj, Andrea. 2014. *Sexual Assault Policies on Campus*. METRAC,
Toronto, Ontario.

Harrison, J., G. Lafrenière, and L.S. Hallman. 2015. "University Campuses
Ending Gendered Violence Final Report and Recommendations."
Waterloo: Wilfrid Laurier University. http://www.sascwr.org/files/www/
change_project/The_Change_Project_Laurier_Final_Report_01_09.pdf.

Jacob, Herbert. 1992. "The Elusive Shadow of the Law." *Law and Society
Review* 26 (3): 565–90. doi:10.2307/3053738.

Kahn, A.S., V.A. Mathie, and C. Torgler. 1994. "Rape Scripts and Rape
Acknowledgement." *Psychology of Women Quarterly* 18 (1): 53–66.

King, Elizabeth. 2015. "The Real Problem with the Tea-Consent
Metaphor." *literallydarling.com*. http://www.literallydarling.com/
blog/2015/05/25/the-real-problem-with-the-tea-consent-metaphor/.

Lalonde, J.S. 2014. "From Reaction to Preventing: Addressing Sexual
Violence on Campus by Engaging Community Partners." Ottawa:
University of Ottawa. https://www.uottawa.ca/president/sites/www.
uottawa.ca.president/files/task-force-report-appendix-1-from-reacting-
to-preventing.pdf.

Laychuk, Riley. 2016. "Brandon University Sexual Assault Victims Forced
to Sign Contract that Keeps Them Silent." CBC News, 5 April. https://
www.cbc.ca/news/canada/manitoba/brandon-university-behavioural-
contract-1.3520568.

Merry, Sally Engle. 1990. *Getting Justice and Getting Even: Legal
Consciousness among Working-Class Americans*. Chicago, IL:
University of Chicago Press.

– 2006. "New Legal Realism and the Ethnography of Transnational Law."
Law and Social Inquiry 31 (4): 975–95. doi:10.1111/j.1747-4469.
2006.00042.x.

Mnookin, Robert H., and Lewis Kornhauser. 1979. "Bargaining in the
Shadow of the Law: The Case of Divorce." *The Yale Law Journal*
88 (5): 950–97. doi:10.2307/795824.

Oliver, M., D. Langan, and R. Godderis. 2015. "Confronting Rape Culture
and Resisting to Anti-Violence Discourse." Waterloo, ON: Wilfrid

Laurier University. https://legacy.wlu.ca/docsnpubs_detail.php?grp_
  id=2465&doc_id=62296.
Ryerson University. 2015. "Report to the Provost: Review of Policies,
  Practices and Protocols related to Sexual Assault at Ryerson University."
Saint Francis Xavier University. 2014. "Preventing Violence against
  Women at Saint Francis Xavier University Project: Policies and
  Procedures Guide." http://awrcsasa.ca/wp-content/uploads/2014/12/
  Policy-Guide-and-Recommendations-Final-3.pdf.
Sawa, Timothy, and Lori Ward. 2016. "Brock University Tells Student to
  Keep Quiet about Sexual Harassment Finding." *CBC News*, 11 March.
  https://www.cbc.ca/news/canada/brock-university-sexual-
  harrassment-1.3485814.
Sexual Assault Centre of Hamilton and Area and YWCA Hamilton. 2014.
  "Key Recommendations – McMaster Project: It's Time to End Violence
  Against Women on Campus."
Sheehy, Elizabeth A., ed. 2012. *Sexual Assault in Canada: Law, Legal
  Practice and Women's Activism.* Ottawa, ON: University of Ottawa
  Press.
Silbey, Susan S. 2005. "After Legal Consciousness." *Annual Review of Law
  and Social Science* 1 (1): 323–68. doi:10.1146/annurev.lawsocsci.
  1.041604.115938.
University of Alberta. 2016. "Review of the University of Alberta's
  Response to Sexual Assault." https://cloudfront.ualberta.ca/-/media/
  ualberta/office-of-the-provost-and-vice-president/vice-provost-and-dean-
  of-students/documents/reports/uofasexualassaultreview.pdf.
University of Ottawa. 2015. "Report of the Task Force on Respect and
  Equality: Ending Sexual Violence at the University of Ottawa." https://
  www.uottawa.ca/president/sites/www.uottawa.ca.president/files/report-
  of-the-task-force-on-respect-and-equality.pdf
University of Toronto. 2014. "Preventing and Reducing Violence against
  Young Women on Post-Secondary Campuses: A Best Practices Guide."
  https://www.utm.utoronto.ca/health/sites/files/health/public/users/
  jankows8/Best%20Practices%20Guide%20Preventing%20and%20
  Reducing%20VAYW%20on%20Postsecondary%20Campuses.pdf.
Young, Cathy. 2015. "Consent: It's a Piece of Cake." *spiked-online.com.*
  https://www.spiked-online.com/2015/11/02/consent-its-a-piece-of-cake/.

12

Towards Acknowledging
the Ambiguities of Sex

Questioning Rape Culture and Consent-Based
Approaches to Sexual Assault Prevention

Tuulia Law

INTRODUCTION

Following the autoethnographic tradition of problematizing one's own observations and experiences (Ellis 2008), this chapter begins with a reflection on my involvement with anti-sexual violence education as a point of departure to (re)considering contemporary approaches centring rape culture and consent. I began to think about these terms after two incidents in 2014 when I was a graduate student at the University of Ottawa – the posting of sexually explicit and violent comments about the then-president of the student government, Anne-Marie Roy; and allegations that members of the hockey team had sexually assaulted a woman on a varsity trip (Andrew et al. 2015). In response, the criminology department held a round table for professors and students about rape culture on our campus. Recalling how the *Consent is Sexy* events I had attended had attracted feminist/queer activists already relatively knowledgeable about sexual violence, and not the straight men whose need for such an intervention was painfully evinced by the aforementioned incidents, I offered to give a workshop to a mixed-gender, captive audience: an undergraduate criminology class. As my familiarity with rape culture was limited, my co-presenter, a community anti-violence activist, defined and led the discussion about rape culture and its pervasiveness, underscoring the importance of consent, while I took the lead on a critique of dominant masculinity. In my subsequent search of feminist activist writings and scholarship, I increasingly saw a resemblance between rape culture and earlier feminist theories otherwise problematized in contemporary feminism.

Preparing and teaching a seminar entitled "Sexual Violence on Campus" provided the opportunity to further this research and reflection. Over the semester we contemplated the interlocking oppressions constructing the university environment (Cabrera 2014), different theories explaining sexual violence (a way to examine various theoretical iterations of and alternatives to rape culture), and policy and activist responses. In one class – with trepidation – I challenged consent as the reigning standard in preventive education through an exercise about personal boundaries and when they should be considered (e.g., only during sex; hugging acquaintances). The exercise was designed to get at why we do things that we do not want to do in various social contexts (e.g., work, romantic relationships, family), and the different reasons why people have sex. For many this was new and unsettling territory; however, with some unease, we concluded that in different configurations of contexts and participants, consent can have different meanings, from willingness, to concession, to compulsion.

This chapter builds on these reflections to reconsider rape culture and consent, two terms so readily and broadly used to characterize the problem of campus sexual violence and its solution as to have become dogmatic. They are discursive forces that, as this chapter argues, draw upon and perpetuate stubborn tropes of female victimhood, and lack of desire and agency. Echoing Vance's (1993) concerns about the stymying effects of orthodoxy, this chapter explores early feminist formulations of rape culture and their relationship to consent, and then critically examines how these terms are deployed by contemporary feminists and contribute to the design of sexual assault prevention education. Challenging the status of these terms as preferred analytical and activist tools, the chapter then revisits the work of feminist scholars who argue that sexual assault should be viewed through a framing of sex as a site of pleasure and danger. This is not to deny either the importance of consent or the prevalence and cultural acceptability of sexual assault, but rather to question whether the issue of sexual violence can be addressed more effectively through other means. To this end the chapter concludes with a reimagined approach to preventive education.

The chapter employs Cohen's (1985) notion of deposits of power. According to Cohen, a deposit of power "is something which is *left behind* and something which is *drawn upon* ... these deposits take the form of descriptions (stories) and causal theories," in this case of sex and sexual assault, respectively, which "leave behind real forms of power" such as institutional policies and programs (89, emphasis in original). As deposits of *power* they are informed by Foucault's (1980) conceptualization of power/knowledge, the mutually constitutive relationship through which knowledge is produced and truths established through the exercise of power, often through relations supporting already dominant social and economic apparatuses – including those with which this volume is concerned, the school and the law (see Smart 1989; Weedon 1987). This lens allows for an analysis of the discursive and concrete effects of the terms "rape culture" and "consent" in the interconnected fields of feminist scholarship, activism, and anti-sexual violence education.

TRACING THE ORIGINS OF RAPE CULTURE

The idea of rape culture has been described as originating in Brownmiller's (1975) famous feminist tome, *Against Our Will* (Rentschler 2014). In it, Brownmiller argues that the "ideology of rape is fueled by cultural values that are perpetuated at every level of our society" (1975, 437). For Brownmiller rape is biologically determined, arising from men's superior physical strength and ability to penetrate, but politically deployed: "a conscious process of intimidation by which *all men* keep *all women* in a state of fear" (ibid., 5, emphasis in original). She offers an important critique of gender roles and sexual norms, and characterizes them as perpetuating aggressiveness among men and passivity, fear, and "a victim mentality" (ibid., 343) among women. As Cahill (2001) pithily notes, Brownmiller's framing of rape as a biological male imperative renders social change around gender norms rather futile. Additionally, Brownmiller's analogy between pornography and "the sadistic pleasures of gassing Jews or lynching blacks" (ibid., 444) problematically reiterates the archaic notion that rape is a fate worse than death. Moreover, as Davis (1981) points out, Brownmiller not only suggests that sexual violence is worse than racist violence, but reproduces the myth of the black rapist by claiming that without access to other privileges of male supremacy black men are more likely to resort to sexual violence. In short, Brownmiller's cultural analysis of rape is at once strategically focused (Cahill 2001) and ignorant of other mechanisms and targets of marginalization (see Crenshaw 1989).

Another contribution to the notion that rape is culturally entrenched
is Sanday's (1981) characterization of some societies as "rape-prone."
According to Sanday, a rape-prone society is "one in which sexual
assault by men of women is either culturally allowable or, largely
overlooked" (15). Going beyond Brownmiller's framing of women as
chattel barred from participation in law-making and enforcement,
Sanday considers women's politico-economic circumstances: not only
are they derided and excluded from public decision-making, but the
"rape prone cultural configuration" (25) occurs in societies already
suffering from resource depletion and socio-economic inequality.
However, Sanday retains binary thinking in characterizing destructive
practices as male, and arguing that "the qualities so often associated
with femaleness ... nurturance, growth, and nature" (26), should be
equally valued. Furthermore, as an anthropological generalization,
the concept of the rape-prone society also overlooks intra-societal
tensions such as racism.

While Sanday and Brownmiller share a reading of rape as a cultural
mechanism of male domination, for Brownmiller, rape is about power
and not about sex. Brownmiller's liberal feminist interpretation is
distinct from radical feminists who instead consider rape to be an
especially violent manifestation of heterosexuality (Cahill 2001),
which is imposed and therefore always already violent – in other
words, because heterosexuality is a socio-cultural norm, power and
(heterosexual) sex are invariably intertwined. For example,
MacKinnon (1982) conceptualizes sex as an effect of, and therefore
never distinct from, power, and specifically of men's transhistorical
domination over women; as a result, "resistance, subversion, and
pleasure are written out of the account" (Valverde 1989, 242).
Similarly, Kelly (1987) situates (hetero)sexual interactions on a continuum of violence extending from sex to rape, which allows her to
characterize all women as victims (including women who do not self-
identify as such), and intimate that all men are offenders. Thus in both
liberal and radical feminist framings, we see that women's agency is
negated to the extent that sexual pleasure itself is virtually unthinkable
(while experiences outside of heterosexual relations between cis men
and women are largely ignored). In other words, in proto-rape culture
analyses, women's consent is meaningless.

In the intervening years between Brownmiller's and MacKinnon's
writings and the refining of the precise term "rape culture" (elaborated
below), feminists fought for and won significant changes in Canada's

criminal justice approach to sexual assault. Reflecting feminist critiques of male socio-economic domination (especially in marriage), gender norms (e.g., the privileging of female chastity), and insistence on the prevalence and myriad forms of sexual violence, in 1983 *rape* was removed from the Criminal Code of Canada and replaced with the gender-neutral *sexual assault*. The latter was expanded into three degrees of violence (now CC ss. 271, 272, and 273) and acknowledged the possibility of sexual assault within marriage; rape shield laws followed a decade later in 1992. Similarly, in the United States, rape laws were broadened to include male victims, the marital exemption was removed, and rape shield laws were enacted (Daigle 2016). It may appear surprising, then, that Buchwald, Fletcher, and Roth retained the term *rape* in coining "rape culture" in 1993, operationalizing it as "a complex of beliefs that encourages male sexual aggression and supports violence against women. It is a society where violence is seen as sexy and sexuality as violent. In a rape culture women perceive a continuum of threatened violence that ranges from sexual remarks to sexual touching to rape itself. A rape culture condones physical and emotional terrorism against women *as the norm*" (vi, emphasis in original).

Speaking to the power of feminist orthodoxy, this operationalization retains a heterosexual, cisgendered focus, and a framing of sexual assault as something men do to women; however, it also develops existing critiques of the restrictions imposed on women and of gender norms. In the same volume, Buchwald (1993) suggests that schools should teach ethical sexual behaviour. In the latter respects, Buchwald, Fletcher, and Roth's (1993) conceptualization allows for the possibility of women's sexual agency; it also, unlike Brownmiller's biologically based understanding of rape and MacKinnon's pessimism, leaves room for change.

THE DEPLOYMENT OF RAPE CULTURE IN CONTEMPORARY FEMINISM

As Rentschler (2014) has observed, young feminists' interventions online are informed by Buchwald et al.'s (1993) definition of rape culture, as well as their assertion that the attitudes and values perpetuating it can change. Rentschler documents how young women identify and shame street harassers; refer to their own experiences to powerfully speak against sexual assault; offer support; and share strategies to combat sexual harassment, assault, and their normalization. In this respect, the term can be seen as rallying contemporary feminist efforts against sexual violence.

However, deposits of rape culture's earlier conceptual shortcomings occasionally manifest in moments of discomfort. For example, while rape culture features in enough articles that *Everyday Feminism* has produced a "best of" list on the topic, the magazine's editors unwittingly highlighted these shortcomings when they included a disclaimer atop an article entitled "25 Everyday Examples of Rape Culture": "While this list demonstrates the pervasiveness of rape by cis men against cis women, Everyday Feminism would like to note that sexual violence and rape culture affect trans and gender non-conforming people (as well as cis men) at an alarming rate. Rape culture is everyone's issue, regardless of gender" (Ridgway 2014).

Another caveat takes up a whole article – Johnson (2016) endeavours to dissociate feminists' use of the term from several popular assumptions, notably the overestimation of the occurrence of sexual violence, the inference that all men are rapists, and the claim that society explicitly promotes rape. Recalling Brownmiller (1975), Kelly (1987), and MacKinnon (1982), however, these assumptions about the entailments of the term "rape culture" are not inaccurate – rather, they highlight the deposits of power that remain embedded in the term.

Recent literature on campus sexual assault and prevention similarly provides cursory updates to rape culture or uses the term as given. While Klaw et al. (2005) do not offer a definition, Lanford (2016) uses rape culture to mean sexist attitudes that encompass victim-blaming and the normalization of male sexual violence, retaining the heterosexual focus of earlier scholars. Similarly, Burnet et al. (2009) argue that victim-blaming, facilitated by rape myths and rape culture, silences women – both through impeding sharing experiences of rape and by not interpreting their own experiences as rape, recalling radical feminist assertions that rape is *the* way to understand heterosexual encounters. For example, Kelly (1987) asked her participants about experiences including feeling "pressured to have sex, and if they picked up sexual messages in the family" (52), to arrive at a broad definition of sexual violence inclusive of incidents that participants may or may not have interpreted as problematic. Analogously, Burnet et al. (2009) grouped together college student participants' articulations of "peer pressure to have sex or the need to 'prove to a male that you like him'" (that is, the weight of cultural norms) with "giving up the fight of consent, 'He was already doing it, so I just lay there'" (that is, the physical violation of sexual boundaries).

Rape culture's continued circulation evinces its powerful narrative sway, and, given that sexual assault continues unabated on campuses and elsewhere, also shows the need for ongoing discussion. I saw this need amongst my students, who employed the term unquestioningly, and lauded its inclusion (or critiqued its inadequate integration or absence) in the newly developed university policies we examined in class. That they did so even after we spent time considering its conceptual shortcomings, including the implications of excluding relations and identities that fall outside of the penetrative, heterosexual sex that *rape* connotes, suggests that second-wave theories of sexual assault continue to be embraced as truth.

CONSENT: A PANACEA?

Consistent with the popularity of consent in efforts to prevent sexual assault at universities and colleges across North America (Beres 2014), my students also frequently articulated consent as a solution to rape culture on campus. Given that feminists like MacKinnon (1982; see also Kelly 1987) asserted that women's experience of (heterosexual) sex is determined by unequal power relations that effectively nullify their capacity to consent (Cahill 2001), this appears to be a significant departure. However, upon closer examination, the same dichotomies remain: consistent with the conceptual pedigree of rape culture, emphasis continues to be placed on women victimized by men (other configurations are exceptionalized when acknowledged) (e.g., Andrew et al. 2015); and, echoing Sanday's (1981) characterization of cultures as "rape free" or "rape prone," sexual relations are framed as either empowering or assault (Wodda and Panfil 2017). From the latter (strangely decontextualized) perspective, consent is the obvious solution.

As Smart (1989) has so persuasively argued, the concept of consent, constructed in and drawing from law, is starkly dichotomous and perpetuates binary gender norms. In contrast to her feminist contemporaries (e.g., MacKinnon) who fought to improve legal and carceral responses to sexual assault (see Halley 2006), Smart highlights how legal discourse and processes construct women's sexuality as a valuable possession that men desire and which women ostensibly do not enjoy except when they shirk their moral responsibilities – sexually assaulted (or indeed, sexual) women are in this way framed as immoral and irresponsible, while pressure from men is viewed as natural. Drawing on these insights, more recent feminist scholars and activists have highlighted the failures of the criminal justice system in responding to sexual assault, including how women are routinely attacked, undermined, stigmatized, shamed, and doubted throughout the process, even after changes were introduced to nuance consent and protect victims (i.e., rape shield laws) (Craig 2016; Gotell 2015). This should lead us to wonder: if women's articulations of non-consent are not respected in court – by defence attorneys, juries, and judges (see Craig 2016) – what is the likelihood that they will be respected interpersonally? Indeed, numerous theories posit that men are socialized to believe rape myths, either through dominant discourses, beliefs, and cultural practices (Sanday 1981; Buchwald 1993), interlocking oppressions (Cabrera 2014; Fellows and Razack 1997), or gendered and sexual scripts and roles (Jozkowski et al. 2013; Godenzi, Schwartz, and Dekeseredy 2001; Carrigan, Connell, and Lee 1985). Furthermore, scholars have found not only that voluntary attendance programs predominantly attract women (as was the case with my course) (Klaw et al. 2005), but also that young men continue to perceive consent as overly complicated or an unreasonably high barrier even after attending preventive education (Worthen and Wallace 2017).

As such, the contemporary framing of consent as a viable counter-strategy to rape culture appears to disregard the entrenched societal norms and beliefs central to rape culture's operationalization. At the same time, the accompanying punitive responses (e.g., legal and scholastic sanctions) advanced by anti-violence activists can be seen as a deposit of power of earlier carceral feminist solutions (Halley 2016). Moreover, as Gotell (2008) argues, an affirmative consent standard, enshrined in law or university policy (see Halley 2016), responsibilizes men to ensure they get consent in order to avoid punitive sanctions rather than out of "respect for [women's] sexual autonomy or recognition of the harmful consequence of coerced sex" (876).

Some contemporary scholars studying sexual practices and assault among young people do however appear to heed Smart's (1989) argument for decentring law. For example, Wodda and Panfil (2017) reject a legalistic understanding, framing consent instead as an affirmation of desire unfolding within overlapping social and interpersonal structures and contexts. Others question the applicability and meaning of consent in sexual interactions. Beres (2014) observes that young people do not necessarily see consent and willingness as synonymous, and in turn view reluctantly agreeing to sex as consent. Similarly, Thomas et al. (2017) examine young women's experiences of unwanted sex, including agreeing to sex to satisfy a partner's expectations and/or to maintain a relationship, faking an orgasm to end unwanted sex, and other situations occurring in the context of unequal power relations. They argue that our cultural focus on consent ignores, invisibilizes, and renders unintelligible various troubling experiences, as well as desire or its absence (284). Together these findings suggest that if women can consent because they are willing, but also concede for reasons other than (or in addition to) fear of violence, the dichotomous connotations of consent do not adequately speak to sexual experiences or the contexts in which they unfold.

In turn, the strategies put forward by contemporary scholars to address sexual assault on campus draw upon second-wave framings of rape culture and critiques of law and legal processes. Lanford (2017), though uncritical of legal definitions and processes, advances the idea that sexual education ought to centre pleasure and communication – but maintains that consent should be included. Arguing that rape culture engenders a lack of understanding of consent in relation to date rape, one of the solutions proposed by Burnet et al. (2009) is improving communication skills and strategies. Somewhat similarly, Jozkowski et al. (2014) suggest that because young people's communication of consent is informed by normative gender roles and sexual scripts (Simon and Gagnon 1986), educational programs should account for these differences. By contrast, Beres (2014, 386) advocates abandoning the focus on consent (see also Thomas et al. 2017), advancing educational materials that are "more direct and straightforward with less room for multiple interpretations," such as the Edmonton campaign poster, "Just because she isn't saying no ... doesn't mean she is saying yes."

It was precisely the issues raised by these scholars – pleasure, (mis)communication, sexual scripts, and their interplay and coexistence – that my seminar students reflected upon when I asked them why we agree to things unenthusiastically (e.g., accepting a cup of tea offered by a host) and how social expectations extend into and play out in sexual situations. This brought us to complex questions of relational obligations, desire, and how people negotiate sexual interactions and assert agency in contexts of unequal power relations, as well as the meanings of these exchanges to their participants – in other words, the ontological ambiguity of sex.

AMBIGUITIES AND POWER RELATIONS

Some scholars have ventured into the uncomfortable territory of ambiguity. Evocatively, Halley (2006, 301–2) describes sex as "an alarming mix of desire and fear, delight and disgust, power and surrender, surrender and power, attachment and alienation, ecstasy in the root sense of the word and enmired embodiedness." Challenging dichotomous conceptions of sex as either consensual and liberatory or non-consensual and assaultive, Wodda and Panfil (2017, 10) argue that, "a vast expanse of bad sex – joyless, exploitative encounters that reflect a persistently sexist culture and can be hard to acknowledge without sounding prudish – has gone largely uninterrogated" (see also Thomas et al. 2017). In examining the gap between consent and willingness to have sex, Beres's (2014) interview-based research takes us to an uncomfortable place that is seemingly overlooked in consent-based education: there are myriad reasons that people agree to engage in sex; these reasons may significantly differ for each party to the interaction; and sexual relations are always shaped by the social contexts in which they unfold. Halley (2016) further argues that, though the two may (often) be interrelated, ambiguity is not reducible to unequal power relations.

These are not new arguments; they too draw on earlier scholarship. Another strain of second-wave feminists took the position that women's sexual desires and experiences contain "elements of pleasure and oppression, happiness and humiliation" (Vance 1992, 6). Often misjudged as advancing an ungrounded and exaggerated conception women's agency, these "pro-sex" feminists or sexual radicals (Rubin 1992) argued that an "exclusive focus on danger ... makes women's actual experiences with pleasure invisible, overstates danger until it monopolizes the entire frame, [and] positions women solely as victims" (Vance 1993, 290). In a similar vein, Dimen (1992, 144) suggests that the intrinsic ambiguity of sexuality confers on it "an inherent novelty, creativity, discovery, and these give it its excitement, its pleasure, its fearsomeness" – a fearsomeness that derives not from a biological risk of male aggression, but from the "loss of self-other boundaries ... [and] confusions about what to do next." These arguments highlight the humanity of sex, framing it as an interaction that is social but also corporeal and subjective, comprising communication and interpretation; insecurities about one's body, skills, and social judgement; and differences of size, strength, experience, needs, and personality.

The concept of rape culture does not allow for this fearsomeness, ambiguity, or discovery. As Halley (2006) suggests, the very pervasiveness of female victimization that it implies may serve to diminish women's agency and exacerbate our fear. Indeed, Buchwald et al. (1993) and even Brownmiller (1975) problematized the paralyzing potential of fear and how it curtails women's activities and use of public space. It seems odd, then, that on university campuses punitive responses (see Nelund, this volume) and services for victims appear to be dominating the conversation: reactive rather than preventive approaches which, like the rape culture they critique, assume sexual assault as normative. In other words, such responses are not focused on longer term goals like the cultural and discursive change that Buchwald (1993) insists are necessary for rape culture's eradication.

Ambiguity also entails that there are myriad personal interpretations and definitions, not only of what constitutes sexual violence – for example, people with different personal boundaries will feel violated by different levels of encroachment, sexual or otherwise – but also of "bad" and "good" sex, and various experiences in between. My students' reflections are telling in this regard: we spent considerable time debating the nature and ethics of "okay" encounters, including half-hearted, conditional, or reluctant participation, and poor or minimally enjoyable sex. This brought us to the issue of discrepant motivations for engaging in a sexual encounter. In this regard, Meston and Buss (2007) uncovered diverse reasons why the parties to an interaction may want to participate. They found 237 reasons why humans have sexual relations and placed them into the following broad categories: physical (e.g., pleasure, stress reduction); goal attainment (e.g., social status, revenge, resources); emotions (e.g., love or companionship, expression of feelings); and insecurity (e.g., better self-esteem, pressure, maintaining a relationship). Meston and Buss also observed that men are more likely to engage in sex for physical or goal-related reasons, while women have sex to express or because they feel love more often than do men. That my students were uncomfortable with these differences speaks to a persistent unwillingness to acknowledge ambiguity.

The varying understandings of, and reasons for, sexual interaction that are implicated in ambiguity bring us to reconsider the oft-repeated feminist mantra (itself a deposit of power decontextualized from its origin in, but nonetheless continuing to draw on, Brownmiller 1975): rape is about power, not about sex. As Cahill (2001, 27) argues, it matters that "the rapist is sexually aroused ... he experiences an erection and, frequently, orgasm. That these sexual experiences may be the result of the violence and the asymmetric power relations inherent in the assault makes them no less sexual in nature." Discomfiting though this proposition may be, thinking about sexual assault being about sex as well as power for the perpetrator allows us to inquire how individuals come to engage in assaultive acts. Here too we can look to extant theoretical and empirical scholarly works addressing a variety of factors underlying sexual assault, including: the pressures of masculinity that both encourage men to enact sexual aggression (Boyle 2015; Godenzi, Schwartz, and Dekeseredy 2001) and invisibilize their experiences of sexual victimization (Weiss 2010); blatant and subtle disrespect for women that intersects with other forms of discrimination, especially racism in the campus context (Cabrera 2014); and the preferential position of male heterosexual experience and pleasure in the definition of sex (Smart 1989). These insights highlight the narrow, interpersonal scope of consent, providing support for a broader approach to anti-violence education that fosters an empathetic understanding of the interests, constraints, scripts, identities, and experience that each party brings to a sexual interaction.

TOWARDS LEAVING BEHIND STAGNATING DEPOSITS: RECOMMENDATIONS FOR FUTURE RESEARCH, POLICY, AND PROGRAMMING

While the concept of rape culture has rallied contemporary feminist efforts against sexual violence, it retains a construction of women's (hetero)sexual lives as passive and dangerous, shaping understandings and practices that in turn have contributed to university policies and programming. Similarly, consent, a dichotomous legal term, is woefully inadequate in a cultural, social, and economic context where soft coercion is pervasive. The ways we labour, consume, and behave are so significantly impacted by structures (e.g., capitalism), ideologies (e.g., neoliberalism), roles (e.g., gender), and expectations (e.g., politeness) that scholars from many disciplines have argued that our choices are never free, but also not wholly determined by our circumstances (e.g., Craig 2006; Westcott, Baird, and Cooper 2006; Weedon 1987). To this end, further research about why students of all genders and sexual orientations engage in sex and how they communicate with, respect, and understand their partners (or not) would enable a more nuanced understanding of sexual interactions occurring in mutually reinforcing contexts of unequal power relations (e.g., women's political underrepresentation, intersecting forms of discrimination, the gendered wage gap and division of labour), which could in turn inform the design of needs-based education.

According to Cohen (1985), stories and systems of thought leave behind particular strategies, programs, or actions; at the same time, multiple systems of thought can shape programming or policies within a shared institutional infrastructure. Indeed, provincial and university policies already mandate preventive education. As this chapter has argued, however, preventive efforts have more heavily drawn on theories centring danger than those emphasizing pleasure or ambiguity. In this regard, shifting the focus toward alternatives presented in contemporary critical studies and drawing from the insights of "pro-sex" feminist scholars could unsettle the stubborn deposits of dichotomous thinking in which consent and rape culture are mired. Approaching sex as neither pure joy nor mere hardship or victimization, but rather as a human activity about which a vast expanse of meanings are made, could de-emphasize its cultural salience and help dispel the notion that a woman's sexual integrity is her most valuable possession. As evinced in the prevalence of feminist critiques from various perspectives, challenging entrenched norms about gender and sex is a significant undertaking, and given the above-noted shortcomings in regard to men's participation in and effectiveness of anti-sexual violence programming, these educational endeavours would have to be mandatory and long-term. Additionally emphasizing mutual pleasure, Wodda and Panfil (2017, 7; see also Klaw et al. 2005) advocate for the expansion of sex positivity into a "more positive relationship with sex" that considers not only pleasure but also "age, race, ability, sexual orientation, and culture" – in other words, intersectionality (Crenshaw 1989). And Burnet et al. (2009) propose resistance training – an approach that Radtke et al. (this volume) found to be an effective way for women not only to defend themselves but also to counter gendered ascriptions of weakness. In short, an approach that grounds sex in intersecting power relations, that unreservedly acknowledges diverse desires and motivations, and that challenges gendered, sexual scripts through discursive and concrete strategies could precipitate sex that is more than merely consensual, or safe(r), but enjoyable.

REFERENCES

Andrew, Caroline, Veronika Bernard, Kelly Gordon, Shari Graydon, Karen Green, Pam Hrick, and Holly Johnson. 2015. "Report of the Task Force on Respect and Equality: Ending Sexual Violence at the University of Ottawa." https://www.uottawa.ca/president/sites/www.uottawa. ca.president/files/report-of-the-task-force-on-respect-and-equality.pdf.

Beres, Melanie Ann. 2014. "Rethinking the Concept of Consent for Anti-Sexual Violence Activism and Education." *Feminism and Psychology* 24 (3): 373–89.

Boyle, Kaitlin M. 2015. "Social Psychological Processes that Facilitate Sexual Assault within the Fraternity Party Subculture." *Sociology Compass* 9 (5): 386–99.

Brownmiller, Susan. 1975. *Against Our Will: Men, Women, and Rape.* New York: Simon and Schuster.

Buchwald, Emilie. 1993. "Raising Girls for the 21st Century." In *Transforming a Rape Culture*, edited by M. Roth, Pamela Fletcher, and Emilie Buchwald, 179–200. Minneapolis, MN: Milkweed Editions.

Buchwald, Emilie, Pamela R. Fletcher, and Martha Roth, eds. 1993. *Transforming a Rape Culture.* Minneapolis, MN: Milkweed Editions.

Burnett, Ann, Jody L. Mattern, Liliana L. Herakova, David H. Kahl Jr, Cloy Tobola, and Susan E. Bornsen. 2009. "Communicating/Muting Date Rape: A Co-Cultural Theoretical Analysis of Communication Factors Related to Rape Culture on a College Campus." *Journal of Applied Communication Research* 37 (4): 465–85.

Cabrera, Nolan León. 2014. "Exposing Whiteness in Higher Education: White Male College Students Minimizing Racism, Claiming Victimization, and Recreating White Supremacy." *Race, Ethnicity and Education* 17 (1): 30–55.

Cahill, Ann J. 2001. *Rethinking Rape.* Ithaca, NY: Cornell University Press.

Carrigan, Tim, Bob Connell, and John Lee. 1985. "Toward a New Sociology of Masculinity." *Theory and Society* 14 (5): 551–604.

Cohen, Stanley. 1985. *Visions of Social Control: Crime, Punishment, and Classification.* New York: Polity Press.

Craig, Elaine. 2016. "The Inhospitable Court." *University of Toronto Law Journal* 66 (2): 197–243.

Craig, Maxine Leeds. 2006. "Race, Beauty, and the Tangled Knot of a Guilty Pleasure." *Feminist Theory* 7 (2): 159–77.

Crenshaw, Kimberlé. 1989. "Demarginalizing the Intersection of Race and Sex: A Black Feminist Critique of Antidiscrimination Doctrine, Feminist Theory and Antiracist Politics." *University of Chicago Legal Forum*: 139–67.

Daigle, Leah E. 2016. *Victimology*. Edited by Lisa R. Muftić. Los Angeles, CA: SAGE.

Davis, Angela Y. 1981. *Women, Race and Class*. New York: Vintage Books.

Dimen, Muriel. 1992. "Politically Correct? Politically Incorrect?" In *Pleasure and Danger: Exploring Female Sexuality*, edited by Carol S. Vance, 138–48. Boston: Routledge and Kegan Paul.

Ellis, Carolyn. 2008. "Autoethnography." In *The Sage Encyclopedia of Qualitative Research Methods*, edited by Lisa M. Given, 49–51. Thousand Oaks, CA: Sage Publications.

Fellows, Mary Louise, and Sherene Razack. 1997. "The Race to Innocence: Confronting Hierarchical Relations among Women." *Journal of Gender, Race, and Justice* 1: 335–52.

Foucault, Michel. 1980. *Power/Knowledge*. New York: Vintage Books.

Godenzi, Alberto, Martin Schwartz, and Walter Dekeseredy. 2001. "Toward a Gendered Social Bond/Male Peer Support Theory of University Woman Abuse." *Critical Criminology* 10 (1): 1–16.

Gotell, Lise. 2015. "Rethinking Affirmative Consent in Canadian Sexual Assault Law: Neoliberal Sexual Subjects and Risky Women." *Akron Law Review* 41 (4): 865–98.

Halley, Janet E. 2006. *Split Decisions: How and Why to Take a Break from Feminism*. Princeton, NJ: Princeton University Press.

– 2016. "The Move to Affirmative Consent." *Signs: Journal of Women in Culture and Society* 42 (1): 257–79.

Johnson, Maisha Z. 2016. "4 Things We're Not Saying When We Say 'Rape Culture.'" *Everyday Feminism*. https://everydayfeminism.com/2016/07/when-we-say-rape-culture/.

Jozkowski, Kristen N., Zoë D. Peterson, Stephanie A. Sanders, Barbara Dennis, and Michael Reece. 2013. "Gender Differences in Heterosexual College Students' Conceptualizations and Indicators of Sexual Consent: Implications for Contemporary Sexual Assault Prevention Education." *Journal of Sex Research* 51 (8): 1–13.

Kelly, Liz. 1987. "The Continuum of Sexual Violence." In *Women, Violence and Social Control*, edited by Mary Maynard and Jalna Hanmer, 46–60. London, UK: MacMillan Press.

Klaw, Elena L., Kimberly A. Lonsway, Dianne R. Berg, Craig R. Waldo, Chevon Kothari, Christopher J. Mazurek, and Kurt E. Hegeman. 2005. "Challenging Rape Culture: Awareness, Emotion and Action through Campus Acquaintance Rape Education." *Women and Therapy* 28 (2): 47–63.

Lanford, Anna. 2016. "Sex Education, Rape Culture, and Sexual Assault: The Vicious Cycle." *Furman Humanities Review* 27 (1): 61–78.

MacKinnon, Catharine A. 1982. "Feminism, Marxism, Method, and the State: An Agenda for Theory." *Signs: Journal of Women in Culture and Society* 7 (3): 515–44.

Meston, Cindy, and David Buss. 2007. "Why Humans Have Sex." *Archives of Sexual Behavior* 36 (4): 477–507.

Rentschler, Carrie A. 2014. "Rape Culture and the Feminist Politics of Social Media." *Girlhood Studies* 7 (1): 65–82.

Ridgway, Shannon. 2014. "25 Everyday Examples of Rape Culture." *Everyday Feminism*. https://everydayfeminism.com/2014/03/examples-of-rape-culture/.

Rubin, Gayle. 1992. "Thinking Sex: Notes for a Radical Theory of the Politics of Sexuality." In *Pleasure and Danger: Exploring Female Sexuality,* edited by Carole S. Vance, 267–319. Boston: Routledge and Kegan Paul.

Sanday, Peggy Reeves. 1981. "The Socio-Cultural Context of Rape: A Cross-Cultural Study." *Journal of Social Issues* 37 (4): 5–27.

Simon, William, and John Gagnon. 1986. "Sexual Scripts: Permanence and Change." *Archives of Sexual Behavior* 15 (2): 97–120.

Smart, Carol. 1989. *Feminism and the Power of Law.* London and New York: Routledge.

Thomas, Emily J., Monika Stelzl, and Michelle N. Lafrance. 2017. "Faking to Finish: Women's Accounts of Feigning Sexual Pleasure to End Unwanted Sex." *Sexualities* 20 (3): 281–301.

Valverde, Mariana. 1989. "Beyond Gender Dangers and Private Pleasures: Theory and Ethics in the Sex Debates." *Feminist Studies* 15 (2): 237–54.

Vance, Carole S. 1992. "Pleasure and Danger: Toward a Politics of Sexuality." In *Pleasure and Danger: Exploring Female Sexuality*, edited by Carole S. Vance, 1–27. Boston: Routledge and Kegan Paul.

– 1993. "More Danger, More Pleasure: A Decade After the Barnard Sexuality Conference." *New York Law School Law Review* 38: 289–318.

Weedon, Chris. 1987. *Feminist Practice and Poststructuralist Theory.* Oxford, UK, and New York: Basil Blackwell.

Weiss, Karen G. 2010. "Male Sexual Victimization: Examining Men's Experiences of Rape and Sexual Assault." *Men and Masculinities* 12(3): 275–98.

Westcott, Mark, Marian Baird, and Rae Cooper. 2006. "Re-Working Work: Dependency and Choice in the Employment Relationship." *Labour and Industry: A Journal of the Social and Economic Relations of Work* 17 (1): 5–17.

Wodda, Aimee, and Vanessa R. Panfil. 2017. "Insert Sexy Title Here: Moving Toward a Sex-Positive Criminology." *Feminist Criminology* 13(5): 583–608.

Worthen, Meredith G.F., and Samantha A. Wallace. 2017. "Intersectionality and Perceptions about Sexual Assault Education and Reporting on College Campuses." *Family Relations* 66 (1): 180–96.

13

The Silos of Sexual Violence

Understanding the Limits and Barriers to Survivor-Centrism on University Campuses

Marcus A. Sibley and Dawn Moore

INTRODUCTION

Much of the attention to campus-based sexual violence focuses on reporting. While reporting may be the "gold standard" of excellence in sexual assault policy reform from the point of view of governing bodies, our research shows that sexual assault survivors are not particularly interested in reporting the violence they experience to an established "authority" (see also Fisher et al. 2003; Walsh et al. 2010). Instead, support, prevention, and unencumbered access to services and accommodations are survivors' top priorities. These priorities are identified by survivors who experienced sexual violence and its aftermath on campus.

Our research reveals several key findings. First, survivors' experiences are shaped by policies and practices within the context of persisting rape myths that continue to govern the way universities address sexual violence (Levenson and D'Amora 2007; Page 2010). Second, we explore how rape myths create institutionalized barriers to reporting and disclosing sexual violence to university administration and police. Third, we suggest that the various campus offices responsible for offering services to survivors (health centres, equity and safety offices, registrars, campus residences, etc.) operate in "institutional silos," often working under the assumption that support for survivors is readily available and easily accessible. On the basis of this assumption, faculty members and administrators will often defer to other units on campus – a key limitation to "survivor-centrism" when faced with a student disclosing sexual assault. We conclude with some recommendations for addressing sexual violence, including reorienting attention from the importance of disclosure, reporting, and evidence collection, and instead focusing on strategies that provide meaningful support to students regardless of whether or not they choose to make a formal report.

The context in which our research was conducted matters a great deal. All of our fieldwork was conducted over a four-month period – a length of time wholly inadequate given our commitment to feminist method and the fact that we were working in a site of great precarity. That our appeals to the Ontario Ministry of Community Safety and Correctional Services (OMCSCS) for adequate time to do the research properly were dismissed we see as an indication that the ministry was more interested in the research "seeming to be done" rather than "being done well." Given that our final report was never published by the ministry, it would appear that, at least at the level of government and in our case, high-quality research into this area was trumped by political interests. The broader context illuminates this point. The spring of 2015 became what we can now see as the backdrop, at least on a national scale, for the #MeToo movement and its offshoots. The politics of *R. v. Ghomeshi* were very palpable. At the same time, universities and colleges had been thrown into varying degrees of scramble as Bill 132 (mandating stand-alone sexual violence polices at all provincially funded colleges and universities) was working its way through the legislature with scant time for post-secondary institutions to meet the legislated requirements of creating "community-informed" policies. This pressure manifested in different ways on different campuses but was certainly present, more or less menacingly, throughout the research. Bill 132 mandates that these new stand-alone sexual violence policies clearly outline how students can report sexual violence, the elements of the investigation process, complainant options, and support services available for those who choose to disclose to designated university officials. Bill 132 also mandated prevention and education as part of these new policies, but those issues, as we discuss below, were generally treated as afterthoughts.[1]

Here we focus on the experiences of the eighteen survivors interviewed. We do not claim that this is a representative sample. Time constraints imposed by the ministry hampered recruitment and made it impossible to establish the relationships mandated by the Truth and

Reconciliation Commission to gather the experiences of First Nations, Inuit, and Métis students. Outside this population, active research coinciding with the end of term made recruitment of the general student population difficult. This research should therefore be taken as a starting point and a justification for a far more expansive study. Despite these limitations, we maintain that this work gives meaningful voice to some of those routinely silenced by the complex and sometimes wavering institutional efforts of universities, with an eye to underscoring the importance of these voices which are all too often absent from both policy and research debates on sexual violence.

SEXUAL VIOLENCE IN THE UNIVERSITY CONTEXT

Rape Myths, Perceptions, and Stigma

The university, as an institution, poses a barrier to support for survivors. Dominant narratives and rape myths pervade institutional logics and, consequently, inform the ways that survivors navigate campus life in the wake of an assault (Sabina and Ho 2014; Sable et al. 2006). A substantial barrier is the "stranger danger" myth. Survivors explained that their own understandings of sexual assault emerged from the "unknown assailant" trope that pre-empts the possibility that sexual violence occurs within intimate relationships.

Emma, for example, did not necessarily realize that what she had experienced was sexual violence. Emma met her assailant during orientation week. The two had been dating for a month before Emma ended the relationship, often questioning and doubting some nonconsensual nature of their sexual encounters: "I let it happen for almost a month and then realized, okay, I'm not happy and then I left. It ended up being what made me leave. But it took a while to get around to it. So, I thought, how could it have been an assault because it wasn't as if someone was in a dark alley. It was someone I knew and someone I had chosen to be with... The [stranger assaults] are the only thing we're taught about."

Zayanya was in her first long-term relationship. Like Emma, she came to understand that she had not been consenting to parts of her sexual relationship. Zayanya experienced sexual abuse within the context of an intimate partner relationship throughout her first year of university. Her partner was older and finishing his degree while she was just starting. Zayanya felt that her lack of experience contributed to her inability to leave her relationship, citing the "very bad power dynamic" that caused her to stay. Though she blames herself for not leaving the relationship earlier and not reaching out for help, she explained that she did not disclose the violence because she was very confused about what she had experienced. Zayanya realized that something was wrong and that many aspects of her relationship were non-consensual, but she feared that those who were ostensibly there to listen to her disclosure, namely authority figures in her life, would tell her that sexual violence could not genuinely occur within the context of her intimate relationship.

Survivors of sexual violence do not always conform to normative configurations of ideal victimhood (Gotell 2002; Randall 2004), and even ideal victims, particularly of sexual violence, are almost always met with disdain and contempt. We have to look no further than the rape trial – as a legal and historical artefact – to illustrate that the focus of legal adjudication focuses largely on the credibility and unwavering cooperation of sexual assault complainants (Larcombe 2002; Randall 2010; Sheehy 2002).

Alex, a student-survivor who runs a consent-training initiative on her campus, described conversations with campus police as filled with understandings of sexual violence fuelled by ongoing rape myths and persistent victim-blaming. Through her own anti-sexual violence research, Alex describes how campus police are largely interested in whether complainants were involved in substance use and what they were wearing at the time of the assault. She notes that perception of "risky" behaviours, including drinking or drug use, are often key factors in whether campus police/security will launch an investigation, liaise with local police, or completely dismiss the matter as unfounded.

Our participants overwhelmingly point us to heightened safety campaigns during the first few weeks of academic orientation, also referred to as "frosh week," which stress the need for risk management and self-responsibilization. Focus group participants cited that while they thought much of the information provided at frosh week was useful, it placed far too much emphasis on women avoiding "risky" situations and employed an individualized characterization of risk management – pertaining to drinking, walking alone at night, and so on – rather than education on sexual consent and how to be clear about the boundaries of consent in the context of intimate relationships.

The information and spatial infrastructure of universities perpetuate these rape myths, complicating definitions or perceptions of what sexual violence looks like from perspective of students, especially those in their first year. Students are told from their initial days on campus to be aware of the blue emergency lights attached to panic buttons on campus if walking alone at night. Residence coordinators offer around-the-clock monitoring of the front entrances, and public transit offers a "night rider" service where people can request to be dropped off at a safe location in between stops if necessary.

Having been sexually assaulted right before the start of her first academic term of university, Ohary describes the information provided at orientation week as having a high reliance on victim-blaming and risk-management. Ohary suggests that any references made to sexual violence prevention were almost exclusively aimed towards female alcohol consumption (Moore and Valverde 2000; Profitt and Ross 2017). Every time Ohary attends a party or a social gathering she tends to be hyper-aware of her alcohol intake and that of her friends in order to minimize the risk of sexual assault. She knows that if she were to get involved in a situation, her alcohol consumption would be scrutinized and thus feels the need to take on a particular risk-management role in order to prevent victim-blaming and ensure self-responsibilization.

Students are made hyper-aware of the kinds of stranger dangers they might face. Alcohol and drug use are policed in ways that heighten a sense of risk that is externalized onto the "unknowns" of university life. The randomness of sexual violence is touted in scripts of sexual violence prevention, presented during orientation week presentations by upper-level students, who, according to many we interviewed, did not always take sexual violence training seriously. Students were told that use of the "buddy system" is an effective way of preventing dangerous situations and can help de-escalate sexual aggression. These strategies, alongside victim-blaming, also promote the fiction that sexual assault is a crime between strangers. Students reported feeling completely unprepared for and uneducated about the realities of intimate partner sexual violence or the undesired outcomes they may encounter in the wake of sexual violence and their own interpersonal relationships, whether it be with current or former partners, acquaintances, or even those in positions of authority on campus (e.g. professors, administrators, counsellors, etc.). From the very outset, the myths around sexual violence form a significant barrier to understanding and internalizing sexual violence as a distinct problem that almost always occurs outside of tropes of the lurking rapist.

Accessing On-Campus Services

Since the university generally speaks of sexual violence through tropes of popular rape myths, students often infer that the university is only interested in disclosures of sexual violence that fit into those normative scripts of victimhood and violence. Because of this, survivors feel as though university employees will not be receptive to their stories and look elsewhere for disclosures. Disclosures to trusted friends and family were often made before any formal disclosures to institutions were made (i.e., university, police, health care provider).

Ashley, however, describes the tension of not knowing whom she should disclose to and the accompanying anxiety and fear. She decided to disclose to a close friend who was mutual friends with her assailant: "I told my friend and she got really mad at me. She said that he was a really nice guy and could never have done anything like that."

Ashley decided months later that she could trust her roommate, who recommended she seek counselling at a women's centre in a suburb outside the city. When asked why she decided against talking to police or campus services, Ashley stated: "I got such a poor response from my friend, where she was saying it was my fault ... and I wasn't in the right set of mind, I just wasn't thinking. It basically took me until I told my roommate to realize what had actually happened, that I thought it was too late and I panicked."

Ashley deferred to off-campus help because she was not very close with her professors and did not feel comfortable disclosing to them. She also did not want to access health services on campus for fear that people would find out about her assault. The conspicuousness of having to wait in the lobby of health services was a sufficient deterrent to seeking medical assistance.

Lilly, Megan, and Cathleen reached out to crisis helplines for counselling and assistance in trying to make sense of what had happened to them. The information leading them to crisis hotlines was readily available through quick internet searches or recommended by their peers. In contrast, the information regarding on-campus services for sexual assault survivors was not as easily accessible. Almost half of our participants indicated that following their assaults they had researched and considered the various on-campus resources but were not necessarily sure how to actually access them. For those who chose not to disclose their assaults to friends and family, not-for-profit crisis helplines were the initial starting point to get assistance on how to understand what had happened to them. Students in our focus groups also reported not knowing how the process works, what it entailed, and what kinds of benefits (if any) services could offer. This black boxing of knowledge often discouraged students from reporting in the first place. When asked what services they knew of that were available to those who have been assaulted, many respondents (both from focus groups and survivors) merely guessed at departments they thought *should* be in charge of dealing with sexual violence.

The majority of our participants displayed resourcefulness following their assault by actively researching the kinds of remedies (both legal and non-legal) that may be available to them. When asked if they were aware of sexual violence assault centres on campus, most respondents (including those in the focus groups) knew of the idea that sexual assault support was offered *somewhere* on campus, though it was not explicitly clear who ran the organization and whether they could trust the system.

Ashley reiterated that the system is overwhelming for first-year students. Having moved away from home for the first time, she described that the stressors of moving to a new city, meeting new people, and dealing with an assault contributes to a sense of overwhelming sensorial experience that is hard to overcome: "It was my first time being away from home. I was just too nervous to do stuff by myself and it was my first time at university ... Now looking at the services, they are great, now I'd use them, and I'd tell other people to go ahead and use them because I feel kind of stupid that I didn't, but I was just so out of it." Now that Ashley is more comfortable with the university, her peer groups, and her living circumstances, she said that she would be more willing to approach services offered by the university to deal with her trauma.

Survivors who attempted to access on-campus health and counselling services cited long wait times, deterring them from returning after their initial appointments. Violet was sexually assaulted by another student whom she had met during orientation week. Having been asked to provide details of the assault to her health care practitioner, Violet was asked questions that made her feel as though she was at fault for the assault, and despite her suicidal ideation, had to wait over two weeks for her next appointment:

When I went to counselling, this was in my first year, I had to go to a desk and fill out questions about how suicidal I was and how I was feeling. And I checked off 'really bad.' And then during my intake, the woman asked me to play out the scenario, like play by play, what happened. So [I relayed what happened] … and the counselor asked, 'Are you sure your choices of hanging out with him were okay? Shouldn't you have thought about that?' Then after I had the intake appointment, I had to wait over two weeks for the next appointment, even though I checked off 'very suicidal.'

Questioning why Violet had returned to refill her anti-depressant prescription, Violet felt pressured into disclosing to the health care professional that she had been sexually assaulted and was continuing to deal with the trauma:

The doctor asked me why I needed the anti-depressants and I said it was because of the incident, I need them. And then she asked me, 'What happened? Did you know the person? Were you drunk? Where was it on campus?' And she was asking me all these questions and I wasn't responding. And she said, 'Are you sure that's what happened? This campus is pretty safe.' So, actually, my friend made an appointment with health services to talk to the Director about that. I didn't expect her to ask me these questions. I think the worst part was that she didn't believe me. She asked me whether I was drunk. And I said I wasn't.

The experience of having to disclose the trauma of sexual violence to health services while simultaneously feeling scrutinized and blamed for one's assault shows the ways in which the barriers to disclosure manifest in their various forms across the university campus. The exposure of disclosing one's lived realities, a concept we develop in the following section, is the result of entrusting institutions to be able to understand and assist in dealing with trauma. Such a project, as Lauren Berlant (2011) suggests, is cruelly optimistic, in that the fantasy of having one's trauma be dealt with in a way that is compassionate, empathetic, and dignified is almost always never delivered.

Choosing Formal Mechanisms

One of the most prominent barriers to reporting sexual violence is the reporting architecture itself. The three university campuses on which we conducted field work, along with other universities whose policies we examined as part of our broader desk study, did not have any formal reporting mechanisms in place to allow survivors to come forward with their experience. Survivors told us that they engaged in substantial research following their assaults in order to weigh the best course of action that would have the most impact on their needs. As noted above, many survivors sought counselling through friends and family, while many also turned to internet searches to vet organizations to which they felt most comfortable disclosing.

Survivors often adopt informal mechanisms of coping with sexual violence and avoiding their assailants on campus. Avoiding certain common areas where specific assailants were known to hang out, skipping classes in which their abusers were enrolled, and distancing themselves from mutual friends are quite common strategies for dealing with the ongoing trauma of sexual violence.

In many cases, disclosures about sexual violence were first made to friends and then to non-profit organizations in the city. Lilly, for example, contacted Planned Parenthood immediately after her assault. Confused about how to make sense of what happened, the representative from Planned Parenthood explained to her, in quite clear terms, that based on Lilly's account she was sexually assaulted.

> Right after it happened I started crying, and I didn't understand why I was crying. I was just trying so much for it to be okay. I didn't talk to my parents. The first person I talked to was [a person] from Planned Parenthood … I talked to her about it and I'm like, 'I don't understand how I'm feeling. I feel like something's wrong; like I did something wrong.' There was a lot of me putting the blame on myself. She asked, 'Did you say no,' 'Did you do make it clear?' She was trying to walk me through my experience. At the time I couldn't understand why I was feeling panicky about it and why I started breathing heavily, but she told me that it sounds like you've been sexually assaulted.

Like the survivors who opt to turn to crisis hotlines and women's centres, Lilly trusted that her disclosure to Planned Parenthood was a logical choice because she had already made connections with the staff through other grassroots organizing and community-based events. The person she spoke with at Planned Parenthood was a trustworthy and reliable point of contact to ensure that her anonymity was kept, and also to provide initial guidance as to how she could navigate the criminal justice system if she chose to do so.

For Lilly, "the thought of going to police terrified me because there is a lot of emotional stress involved with that because you have to recount your story over and over and over and over again." Her perception of the criminal process was already influenced by ongoing media representation of sexual violence. Having heard horror stories of survivors being ignored and discredited by police, blamed by their friends and family, and having to endure their trauma over again, Lilly strategically chose to avoid criminal justice involvement. Similar to Lilly's experience, Emma could not bear to think of reporting to the police or anyone at the university after her assault. After disclosing her experience to a friend, she experienced victim-blaming, shaming, and betrayal.

Not wanting to discuss the assault with anyone, it took Emma a year before she told anyone else what had happened to her. It was not uncommon for some survivors to receive some form of pushback or denial from those closest to them, including friends, family, and health care professionals. Citing the Jian Ghomeshi case as an example of how survivors of sexual violence are scrutinized in the public realm, Emma felt it was best to keep her experiences to herself in order to consider the benefits and harms of officially reporting. This experience is remarkably consistent throughout most interviews. Not only are survivors unsure of where to turn first, they are also suspicious of a system that continues to silence their experiences and question their motives. When asked about coming out as a survivor on campus, Lilly stated that she has considered it and would never do it. She told us, "I don't want to be perceived as damaged or fragile, or anything less than a human being. I just don't want to give anyone my secret." Her secret is one for her to keep, not to be mishandled by the bureaucracies of the university. Lilly stated that she has not come out on campus because she is fearful of being perceived as something other than human. She knows, from experience, that her voice will be silenced, and she is afraid of having her dignity and reputation dragged through the mud by "meninists" who make it their objective to delegitimize the experiences of sexual assault survivors and often harass them. She states that there is no indication on the part of the university that they are taking measures to prevent the re-traumatization of victims, particularly with those who cannot or will not follow expected scripts related to survivorship. Not all survivors held the same degree of cynicism as Lilly, but all were aware of the institutional mechanisms that were already in place that would provide barriers to any form of healing, redemption, or "justice" that survivors may seek.

Exposing Oneself through Disclosure: Institutional Silos and the Trauma of Sexual Violence

In this section, we offer insight into what happens when students decide to disclose and report, either to university staff and administration, or to their local police service. The survivor accounts we put forward are often couched in a deep skepticism towards the way universities and the criminal justice system can provide any kind of recourse. Our participants were almost always hesitant to bring their disclosures forward to those in positions of authority, mainly due to their cognizance of the ways in which complainants of sexual violence are treated in the media, by police, and how their accounts could never live up to the expectations of what it means to be the ideal complainant.

After what she describes as hopeless and degrading attempts to report sexual violence to police, Megan focused her attention on trying to seek support through her university. As a graduate student, Megan approached the head of her department to disclose her assault and seek guidance on how she could access accommodations and increased support for her affected academic work. Megan had hoped for guidance on how she could access accommodations, but the department head simply stated that they were sympathetic to her situation and never offered her any additional support or accommodations to assist in the completion of her studies. Though Megan was open about what had happened to her, professors were quite unaccommodating. She felt as though the confrontational style of questions by professors during class presentations was like reliving her police interviews, and one professor noted that her academic performance was suffering. Rather than developing strategies on how to best address her trauma in relation to her work, the professor simply stated, "Perhaps it's best if you drop the class." Megan recounts the times she heard office administrators discussing her assault in front of other people, noting that she was not afforded the respect and confidentiality that would be given if the topic was a private academic matter, such as a student's grades, for example.

After going to the dean of her faculty about this treatment, Megan describes the complete disinterest on the part of faculty members to provide any form of alternative coursework evaluations or accommodations, let alone any meaningful support. She concluded, "the solution is to push the student out of academia." This experience represents a failure at all levels. Though some of our respondents suggest that there were some professors who would help and keep their stories confidential, most survivors oriented themselves around the feeling that faculty members could not even be approached – for fear of exposing their stories or trauma – let alone trusted to provide the necessary accommodations. In our experience, many university faculty and administrators do not see it as their role to address sexual violence.

Zayanya expresses similar frustrations with her experience in seeking help from on-campus counsellors and administrators:

> My counsellor was really helpful in working with the registrar's office. But my department was meaner. It was a different [academic member of staff in charge] at the time. But, I went to them saying, "I'm not going to be able to fulfill this academic requirement and I know this because I'm really, really struggling. And he said, 'Well, you're going to have to figure this out because there's nothing I can do for you.' And then when I went back a few weeks later, he said, '-------, you should have come to see me before, because now your degree is all messed up.' And I said, well, I tried, but you didn't want to help me, so what could I do. And I was forced to take a year off because of the academic things that were going on in my department, not so much the registrar's office.

She described being bounced around between the registrar's office, various professors, and the undergraduate chair of her department, and was left having to advocate on her own behalf for academic support.

Like Megan and Zayanya, Maddie's attempts to access academic accommodation was extremely difficult and fraught with reliving the trauma of sexual violence. Knowing that she would have to disclose her rape to her professor, Maddie was reluctant to share too many details about the assault. She was worried that her professors would not be accommodating as her story might come across as too "vague" and that she "wouldn't sound convincing":

> [crying] For me what was really difficult was that I had to look at this professor and he knew. It would have been better if there was a middleman to do that for you so that professor didn't

know specifically what happened to me. I felt that afterwards he kind of realized that his response wasn't ideal emotionally. And he kept trying to check in, but he was still very awkward and fumbly about the whole thing. Or [in class], he would check in when there were other people in the room. And he wouldn't say anything specifically, but he would say, 'Are you okay?' But then all my classmates [would notice] and try to figure out what happened. If there was a middleman where I didn't have to tell him what happened [that would have made it easier].

Pointing to a lack of clarity about where she could go for support, disclosures to professors are often required in order to receive any consideration for academic accommodation, the guarantee of which is virtually impossible and dependent on the willingness of the professor to accommodate. For professors willing to help, survivors tell us that many professors lack the necessary knowledge of the kinds of services offered to students and how students may access these.

Forrest and Senn (2017) suggest that many university employees think the task is up to student affairs or other related departments to offer students the necessary tools to deal with the effects of the trauma. At each of these universities, there was no singularly identifiable point-person or dedicated office that could provide accurate information on academic accommodations, university policies, or prepare students for the possibility of criminal justice involvement. Having a designated person who could help coordinate academic accommodations, health counselling treatment, and any other support survivors need would have helped alleviate much of the stress of having to navigate the system alone. It also points to the fact that these decentralized academic and institutional units are in no way capable of coordinating with each other on how best to support the student in all aspects of their social and academic life.

Ashley stated that putting a face to the services provided to students would be an excellent way of ensuring that survivors know which university services are available, who they can turn to, and who they can trust to listen to them and advocate on their behalf. Consideration must also be given to those who wish to do this without drawing attention to themselves from other university faculty, staff, colleagues, or friends. Ashley recommends that these services be dedicated and easily identifiable to survivors but not so easily surveyed by the rest of the campus population, including their abusers, as to draw attention or stigma to the site. She herself did not want to access health services on campus because she feared that people would find out about her assault.

The disclosure of sexual assault is an exposure of the self to others that may otherwise go untold. This exposure places students in a precarious and vulnerable position in which they must trust that their trauma will be dealt with care and in meaningful ways. The siloing effect of these departments within the university creates the semblance of a disjointed and disconnected reporting architecture.

CONCLUSION

For universities to effectively address sexual violence, they must actively adapt to the changing needs of survivors. While the universities all subscribe to survivor-centred approaches, we also acknowledge that this approach limits the kinds of interventions that are possible. Though some academic and non-academic units on campus can provide meaningful support to survivors, they lack coordination with each other. As evidenced by the stories above, survivors are often left to navigate support services on their own. This is in large part because of a lack of communication among various departments on campus, but also a by-product of survivor-centred models of support. Having survivors control their own experiences is an important part of dealing with sexual violence, but often creates a sense of uneasiness about how to proceed. Survivors may choose to withdraw their complaints, or they may ask professors or administrators to keep their disclosures confidential. These are significant elements of a survivor-centred approach, but also contribute to the further isolation and siloing of survivors' experiences within the labyrinth of the university architecture.

We've learned that although survivor-centred approaches can sometimes exacerbate the conditions which contribute to institutional silos, survivors are fully capable of identifying the resources that are available to them. They are aware that outing themselves as survivors in our contemporary political climate can be a risky thing to do. Some are willing to traverse this landscape while others prefer to navigate quietly. Supporting both of these trajectories is equally important. Perception and visibility are profoundly impactful issues.

Recommendations

(1) Survivors would benefit from the implementation of easily identifiable sexual assault support coordinators on post-secondary campuses.

These coordinators should have a very broad purview and direct access to all related departments within the university (registrar, housing, health and counselling, academic departments). Instead of serving a mandate set by the university, the mandate of these coordinators should reflect the localized needs of students on that particular campus as reflected through thorough research with survivors and other students. One might imagine this role as a sort of "sexual assault midwife" who offers holistic care to survivors and has the resources and authoritative capacity to both support and advocate for the student.

(2) Universities must abandon reporting as their top priority in reforming responses to sexual violence. In its stead, prevention, sex positive, consent-driven education throughout the university career and comprehensive supports and infrastructures for survivors should be the priorities.

(3) Sexual assault coordinators (or sexual assault midwives) should have a thorough understanding of the implications of every form of disclosure at their particular institution. Institutional cultures vary and students need to rely on someone who understands their own campus in order to help them make decisions about disclosure, under what circumstances and to whom.

(4) Independent oversight of sexual violence policies and a degree of independence for sexual assault coordinators (similar to an ombudsperson position) is vital to ensure ongoing quality of services provided to students and also to reveal when gaps or problems in service provisions appear. This body should be made up of representatives from all facets of the university community and report, at least annually, to the Board of Governors. Legislative changes should be made to university governance structures to place the onus on governing boards to detail how they have responded to oversight reports and what steps the university is taking to actively address concerns that are raised in these reports.

ACKNOWLEDGMENTS

We would like to thank our research team, Doris Buss, Diana Majury, George Rigakos, and Rashmee Singh, as well as our research assistants Aysegul Ergul, Kanatase Horn, Leanna Ireland, David Meinen, and

Elise Wohlbold. This research was funded by a grant from the Ontario Ministry of Community Safety and Correctional Services.

NOTE

1 This chapter emerges out of a larger project funded by the Ontario Ministry of Community Safety and Correctional Services (OMCSCS). This is the first problem. Our research team of five Principal Investigators (PIs) responded to OMCSCS's 2015 call for proposals for research on campus sexual violence. We assumed, wrongly as it turned out, that the ministry's research funding would feed into the implementation of Bill 132, legislation that came jointly from the Ministries of Education and Labour. We were awarded the grant swiftly and the research was announced provincially via a press conference held at the lead PI's university. At that event, Moore, the PI, asked the minister to explain the connection between this grant and the MEL's bill, wanting to ensure that the research would be seen by both ministries and at least considered by the lawmakers moving swiftly to enact and enforce Bill 132. The minister responded that he was not aware of Bill 132 but would "look into it." To our knowledge, neither ministry has published, referred to, or even read the report. Its only circulation came through the research team. The broader project funded by OMCSCS was conducted by a team of seasoned scholars in policing, gender-based violence, governance, public institutions, and feminist research. The faculty investigators were supported by a team of ten graduate students chosen collectively by the lead researchers based on their research experience. The research team produced a comprehensive overview of contemporary sexual violence literature and completed interviews at three Ontario universities with executive administrators, support staff, campus security, and local police, and survivors who had either experienced sexual violence on campus or were dealing with its aftermath during their university careers.

REFERENCES

Berlant, Lauren Gail. 2011. *Cruel Optimism*. Durham, NC: Duke University Press.

Fisher, Bonnie S., Leah E. Daigle, Francis T. Cullen, and Michael G. Turner. 2003. "Reporting Sexual Victimization to the Police and Others: Results from a National-Level Study of College Women." *Criminal Justice and Behavior* 30 (1): 6–38.

Forrest, A., and C.Y. Senn. 2017. "Theory Becomes Practice: The Bystander Initiative at the University of Windsor." In *Sexual Violence at Canadian Universities: Activism, Institutional Responses, and Strategies for Change*, edited by Elizabeth Quinlan, Andrea Quinlan, Curtis Fogel, and Gail Taylor, 175–92. Waterloo, ON: Wilfrid Laurier University Press.

Gotell, Lise. 2002. *The Ideal Victim, the Hysterical Complainant, and the Disclosure of Confidential Records: The Implications of the Charter for Sexual Assault Law*. Vol. 40 HeinOnline.

Larcombe, Wendy. 2002. "The 'Ideal' Victim v Successful Rape Complainants: Not What You Might Expect." *Feminist Legal Studies* 10 (2): 131–48.

Levenson, Jill S., and David D'Amora A. 2007. "Social Policies Designed to Prevent Sexual Violence: The Emperor's New Clothes?" *Criminal Justice Policy Review* 18 (2): 168–99.

Moore, Dawn, and Mariana Valverde. 2000. "Maidens at Risk: 'Date Rape Drugs' and the Formation of Hybrid Risk Knowledges." *Economy and Society* 29 (4): 514–31.

Page, Amy Dellinger. 2010. "True Colors: Police Officers and Rape Myth Acceptance." *Feminist Criminology* 5 (4): 315–34.

Profitt, Norma Jean, and Nancy Ross. 2017. "A Critical Analysis of the Report Student Safety in Nova Scotia: Co-Creating a Vision and Language for Safer and Socially Just Campus Communities." In *Sexual Violence at Canadian Universities: Activism, Institutional Responses, and Strategies for Change*, edited by Elizabeth Quinlan, Andrea Quinlan, Curtis Fogel, and Gail Taylor, 193–18. Waterloo, ON: Wilfrid Laurier University Press.

Randall, Melanie. 2004. "Domestic Violence and the Construction of Ideal Victims: Assaulted Women's Image Problems in Law." *Saint Louis University Public Law Review* 23: 107.

– 2010. "Sexual Assault Law, Credibility, and 'Ideal Victims': Consent, Resistance, and Victim Blaming." *Canadian Journal of Women and the Law* 22 (2): 397–433.

Sabina, Chiara, and Lavina Y. Ho. 2014. "Campus and College Victim Responses to Sexual Assault and Dating Violence: Disclosure, Service Utilization, and Service Provision." *Trauma, Violence, and Abuse* 15 (3): 201–26.

Sable, Marjorie R., Fran Danis, Denise L. Mauzy, and Sarah K. Gallagher. 2006. "Barriers to Reporting Sexual Assault for Women and Men:

Perspectives of College Students." *Journal of American College Health* 55 (3): 157–62.

Sheehy, Elizabeth. 2002. "Evidence Law and Credibility Testing of Women: A Comment on the E Case." *Queensland University of Technology Law Journal* 2: 157.

Walsh, Wendy A., Victoria L. Banyard, Mary M. Moynihan, Sally Ward, and Ellen S. Cohn. 2010. "Disclosure and Service Use on a College Campus after an Unwanted Sexual Experience." *Journal of Trauma and Dissociation* 11 (2): 134–51.

PART FOUR

Interrupt

14

Instructor-Student Sexual Misconduct

The Fraught Silences of Liminal Policy Spaces at Canadian Universities

Richard Jochelson, David Ireland, Leon Laidlaw, and Anna Tourtchaninova

INTRODUCTION

It was not the type of file we expected or hoped to see. As a senior member of a faculty union,[1] one expects to rail against the administration, fight for fair workload and wages, and pursue other noble markers of equality and justice. Nobody prepares you for the first time *that case* comes across your desk – the file that describes a colleague's sexual relationship with a student.

In this chapter, we summarize the union and university responses to the situation, and place the incident in a larger socio-legal context. We review some policies and protocols from Canadian universities and several reported tribunal and case decisions. We argue that all post-secondary institutions should develop cogent workplace and learning environment relationship policies in order to foster clarity and to create a culture of consent and boundaries in the work and learning spaces of Canada's universities.

In matters of sexual misconduct or violence on campus, criminal investigations are often obfuscated by a muddle of university-controlled systems. Sexual misconduct cases often implicate various university policies and investigatory powers and can result in discipline for the perpetrator. In the case of an instructor-perpetrator, an investigation can lead to remedies ranging from a warning through to termination. The prevalence of professor-student sexual misconduct remains hidden from view, in terms of the alleged actors, as privacy legislation protects the vast majority of information. But, once in a while, cases materialize as arbitral or human rights decisions, and, rarer still, as criminal cases. Some studies have shown that between 20–30 per cent of female students suffer sexual harassment by instructors in their university careers (Weiss and Lalonde 2001; Dzeich and Weiner 1984). Others have suggested that half of women students experience harassment by male faculty (Pyke 1996). Reporting rates are suspected to be low (ibid.). These figures suggest a context in which harassment and respectful workplace policies alone cannot manage instructor-student relationships. These relationships are inherently fraught with power dynamics, conflict, bias, and, from a university's perspective, risk.

As other chapters in this volume demonstrate, rape culture is described as a manifestation of the sexism that is deeply embedded in the social structures of Western society. When institutions and their staff adopt cultural attitudes and create policy and procedures that overtly or covertly disadvantage women, institutional sexism occurs (Andreasen 2005). Institutional sexism is embedded in the campus environment, reflected in gendered pay inequities, sexist comments from instructors, sexual harassment of employees, and administrations' attempts to cover up sexual violence (Vaccaro 2009, 2010). Because sexist environments allow rape culture to flourish, there are concerns over whether university faculty are reflecting the attitudes of the culture that surrounds them. In the tradition of reflexive analysis (Frauley 2009; Haggerty 2004; Jochelson et al. 2013), we use *that case* to exemplify how sexual misconduct allegations against an instructor can progress in a unionized environment. Before exploring the case in question, a brief review of the Canadian post-secondary policy landscape and some attendant cases will aid in understanding the context of the discussion.

POLICY AND CASE REVIEW

Canadian post-secondary institutions regulate faculty-student relationships in various ways. Universities have adopted policies to address situations falling anywhere from consensual relationships to sexual violence. Most commonly, universities rely on conflict of interest or sexual harassment and violence in the workplace policies to address faculty-student relationships. These policies vary greatly among universities, both in their specificity and applicability.

Conflict of Interest Policies

Although the power imbalance inherent in faculty-student involvement has the potential to negate consent (Sandler and Hall 1986; Hall and Sandler 1982), not all such relationships can be considered nonconsensual. Universities have developed conflict of interest policies to address situations where relationships have a detrimental effect on university governance, learning, research, or decision-making. Many make a point of assuring the reader that a conflict reflects the status of a situation, not the character of the person, and that disclosing the conflict (a requirement in virtually all of the policies) is not a punitive measure, but a protective one. The polices generally expect that instructors will declare conflicts of interest to the administration. These conflicts usually refer to financial conflict or familial conflicts and rarely refer to sexual relationships explicitly. The policies may direct that relationships of animus and closeness necessitate disclosure when a university employee is a decision-maker or assessor of merits (e.g., in class or on a committee). Consequences for failing to disclose vary depending on the collective agreement or policy. The most common consequence is recusal from decision-making, but in egregious situations suspension and termination become possibilities. Many policies do not explicitly define faculty-student involvement as a conflict, which leads to an added level of complication and ambiguity.

For example, the Athabasca University Conflict of Interest Policy (Athabasca University 2013) provides that conflict is defined as:

> A situation in which a Member or a Member's Related Party has a personal or financial interest which in the opinion of a reasonably informed and well advised person is sufficient to call into question the ability of the Member to maintain the impartiality, independence, and objectiveness that the Member is obliged to exercise in the performance of the Member's duties on behalf of the University, or call into question the ability of the Member to act in the best interests of the University, and includes a Conflict of Commitment ... All persons have personal interests, some of which are financial and some of which are non-financial. Those personal interests may be direct, or may arise from the person's

relationship with a Related Party. Such personal interests are natural and often facilitate personal and professional growth and development. However, given the obligations that Members have to the University it is inevitable that on occasion, some Members will have personal interests that may reasonably be perceived to be such as to interfere with independence, impartiality, and objectiveness that the Member is obliged to exercise in the performance of the Member's duties on behalf of the University, or with the ability of the Member to act in the best interests of the University.

As another example, the University of Prince Edward Island's Conflict of Interest in Research Policy[2] states that it is a conflict to supervise a student who is a "closely associated person" (defined as a spouse or adult interdependent partner), or dependent children, or any other family members or adult interdependent partners of individuals living in the person's household. It seems that a student romantically involved with a faculty member, but not married or living interdependently, are excluded from this policy. Similarly, Okanagan College, in its policy documents, explains that "a conflict of interest occurs when a situation arises where there is a divergence between the private interests of a College researcher and that researcher's obligations to the College, such that an impartial observer might reasonably question whether actions or decisions taken or made by the researcher relating to that situation would be influenced by consideration of the researcher's private interest. Competing interests may arise from family relationships, financial partnerships or other economic interests" (2014).[3]

The absence of faculty-student relationship prohibitions can create problems. The case of *Okanagan University College v Okanagan University College Faculty Assn*[4] involved a fine arts instructor who had consensual relationships with two students who complained of harassment. Allegations were also made about relationships with another two students who did not complain formally. After the relationships ended, each student launched a sexual harassment complaint against the instructor. Termination of the relationships created a hostile study environment for the students and led one to become depressed and withdraw from the arts program.

Arbitrator Stan Lanyon noted that sexual intimacy removes all professional boundaries between teacher and student and that there is a presumption of a breach of trust for any such involvement. Despite this, the arbitrator could not find that the difference in power vitiated consent sufficient to trigger formal university policy. The university was nonetheless justified in terminating this professor, according to Lanyon. The arbitrator upheld the instructor's termination, finding that the relationships constituted a breach of trust because the instructor initiated the relationships and was determined to keep them secret.

The path to a decision in this case had been made notably more difficult due to the absence of appropriate policies to provide guidance on such matters. The arbitrator had to found his decision in implicit contractual terms – a matter that requires considerable analytical contortions compared to the application of university policy. Importantly, Lanyon found that breach of trust was an implied condition of the collective agreement and thus his decision to uphold the termination was undergirded by an implied duty to avoid conflicts with students by virtue of engaging in sexual relationships. The violation of the duty of trust provided grounds for discipline in this case.

Whether a faculty-student relationship is consensual or not, the possibility of misusing a power imbalance is always present. The University of British Columbia acknowledges this potential in its Conflict of Interest and Conflict of Commitment Policy.[5] The policy states that a conflict arises where one's responsibility to instruct and evaluate students in a fair, unbiased, and effective manner is, or could be, compromised (2012, s.3.1.1). It goes on to state that "the inherent power imbalance that exists between a UBC Person and a student must not be used for personal benefit." Likewise, the University of Toronto's Conflict of Interest and Close Personal Relations Memo[6] suggests that a conflict of interest arises almost inevitably if staff are involved in personal and intimate relationships with a student. The University of Toronto policy goes even further to explicitly warn that such involvement exposes staff to sexual harassment complaints. At McGill University, both the Policy against Sexual Violence[7] and the Recognizing Conflicts Policy[8] have clauses addressing faculty-student relationships. The former considers the relationship between an instructor and student as a potential obstacle to consent (2016, s.4.1), and the latter explicitly lists instructor-student involvement as a conflict of interest (2015, s.A.1). Capilano University's Policy on Faculty Member-Student Conflict of Interest[9] addresses the conflict that arises from student-professor relationships by advising that alternate arrangements must be made for assessment as much as is feasible.

York University's Personal Relationships between Instructors and Students Policy[10] states that "if no appropriate alternative arrangements for evaluation can be agreed upon, the student may not enroll in the course."

Regardless of whether formal complaints are issued, universities need ways to resolve potential conflicts that can stem from real or perceived bias on behalf of students outside the relationship who believe that their learning environment has been negatively affected. For example, Aurora College's Conflict of Interest Policy[11] acknowledges that "personal relationships between staff and students or staff and staff may be perceived as creating an advantage for one of the parties" (1999, s.43).

In some instances, cases of sexual harassment and conflicts of interest are not immediately extricable from one another. The policies addressing one or the other are therefore not mutually exclusive. For example, Memorial University's Sexual Harassment Policy[12] addresses overlap by stating that the policy must be construed together with the Conflict of Interest Policy,[13] amongst others.

Sexual Behaviour: Sexual Violence and Sexual Harassment Policies

The importance of a uniform and clear definition of consent and sexual harassment is highlighted in cases where circumstances surrounding the activity could be interpreted, perhaps mistakenly, as a person giving consent. Many of the sexual behaviour policies contain definitions of consent. One particularly cogent example of such a policy is the Memorial University's Sexual Harassment and Sexual Assault policy.[14] The policy outlines the scope of consent, harassment, assault, and power. It also cross-references the conflict of interest policies and collective agreements of the university. The Sexual Harassment and Sexual Assault Policy defines *consent* as "an active, direct, voluntary, unimpaired, on-going and conscious choice and agreement, expressed by word or conduct, between and among persons to engage in sexual activity. A person can only consent for themselves. Consent cannot be given or received while under the influence of alcohol or drugs, while incapacitated, unconscious or otherwise incapable of consenting. Consent cannot be induced by abusing a position of power, trust or authority. Consent can be withdrawn at any time. In addition, silence is not consent" (2017, preamble).

It defines *sexual assault* as being concordant with Canada's criminal prohibition on sexual assault and notes that *sexual harassment* includes "conduct or comments of a sexually-oriented or gender-oriented nature based on gender expression, gender identity, sex or sexual orientation directed at a person or group of persons by another person or persons, who knows or ought reasonably to know that such conduct or comments are unwelcome or unwanted. It includes Sexual Assault and assisting in Sexual Harassment" (ibid.).

The policy also explains the role of *power differences* in the context of consent and harassment, noting that a "Power Differential may be construed against the person in power" and that "sexual solicitation by a person in a position to confer, grant or deny a benefit or advancement to another person shall not engage in sexual solicitation or make a sexual advance to that person. A person who is in a position to confer or deny a benefit or advancement to another person shall not penalize, punish or threaten reprisal against that person for the rejection of a sexual solicitation or advance" (ibid., s.3.3).

Not all university policies assert that consensual relationships between students and faculty must be avoided at all costs. The University of Northern British Columbia's Harassment and Discrimination Policy,[15] while warning that student-faculty relationships are "particularly susceptible to exploitation," does not intend to "inhibit normal social relationships" (2015, s.2.10). Rather, the policy instructs faculty to decline supervisory or evaluative roles and inform superiors about any romantic relationships with students so that appropriate arrangements can be made to have the student's work evaluated by someone else. In some cases, a student must enroll in a different section of the course. The policy urges alternative arrangements but recognizes that a student's access to education may be affected where no reasonable alternative exists, and it does not prohibit a student in all circumstances from registering in a course taught by their romantic partner.

In *Re Memorial University of Newfoundland and MUNFA (I-12-20)*,[16] a graduate student ("C"), who was originally from China and had limited understanding of English, was touched inappropriately by her supervisor, initially on the face and hands, over the course of several meetings. C was told by friends to regard this as similar to behaviour from a grandfather figure, and she did so, not realizing that this could constitute sexual harassment. Only when the touching escalated to sexual touching did she feel justified in reporting it to the Sexual

Harassment Advisor, to whom she expressed concern that if she had not acquiesced to his touching, he would have failed her out of the program. The instructor was terminated and his subsequent grievance was arbitrated. The board ultimately concluded that "the conduct of the investigation by the Investigator did not violate the Procedures or the Collective Agreement. The Board accepts the credibility of C with respect to the events that are the subject of the sexual harassment complaint. The Employer has proven the inappropriate conduct ... and has proven that the Grievor's conduct amounted to sexual harassment as defined in the Sexual Harassment Policy. The Employer had just cause to discipline the Grievor and to impose the penalty of a 20 day suspension without pay" (2015, para. 74).

Re Memorial serves to highlight a recurring issue in cases of harassment by faculty members against students: the latter's fear of rejecting or speaking out against the unwanted conduct, and their subsequent concern that their inability to do so constituted consent to the harassment. This type of concern is often reflected in sexual behaviour policies – for example, in 2017, the University of Manitoba's Sexual Assault Policy[17] stated that no consent is obtained when "the person submits or does not resist by reason of the exercise of authority" (2016, s.2.1(e)).

Not only can it be difficult for policy-makers to identify the boundaries of consent in higher education settings, but it can be difficult to ascertain at which point the actions of university employees and students are no longer under the institution's jurisdiction (particularly when incidents occur off campus). Some policies, such as Thompson River University's Sexual Violence Policy,[18] offer an extension to the policy's applicability – which was usually applicable only on campus or during university-sponsored events – "when the respondent was in a position of power or influence over the survivor's academic or employment status" (2017, s.3(c)).

The case of *Mahmoodi v Dutton*[19] showcases an example of such off-campus conduct. In *Mahmoodi*, Donald Dutton, a psychology instructor at the University of British Columbia, met with a student at his home to discuss her involvement in a project for him, which he claimed was customary in order to foster an environment of mentorship. However, the meeting took on a sexual tone, with candles, romantic music, and wine, and Dutton was alleged to have made several sexual advances towards the student. After two such encounters, the student was soon under the impression that if she continued to provide companionship to him, then he would assist her in getting into the graduate psychology program. Although the incidents were occurring off campus, many of the aspects, such as the promise of admission to graduate studies and Dutton's leverage over the complainant by virtue of his role as instructor, directly pertained to the university. In fact, the university was later held to be vicariously liable for Dutton's conduct: despite occurring off campus, it had occurred through the course of his employment at the university, and he had utilized the faculty-student power differential to his advantage. As illustrated by *Mahmoodi*, sexual misconduct perpetrated in the course of employment does not always stop at the physical boundaries of university campus, and policies clarifying attendant procedures and penalties give an important level of protection to victims. Ultimately, the victim in this case was awarded damages. The board per Commissioner Gordon noted its considerations in awarding monetary damages:

> I have considered that the proven harassment was in the form of a sexualized environment into which Dutton thrust Mahmoodi to discuss her academic pursuits, and that none of the allegations of sexual touching were established by the evidence. As Dutton's student, Mahmoodi was in a position of significant dependence and vulnerability. She turned to him for guidance and he let her down. I have also considered that Mahmoodi's personal circumstances and her sense of isolation in Canada made her particularly vulnerable. These facts were well-known to Dutton who, I find, chose to ignore them ... I find that these abuses of his position as a professor resulted in injury to Mahmoodi's dignity, feelings and self respect (1999, para. 311).

Many policies, including the University of Northern British Columbia's Harassment and Discrimination Policy,[20] consider it sexual harassment to make submission to sexual conduct a condition of employment or study, or the basis for academic performance decisions. In other words, the making of threats or promises pertaining to academics or employment in exchange for sexual acts constitutes sexual harassment, presumably due to the abuse of power in making such threats or promises. The use of threats and promises is a recurring element in some cases of faculty sexual misconduct, such as *York University v YUFA*,[21] where Paul Laurendeau, an instructor of French linguistics, offered to improve a student's grade in a course in exchange for sexual favours. The student then lodged a formal complaint of sexual harassment against Laurendeau, who was subsequently terminated.

This review of sample sexual misconduct cases and policies emerging from higher educational institutions across Canada is demonstrative. Properly made policies are an essential first step in addressing issues of sexual harassment and violence in the academic workplace and learning environment, and in keeping both employees and students safe.

That Case

The above policy contexts delineate the patchwork quilt of protections that exists across Canada for students who engage in relationships with professors. The policy network is strong on delineating conflict and harassment. The network becomes weaker in the context of regulating professor-student relationships that involve conduct that is not completely within the definitions of conflict and harassment. It may be the case that some professors involved with students may be unaware of the nature of conflict, or when their behaviour has moved into the realm of harassment. Similarly, students might not know the protections that conflict and harassment policies give them when they engage in what they believe are consensual relationships with professors. While these behaviours should be common sense in terms of their perils, the absence of specific policies regulating professor-student relationships can become confusing and may contribute to protracted university investigation when these relationships come to an end. These contexts may well have contributed to the circumstances that led to *that case*.

The union member in question had made an appointment with the union regarding what he believed to be unjust disciplinary action by the university; he was facing paid suspension pending investigation. As an instructor, he was frequently overloaded with up to eight courses a year; he was a contract faculty member who had worked for many years at the university. His contract status meant that he had limited rights with respect to a guarantee of teaching his preferred classes; there was no requirement that his contract would be renewed.

One former and one current student alleged sexual misconduct. The instructor had begun a sexual relationship with a student in his class, and he had also hired a teaching assistant (another former student) with whom he was sexually involved as well. He had not told either person about the other, nor did they know about his common-law relationship with another person. Once the relationships with the students terminated, each student filed respectful workplace complaints.

One student alleged that the instructor had promised her a higher grade than she ultimately received. The instructor countered this claim with an admission that he had already given that student a higher grade than he thought she deserved because of their relationship. The other student claimed that the relationship was premised on a coercive power dynamic, and that it occurred due to manipulation by the instructor.

The university held an investigatory meeting within a year of the complaints, embarked on multiple interviews with the parties, and, within the first several meetings, established that the instructor had engaged in intimate sexual relationships with both students. While a union representative was allowed to attend, the representative was not permitted to intervene or advise the instructor during university questioning. The union representative's role was limited to notetaking. Despite the early admission of his conduct, it would take one more year before any final discipline emerged. Why did it take so long?

University policy, or lack thereof, contributed to the delay. The university was unclear on whether it was choosing to respond to a respectful workplace violation, a conflict of interest problem, or something else that was not in any formal policy document. The respectful workplace policy stipulated that no university community member could harass, sexually or otherwise, any other university community member. The conflict of interest policy required that no university employee could provide or deny a university-based material benefit to someone with whom they have a relationship. Although the former student was hired as a research assistant, she and the instructor were in a relationship at the time of her hire. This may have given rise to a conflict of interest. In the case of the current student, the instructor was in a conflict by potentially assessing the academic work of a romantic partner. The remedy for such conflicts under university policy was, historically, a recusal from assessment or decision-making, and thus the conflicts were not an ideal path towards termination by the university.

The students alleged that the instructor was deceitful about his other relationships, and, being in a position of relative power, abused that position to obtain sexual gratification. However, the respectful workplace policy did not contemplate retrospective reflections on misuse of power dynamics: it never directly considered that relationships which at the time of their inception appeared to be consensual could later be viewed as problematic, in light of the power relations in place and the conflicts that the situation created. A review by the university of texts, direct messages, and shared photos revealed active participation by all parties in the sexual activities of the relationships, but the university was reluctant to pursue respectful workplace discipline without an exhaustive investigation. Though the university had enough information to confirm the relationships quite early on, it nonetheless launched a formal process of investigation that would last almost a full year.

The initial investigation, in response to a respectful workplace complaint, began with the employer meeting the instructor. At or around the first meeting, the instructor admitted to relationships with the students. Nonetheless, the university arranged numerous subsequent meetings (including with the students), requested all digital communications, and cross-examined the instructor extensively on the context and content of these digital communications. The remarkable aspect of the investigation was not only its length and comprehensiveness, but also the fact that it occurred in the context of contract teaching, where little in the way of ongoing obligations were owed by the university to the instructor. The length of the process took its emotional tolls on all parties; one of the students took to social media to express her trauma. In response, the instructor made an unwelcomed comment about the student on social media. As the social media battles unfolded, the university finally found its footing, casting the threatening comments as a prohibited reprisal under its respectful workplace policy. Throughout the process, the union provided the instructor, as was its statutory duty, with a representative to take notes at each meeting. Almost at the same time, external counsel was retained.

Approximately eight months later, the university delivered its definitive disciplinary measures. The instructor member would never teach again at the university. The union engaged its external counsel relatively early in the process – first to examine the way tribunals had adjudicated professor-student relationships, and later to grieve the university's decision, which then allowed counsel to negotiate the terms of final settlement of the matter. Until the instructor's act of social media reprisal, counsel had considered the possibility of seeking arbitration. Once the reprisal came to light and once the case review established demonstrative and diminishing possibilities of success for moving the process forward, counsel advised that settlement negotiations would be the best path forward. After the diligent work of counsel, the instructor received a modest parting sum and the university told the victims that the matter was complete and that the professor would no longer be working at the university.

The union's staff were aware of other cases in the past where its members had received no real consequences for similar conduct. Most of these instances had occurred years before the case in question. Indeed, despite several similar incidents coming to the union's attention within the last twenty years, no professor had ever been dismissed for the behaviour. In other cases, the university sought no redress, or simply issued warnings or reorientation of working relationships. In one case, the university merely prohibited a professor from supervising their love interest. In another, the university warned a professor that he could no longer date his students. Sometimes warning letters were issued. In one past case, the university moved a professor's office across campus when a neighboring instructor complained that he was engaging in loud coitus with a student during office hours. These cases, though, were materially different, counsel advised us. First, they had occurred years earlier. Each of these cases involved tenured professors, as opposed to tenuous contract teachers. Further, counsel advised the union, the culture at universities had changed and jurisdictions were now mandating universities to develop sexual violence policies in addition to respectful workplace policies. The changing legal and cultural context, together with the weak labour-law status of employees working on contract, provided little impetus for the university to be lenient. This in turn provided little-to-no room for legal counsel to maneuver in favour of the instructor. Once legal counsel advised the union of the possibilities, the union had little choice but to accept their advice and seek settlement.

At the end of the process, the union decided there should be a university policy containing a presumption against faculty-student relationships, adopting a formal resolution to this effect. We agreed that power dynamics and students' unique vulnerability, particularly undergraduate students, made sexual faculty-student relationships inappropriate. Other prominent schools, most notably Harvard (Rhodan 2015), had developed statements restricting instructor-student relationships. In Canada, such prohibitions, where they exist, vary from school to school.[22]

On at least three occasions after the settlement was concluded, we approached the university administration to see if they would be open to developing a policy specifically on the issue of student-professor relationships, especially in light of the provincial requirement for universities to develop sexual violence policies. The university was reluctant for several reasons. They cited the storied history of instructors, chairs and deans marrying former students. They argued that they had policies in place that could deal with the professor-student relationships obliquely. The university did not want to "legislate love." Ultimately, they argued that the phenomenon was uncommon. The union found itself in the very odd position of wanting *more* formal policy to direct professors' conduct, and the university wanted to maintain the status quo.

Analysis of the Case: An Argument for Policy

University policy, we argue, works just as administrative tendencies operate in other legal contexts. Administrative delegation can be quite specifically limited and delineated through precision, or, alternatively, it can provide for unfettered discretion. Opaque definitions in amorphous policies provide delegated power to appointed decision-makers, with the power of unbounded discretion. As a result, decision-makers can make ad hoc decisions of little precedential value. This policy landscape can generate incongruous results even in similar case scenarios.

In our case, the absence of cogent policy on faculty-student relations left the university adrift. The university did not want to create any policy that could restrict its administrative flexibility. One could argue that clear policy prohibiting and punishing instructor-student relationships could have negative financial consequences for universities. One example might be if a professor holds substantial seven-figure research grants, and a student relationship threatens their employment. Rigid policies would imperil this revenue stream, whereas flexibility would provide the university with opportunities to preserve the monies. In the case of itinerant, contract faculty, such situations are rarely engaged. Tenured professors are more likely to hold this type of value for universities. Thus, flexibility allows universities to pick and choose their disciplinary battles.

While cogent policy on faculty-student relationships may not have prevented the unfortunate events in our case, clear policy would at least have guided the behaviour of the power-holding parties. Whether this policy void achieves the flexibility that a university requires to deal with such matters is an open question, but vacuums tend to be spaces where cultural norms flourish. When those norms reflect cultural biases, we may see actions that harm victims.

Our case illustrates the university's failure to recognize that its silence tacitly endorsed the harms that inure from ungoverned professor-student relationships. Ensuring inconsistent treatment of instructor-student relationships based on the inherent institutional values of flexibility and sometimes financial expediency undergirds policy responses that resist formal policy infrastructure. Formal policies on professor-student relationships undercut flexibility, and flexibility allowed the university the power to avoid our case from becoming a spectacle. It led to non-disclosure agreements. It maintained the university's good name in the media. It failed to shine a light on a real problem – that professor-student relationships occur, and that they too often are informally regulated by universities. This in turn maintained the brand reputation of the university and avoided any financial backlash that might arise from the university being perceived as a haven for predators.

The fact that the students had to initiate a respectful workplace complaint provided an oblique opportunity for redress. The university at the end of the day found no sexual harassment, misconduct, or abuse, but, instead and most significantly, found a violation of the reprisal sections of the respectful workplace policy. Had the university developed policy prohibiting and regulating professor-student relationships in a cogent fashion, the university would have found a violation at the point of the development of the instructor-students relationships and could have argued that its policies redressed the situation. This would have allowed a stronger advocacy position for the university than mere conflict of interest policies which seek administrative redress (such as recusal). In our case, the instructor's response to the post-offence behaviour, through social media reprisal, led to a respectful workplace violation and was one of the pivotal instances of malfeasance that the university used to ground its discipline. Yet, a clearer path would have been to start from a formal prohibition against professor-student relationships through policy. Such a formal declaration would acknowledge that these relationships exist, however, and that acknowledgment might send the wrong branding message for the university – a matter that could lead to rational university fear in respect of fiscal consequences through diminished enrolments and donations. A failure to make such policies may be a reflection of these university values and of these fears. The failure to make policy creates the invisibility of these relationships, fostering silence (by professors, students, and administration) and maintaining university brand integrity. Ad hoc responses to gendered social problems reify power structures. In cases of instructor sexual misconduct towards students, this ad hoc approach further marginalizes student victims.

Considering faculty members' significant influence over students' educational development, relationships between students and instructors are inextricable from students' academic success (Cortina et al. 1998, 419–41). Permitting female students to be assessed not on the basis of academic or professional merit, but on the basis of gender, is a symptom of the "chilly climate" that plagues universities; an environment in which the devaluation, sexualization, and objectification of women flourishes (Weiss and Lalonde 2001; Dzeich and Weiner 1984)

That is not to say an outright ban on instructor-student relationships in the only solution. Rather, crafted policy with limits and contours could aid parties who find themselves in such relationships. Absolute prohibitions may drive student-instructor relationships underground, and so an outright prohibition with stiff penalties could actually lead to more secrecy and hidden abuses. A logical policy should allow faculty to declare these relationships and provide them the ability to foster alternate arrangements of student supervision and grading that avoids bias and conflict of interest. These flexibilities allow some room for pre-existing relationships, or consensual relationships. A good policy should include consequences for relationships deliberately withheld from the employer, those that raise issues of power dynamics, or worse, hidden behaviours that may contain criminal elements.

Concomitantly, each university policy that deals with conflicts, harassment, workplace and learning environment, and instructor-student ethical interactions should reflect the values of the presumption of impropriety and the duty of disclosure and alternate arrangement: these policies should contain a qualified prohibition against sexual relationships with students and subordinates, should require that professors inform the administration of the relationship in a formal declaration, and should outline the steps that the instructor has taken to ensure that the student is not assessed by the instructor or is otherwise removed from a learning environment that the instructor leads.

A formal policy will serve as notice to the university community and wider public (any of whom can access a policy on the internet) of a university-wide approach to these issues. A university's approach to handling instructor-student relationships should be openly discussed and made accessible to all university stakeholders: most importantly, instructors, administration, students, research assistants, teaching assistants, and staff. Policies should raise calls to strengthen campus sexual harassment best practices, and for universities to reorient the policies from legally protecting the university and towards fostering an institution's commitment to safe and productive educational environments (Hutchens 2003, 411).

At the same time, we must accept that instructor-student relationships are complex and that singular, inflexible approaches also raise concerns. In a recent interview, Laura Kipnis reflects on instructor-student relationships and argues that prohibitions of these relationships in campus policies turns the professorate into "would-be harassers all, sexual predators in waiting," expressing concerns for "all those she knew who are married to former students, or who are the children of such couples, and wondered where this left them" (Cooke 2017). Kipnis warns that such policies can create paranoia and an environment where office-hour teaching occurs only with open doors, where off-campus teaching is discouraged, where coffee and deep discussions with students are prohibited. She sounds the death knell for, in her view, the best learning contexts – informal learning environments (Kipnis 2017).

If these problematizing elements sound similar to the prognostications and protestations of the university's response to our union's calls for cogent policy, it is because the similarities are jarring. The absence of tangible and material policy to regulate these relationships preserves the flexibility of informal learning: the void provides maximum institutional flexibility. The void permits professor-student relationships, when they lead to "success" under the Kipnis definition – relationships which last and lead to happy families. These values accord with what the union heard when it asked for formal policy from the university; the university responded that there were faculty that had long-term relationships with former students, that this was nonetheless a rare occurrence, and that legislating love was not a valid policy concern.

A policy network that mandates declaration and amelioration, as we have suggested above, does not assume that all instructors are predators and that all students lack agency, as Kipnis fears. Rather, it suggests that instructors have a duty to ensure basic fairness in evaluation and learning environments and that student agency can be maximized through the mandated visibility of the relationship.

CONCLUDING THOUGHTS

Opaque policy can act similarly to traditional open-ended law (for example, legal tests requiring that one conduct a reasonable person assessment to ascertain culpability). Here, we refer not to law's coercive aspects but to its ability to make "knowledge claims," including the ability of policy to exercise "power on recalcitrant subjects" (Golder 2009; Jochelson 2015, 247). In this context, policy can be looked at as a "rebooting system of social control" by having "clear" yet "malleable" boundaries (Jochelson 2015, 247). Thus, policy or its absence can both reflect the institutional culture of universities and create it anew. Policy can and should change in step with progressive institutional cultures.

The relationship of the social world to policy is complex. The social world informs policy, and policy in turn informs society. Policy can "shore up limits in cases of social anxiety, and it can bend and warp in response to push back from society" (ibid., 249). Law and policy may reflect and refract the social world. Thus, policies that exacerbate inequalities, or remain silent on them, can be iterative of the injustice of power differentials.

The policy framework governing instructor-student relationships in Canada remains a potpourri of multivalent and inconsistent policies. We have explored a variety of policies governing these relationships and used our experiences in *that case* to demonstrate problems that manifest when universities fail to enact policy that directly implicates instructor-student relationships. If the university's desire for flexibility prolongs the agony of student complainants, exposes the most intimate details of such relationships, and provides no intellectual guidelines for future benchmarks in the university's adjudication of these matters, then the university investigative process will reproduce the inequalities faced by sexual assault victims in the criminal justice system. Victims will wait in purgatory as university investigators pick through the bones of the evidence left behind – sexts and social media posts. More vulnerable perpetrators will have justice meted out against them, while tenured instructors with material value to the university may be given less strict admonitions, or perhaps face no consequences at all.

Conceptions of rape culture, indeed the usefulness and meaning of the phrase itself, are problematized in this volume. We observe that the phrase describes inequality: the rampant objectification and utilitarianization of women in society's formal and informal structures. The term also connotes antipathy towards the many and diverse experiences of victimization, an ignorance of the political economy of itinerant employment, and it points to the role of legal and policy vacuums in reproducing misogyny and in denying the agency of women. If this is an accurate portrait of the term, then universities that choose silence in delineating relationships between instructors and students can expect to see these vacuums filled with exploitation, suffering, and a culture of victimization.

Rules, indeed laws, do not alone ameliorate inequalities or balance power differentials. People must act in accordance with these rules. Consequences must be seen to be meted out fairly and consistently. The absence of rules exacerbates problems of consistency and injustice. Ad hoc decision-making has been at the fore of many cases of state sponsored actions which have denigrated the values of equality. In reflecting on our case, we see one example where a lack of university policy prolonged the suffering of the student victims. The silence motivated the union to respond by defending the member perpetrator. The protracted institutional wrangling that followed yielded a result that could have been determined within a day of investigation under a more formal policy framework. Professor and student relationships should be frowned upon from a policy perspective; a presumption against these relationships with the possibility of declarations and conflict ameliorations allows sunlight to be the best disinfectant. It also sends a formal message that power imbalances exist in the university environment; that universities are concerned about equality, fairness, accessibility, and consistency; and that adult humans are complex and varied agents who, with clarity and consent, can chart their own course through difficult waters.

CODA: RECOMMENDATIONS FOR MOVING ON

More recently, student activism has resulted in some policy changes on some campuses. A recent example is the lobbying of the University of Manitoba Students Union (UMSU) when it comes to professor-student relationships. The UMSU called for the University of Manitoba to prohibit sexual relationships between students and staff in situations of direct supervisory power imbalance. This demand occurred in the wake of two sexual misconduct cases dealing with high-profile professors and the ongoing investigation of five separate sexual harassment investigations (McGuckin 2019). The University of Manitoba responded by raising tuition to help cover a budgeted $250,000 to combat sexual violence (Rollason 2019). New University of Manitoba policies were subsequently drafted. The approach was not to ban professor student relationships but to strongly discourage them and to insist that staff avoid intimate relationships with students when power differentials exist. The president of the University of Manitoba, David Barnard, noted that administrators at the university "have some concerns that an outright ban could infringe on the legal rights of adults to enter into consensual relationships," and that "anyone who breaches policies would be subject to different disciplinary measures depending on their roles at the school and their respective collective agreements" (Botelho-Urbanski 2019).

The University of Manitoba Policy between University Employees and Students (University of Manitoba n.d.) contains a number of provisions that provide a useful path forward for mediating the tensions in the fraught situation of professor-student relationships that appear consensual. The policy identifies the conflicts of interest that could arise in supervisory or evaluative relationships. The policy mandates disclosure by the employee immediately. Even where there is no teaching or supervisory relationship, the policy recommends that the employee write the department head immediately and disclose the relationship. The policy strongly discourages intimate relationships between employees and students, noting that they should be avoided. The policy then sets out situations where employee behaviour might be perceived by a student to cross the professional boundaries. Examples include social invitations, commenting on appearance and dress, invitations to one's home, sharing conference accommodations, personal questions or disclosures, and physical contact of any kind. The policy provides "helpful" advisory "boxes" rendering advice such as the avoidance of geo-dating apps that encourage casual sexual encounters and are more likely to include student users. The policy also cross-references other university policies on respectful work and learning and sexual assault, and provides links to sexual violence and education support.

This sort of policy might point a way forward for other universities struggling with these issues. For one thing, it represents the results of protracted personnel and institutional investigations as well as direct conversations with student union representation. The policy is apprised of prudential logics and offers a human resources approach to management: caution, disclosure, and consequence. Potential pitfalls remain. The university is acting as a regulator of social interaction between potentially consenting adults, going so far as to intercede in online dating behaviours and in proscribing the conversations adults have in learning environments, including the potentially positive social dialogues that occur during teaching moments outside of the classroom.

The high wire act necessary to navigate such terrain is delicate. There remain strongly held beliefs that neither the state nor the university ought to regulate consensual adult relationships.[23] Yet in an era where power dynamics in sexual relations are the subject of more scrutiny than ever before, and in an arena where universities seek to avoid potential liability, the policy momentum seems to require disclosure of all professor-student intimate relationships, at a minimum. Whether such prescriptions ought to bear on professor-student conversations, or digital dating platform behaviours outside of a university, they do veer the needle closer to abject sexual regulation.

Regulation of the workplace through policing adjunct behaviour is unlikely to change the social forces that undergird a culture of exploitation, but disclosure of power dynamic relationships between employers and students does at least establish a potential professional standard that can be demanded from all employees. A uniformity of such rules across post-secondary institutions could set an important baseline for professional behaviour for the professorate. Perhaps stating the obvious in the black letter of policy seems like a meagre step, but it is nonetheless important. More nuanced developments are unlikely to inure in contexts of silence. Making visible the professor-student relationship that crosses workplace guidelines has the value of countenancing dialogue and fostering further debate.

NOTES

1 The authors variously worked with university faculty unions and one worked with a union closely for almost a decade. This article summarizes their experience. Care has been taken to anonymize all parties. Some events have been described opaquely for this purpose.
2 See University of Prince Edward Island (2018).
3 See Okanagan College (2011).

4   *(1997), 64 L.A.C. (4th) 416* (B.C. Arb.) (Lanyon): 444

5   See University of British Columbia (1992).

6   See University of Toronto (n.d.).

7   See McGill University (2016).

8   See McGill University (n.d.).

9   Capilano University n.d.

10 See York University (1989).

11 See Aurora College (1999).

12 See Memorial University (2017).

13 See Memorial University (2013).

14 See Memorial University (2017).

15 See University of Northern British Columbia (2015).

16 2014 CarswellNfld 456; 125 C.L.A.S. 164; See also *Memorial University of Newfoundland Faculty Assn. v Memorial University of Newfoundland (Sutradhar Grievance)*, [2015] N.L.L.A.A. No. 13, 2015 CarswellNfld 295, 124 C.L.A.S. 82, 258 L.A.C. (4th) 57.

17 See University of Manitoba (2016).

18 See Thompson Rivers University (2017).

19 1999 CarswellBC 3088; [1999] B.C.H.R.T.D. No. 52; 36 C.H.R.R. D/8. Instructor Dutton brought a judicial review of the tribunal decision that was dismissed by Boyd J.: 2001 BCSC 1256, 2001 CarswellBC 2016.

20 See University of Northern British Columbia (2015).

21 *York University Board of Governors v York University Faculty Assn. (Laurendeau Grievance)*, [2009] O.L.A.A. No. 270

22 For example, some schools, like St Thomas University, explicitly govern consensual relationships between students and teachers – at https://www.stu.ca/media/stu/site-content/academics/bachelor-of-social-sciences/policies/docs/policies.pdf; see also s.5.3.3 of University of King's College (2016); other policies only mention warnings about conflicts from "closely associated persons – see Saint Mary's Conflict of Interest in Research Policy (Saint Mary's University 2009) and its Policy on Conflict Resolution and the Prevention and Resolution of Harassment and Discrimination (Saint Mary's University 2015) which only provide guidelines for amelioration on conflict rather than prohibitions on professor-student relationships; all accessed 19 February 2018.

23 See the opinions of law professor Heidi Matthews (@Heidi__Matthews) on what she has termed "age-gap phobia," and in particular her tweet at https://twitter.com/Heidi__Matthews/status/1155194134782795776 (accessed 29 June 2019): "When I was 19 I dated my former philosophy prof (then 35) for nearly 4 years. I came on to him (he's a radical

feminist). I remember how awesome it was to get a glimpse of the academic life I wanted to lead, as well as many tips on how to get there. It was positive & validating."

REFERENCES

Andreasen, Robin O. 2005. "Institutional Sexism." *Journal of Philosophical Research* 30: 147–63.

Athabasca University. 2013. "Athabasca University Policy: Conflict of Interest." http://ous.athabascau.ca/policy/humanresources/150_002.pdf.

Aurora College. 1999. "Conflict of Interest Policy." http://www.auroracollege.nt.ca/_live/documents/content/Policies/F04%20Conflict%20of%20Interest%20-%20January%201999.pdf.

Botelho-Urbanski, Jessica. 2019. "U of M Decides Not to Ban Relationships between Employees and Students." *Winnipeg Free Press*, 15 March. https://www.winnipegfreepress.com/local/u-of-m-decides-not-to-ban-relationships-507174162.html.

Capilano University. n.d. "Employee-Student Relationships Procedure." https://www.capilanou.ca/media/capilanouca/about-capu/governance/policies-amp-procedures/board-policies-amp-procedures/B.311.1---Employee-Student-Relationships-Procedure.pdf.

Cooke, Rachel. 2017. "Sexual Paranoia on Campus – and the Professor at the Eye of the Storm." *Guardian*, 2 April.

Cortina, Lilia M., Suzanne Swan, Louise F. Fitzgerald, and Craig Waldo. 1998. "Sexual Harassment and Assault." *Psychology of Women Quarterly* 22 (3): 419–41.

Dzeich, Billie W., and Linda Weiner. 1984. *The Lecherous Instructor*. Boston, MA: Beacon Press.

Frauley, Jon. 2009. "The Fictional Reality and Criminology: An Ontology of Theory and Exemplary Pedagogical Practice." *Current Issues in Criminal Justice* 21: 437–59.

Golder, Ben. 2009. *Foucault's Law*. Edited by Peter Fitzpatrick. Abingdon, UK, and New York: Routledge.

Haggerty, Kevin. 2004. "Ethics Creep: Governing Social Science Research in the Name of Ethics." *Qualitative Sociology* 27 (4): 391–414.

Hall, Roberta M., and Bernice Resnick Sandler. 1986. *The Campus Climate Revisited: Chilly for Women Faculty, Administrators, and Graduate Students*. Washington, D.C.: Project on the Status and Education of Women, Association of American Colleges.

Hutchens, Neal. 2003. "The Legal Effect of College and University Policies Prohibiting Romantic Relationships between Students and Professors." *Journal of Law and Education* 32: 411–43.

Jochelson, Richard. 2015. "Let Law Be Law, and Let Us Critique: Teaching Law to Undergraduate Students of Criminal Justice." *IJR* 4–14. https://ssrn.com/abstract=2995851.

Jochelson, Richard, Steven Kohm, and Michael Weinrath. 2013. "Mitigating the Protective-Services Orientation in Criminal Justice: An Opening Salvo at the University of Winnipeg." *Canadian Journal of Criminology and Criminal Justice* 55 (1): 1–32.

Kipnis, Laura. 2017. *Unwanted Advances: Sexual Paranoia Comes to Campus.* New York: Harper.

McGill University. n.d. "Recognizing Conflicts." https://mcgill.ca/secretariat/files/secretariat/recognizing-conflicts-jan_2015.pdf.

– 2016. "Policy against Sexual Violence." https://www.mcgill.ca/secretariat/files/secretariat/policy_against_sexual_violence.pdf.

McGuckin, Amber. 2019. "University of Manitoba Students Union Calling for Ban of Student-Faculty Relationships." *Global News*, 12 December. https://globalnews.ca/news/4754649/university-of-manitoba-students-union-calling-for-ban-of-student-faculty-relationships/.

Memorial University. 2013. "Conflict of Interest Policy." https://www.mun.ca/policy/browse/policies/view.php?policy=322.

– 2017. "Sexual Harassment and Sexual Assault Policy." https://www.mun.ca/policy/browse/policies/view.php?policy=321.

Okanagan College. 2011. "Conflict of Interest in Research Policy." http://www.okanagan.bc.ca/Assets/Departments+(Administration)/Legal+Affairs/Conflict+of+Interest+in+Research+Policy.pd.

Pyke, Sandra W. 1996. "Sexual Harassment and Sexual Intimacy in Learning Environments." *Canadian Psychology/Psychologie Canadienne* 37 (1): 13–22.

Rhodan, Maya. 2015. "Harvard Bans Sexual Relationships between Students and Professors." *Time Magazine*, 5 February. https://time.com/3697799/harvard-sexual-relationships-students-professors/.

Rollason, Kevin. 2019. "Tuition Increase, Funding to Combat Sexual Violence Highlight U of M Budget." *Winnipeg Free Press*, 22 May. https://www.winnipegfreepress.com/local/tuition-increase-funding-to-combat-sexual-violence-highlight-u-of-m-budget-510296592.html.

Saint Mary's University. 2009. "Conflict of Interest in Research Policy." https://smu.ca/webfiles/8-1004_Senate_ResearchConflictInterest.pdf.

– 2015. "Policy on Conflict Resolution and the Prevention and Resolution of Harassment and Discrimination." https://smu.ca/webfiles/6-2013 ConflictResolutionHarassmentDiscrimination.pdf.

Sandler, Bernice R., and Roberta M. Hall. 1986. "The Campus Climate Revisited: Chilly for Women Faculty, Administrators, and Graduate Students."

Thompson Rivers University. 2017. "Sexual Violence Policy." https://www.tru.ca/__shared/assets/Policy_BRD_25-0_Sexual_Violence40359.pdf.

University of British Columbia. 1992. "Conflict of Interest and Conflict of Commitment Policy." https://universitycounsel.ubc.ca/files/2012/02/policy97.pdf.

University of King's College. 2016. "Policy on Conflict of Interest." https://policies.ukings.ca/wp-content/uploads/2017/01/Kings2016ConflictInterestPolicy.pdf.

University of Manitoba. n.d. "Relationships between University Employees and Students." http://umanitoba.ca/student/media/Relationships-Between-Employees-and-Students.pdf.

– 2016. "Sexual Assault Policy." http://umanitoba.ca/admin/governance/media/Sexual_Assault_Policy_-_2016_09_01.pdf.

University of Northern British Columbia. 2015. "Searchable Policies." https://www.unbc.ca/sites/default/files/sections/policy/unbcsearchable policies-2015.pdf.

University of Prince Edward Island. 2018. "Conflict of Interest Policy." http://files.upei.ca/policy/conflict_of_interest_policy_govbrdgnloo18.pdf.

University of Toronto. n.d. "Conflict of Interest and Close Personal Relations Policy." https://www.provost.utoronto.ca/planning-policy/conflict-of-interest-close-personal-relations/.

Vaccaro, Annemarie. 2009. "Third Wave Feminist Undergraduates: Avoiding Ivory Tower Bureaucracy by Fighting for Social Justice Off Campus." *Journal about Women in Higher Education* 2: 1–25.

– 2010. "What Lies Beneath Seemingly Positive Campus Climate Results: Institutional Sexism, Racism, and Male Hostility toward Equity Initiatives and Liberal Bias." *Equity and Excellence in Education* 43 (2): 202–15.

Weiss, Deena S., and Richard N. Lalonde. 2001. "Responses of Female Undergraduates to Scenarios of Sexual Harassment by Male Professors and Teaching Assistants." *Canadian Journal of Behavioural Science/ Revue Canadienne Des Sciences Du Comportement* 33 (3): 148–63.

York University. 1989. "Personal Relationships between Instructors and Students Policy." http://secretariat-policies.info.yorku.ca/policies/personal-relationships-between-instructors-and-students-policy/.

15

"Calling Out" Campus Sexual Violence

An Analysis of Anti-Rape Student Activism and Media Engagement at McGill University

Ayesha Vemuri

INTRODUCTION

Over the last several years, campus sexual violence has risen to prominence in mainstream discourse across North America. Stories from survivors and victims[1] about mishandled cases and failures of justice have drawn attention to universities' failure to adequately address the problem (Kane 2016; Kingkade 2014). One of the most widely publicized cases is that of Emma Sulkowicz, a visual arts major at Columbia University, who filed a sexual violence complaint against a fellow student, detailing a non-consensual sexual encounter. A university inquiry, and subsequent police investigation, both found the accused student not responsible due to lack of reasonable evidence (Kutner 2015). To reflect upon the failures of justice through this process, Sulkowicz created an endurance performance piece, *Carry that Weight*, for their senior thesis, in which they carried a twin mattress everywhere they went on campus. *Carry that Weight*, which received enormous public attention, reflects upon the enormous emotional, psychological, and physical burden that sexual assault survivors must carry, and calls attention to Columbia's failure to support Sulkowicz's education over their rapist's (Jackson and Mazzei 2016; Mitra 2015; Smith 2014).

In Canada, numerous survivors of sexual and gendered violence across the country have spoken publicly about their experiences, discussed unfair university processes and their mishandled sexual assault complaints, and in some cases, filed human rights complaints against their universities. In this chapter, I argue that this recent spate of students' public statements, mediatized critiques, and artistic performances regarding campus sexual violence can be seen as a form of "call out culture." While public critiques of institutional power are by no means a new phenomenon, students' specific use of the internet and social media platforms positions their critiques within the realm of "calling out," a common online phenomenon amongst social justice advocates. Here, students' calling out is typically focused on drawing attention to inadequate, unfair, and sometimes absent university responses to sexual violence, but also the larger institutional structures that support or tacitly condone gendered violence or "rape culture" on campus. Students are therefore calling out universities for their failure to take the issue seriously or offer redress to those who have experienced sexual violence on campus, and for perpetuating a culture that ignores sexualized and gendered violence.

In this chapter, I describe how student activists use different modes of calling out rape culture at McGill University in Montreal, Canada. I first describe McGill's institutional response to sexual violence and student activists' contribution to the university's Policy against Sexual Violence, released in late 2017. Following the work of Amanda Nelund (this volume), I view university policies and processes as an alternative forum for justice that lies outside the court system but nonetheless aims to adjudicate cases of sexual violence and offer redress to survivors. I focus specifically on how some student activists have used public forums to reveal what they argued was a failure in the institutional response to sexual violence. I analyze Facebook groups, blog posts, campus newspapers, and news articles to describe how student activists have publicly critiqued the university and shared their experiences. Taken together, I view these texts as different manifestations of call-out culture. I argue that the students' public declarations aim to garner accountability of the institution and justice for victims and survivors.

CALL-OUT CULTURE

Asam Ahmad defines call out culture as "the tendency among progressives, radicals, activists, and community organizers to publicly name instances or patterns of oppressive behaviour and language use by others" (2015). While the phrase typically describes interactions between two individuals, I argue that when student activists publicly reveal inadequate and harmful responses to sexual violence, they participate in call out culture. Rather than calling out individuals, student activists focus attention on the university, or on bodies with power within the university (including student governments), and for this reason the impact may be more far reaching. As Ahmad points out, calling out is a "public performance" to openly demonstrate one's politics and positionality to an audience. It is this performativity that can render call out culture so toxic, in Ahmad's view: people can "demonstrate their wit or how pure their politics are," while the actual content of the call out is rendered less relevant (ibid.). For Ahmad, one of the most harmful effects of call out culture is the loss of empathy and the tendency to forget that the individual being criticized is also a human being, with emotions and imperfections.

The dismissal and criticism of call out culture based on its toxicity has now become commonplace, and many thoughtful commentaries articulate its ineffectiveness as an activist tactic. Maisha Z. Johnson (2016) writes that although calling out can be an effective tactic for activists and social justice advocates, it can often manifest as a form of public punishment, shaming, and silencing another individual. Michael O'Neill (2016) discusses the ways in which calling someone out may inadvertently backfire by directing excessive public attention to a misogynistic or racist individual. Other articles stress that call out culture may result in less nuanced debates and discussions (Friedersdorf 2017).

While all these articles point to important negative effects of call out culture, their examples tend to be limited to interpersonal communication and calling out one's peers. In the context of students calling out an institution (or indeed other powerful entities), this public performance may draw a level of public scrutiny that induces the institution to respond. Indeed, in a follow-up article, Ahmad writes that even while call out culture may have shortcomings, "sometimes the only way we can address harmful behaviours is by publicly naming them, in particular when there is a power imbalance between the people involved and speaking privately cannot rectify the situation" (2017). Ahmad goes on to write that call out culture is often equated with survivors of sexual violence calling out their abusers, a comparison he regards as dangerous because it ignores the fact "that survivors going public often do so at an incredible personal cost, and often after years of having tried to privately rectify the situation" (ibid.). However,

I view many student activist tactics in just this light: survivors and allies assume great personal risk to their reputations and careers in an attempt to hold institutions accountable despite a significant imbalance of power.

I argue that these critiques draw attention to the university's shortcomings as an alternative adjudicator of justice, and seek to improve university policies and processes so that survivors in the future may have better experiences. In the next sections, I provide a brief history of anti-sexual violence activism in Canada, as well as some of the recent cases that have deepened attention to the issue. I then move to a more detailed account of student activism related to the sexual violence policy at McGill University, focusing on events in the last five years, to describe how student activism to call out the university constitutes a form of informal justice.

CAMPUS SEXUAL VIOLENCE AND STUDENT ACTIVISM IN CANADA

In Canada, several notorious stories of sexual assault and rape culture on university campuses have been brought to light. These include the explicit and violent Facebook page of the so-called Gentlemen's Club at Dalhousie University's dentistry program, a series of sexual assaults at Laval University, and rape chants during frosh events at Saint Mary's University (Enos 2017; Canadian Press 2016; Tutton 2013; Anonymous 2014). In addition, survivors of sexual assault in several universities have spoken out about how their university did not support them, or even deterred them from reporting (Denton 2017; Reuss 2016). Many of these events have come to media attention, and therefore into the public view, because of individual survivors who have publicly spoken about their experiences, and because of the outrage of student activists and allies.

It is important to state here that attention to campus sexual violence is by no means a new issue, and anti-rape activism on college and university campuses has been in progress throughout the 1970s and 1990s (Gold and Villari 2000; Heldman and Brown 2014). During the 90s, a particularly active time for feminist activism on campus, universities across Canada saw numerous protest marches, including *Take Back the Night* marches (Strong-Boag n.d.), anti-date rape activism (*McGill Daily* 1993), and calls for sexual violence policies on campus (Draho 1995; Stewart 1991). At McGill University, for instance, students demanded a sexual violence-specific policy in the early 1990s (Stewart 1991).[2] Similarly, accounts of student-led activism against campus sexual violence at the University of Saskatchewan (Quinlan and Lasiuk 2017) and at York University (MacKay, Wolfe, and Rutherford 2017) show that students – often from feminist-identified activist collectives – have worked to garner institutional accountability for gender-based violence for several decades.

The last several years have seen resurgence in this activism, primarily as a consequence of survivors speaking out publicly about the high incidence of sexual violence in universities. As journalist Tyler Kingkade writes, "The reason this issue has gotten so much attention, rather [than statistics and data], is because students started speaking out and criticizing how their colleges and universities handled their sexual assault cases" (2014). At the heart of the attention to sexual violence, then, are survivors who share their narratives, often overcoming enormous sociocultural barriers in order to do so. These numerous cases have highlighted the prevalence of campus rape culture, as well as the inconsistencies and gaps in institutional responses to sexual violence. These public testimonials can be viewed as instances of survivors calling out their universities in an effort to draw attention to failed, or unavailable, avenues for justice. Indeed, several survivors have reported that they felt more victimized by the institutional response to the assault than by the assault itself, compounding the trauma of the experience (Khosroshahy 2016a, 2016b; Quinlan 2017a).

Survivors are pointing not only to a culture of sexual violence, but to a failure of institutional care (Noddings 2012). Elizabeth Quinlan argues that the increasing corporatization of universities results in this lack of care, as the corporate university views students as "revenue generating units," and sexual violence prevention programs are guided by principles of cost-efficiency (2017a, 62–3). However, she notes, "The calculus of corporatization both encourages and dissuades universities from implementing … sexual violence prevention and response initiatives" (64). On one hand, concerns with cost-efficiency leads universities to treat sexual violence as an individualized problem and deters them from implementing long-term prevention campaigns to change the culture in the university. On the other hand, "unfavourable reports, such as incidents of campus sexual violence, are blemishes on universities' images as good corporate citizens" (ibid.). It is here that call out culture becomes a particularly impactful strategy, as survivors and anti-rape activists recognize the effect of their public testimonials on the university's reputation and use highly visible media reports to draw attention to the university's insufficient care and provoke a response.

In response to media reports and criticisms, several universities have instated or initiated the creation of sexual violence policies. Many others have also undertaken campus-wide studies to better understand the prevalence of sexual violence on their campuses. McGill University conducted a campus-wide climate survey in 2015, and approved a stand-alone policy to address campus sexual violence in 2016. In the following section, I provide an account of McGill's Policy against Sexual Violence, centring the many interventions that led to its creation. I focus on the policy because it provides a useful structure to this narrative; however, it is important to note that student activism against sexual violence extends beyond the policy to address other aspects of university culture. I conclude with an analysis of how call out culture constitutes a means of debating and achieving justice.

Student Activism and McGill's Sexual Violence Policy

At McGill University, where I studied and continue to work on a research project that examines rape culture in universities, the relationship between university administrators and student activists can be described as tense, even adversarial. Indeed, it often appears as though the university's attempts to address campus sexual violence is viewed by survivors as arising primarily from legal and PR necessities, rather than a true desire to support those students who have been victims of sexual assault (Bejar 1991; Khosroshahy 2016a, 2016b; Lalonde 2014; Reuss 2016). In this section, I provide an account of the development of McGill's sexual violence policy alongside the student activism that has catalyzed its creation.

I view the McGill sexual violence policy as an assemblage made up of administrative decision-making as well as student activism. Assemblage provides us with a framework, or way of seeing,[3] in which policy can be viewed as a *process* that emerges out of the frictions and relations of activist networks and institutional response, rather than as a final *product*, which does not acknowledge the ongoing process of its creation and implementation. Assemblages de-privilege the discrete body or object of study, to consider instead how they come into being through "events, actions, and encounters" (Puar 2012, 58). They allow us to look beyond the fixed, binary notions of subject/object, context/action, past/present, to show how these are deeply interconnected and entangled with one another (Barad 2007; Puar 2012; Slack 2012). By viewing policy as assemblage, I hope to be able to situate the specific events and conversation at McGill within a larger social and political effort to address sexual violence through formal and informal processes. I turn to the process of activist interventions and student engagement that led to the creation of McGill's policy, but first, I provide a brief note about whom I refer to when I talk about student activists.

Anti-Rape Student Activism at McGill

It is important to account for the varying perspectives of the different individuals and groups I refer to within the larger rubric of "student activism" at McGill University, in order not to represent a diverse group of actors as an undifferentiated entity. I classify anti-rape student activists and advocates into two broad groups: institutionalized student societies, and independent student activists and organizations.[4] Whilst student societies do not necessarily have institutional power in their dealings with the university, they are quasi-political organizations that are institutionally recognized. Here I include groups as varied as the Student Society of McGill University (SSMU), the volunteer-run Sexual Assault Centre of the McGill Students' Society (SACOMSS), Queer McGill, and more. Although they can collectively be considered student societies, these groups have differing amounts of power and influence on the campus, an analysis of which would be a useful subject for further research.

Within the frame of independent groups and individual activists, I include survivors of sexual violence who have spoken and written publicly about their experiences at the university. I also include individuals who have spoken out about sexual violence and rape culture on campus, either as anonymous posts on online forums, or as contributors to student newspapers on campus. As well, I include independent student groups such as Silence Is Violence, Independent Women for Equality at McGill, and the Community Disclosure Network. These groups can emerge ad hoc in response to a particular situation, or have regular membership. They can also be an ongoing initiative with the various apparatus of organizational presence, such as a website, events, and so on, or be a more informal presence, existing solely as a blog or Facebook group.

The Creation of McGill's Sexual Violence Policy

Viewing policy as assemblage helps us trace the connections between the ways in which student activism and university policy-making are constituted in relation and in response to one another. In the case of McGill University's sexual violence policy, negotiations between student activists and university administrators over the course of several years finally yielded a policy that was accepted by the university. SACOMSS provides a timeline of the policy creation process (SACOMSS 2016). They begin by recognizing historical activism against sexual violence at the university, designating a "pre-2013" period during which there was "on and off organizing by SACOMSS (starting in the 90s)" (ibid.; see also Staggenborg and Lang 2007). Archives of the *McGill Daily* show student-authored letters that critique the lack of transparency in the university's response to assault, notably in fraternity-related events including a gang rape at a Zeta Psi frat party in 1988 and an accusation of date rape against a Phi Delta Theta member in 1990 (Bejar 1991; Stojsic 2001). In the letter, the authors write, "While we can find out what happens in the courts, we haven't a clue what goes on when a student goes through university channels" (*McGill Daily* 1991). While student activists in the 1990s also proposed a sexual assault policy, McGill refused, claiming that a general student code of conduct was sufficient (Khosroshahy 2016b; Stewart 1991). The criticism of the lack of institutional accountability for campus sexual violence thus has a long history at the university, signalling a deep-seated mistrust of the institution.

In 2013, three members of McGill's football team were accused of sexually assaulting a female student at Concordia University, but they had been allowed to remain at the university and on the team (Shields 2013). The incident prompted SACOMSS and other student societies at McGill to call for a special policy to address sexual violence (*McGill Daily* 2014). In 2014–15, a Sexual Assault Policy Working Group (SAPWG) was created, consisting of student representatives from SACOMSS, SSMU, and a host of feminist, queer, and social justice-oriented student societies. Over the course of two years, the SAPWG proposed two draft sexual violence policies, both of which were rejected by the university administration. Around the same time, a CBC investigation revealed that universities' published statistics of the prevalence of sexual violence was worryingly low, indicating that the schools were doing a poor job of encouraging people to come forward and file complaints (Sawa and Ward 2015). Later, a *Globe and Mail* investigation revealed that most Canadian universities did not have formal procedures to respond to sexual assault on campus (Chiose 2016).

In early 2016, a series of meetings between SAPWG, the former dean of students Andre Costopoulos, and the associate provost (Policies, Procedures, and Equity) Angela Campbell, were intended to finalize a sexual assault policy to bring to Senate. However, there was a breakdown of negotiations, followed by student-led actions, which included demonstrations and media outreach. The SAPWG also released an open letter to the community about the breakdown, stating that the "administration's refusal sends a clear message that McGill does not support survivors of sexual assault and is unwilling to commit the resources required to adequately support survivors and address sexual violence on campus" (SAPWG 2016). In the letter, the working group also makes a scathing critique of the university's appropriation of their labour by stating that, "throughout the process, the working group has been used to bolster the University's reputation. The administration has publicly credited Dean Costopoulos as being 'instrumental in seeing the draft sexual assault policy progress through the system.' Despite positioning itself as a leader in addressing sexual violence, the University has been disingenuous at best and obstructive at worst in its efforts" (ibid.).

Later in 2016, a draft Policy against Sexual Violence, written by the associate provost (Policies, Procedures, and Equity), was circulated to stakeholders for feedback, released for community-wide feedback, and subsequently passed by the McGill Senate and Board of Governors in December.

As is evident in this brief timeline, the development of the policy was primarily driven by the activism of student societies, especially SACOMSS and feminist, queer, anti-racist, and other social justice groups. Their activism often uses open letters, which I argue can be seen as a form of activist performance (Mitra 2015). Open letters, though long used by activists and writers, have become an increasingly popular mode of literary activism, perhaps even "the internet's opinion genre of choice" (Lordi 2017). They can provide a means of publicly declaring one's politics, but also of holding institutions and people in power to account, and can create meaningful "networks of support over time and space" (ibid.). In the context of the intimate, bounded setting of university, the open letter can be a powerful political tool in calling out institutional silences.

Although these letters are addressed to the administration at McGill, it can be argued that they are intended for a much larger audience: the student body at McGill, staff and faculty members not involved in creating the policy, and also the general public in Montreal and beyond. These letter and survivor testimonies, most often published in campus newspapers or distributed across campus emails and list-servs, are circulated online and in print, and are often republished by journalists and newspapers (for instance, see D'Amours 2016; Scott 2017; Seidman 2016). As Julie Lalonde notes, it often takes a "media frenzy" for universities to begin to address campus sexual violence (2014, 11). Negative media attention impacts the university's reputation and can make it less desirable for prospective students and funders alike. In essence, these letters are a form of calling out the university's unwillingness to respond to a subject as grave and pressing as campus sexual assault. Publicly calling out the university administrators for ignoring student demands and appropriating student labour is a powerful tool to provoke the institution to respond.

Responses to the Policy

Although the instatement of McGill's policy to address campus sexual violence was widely lauded, many remain critical or only cautiously optimistic. Even as several activists and survivors acknowledge the policy as a necessary first step, they note its shortcomings. For instance, the policy does not clearly state the process for reporting sexual assault, or how the university will handle such cases. Another issue is that it focuses more on prevention than on addressing incidents of sexual assault (Desai 2016). These prevention programs typically take the form of consent and bystander education, both of which have been heavily critiqued even as they continue to be touted as the most effective means of preventing sexual violence (Elk and Devereaux 2014; Bailey et al. this volume; Quinlan 2017a).

Critics note that consent education is unhelpful, not only because it does not reflect the reality of how young people negotiate sexual consent (Powell 2010). Some critics argue that it "overshadows and replaces institutional transparency and accountability" (Khosroshahy 2016b), and places the responsibility of communication on survivors (Anonymous 2015; see also Ikeda and Rosser 2010). A survivor who was sexually assaulted by a student staff member at a McGill residence recalls, "[My rapist] had already had two years of floor fellow training (around 60 hours of training each year) and had facilitated at least four Rez Project workshops, so he should have known better, right? Hell, he should have been an expert on consent!" (Khosroshahy 2016b). This reveals a gap between the expected outcomes of consent education and the reality of how sexual assault happens (Powell 2010).

Others critique the policy for depoliticizing the issue and divorcing it from a gendered analysis. In an open letter, three students from Independent Women for Equality McGill remind the reader that while men can be victims of sexual violence, it is overwhelmingly the case that victims are girls and women. Moreover, they write, "As the discussion of a 'pro-survivor focused model' [in the policy] against sexual assault progressed, one troubling oversight became clear: the perpetrators of sexual violence, and the responsibility they bear in committing sexist behavior, are disappearing from the discussion" (Yiannoutsos, Mah, and Gordiychuk 2016). Whilst they commend the policy for describing the support systems for survivors of sexual violence, they ask that the university policy address "what must be done to hold perpetrators of sexual assault, accomplices and bystanders accountable for their actions (or lack thereof)" (ibid.).

These critiques reveal a tension between the role of the university as educational institutions that are responsible for teaching about sexual assault awareness and prevention, and the role of universities as agents for providing survivor support and acting as mediators of justice. Student-activist critiques show that even while the university may have progressive educational practices, the processes for reporting sexual violence are confusing and cloaked in secrecy, and so often fail survivors in terms of both delivering justice as well as providing support. This failure results in a lack of trust and a disbelief in the ability and willingness of the university to support survivors of sexual violence, despite the "pro-survivor" language mobilized around the policy itself.

Survivor-Activist Testimonials and Public Advocacy

Testimonials and stories of individual survivor-activists permeate and catalyze the policy discourse outlined above, particularly when such personal accounts publicly call out the university's (mis)handling of their sexual assault complaints. Khosroshahy, arguably one of the most outspoken student survivor-activists at the university, writes, "If I hadn't reported, I would have still suffered, but I would have at least

suffered without feeling disposable to, and dehumanized by, my university" (2016a). Another story of an unnamed survivor at McGill
tells the same tale following her experience of sexual assault after the
NeuroAnatomy Grad Ball in March 2015 (Dawadi 2015). The *McGill
Tribune* reports her saying, "It was incredibly hard to know what to
do. There was no streamlined, obvious path to take" (ibid.).

Although this survivor felt supported by the administration at
McGill, she notes that "there's a problem with McGill policy" (Dawadi
2015). On the other hand, Khosroshahy feels betrayed by the institutional culture at McGill, writing, "It has become abundantly clear to
me that, following the shameful example set by the Canadian justice
system, McGill breeds predators, lacks adequate mechanisms to support its students, and refuses to put any in place" (2016a). While they
each had different experiences with individual members of the administration, they both identify institutional gaps, such as the definitions
of the "McGill context," the university's ability to support survivors
meaningfully, and the unclear processes for reporting and processing
sexual assault complaints.

The political impact of calling out the university can be seen in the
public disruption of a recent event, the Journée de Réflexion – a series
of formal consultations run by Quebec's Minister of Post-Secondary
Education's Office about the creation of a new policy for sexual violence on campuses. During the event, survivors from Silence Is Violence
McGill[5] (SiV) asserted their presence, calling "for their voices to be
included in this space"; "in one case, [they] publicly called out particular members of the McGill administration for mishandling and/or
dismissing their cases" (Spencer 2017). In this act of disruption, survivors demonstrated their mistrust of the university. One survivor,
Nina Hermes, states that she did not disclose her assault to McGill
because during her four years at the university she witnessed "a pattern of institutionalized violence."[6] Another, Amy, says she chose not
to come forward about her assault because "McGill does not have the
best track record when it comes to helping survivors"[7].

The affective and political power of survivor testimony galvanizes
the creation of survivor support groups and activist communities who
call out the institution as well as support one another (Lewis, Marine,
and Kenney 2016; Powell 2015; Salter 2013). Carrie Rentschler writes
that young feminists "utilize social media in order to respond to rape
culture, and hold accountable those responsible for its practices when
mainstream news media, police and school authorities do not" (2014,

67). At McGill, survivors use a combination of public testimonials, articles in student newspapers, open letters, and social media platforms to call out the university for its inadequate response to sexual violence. Collectively, these discussions can be seen as a public negotiation of justice and an effort to garner institutional accountability.

Call out culture in this respect can be seen as an avenue for informal justice, and as a first step towards garnering institutional accountability. Oftentimes, the public complaint about the institution is a last resort, one that is taken after coming up against many institutional walls (Ahmed 2015). As Sara Ahmed (2017) explains, "Stories of complaint are often stories about the exhaustion of a process." Yet complaint or calling out may also be about wanting to make a change, and to see the potential for a change. In this sense, one may make a complaint "because you have a sense of optimism about how things *could* happen differently" (ibid.). In the case of campus sexual assault, calling out the institution can act as an avenue for changing the culture of the university in order to ensure that the same injustices in procedure and treatment of victims/survivors do not recur.

CONCLUDING THOUGHTS

In this chapter, I have argued that student activists at McGill University have used a combination of media platforms to critique the university's policies, testify to their experiences, voice their concerns, and speak to the student body as well as to university administrators. Publicly aired grievances, which constitute a form of call out culture, are deployed to draw attention to the university's shortcomings, and to encourage an improved institutional response to sexual violence. This assemblage of activists, media platforms, audiences, and incidents reveals the ways in which policy and justice frameworks, as well as the larger discourse surrounding campus sexual violence, comes into being through publicly performed activism. In other words, this assemblage of activist call out culture "asks what is prior to and beyond what gets established" (Puar 2012, 63). It makes visible the different positions of student activists, survivors, administrators, and others, and reveals the frictions between their varied priorities. It is within and through this friction, perhaps, that the transformation of institutional culture is made possible.

As Amanda Nelund writes in this volume, although university processes to address campus sexual violence can provide an alternative site for justice, they can also replicate the criminal justice system's shortcomings, whilst lacking transparency and not being subject to public scrutiny. Viewing call out culture as an avenue for *informal justice* allows us to see one manifestation of what justice beyond the law might look like. Nicola Henry, Anastasia Powell, and Asher Flynn argue that, given the inherent limitations of criminal and formal justice systems, we should acknowledge the emerging "'counterpublic spaces' for seeking justice," including "online and offline activism and consciousness-raising" (2015, 7; see also Salter 2013; Sills et al. 2016). I would argue that student activists' public critiques of the university use testimonials and public statements, but function in the institutional context as a form of whistleblowing. In calling out the university, they reveal details about the internal, private, processes of sexual assault reporting procedures, as well as policy-creation processes. Student activists participating in this institutional calling out may be doing so as a means of attaining justice for themselves, but also aim to transform the culture of the institution as a whole by holding it up to public scrutiny.

RECOMMENDATIONS FOR CHANGE

The story of student activism at McGill is by no means a unique one. I offer this narrative not as a means of drawing attention to one institution, but rather as a means of exploring a common issue across many universities in Canada. The calling out of inadequate university approaches to campus sexual violence is visible nationwide, and is indicative of universities' failures in their roles as adjudicators of justice, but also their lack of institutional care for those students who have experienced sexual violence on campus. While calling out may be an effective tactic for student activists, it is also an adversarial one, necessitated by trauma-inducing responses and a breakdown in communication. If the university response to campus sexual violence took these complaints seriously and adopted a feminist ethics of care in their response to survivors and allies, one imagines that these instances of calling out would no longer be necessary. While further research is needed to better understand how the specific demands and needs of survivors and activists can be better met by the university in order to mend fractured relationships of mistrust, two specific approaches to policy may be useful to consider.

First, as Claudia Mitchell noted in a recent keynote address, policy is a form of speculative writing – it is a means of imagining the world otherwise. In the case of McGill's policy, it is apparent that student activists are often in the position of identifying critical social issues, the gaps in university policy, and developing means of responding to these gaps. Yet, rather than recognizing this crucial role, university administrators have often responded with stonewalling, ignoring, or even appropriating student work without giving due credit. This reveals a gap between the administration's and students' orientation towards social change, as well as administrators' lack of imagination about what a more just university process might be. In this case, it would be useful to undertake research to better understand the nuances of administrative and activist positions, and make visible the reasons for the breakdown of trust. Only through understanding why the friction exists can we begin to address its root causes.

A second, related policy change pertains to the process of negotiations. Student activists repeatedly voice their frustration and their sense of powerlessness in dealing with administrators. This points to a deep and structural imbalance of power. While the question of power is frequently raised in the context of student-professor intimate relationships, it is rarely considered within the context of activist work. However, as I have argued, call out culture stems from a breakdown of communication that often originates in institutional silence. Thus, a second recommendation would be to treat students not merely as beneficiaries or stakeholders but as a second party in a process of negotiation. In other words, an important means of moving towards a more just policy is to treat students as equals who are equally invested in a safe campus environment free of sexualized violence.

NOTES

1   The terms "survivor" and "victim" are both used to describe people who have experienced sexual violence, but each of these terms carries different political and historical meanings. Whilst historically the term "victim" was used to refer to anyone who had suffered a crime, anti-sexual violence activists in the 1980s popularized the term "survivor" in order to emphasize their agency and resilience (see Kelly 1988). Although the term "survivor" and derivatives such as "survivor-centric" are often used today, it is important to note that many individuals who have experienced sexual violence do not identify as survivors. Some prefer the term "victim" because "it places the focus back where it belongs: on the fucking rapist" (Anonymous 2016), and "recognizes the enormity of the system we are up

against" (Gupta 2014). While I recognize the shortcomings of the term, I use the term "survivor" and "survivor-activist" in this chapter, following the self-identification of several of the activists I write about.

2 Anecdotal evidence and some reports indicate that anti-sexual violence activism on university campuses in Canada has a long history, but it is difficult to find a detailed history of feminist student activism. One of the goals of the IMPACTS research project is to create a timeline and archive of student activism against sexual violence in university campuses. Researchers involved in this project are beginning to trace this history, starting with McGill University, but hope to crowdsource this information once an active digital archive is created.

3 Haraway writes, "It matters which ideas we think other ideas with" (2016, 14). I agree, and although it may be possible to view student activism, campus sexual violence, and policy-making through other lenses, assemblages help me see them as being intertwined, becoming-with one another, whilst also taking into account all the contextual, historical, and affective factors that inform them.

4 Even as I seek to account for the varying perspectives of different student activists, I recognize that my categorization necessarily involves a partial perspective that will not capture every nuance of student activists' experiences.

5 Silence Is Violence (SiV) is an informal advocacy group made up of survivors from universities across Canada. SiV describes itself as an intersectional anti-carceral feminist group that aims to "radically alter the culture of institutional violence on university campuses across Canada" (Silence is Violence n.d.). In 2016, a group of activist-survivors at McGill launched a local chapter of Silence Is Violence (Rougeaux 2016).

6 Nina provided a statement at the Journée de Reflexion (Spencer 2017), a video of which was made available on the Silence Is Violence McGill Facebook page.

7 Amy also provided a statement at the Journée de Reflexion (Spencer 2017), a video of which was posted on the Silence Is Violence McGill Facebook page.

REFERENCES

Ahmad, Asam. 2015. "A Note on Call-Out Culture." *Briarpatch Magazine* (blog), 2 March. https://briarpatchmagazine.com/articles/view/a-note-on-call-out-culture.

– 2017. "When Calling Out Makes Sense." *Briarpatch Magazine* (blog), 29 August. https://briarpatchmagazine.com/articles/view/when-calling-out-makes-sense.

Ahmed, Sara. 2015. "Sexual Harassment." *Feminist Killjoys* (blog), 3 December. https://feministkilljoys.com/2015/12/03/sexual-harassment/.

– 2017. "Complaint as Diversity Work." *Feminist Killjoys* (blog), 10 November. https://feministkilljoys.com/2017/11/10/complaint-as-diversity-work/.

Anonymous. 2015. "Beyond 'Yes' and 'No.'" *McGill Daily*, 28 September. https://www.mcgilldaily.com/2015/09/beyond-yes-and-no/.

Anonymous. 2016. "UNPOPULAR OPINION: I Am a Rape Victim, Not a Survivor." *XoJane: Women's Lifestyle and Community Site*, 27 April. http://www.xojane.com/issues/i-am-a-victim-not-a-survivor.

Barad, Karen Michelle. 2007. *Meeting the Universe Halfway: Quantum Physics and the Entanglement of Matter and Meaning*. Durham, NC: Duke University Press.

Bejar, Susana. 1991. "A Matter of Principle." *McGill Daily*, 20 March. https://archive.org/details/McGillLibrary-mcgill-daily-v80-no84-march-20-1991-13644/page/n3.

Canadian Press. 2016. "Hundreds Gather at Université Laval Rally as Dorm Break-In Reports Increase to 15." *Montreal Gazette* (blog), 19 October. https://montrealgazette.com/news/local-news/quebec-city-police-set-up-command-post-at-universite-laval-in-wake-of-break-ins.

Chiose, Simona. 2016. "Harassment on Campus: 90 Percent of Cases Kept Quiet." *Globe and Mail*, 2 April. https://www.theglobeandmail.com/news/national/education/canadian-universities-under-pressure-to-formalize-harassment-assaultpolicies/article29499302/.

D'Amours, Matt. 2016. "Are Concordia and McGill Doing Enough to Deal with Sexual Assault Allegations?" *CBC News*, 23 October. http://www.cbc.ca/news/canada/montreal/mcgill-concordia-sexual-assault-1.3817797.

Dawadi, Shrinkhala. 2015. "Sexual Assault Allegation Raises Concern over Redress Procedures at McGill." *McGill Tribune*, 9 September. http://www.mcgilltribune.com/news/sexual-assault-allegation-raises-concern-over-redress-procedures-at-mcgill-992015/.

Denton, Jack O. 2017. "Sexual Assault Survivors Feel Silenced after Posters Removed at University of Toronto." *Torontoist*, 4 April. http://torontoist.com/2017/04/sexual-violence-survivors-feel-silenced-posters-removed-university-toronto/.

Desai, Saima. 2016. "How Canadian Universities are Failing Sexual Assault Survivors." *NOW Magazine*, 9 August. https://nowtoronto.com/api/content/518cdff4-5e2a-11e6-aed1-12955eaaf839/.

Draho, Lisa. 1995. "Sexual Harassment Policy Amendment under Fire." *McGill Daily,* 13 February. http://archive.org/details/McGillLibrary-mcgill-daily-v84-n058-february-13-1995-14017.

Elk, Lauren Chief, and Shaadi Devereaux. 2014. "The Failure of Bystander Intervention." *New Inquiry* (blog), 23 December. https://thenewinquiry.com/failure-of-bystander-intervention/.

Enos, Elysha. 2017. "Sexual Violence Widespread at Quebec Universities, Study Finds." *CBC News*, 16 January. http://www.cbc.ca/news/canada/montreal/sexual-assault-campus-quebec-victimization-1.3937527.

Friedersdorf, Conor. 2017. "The Destructiveness of Call-Out Culture on Campus." *The Atlantic,* 8 May. https://www.theatlantic.com/politics/archive/2017/05/call-out-culture-is-stressing-out-college-students/524679/.

Gold, Jodi, and Susan Villari. 2000. *Just Sex: Students Rewrite the Rules on Sex, Violence, Equality and Activism*. Lanham, MD: Rowman and Littlefield Publishers.

Gupta, Rahila. 2014. "'Victim' vs 'Survivor': Feminism and Language." *OpenDemocracy,* 16 June. http://www.opendemocracy.net/5050/rahila-gupta/victim-vs-survivor-feminism-and-language.

Haraway, Donna J. 2016. *Staying with the Trouble: Making Kin in the Chthulucene*. Durham, NC: Duke University Press.

Heldman, Caroline and Baillee Brown. 2014. "A Brief History of Sexual Violence Activism in the U.S." *Ms. Magazine Blog* (blog), 8 August. http://msmagazine.com/blog/2014/08/08/a-brief-history-of-sexual-violence-activism-in-the-u-s/.

Henry, Nicola, Asher Flynn, and Anastasia Powell. 2015. "The Promise and Paradox of Justice: Rape Justice beyond the Criminal Law." In *Rape Justice: Beyond the Criminal Law*, edited by Nicola Henry, Anastasia Powell, and Asher Flynn, 1–17. Houndmills, UK: Palgrave Macmillan.

Ikeda, Naoko, and Emily Rosser. 2010. "You Be Vigilant! Don't Rape! Reclaiming Space and Security at York University." *Canadian Woman Studies* 28 (1): 37–43.

Jackson, Alecia Youngblood, and Lisa A. Mazzei. 2016. "Thinking with an Agentic Assemblage in Posthuman Inquiry." In *Posthuman Research*

Practices in Education, edited by Carol A. Taylor and Christina Hughes. 93–107. Houndmills, UK: Palgrave Macmillan.

Johnson, Maisha Z. 2016. "6 Signs Your Call-Out Isn't Actually about Accountability." *Everyday Feminism* (blog), 6 May. https://everydayfeminism.com/2016/05/call-out-accountability/.

Kane, Laura. 2016. "Feeling Let Down by Universities, Survivors Meet to Fight Campus Sex Assaults." *Globe and Mail*, 19 July. https://www.theglobeandmail.com/news/national/feeling-let-down-by-universities-survivors-meet-to-fight-sex-assaults/article30989317/.

Kelly, Liz. 1988. *Surviving Sexual Violence*. Minneapolis: University of Minnesota Press.

Khosroshahy, Paniz. 2016a. "#ThisIsNotHelping." *McGill Daily* (blog), 19 September. http://www.mcgilldaily.com/2016/09/thisisnothelping/.

– 2016b. "McGill Feeds a Cycle of Sexual Violence." *McGill Daily* (blog), 20 April. http://www.mcgilldaily.com/2016/04/mcgill-feeds-a-cycle-of-sexual-violence/.

Kingkade, Tyler. 2014. "Sexual Assault Statistics are Not the Point." *HuffPost Canada,* 15 December. http://www.huffingtonpost.com/2014/12/15/sexual-assault-statistics_n_6316802.html.

Kutner, Max. 2015. "Accused Student in Mattress Protest Sues Columbia." *Newsweek*, 28 April. http://www.newsweek.com/anti-mattress-protest-paul-nungessers-lawsuit-against-columbia-university-326319.

Lalonde, Julie S. 2014. *From Reacting to Preventing: Addressing Sexual Violence on Campus by Engaging Community Partners*. Ottawa, ON: University of Ottawa.

Lewis, Ruth, Susan Marine, and Kathryn Kenney. 2016. "'I Get Together with My Friends and Try to Change it': Young Feminist Students Resist 'Laddism', 'Rape Culture' and 'Everyday Sexism.'" *Journal of Gender Studies* 27 (1): 56–72. doi:10.1080/09589236.2016.1175925.

Lordi, Emily. 2017. "The Intimate, Political Power of the Open Letter." *The Atlantic*, 15 May. https://www.theatlantic.com/entertainment/archive/2017/05/the-intimate-political-power-of-the-open-letter/526182/.

MacKay, Jenna M., Ursula Wolfe, and Alexandra Rutherford. 2017. "Collective Conversations, Collective Action: York University's Sexual Assault Survivors' Support Line and Students Organizing for Campus Safety." In *Sexual Violence at Canadian Universities: Activism, Institutional Responses, and Strategies for Change*, edited by Elizabeth Quinlan, Andrea Quinlan, Curtis Fogel, and Gail Taylor, 237–53. Waterloo, ON: Wilfrid Laurier University Press.

McGill Daily. 1991. "The Best Kept Secret." *McGill Daily*, 20 March. http://archive.org/details/McGillLibrary-mcgill-daily-v80-no84-march-20-1991-13644.

– 1993. "Professor Suspended over Rape Article." *McGill Daily*, 22 November. https://archive.org/details/McGillLibrary-mcgill-daily-v83-no43-november-22-1993-13921/page/n7.

– 2014. "An Open Letter on the Sexual Assault Policy." *McGill Daily*, 24 March. https://www.mcgilldaily.com/2014/03/an-open-letter-on-the-sexual-assault-policy/.

Mitra, S. 2015. "'It Takes Six People to Make a Mattress Feel Light…': Materializing Pain in Carry that Weight and Sexual Assault Activism." *Contemporary Theatre Review* 25 (3): 386–400. https://doi.org/10.1080/10486801.2015.1049845.

"Misogynistic, Sexually Explicit Facebook Posts Probed at Halifax University." 2014. *CBC News*, 15 December. http://www.cbc.ca/news/canada/nova-scotia/dalhousie-university-probes-misogynistic-student-gentlemen-s-club-1.2873918.

Noddings, Nel. 2012. "The Caring Relation in Teaching." *Oxford Review of Education* 38 (6): 771–81.

O'Neill, Michael. 2016. "The Pitfalls of Call-Out Culture." *Brown Political Review* (blog), 6 May. http://www.brownpoliticalreview.org/2016/05/26760/.

Powell, Anastasia. 2010. "Consent: Negotiating Consensual Sex." In *Sex, Power and Consent: Youth Culture and the Unwritten Rules*, 86–105. Cambridge and New York: Cambridge University Press.

– 2015. "Seeking Informal Justice Online: Vigilantism, Activism and Resisting a Rape Culture in Cyberspace." In *Rape Justice: Beyond the Criminal Law*, edited by Anastasia Powell, Nicola Henry, and Asher Flynn, 218–37. London: Palgrave Macmillan.

Puar, Jasbir K. 2012. "'I Would Rather Be a Cyborg than a Goddess': Becoming-Intersectional in Assemblage Theory." *philoSOPHIA: A Journal of Continental Feminism* 2 (1): 49–66.

Quinlan, Elizabeth. 2017. "Institutional Betrayal and Sexual Violence in the Corporate University." In *Sexual Violence at Canadian Universities: Activism, Institutional Responses, and Strategies for Change*, edited by Elizabeth Quinlan, Andrea Quinlan, Curtis Fogel, and Gail Taylor, 61–75. Waterloo, ON.: Wilfrid Laurier University Press.

Quinlan, Elizabeth, and Gail Lasiuk. 2017. "The Coalition of Sexual Assault: Activism Then and Now at the University of Saskatchewan." In *Sexual Violence at Canadian Universities: Activism, Institutional*

Responses, and Strategies for Change, edited by Elizabeth Quinlan, Andrea Quinlan, Curtis Fogel, and Gail Taylor. Waterloo, ON: Wilfrid Laurier University Press.

Rentschler, Carrie A. 2014. "Rape Culture and the Feminist Politics of Social Media." *Girlhood Studies* 7 (1): 65–82.

Reuss, Sophia. 2016. "New Campus Sex Assault Policies Show Canadian Universities Still Aren't Listening to Survivors." *Rabble.ca* (blog), 6 December. http://rabble.ca/blogs/bloggers/campus-notes/2016/12/new-campus-sex-assault-policies-show-canadian-universities-still.

Rougeaux, Alice. 2016. "'Silence Is Violence' Launches at McGill." *McGill Daily*, 12 September. https://www.mcgilldaily.com/2016/09/silence-is-violence-launches-at-mcgill/.

SACOMSS. 2016. "McGill Policy against Sexual Violence: A (Recent) Timeline of Student Advocacy." https://ua.ssmu.ca/wp-content/uploads/2016/10/Sexual-Violence-Policy-Timeline.pdf.

Salter, Michael. 2013. "Justice and Revenge in Online Counter-Publics: Emerging Responses to Sexual Violence in the Age of Social Media." *Crime, Media, Culture: An International Journal* 9 (3): 225–42.

SAPWG. 2016. "McGill Administration Continues to Fail Survivors of Sexual Assault: An Open Letter to the Administration of McGill University." https://ssmu.ca/wp-content/uploads/2015/07/SAP-Open-Letter-2016-04-07.pdf.

Sawa, Timothy, and Lori Ward. 2015. "'Utterly Shocking': Sex Assault Reporting on Campuses Worryingly Low." *CBC News*, 6 February. https://www.cbc.ca/news/canada/sex-assault-reporting-on-canadian-campuses-worryingly-low-say-experts-1.2948321.

Scott, Marian. 2017. "Is McGill Failing Crisis Management 101?" *Montreal Gazette* (blog), 15 April. http://montrealgazette.com/news/local-news/is-mcgill-failing-crisis-management.

Seidman, Karen. 2016. "Students Slam McGill for Refusal to Proceed with Sexual Assault Policy." *Montreal Gazette* (blog), 8 April. http://montreal gazette.com/news/local-news/students-slam-mcgill-for-refusal-to-proceed-with-sexual-assault-policy.

Shields, Billy. 2013. "McGill Campus Football Team at Centre of Sex Assault Controversy." *Global News*, 22 November. https://globalnews.ca/news/985364/mcgill-campus-football-team-the-centre-of-sex-assault-controversy/.

Silence Is Violence. n.d. "About Silence Is Violence." *Silence Is Violence.* Accessed 22 June 2017. http://www.silenceisviolence.ca/about/.

Sills, Sophie, Chelsea Pickens, Karishma Beach, Lloyd Jones, Octavia Calder-Dawe, Paulette Benton-Greig, and Nicola Gavey. 2016. "Rape Culture and Social Media: Young Critics and a Feminist Counterpublic." *Feminist Media Studies* 16 (6): 935–51.

Slack, Jennifer Daryl. 2012. "Beyond Transmission, Modes, and Media." In *Communication Matters: Materialist Approaches to Media, Mobility and Networks*, edited by Jeremy Packer and Stephen B. Crofts Wiley, 143–58. London: Routledge.

Smith, Roberta. 2014. "In a Mattress, a Lever for Art and Political Protest." *New York Times,* 21 September. https://www.nytimes.com/2014/09/22/arts/design/in-a-mattress-a-fulcrum-of-art-and-political-protest.html.

Spencer, Connor. 2017. "Reflections on La Journee De Reflexion." *McGill Daily,* 3 April. http://www.mcgilldaily.com/2017/04/reflections-on-la-journee-de-reflexion/.

Staggenborg, Suzanne, and Amy Lang. 2007. "Culture and Ritual in the Montreal Women's Movement." *Social Movement Studies* 6 (2): 177–94.

Stewart, Kate. 1991. "University Needs Active Sexual Assault Policy." *McGill Daily*, 22 November. https://archive.org/details/McGillLibrary-mcgill-daily-v81-n044-november-22-1991-13737.

Stojsic, Leslie. 2001. "Changing Times for the Lettered Crowd." *McGill Reporter* 33 (10). http://www.reporter-archive.mcgill.ca/33/10/frats/index.html.

Strong-Boag, Veronica. "Women's Movements in Canada: 1969–85." *The Canadian Encyclopedia.* https://www.thecanadianencyclopedia.ca/en/article/womens-movements-in-canada-196085.

Tutton, Michael. 2013. "Saint Mary's University Frosh Chant Cheers for Rape, Underage Sex." *Global News,* 4 September. https://globalnews.ca/news/819744/saint-marys-university-frosh-chant-cheers-for-rape-underage-sex/.

Yiannoutsos, Alexandra, Sarah M. Mah, and Kateryna Gordiychuk. 2016. "An Open Letter on McGill's New Policy against Sexual Violence: A Renewed Commitment to End Violence." *MIR* (blog), 6 December. https://www.mironline.ca/mcgills-new-policy-sexual-violence-renewed-commitment-end-violence-women/.

16

Countering Rape Culture
with Resistance Education

H. Lorraine Radtke, Paula C. Barata, Charlene Y. Senn,
Wilfreda E. Thurston, Karen L. Hobden,
Ian R. Newby-Clark, **and** *Misha Eliasziw*

INTRODUCTION

Focusing on *rape culture* opens up the analysis of sexual assault from
a relatively narrow focus on single incidents, the individual
perpetrator(s), and the individual victim(s) to a consideration of how
social processes enable rape and other forms of sexual violence.
Interventions aimed at preventing sexual violence then need to be
directed at wide-ranging concerns, including social norms related to
femininity, masculinity, and sexuality, and the habitual patterns of
individual action and relationships that arise in the face of the sex/gen-
der and sexuality categories and personal identities. In this paper, we
address how a sexual assault resistance education program directed
at first-year university women – the Enhanced Assess, Acknowledge,
and Act program (EAAA) – is informed by an understanding of rape
culture and is effective precisely because it confronts the cultural scaffolding of rape (Gavey 2005). In so doing, we also speak directly to a
debate within the feminist community regarding the ethics of sexual
assault prevention programs aimed at women. The disagreement
relates to the following question: Are *all* sexual assault prevention
programs for women necessarily woman-blaming? Our position is
that it is both possible and necessary in this time and place (i.e., 2020
in Canada) to provide young women with an empirically supported
sexual assault resistance educational program grounded in feminism.

Such a program must be aimed at resisting sexual assault perpetrated by an acquaintance, and must not hold women responsible for any sexual assaults that they may have experienced in the past or may experience in the future.

Blaming women in general, and the particular women who have been victimized, is a critical element of rape culture. So, to develop an implicitly or explicitly woman-blaming program would be to feed into rape culture rather than to oppose it. Thus, in an effort to provide a feminist-grounded, empirically supported educational program for women, we have had reason to be particularly reflective about how exactly each program component targets rape culture. The challenge has been to respond effectively to an often informally expressed, frequently precipitant reaction that any such program for women is inherently woman-blaming. Our claims in this chapter are that educating young women (1) is an important and effective strategy for undermining rape culture, and (2) can be accomplished without holding women responsible for the sexual aggression of others.

We begin with a brief introduction to EAAA and our research on its effectiveness, followed by our response to the feminist critique of educational programs for women, including our arguments about the necessity of educating young women, and an explication of how EAAA subverts rape culture.

THE EAAA PROGRAM: ITS MAKEUP AND EFFECTIVENESS

In 2005–06, Charlene Senn (with the assistance of graduate students Stephanie Gee and Kristin Saunders) developed EAAA. She drew on feminist and social psychological theories and the advice of leading feminist rape researchers Patricia Rozee and Mary Koss (Rozee and Koss 2001; see also Senn 2013), aiming to provide young women with knowledge and skills needed to defend themselves against sexual assault perpetrated by men they know. From the outset, Senn was guided by feminist values to develop a program designed for women that recognized sexually coercive men as responsible for their actions and which would be well received by anyone who identifies as a woman, including sexual violence survivors.

The program presents a mix of information and activities requiring participants to solve problems related to assessing a situation as dangerous and taking action, reducing emotional obstacles to taking action, and defending themselves verbally and physically. They also apply the provided information to scenarios that reflect commonly encountered situations. The program is organized in four three-hour units. Unit 1, Assess, presents evidence about risk. Participants learn about specific behaviours and aspects of social situations that may signal danger from an acquaintance. The unit expands women's strategies for reducing risk by undermining perpetrators' advantages, for example, managing a situation where the woman has become separated from her friends at a party. Unit 2, Acknowledge, focuses on teaching participants to recognize, as soon as possible, the potential danger related to escalating coercion. This unit also deals with emotional barriers to action, for example, overcoming concerns about being rude and acknowledging that a man you know and like may be attempting to sexually assault you. Importantly, the unit refutes the miscommunication hypothesis – that is, the claim that sexual assault may occur because women fail to communicate their refusals or really mean "yes" when they say "no" (see also Beres, Senn, and Mccaw 2013; McCaw and Senn 1998). Unit 3, Act, centres on effective resistance tactics against known men, including verbal and physical self-defence based largely on the feminist Wen-Do Women's Self Defence program.[1] The selective use of various tactics, both verbal and physical depending on the situation, is discussed with an eye toward successful resistance against acquaintances, including intimate partners. The resistance tactics described and practised in this unit are based on the strategies known to lead to the best outcomes for women (Tark and Kleck 2014; Ullman 2014). Emotional barriers to self-defence in these contexts, such as reluctance to physically confront or harm someone you know, are also an important topic. Unit 4, Relationships & Sexuality, concentrates on basic, positive sexual education.[2] This includes exploring a full range of sexual practices, identifying one's own sexual values and desires, and discussing ways to communicate with a partner about particular sexual activities and safer sex practices. Importantly, like all the EAAA units, the sexual education provided is never proscriptive, but rather is aimed at making participants' own relationship and sexual values visible.

Our research has shown the EAAA's effectiveness using a randomized controlled trial (RCT), the gold standard for demonstrating treatment efficacy. At one-year follow up, the relative risk of rape,[3] defined as oral, vaginal, or anal penetration through a man's use of threats, force, or drug/alcohol incapacitation, was reduced significantly (by

46 per cent) for women who completed the EAAA program, compared to a group of women who had not completed the program (Senn et al. 2015). The results were consistent for other forms of sexual assault and program effectiveness lasted for at least two years (Senn et al. 2017). The program also had a number of other positive outcomes. It increased self-confidence related to self-defence, and, most importantly for our argument in this chapter, decreased rape myth acceptance and victim-blaming (ibid.). To date, EAAA is the only currently available campus intervention that has proven to decrease the sexual violence that women experience through the rigorous test of a RCT.

Negative Feminist Reactions to EAAA

In developing the EAAA, Charlene Senn believed that the non-feminist, woman-blaming educational programs for women that were offered at the time were problematic. Her objective was to build a program that was feminist to the core and would educate women about victim-blaming in the context of sexual assault. Having done just that, she was surprised when she encountered the feminist argument that *all* programs for women, including feminist self-defence programs, were necessarily woman-blaming. She responded to this criticism (Senn 2011; Senn, Saunders, and Gee 2008), but we had to contend with it again when we conducted the RCT assessing EAAA's effectiveness.

In fall 2011 when we launched the study, we confronted concerns that were expressed both directly and indirectly. Although they were few in number, it made us aware of an ongoing difference of opinion regarding how to fight rape culture. Direct concerns were relayed to us primarily by email, and we were able to satisfy these individuals. Email correspondence with us raised the following issues, which were based on having viewed our recruitment posters: (a) our recruitment of women only, when men too could be victims, and (b) the perception that we blamed women for sexual assault. In each case, we responded respectfully with an email detailing the make-up of the program and its theoretical foundations, and offered a face-to-face meeting if desired. We received satisfied email replies in return and no requests for in-person meetings. We took this as evidence that with more information about the program, critics no longer saw the program as woman-blaming.

Indirectly expressed concerns were more dissatisfying for the research team, in that we had no opportunity for dialogue with the troubled parties. These are the "precipitant reactions" that we referred to at the beginning of the chapter – a label that highlights the concerns as not inviting discussion of varied viewpoints. One instance was a private online discussion, including students and a few faculty, that we learned about through a faculty member. Someone also took down recruitment posters across campus, a form of activism that we read as critique. Although we completed the study with highly satisfactory results, these actions, and similar arguments emerging on social media after widespread media coverage of the research, served as reminders that, our feminist intentions and study results aside, we needed to engage with the debate.

Indeed, scientific evidence of the program's effectiveness does not address the ethical concerns raised by those who would argue that EAAA is simply another way to blame women and hold them responsible for their own victimization. After all, we have provided evidence that the program reduces women's acceptance of rape myths and victim-blaming in our published peer-reviewed articles. Those who charge EAAA with woman-blaming despite the published research are fixated on the education program being for women only. Concerns about leaving out men victims can be easily deflected by highlighting studies that document the qualitatively different experiences of men victims (e.g., Bullock and Beckson 2011; Stern, Cooper, and Greenbaum 2015). Nevertheless, this still leaves the objection that men are the perpetrators, and hence interventions should focus on "curing" men. In the spirit of dialogue with those who take this position – especially people we have not had the opportunity to communicate with directly – we aim to show how EAAA can be an effective tool in not just resisting, but dismantling, rape culture, and that to do so by these means is not to blame women, but rather to provide them with knowledge and skills they can use to actively participate in rape culture's demise.

THE ETHICS OF SEXUAL ASSAULT RESISTANCE: UNDERMINING RAPE CULTURE

In this section, we lay out a series of arguments, rooted in feminist scholarship, that make the general case that resistance education for young women is a way of undermining rape culture. This background is critical to an appreciation of how EAAA in particular contributes to this project. Effective resistance education is characterized by two features. First, it ensures that women are empowered to act in their own defence, while placing full responsibility for sexual violence on those who perpetrate it. Second, it enables women to hear and understand counter-discourses to the dominant, rape culture-supporting discourses. By counter-discourses, we allude to alternative meanings of sex/gender and sexuality that do not serve to reinforce rape culture. Taken together, these two "lessons" of resistance education, and EAAA specifically, invite women to reflect on rape culture in the context of their own lives. In these ways, the program, as a particular manifestation of resistance education, contributes to social and political change.

Empowering Women to Defend Themselves against Sexual Coercion

We are not the first to point out that women's resistance to sexual coercion is one strategy for undermining rape culture. Ullman (2010), for example, drew on Gavey (2007) to suggest a *refusal paradigm*. Two of her recommendations are relevant to EAAA: (1) the need to address the social context, that is, the social norms and institutional and organizational practices that enable and maintain sexual assault of women and girls by men; and (2) the inclusion of self-defence training, both to counter many women's inclination to be passive and to support a new norm where women's judgement is respected and they have the recognized right to defend themselves in all ways necessary. In short, what is central is not self-defence training per se, but self-defence training that incorporates Ullman's two recommendations.

EAAA is consistent with Ullman's suggestions. The overall aim of EAAA is to assist women in learning to trust and help themselves while maintaining a clear focus on men's responsibility for their actions (Senn 2011). Although deceptively simple, this objective means profoundly questioning culture and what is considered ordinary. Most women do not grow up being positioned as powerful. They do grow up with the cultural assumption that normal masculinity involves coercive behaviour. Given this context, challenges for the program include: (a) fostering women's sense of their strengths, ability to act, and confidence in their powers, while avoiding woman blaming; (b) enabling women to identify risk, while not making them more fearful for their safety, and (c) questioning heterosexual norms for straight and bisexual women, while being inclusive of lesbians and other women who may not date men for other reasons (e.g., asexual identity, culture). These challenges, which EAAA has successfully overcome, are connected to culturally contingent meanings of sex/gender and hence are relevant to concerns about undoing rape culture.

Confronting Patriarchal Meanings of Sex/ Gender and Sexuality through Resistance Education

The idea that culture supports the sexual assault of women by men and is tied to the cultural meanings of sex/gender is at least as old as the feminist movement arising in the mid-twentieth century (e.g., Burt 1980; Brownmiller 1975). Feminists, such as Martha Burt (1980, 229), noted the significance of gender, understood as a social and cultural phenomenon, for sexual assault:

> the data reported here imply that changing adherence to rape myths will not be easily accomplished, since they are so closely interconnected with other strongly held and pervasive attitudes. They do suggest that a fruitful long-range strategy would begin by fighting sex role stereotyping at very young ages, before it is complicated by sexual as well as sex role interactions ... Only by promoting the idea of sex as a mutually undertaken, freely chosen, fully conscious interaction, in contradistinction to the too often held view that it is a battlefield in which each side tries to *exploit* the other while avoiding exploitation in turn, can society create an atmosphere free of the threat of rape. Rape is the logical and psychological extension of a dominant-submissive, competitive, sex role stereotyped culture.

Almost forty years later, the dominant meanings of sex/gender and sexuality have not been sufficiently altered to eliminate sexual coercion. Indeed, in present times, we find C.J. Pascoe and Jocelyn Hollander (2016, 68) raising the concern that "young men can simultaneously position themselves as 'good guys' who don't rape while symbolically engaging with sexual assault to signal the dominance that is constitutive of Western masculinity at this historical moment." To exemplify their point, they describe events associated with the 2015 Rose Bowl game. The winning team sang "No means no" to a tune routinely used by the fans of that year's losing team. The taunt was a reference to the losing team's quarterback, who had been accused of rape prior to the game. The chant celebrated victory and

simultaneously asserted the winning team's sports prowess and domination over the losers. After all, to take that which belongs to the
losers, in this case their chant, is the ultimate form of domination.
Pascoe and Hollander refer to this example as *mobilizing rape* as "a
way of doing gender" (69). Their argument echoes Burt's (1980)
emphasis on sex roles, stereotypes, and in particular, the cultural equa-
tion of masculinity with dominance and femininity with submissive-
ness. In mobilizing rape, men reproduce the form of masculinity that
is all too familiar: dominance over women, and, as in Pascoe and
Hollander's (2016) example, other men.

Gender inequality and masculinity defined as dominance have continued despite societal shifts in attitudes about sexual assault (ibid.).
Moreover, masculinity and femininity continue to be defined in opposition to one another. Attempts to break down the sex/gender binary
remain largely unsuccessful, despite the very public and political
struggles related to transgender people and other diversities associated
with sex/gender and sexuality. At stake here is a drastic shift in what
it means to be human, and this includes those identified with the sex
category male or female, as well as those who resist and challenge this
binary. It makes sense, then, that any primary intervention into rape
culture necessarily requires efforts to alter the social relations and
psychology associated with all sexes, all genders, and all sexualities.

Understanding rape culture as built on a foundation of sex/gender
and sexuality norms opens a space for educating young women who
have grown up in a time well past the struggles of second-wave feminists, and who may not yet appreciate the limits on gender equality
in Canadian society. If the sex/gender binary and its connections to
sexuality are the problem that underlies rape culture, then focusing
solely on masculinity and men as perpetrators misses an important
opportunity to question and transform the meanings of being feminine
and female. More importantly, why should women wait for men to
change before they consider their own futures? If undermining rape
culture entails changing social relations and individual psychology,
then shouldn't young women be encouraged to actively participate in
those transformations and consider their own circumstances and possibilities? Given the challenges of undermining rape culture, shouldn't
feminists use available knowledge to help young women consider how
to resist those constraints without limiting their choices in the usual
way (e.g., no alcohol, no "sexy" clothing, and no being out late at
parties)? In retitling EAAA the Flip the Script™ program, Sarah

Deatherage and Student Affairs Marketing and Communication at Florida Atlantic University drew on this feminist agenda embedded within EAAA to succinctly name its objectives regarding sex/gender.

There is a further compelling reason to educate young women as a strategy for ridding society of rape culture. Research has shown us the insidious ways in which presupposed social norms and beliefs related to femininity, masculinity, and heterosexuality produce a blurry boundary between "just sex" and rape, and constitute a "cultural scaffolding of rape" (Gavey 2005). In exploring women's accounts of unwanted sex, Nicola Gavey showed how women's choices are limited by cultural meanings that make it difficult for women to resist men's sexual desires. For example, some of her participants constructed saying "no" as virtually impossible if the woman previously had had sex with the man, and sometimes women positioned themselves as nurturing men by consenting to sex that the women did not want, but the men "needed." Gavey's research highlighted how mundane acts of heterosexuality are nonetheless political: they involve power relations, which enable certain ways of being (in this case, a heterosexual relationship where men's needs and expectations take priority over women's), and constrain other ways of being (women do not see any viable options). Thus, the same norms and meanings operate for women and men in the context of "just sex" and in the context of coerced sex. Importantly, how those power relations are negotiated depends on available cultural meanings, which again both enable and constrain women's (and men's) actions. Providing discourses and meanings (e.g., feminist ones) that compete with the ones that are part of rape culture offers the possibility of social change. Gavey's account rests on the recognition that we – researchers and other women (and men) alike – cannot escape culture. So again, women, like men, must be part of the process of socio-cultural change, and feminist interventions addressed to women are one way of attempting to influence the direction of that change.

Confronting the Meaning of Rape

The meaning of rape is connected to cultural meanings of sex/gender and sexuality. Therefore, negotiations of its meanings are also important if we are to undermine a rape-supportive culture (Marcus 1992). In treating rape as a *linguistic fact*, Sharon Marcus (ibid.) underlined how normative understandings of rape make women "rapeable" through the assumptions that rape is enabled by men's physical size and strength and that women are vulnerable to rape for all the usual reasons, including those identified as rape myths. Instead, Marcus imagined empowering women "to take the ability to rape completely out of men's hands" (388). Emphasizing that rape is a process open to analysis and undermining as it unfolds, she noted that it entails both verbal and physical interactions:

> The language of rape solicits women to position ourselves as endangered, violable, and fearful and invites men to position themselves as legitimately violent and entitled to women's sexual services. This language structures physical actions and responses as well as words, and forms, for example, the would-be rapist's feelings of powerfulness and our commonplace sense of paralysis when threatened with rape ... I am defining rape as a scripted interaction which takes place in language and can be understood in terms of conventional masculinity and femininity as well as other gender inequalities inscribed before an individual instance of rape (390).

To defend oneself against rape through words and actions, is, according to Marcus, not only a practical strategy for the moment, but "strikes at the heart of rape culture" (400). Furthermore, current media culture suppresses knowledge of women's resistance and its effectiveness (Hollander and Rodgers 2014), which means that programs such as EAAA serve an important role in making that knowledge available to women.

A central element of rape culture is the tendency to blame women for not avoiding rape because, for example, they consumed too much alcohol. Another is the tendency to disbelieve that a woman was assaulted. A recent exposé published in the *Globe and Mail* established that one in five sexual assault cases reported to the police in Canada are deemed to be unfounded, a category that has been used inconsistently but presumably indicates that the women's claims were not believed and the police concluded that a rape had not occurred (Doolittle 2017). Among the cases described over several weeks of coverage were those of many university women. When women's accounts of their actions are scrutinized retrospectively and found wanting, end of case! Attention is taken away from the men perpetrators and women are left to deal with the consequences of being accused of having lied, or of having been unclear about their wishes, or of having miscommunicated.

Sexual assault resistance education grounded in feminist theory about rape prepares young women to confront the cultural meaning and dismissal of rape in their own lives or the lives of other women. Specifically, it is an effective way to counter victim-blaming by others and to offer perspective when one is the target of victim-blaming. This serves to undermine rape culture, in that resistant women may refuse to blame victims or allow victim-blaming to keep them passive and submissive. To arrive at this conclusion requires an understanding of how sex/gender plays out in our social world in a way that facilitates rape and other forms of sexual violence. We and others who favour resistance education, such as Gavey, Ullman, Hollander, Rozee, Koss, and Cermele, recognize this central connection between the meanings of sex/gender, sexuality, and rape.

THE EAAA IN ACTION: SUBVERTING RAPE CULTURE

How, though, does the EAAA program work to undermine rape culture? In this section, we build on the theoretical arguments made in the previous section to highlight the ways in which EAAA contributes to undermining rape culture and argue that the program has proven to be effective precisely because it weakens some of the underpinnings of that culture.

Reconstructing Sex/Gender

The social construction of sex/gender is clearly a central aspect of rape culture, and any critical analysis, whether at the level of individual psychology or the social world, must involve both masculinity and femininity because they are defined as opposites. Thus, any efforts to intervene in rape culture necessarily entail women reconsidering who they are and how they can live their lives.

EAAA guides women to critically question dominant meanings of femininity and masculinity in order to address barriers to responding forcefully to sexual coercion. The Acknowledge unit, in particular, takes issue with norms that encourage women to be "nice" and to value relationships over their own sexual desires and rights. Their right to not be sexually assaulted is pitted against societal expectations for pleasant or passive feminine behaviour. This unit helps them see the social pressures that constrain their behaviour. For example, they are asked to consider realistic situations: being pinned against a wall in a semi-public place by a friend's boyfriend, and being alone in a dorm room with a man they like when he starts to act differently. They then think through what their emotional reactions would be in that situation (e.g., embarrassed, confused, etc.) and how their goals (e.g., to avoid a scene, build a relationship) might realistically affect what they do next. The discussion of the constraints on their behaviour that follows is aimed at recognizing their responses as normal but then challenging those very responses because their right to safety super-sedes the discomfort that comes with challenging gender norms.

The Act unit makes women's physical capabilities – no matter her size, shape, fitness, or ability – visible, and narrates the success stories of women with no or little self-defence training. The unit includes research showing that when women fight back verbally and physically they are usually effective (e.g., Tark and Kleck 2014). It encourages women to focus on the future and not to ruminate about what they might have done or not done in the past. As well, the temporary freeze response, so commonly experienced when women are confronted by men's sexual violence, is treated as normal, but then women are given tools to change fear into anger, such as yelling to access the oxygen and adrenaline required to act. Women's self-knowledge and unique positioning to decide what they should do or could do in a particular situation, whether in the past or the future, is emphasized. Every woman leaves with a toolbox that includes effective verbal and physi-cal strategies that she would be willing to use against a man she knows who threatens her bodily integrity. This is particularly important in dealing with acquaintances, because women are especially reluctant to fight back when the coercive man is someone they know. Like the other units, Act also makes norms related to women and gender explicit. Media images of helpless women who can do no more than wait to be saved or pound lightly on an attacker's chest are contrasted with unrealistic images of "tough girls" who defy gravity with super-human strength and skill. By exposing these stereotypes as constrain-ing women's behaviour, room is made for verbal and physical self-defence that women can engage in.

Reconstructing Sexuality

The sex/gender binary with its polar opposites has its counterpart in heterosexual sexuality constructed as a relationship between compatible partners: the active, desiring, dominant man and the passive, receptive, subordinate woman. Arguably, this heterosexual norm shapes the meanings of rape, regardless of the sexual identities of perpetrator and victim. Women who do not identify as heterosexual or as sexual must account for their "deviance" and are also at risk of sexual assault by a man (e.g., Balsam, Rothblum, and Beauchaine 2005). Thus, the norms of sexuality that underlie rape culture are relevant to everyone.

The final unit, Relationships and Sexuality, challenges rape culture through its focus on desired sexual activity. Here, feminine norms of submission and passivity with regards to sexual desire are challenged in a number of ways. For example, women are given time to think about their own sexual desires and the kinds of activities that they enjoy or would be interested in trying, if any. This helps deconstruct the definition of "having sex" and opens up possibilities that extend beyond intercourse or nothing. This unit includes a number of role-playing activities that put women in an active role, initiating desired sexual activity or making their needs clear (e.g., arguing for the use of a condom/latex dam when faced with a partner's refusal). These activities directly combat rape culture by challenging norms about women's passivity and men's dominance when it comes to sexual activity, and by reinforcing women's right to pleasure.

Reconstructing Rape as a Process

EAAA was founded on the assumption that men perpetrators are responsible for their coercive and harmful actions (Senn 2011). Women may be able to undermine rape culture by being better equipped to assess situations associated with higher risk of sexual assault. The first unit of the program, Assess, takes up this issue, which echoes Sharon Marcus's insight that rape is a process to be analyzed. The emphasis on *recognizing* risk rather than *avoiding* risk acknowledges that young women can benefit from knowing about behaviours and situations associated with higher risk of sexual assault. The program encourages them to understand risk factors rather than avoid them. It gives them a repertoire of strategies that suit them personally and are likely to *reduce* the coercive man's advantage, thereby altering the social relations between the woman and that coercive man. She is now positioning him as a potential, but not infallible, danger and may be able to take steps to resist his efforts to control the situation. Thus, she positions herself as an actor, who has resources at her disposal that she knows how to use.

In the Assess unit, participants watch two versions of a similar video that depicts a dating situation between a young man and woman.[4] In both versions, the man is coercive and attempts to control the situation in various ways. Having already discussed risk cues and protective strategies, the program participants work as a group to identify the risk cues present in the first version that ends in a sexual assault. They then view the second version and identify the strategies the woman in the video uses to undermine the man's advantages in various ways, which interrupts his ability to progress in his coercive behaviour. Thus, participants come to understand sexual assault as unfolding over time. The videos present the coercive man as a problem, and the woman as actively analyzing the situation and making decisions based on her evolving assessments of the situation. This disrupts the assumption that women are powerless in the face of men's desires and need to remain passive and polite. It also disrupts the assumption that coercive men are simply acting on their sexual desires, instead positioning them as strategically creating a situation in which they have the required advantage to coerce and if necessary force a woman to engage in sexual activities that she does not want. Like the Act unit, the dialogue with the women is not prescriptive, and it is assumed that each woman knows best what she could or should do when faced with a coercive acquaintance.

The sexual assault process includes what happens after a woman has been raped, and thus rape culture is implicated further. Rape culture shapes women's actions after they have been raped and how others respond to them. As well, laws and policies may reflect rape culture and help perpetuate low reporting rates. EAAA can protect against this to some extent. As we have shown, women who participated in the program and were subsequently raped reported less self-blame (Senn, Hobden, and Eliasziw 2016), which may remove one barrier to reporting (Zinzow and Thompson 2011). As well, the program provides women with resources that can help them seek support or services and understand reporting procedures if they or their friends should need them.

To undermine societal expectations that rape victims should immediately report a sexual assault, EAAA presents reporting as only one possible option, and facilitators challenge the presumption that reporting is necessary. The small group size and women-only context implicitly and explicitly supports greater bonds and solidarity between women regardless of their decisions. This means that women who do report and are subsequently blamed have the knowledge and resources to challenge the victim-blaming that they may experience. Further, this aspect of EAAA works to undermine rape culture by calling into question existing judicial and administrative processes and creating a space for social and institutional change.

RECOMMENDATIONS FOR FUTURE RESEARCH AND POLICY

We recommend that policies on sexual violence include prevention strategies aimed at undermining rape culture. Our research on EAAA has demonstrated that this particular program does prevent rape, and as we have argued, also undermines rape culture in other ways. Thus, universities ought to feel as obligated to offer EAAA as they do to provide appropriate processes for responding to sexual assault. Resources must be tied to such policies, however. Complex programs like EAAA are resource intensive and challenging to implement. Without policies that support implementation of effective programs and the resources to do so, it is simply not feasible for universities to take them up. That said, in assessing the merits of funding programs like EAAA, universities also need to consider the foreseeable costs of not doing so, such as having women who experience sexual assault on campus seek legal redress against the university for its failure to offer what has proven to be an effective prevention program. They must also consider the costs of bad publicity generated by members of their community who perpetrate sexual assault. In general, policies and accompanying resources need to keep an eye on the long-term outcomes, broadly defined.

One further policy recommendation is for universities and colleges to adopt a multifaceted action plan to ending sexual assault and undermining rape culture that incorporates EAAA together with other evidence-based strategies. As we have tried to make clear in this chapter, we believe that EAAA is part of the solution even though it does not provide *the* solution. The educational information and opportunities for critical reflection and practising resistance provided by EAAA can work with, rather than against, other approaches, and can also make up for deficits in those other approaches. Because sexual assault by an acquaintance most commonly occurs in private, promising programs like bystander intervention (Coker et al. 2017; Moynihan et al. 2015) leave a gap that can only be filled by an initiative, like

EAAA, that equips women to act on their own behalf. Bystander approaches also have a variety of potential weaknesses that are explored elsewhere in this volume. In particular, they may reinforce benevolent sexism, or the notion that women need to be rescued. While all of us require the support of other individuals in our communities at times, EAAA focuses attention on women's own strengths beyond their capacity to help others.

Interventions that focus on men and combine bystander approaches with dedicated messaging about masculinities, male privilege, and social norms are also an important way to challenge rape culture (e.g., Gidycz, Orchowski, and Berkowitz 2011; Katz, Heisterkamp, and Fleming 2011; Barone, Wolgemuth, and Linder 2007; Katz 1995). EAAA, which helps to undo the female socialization that renders women unprepared for sexual assault by men they trust, complements the most effective men's programs, such as the Men's Workshop (Gidycz, Orchowski, and Berkowitz 2011). In fact, all policies that promote mutual respect and tolerance and which recognize gender as a social construct that promotes sexual assault can contribute to ending rape culture.

Appreciating the complementary nature of these various interventions and working in a collaborative environment may be the most effective political strategy today. Recent gains in societal and institutional buy-in concerning the need to combat rape culture on college and university campuses are easily eroded. For example, in September 2017, the Education Department in the United States rolled back President Obama's initiative on how post-secondary institutions were to institute policies and procedures aimed at preventing and handling cases of alleged sexual assault (Tatum 2017). Universities in Canada have also pointed to a backlash against efforts at sexual violence education and prevention that predate recent campaigns to ensure that post-secondary institutions have effective sexual assault policies (Godderis and Root 2017; Kingston 2013). These are compelling reasons to implement EAAA alongside other programs. Clearly, rape culture is an old phenomenon that requires "new" strategies if it is to be even diminished.

A final policy recommendation applies more broadly to any services (from legal to medical and non-governmental) that provide interventions for women who experience sexual assault. Such services should critically examine their existing policies and practices for aspects that support the myth that victims of sexual assault are weak, naïve, or somehow damaged. This requires attending to the subtle sexism that is associated with rape culture. We also need to be vigilant that as EAAA and other effective interventions become more readily available, women who are sexually assaulted are not blamed if they chose not to participate in a campus program.

Future research must consider how policies, procedures, survivor supports, and different programs may most effectively work together to undermine rape culture (for examples of programs, see Orchowski et al. 2018). However, collaboration does not negate the significance of attending to the effectiveness of individual programs before they are launched; only adding *effective* programs together will result in deeper knowledge of what works when and why, thus creating sustainability of outcomes. Further, while an RCT may be the gold standard for assessing treatment effectiveness, studying how programs fare when implemented under non-controlled conditions is also critical (see, e.g., Hollander 2014). In the case of EAAA, although there are manuals to guide new users and an established and required training program for those wishing to offer the program, there will inevitably be some gap between how the program was implemented in the controlled research context and how it is implemented in practice in universities across Canada. Besides assessing program effectiveness in this more fluid context, implementation research may identify the conditions critical to program effectiveness, and produce important information to guide ongoing development of the program to meet the specific and changing needs of the population being served. Our research team is currently conducting such a study on a number of Canadian university campuses where EAAA is being implemented to answer these questions.

Additionally, although it is important to study the impact on program participants, it would also be valuable to explore the influence of the program participants on their peers, who may not have participated themselves. Studying possible changes in the attitudes and conduct of men and women non-participants in a university setting where a program like EAAA is offered focuses on the broader consequences of undermining rape culture. As well, studying how delivering the program affects the graduate student facilitators would be a worthy endeavour. Knowing the program content intimately and interacting with numerous program participants is likely to shift the facilitators' perspectives of the culture and encourage political engagement with the forces that maintain rape culture. Being able to demonstrate these wider circles of influence would strengthen the resolve of those committed to countering the forces that enable sexual violence. Undermining rape culture through prevention, however, will take time, and thus longitudinal research assessing both individual change and campus cultural change is needed to document the long-term effects of prevention programs.

CONCLUSION

In this chapter, we have unpacked how a sexual assault resistance program that is supported by evidence targets rape culture. Our motivation for doing this arose in the context of a debate about the ethics of sexual assault prevention programming for women. By bringing this debate into the public arena, we aimed to provoke a shift away from opposition to programs for women or, at the very least, to open a dialogue with the objective of establishing a feminist consensus. We have argued that such programming is not only ethical but essential, if the ultimate goal is to erode the foundations of rape culture. The underpinnings of rape culture are implicated in the humdrum of everyday life, the taken-for-granted and mundane. EAAA invites young women to reconsider this by reimagining themselves and their intimate relationships with others. Further, it equips them with knowledge and skills to bring those imaginings to life. In this way, young women's actions may contribute to the radical transformations required to replace rape culture with a culture shaped by principles such as equal rights and social justice.

NOTES

1 Wen-Do is a self-defence program for women, originating in 1964. Taught only by women, it reflects feminist, anti-racist, and anti-oppression values and analysis. Girls as young as ten years old may also participate. It is transgender woman inclusive. The program includes discussion alongside acquiring physical and verbal techniques and strategies. Importantly, the program assumes that the attacker will often be physically larger and stronger than the woman. It does not assume that women are physically fit or without physical limitations and disabilities. See www.wendo.ca.

2 Activities are adapted with permission from the *Our Whole Lives* sexuality curriculum (Goldfarb and Casparian 2000; Kimball and Freidani 2000).

3 Relative risk of rape refers to the probability of being raped after participating in EAAA compared to the control condition (i.e., receiving information about sexual assault in the form of brochures and having the ability
to ask questions). It is calculated by dividing the proportion of participants in the EAAA condition who reported an incident of rape post-
program by the proportion of participants in the control condition who
reported an incident of rape post-program. When this ratio is less than
1.00, as it was in this case, the ratio is subtracted from 1.00 to yield the
relative risk reduction. A relative risk reduction of 46 per cent means that
the probability of a woman being raped after participating in EAAA is
reduced by 46 per cent compared to the probability of being raped had
she received information about sexual assault through brochures
(brochures are available on almost all university campuses).

4 The videos were adapted/updated from ones developed by Hanson
and Gidycz (1993).

REFERENCES

Balsam, Kimberly F., Esther D. Rothblum, and Theodore P. Beauchaine.
2005. "Victimization over the Life Span: A Comparison of Lesbian,
Gay, Bisexual, and Heterosexual Siblings." *Journal of Consulting and
Clinical Psychology* 73 (3): 477–87.

Barone, Ryan P., Jennifer R. Wolgemuth, and Chris Linder. 2007.
"Preventing Sexual Assault through Engaging College Men." *Journal of
College Student Development* 48 (5): 585–94.

Beres, Melanie A., Charlene Y. Senn, and Jodee Mccaw. 2013. "Navigating
Ambivalence: How Heterosexual Young Adults Make Sense of Desire
Differences." *Journal of Sex Research* 51 (7): 1–12.

Brownmiller, Susan. 1975. *Against Our Will: Men, Women, and Rape.*
New York: Simon and Schuster.

Bullock, Clayton M., and Mace Beckson. 2011. "Male Victims of
Sexual Assault: Phenomenology, Psychology, Physiology." *The
Journal of the American Academy of Psychiatry and the Law* 39 (2):
197–205.

Burt, Martha R. 1980. "Cultural Myths and Supports for Rape." *Journal
of Personality and Social Psychology* 38 (2): 217–30.

Coker, Ann L., Heather M. Bush, Patricia G. Cook-Craig, Sarah A. DeGue,
Emily R. Clear, Candace J. Brancato, Bonnie S. Fisher, and Eileen A.
Recktenwald. 2017. "RCT Testing Bystander Effectiveness to Reduce
Violence." *American Journal of Preventive Medicine* 52 (5): 566–78.

Doolittle, Robyn. 2017. "Unfounded: Why Police Dismiss 1 in 5 Sexual Assault Claims as Baseless." *Globe and Mail*, 3 February. https://www.theglobeandmail.com/news/investigations/unfounded-sexual-assault-canada-main/article33891309/.

Gavey, Nicola. 2005. *Just Sex? The Cultural Scaffolding of Rape*. New York and London: Routledge.

Gidycz, Christine A., Lindsay M. Orchowski, and Alan D. Berkowitz. 2011. "Preventing Sexual Aggression among College Men: An Evaluation of a Social Norms and Bystander Intervention Program." *Violence against Women* 17 (6): 720–42.

Godderis, Rebecca, and Jennifer L. Root. 2017. "Addressing Sexual Violence on Post-Secondary Campuses is a Collective Responsibility." *Transformative Dialogues: Teaching and Learning Journal* 9 (3): 1–9.

Goldfarb, Eva S., and Elizabeth M. Casparian. 2000. *Our Whole Lives: Sexuality Education for Grades 10–12*. Boston: Unitarian Universalist Association of Congregations.

Hanson, Kimberly A., and Christine A. Gidycz. 1993. "Evaluation of a Sexual Assault Prevention Program." *Journal of Consulting and Clinical Psychology* 61 (6): 1046–52.

Hollander, Jocelyn A., and Katie Rodgers. 2014. "Constructing Victims: The Erasure of Women's Resistance to Sexual Assault." *Sociological Forum* 29 (2): 342–64.

Katz, Jackson. 1995. "Reconstructing Masculinity in the Locker Room: The Mentors in Violence Prevention Project." *Harvard Educational Review* 65 (2): 163–75.

Katz, Jackson, H. Alan Heisterkamp, and Wm Michael Fleming. 2011. "The Social Justice Roots of the Mentors in Violence Prevention Model and Its Application in a High School Setting." *Violence against Women* 17 (6): 684–702.

Kimball, Richard S., and Judith Frediani. 2000. *Our Whole Lives: Sexuality Education for Adults*. Boston: Unitarian Universalist Association of Congregations.

Kingston, Anne. 2013. "The Real Danger for Women on Campus." *Maclean's*, 27 November.

Marcus, Sharon. 1992. "Fighting Bodies, Fighting Words: A Theory and Politics of Rape Prevention." In *Feminists Theorize the Political*, edited by Judith Butler and Joan W. Scott, 385–403. New York: Routledge.

McCaw, Jodee M., and Charlene Y. Senn. 1998. "Perception of Cues in Conflictual Dating Situations: A Test of the Miscommunication Hypothesis." *Violence against Women* 4 (5): 609–24.

Moynihan, Mary M., Victoria L. Banyard, Alison C. Cares, Sharyn J. Potter, Linda M. Williams, and Jane G. Stapleton. 2015. "Encouraging Responses in Sexual and Relationship Violence Prevention: What Program Effects Remain 1 Year Later?" *Journal of Interpersonal Violence* 30 (1): 110–32.

Orchowski, L.M., K.M. Edwards, J.A. Hollander, V.L. Banyard, C.Y. Senn, and C.A. Gidycz. 2018. "Integrating Sexual Assault Resistance, Bystander, and Men's Social Norms Strategies to Prevent Sexual Violence on College Campuses: A Call to Action." *Trauma, Violence, and Abuse.* https://doi.org/10.1177/1524838018789153.

Pascoe, C.J., and Jocelyn A. Hollander. 2016. "Good Guys Don't Rape: Gender, Domination, and Mobilizing Rape." *Gender and Society* 30 (1): 67–79.

Rozee, Patricia D., and Mary P. Koss. 2001. "Rape: A Century of Resistance." *Psychology of Women Quarterly* 25 (4): 295–311.

Senn, C.Y., Kristin Saunders, and Stephanie Gee. 2008. "Walking the Tightrope: Providing Sexual Assault Resistance Education for University Women without Victim Blame." *Violences Faites aux Femmes: Problemes Sociaux et Interventions Sociales,* edited by Suzanne Arcand, Dominique Damant, Sylvie Gravel, and Elizabeth Harper, 353–72. Quebec City: Les Presses de Université du Québec.

Senn, Charlene Y. 2011. "An Imperfect Feminist Journey: Reflections on the Process to Develop an Effective Sexual Assault Resistance Programme for University Women." *Feminism and Psychology* 21 (1): 121–37.

– 2013. "Education on Resistance to Acquaintance Sexual Assault: Preliminary Promise of a New Program for Young Women in High School and University." *Canadian Journal of Behavioural Science/Revue Canadienne Des Sciences Du Comportement* 45 (1): 24–33.

Senn, Charlene Y., Misha Eliasziw, Paula C. Barata, Wilfreda E. Thurston, Ian R. Newby-Clark, H. Lorraine Radtke, and Karen L. Hobden. 2015. "Efficacy of a Sexual Assault Resistance Program for University Women." *New England Journal of Medicine* 372 (24): 2326–35.

Senn, Charlene Y., Misha Eliasziw, Karen L. Hobden, Ian R. Newby-Clark, Paula C. Barata, H. Lorraine Radtke, and Wilfreda E. Thurston. 2017. "Secondary and 2-Year Outcomes of a Sexual Assault Resistance Program for University Women." *Psychology of Women Quarterly* 41 (2): 147–62.

Senn, Charlene Y., Karen L. Hobden, and Misha Eliasziw. 2016. "Effective Rape Resistance Training: Can It Reduce Self-Blame for Rape

Survivors?" Presentation at the Annual Convention of the American Psychological Association, 4 August, Denver, CO.

Stern, Erin, Diane Cooper, and Bryant Greenbaum. 2015. "The Relationship between Hegemonic Norms of Masculinity and Men's Conceptualization of Sexually Coercive Acts by Women in South Africa." *Journal of Interpersonal Violence* 30 (5): 796–817.

Tark, Jongyeon, and Gary Kleck. 2014. "Resisting Rape: The Effects of Victim Self-Protection on Rape Completion and Injury." *Violence against Women* 20 (3): 270–92.

Tatum, Sophie. 2017. "Education Department Withdraws Obama-Era Campus Sexual Assault Guidance." *CNN*. https://www.cnn.com/2017/09/22/politics/betsy-devos-title-ix/index.html.

Ullman, Sarah E. 2010. *Talking about Sexual Assault: Society's Response to Survivors*. Washington, DC: American Psychological Association.

– 2014. "Reflections on Researching Rape Resistance." *Violence against Women* 20 (3): 343–50.

Zinzow, Heidi M., and Martie Thompson. 2011. "Barriers to Reporting Sexual Victimization: Prevalence and Correlates among Undergraduate Women." *Journal of Aggression, Maltreatment and Trauma* 20 (7): 711–25.

17

Telling Stories and Making Sense of Campus Culture

Diane Crocker

INTRODUCTION

In fall 2013, the participation of Saint Mary's University students in a pro-rape chant surfaced on the internet and exploded in the mainstream media. Like other universities faced with similar incidents, the university reacted quickly. Administrators appeared on media outlets apologizing and vowing to do better. The campus community held meetings, workshops, and town halls to grapple with the event. The president established a task force to explore what happened and to propose ways to ensure that something similar would not happen again.

Student responses were diverse. Some who had participated in the chant were devastated by their actions' consequences. Others expressed confusion over the controversy. While admitting that it may have been in poor taste, some students minimized it as "just a chant." Many disagreed with the faculty consensus that the chant was a manifestation of campus rape culture. To faculty, as well as some students highly engaged with issues relating to gender, any failure to understand the relationship between the chant and rape culture was a way of thinking that needed to change. There was a clear disconnect between, on the one hand, many students' understandings of the event and what it represented, and, on the other hand, the prevailing views among faculty and administrators.

The President's Council produced a report that included policy and program improvements to promote "broad culture change" (Saint Mary's University President's Council 2013). The report recommended policy improvements, changes in orientation week, and increases in training and available resources for anyone affected by sexual violence. An action team pursued these recommendations in subsequent years.

In my view, however, we have moved forward without having adequately understood the culture we want to change. We need to better understand the complexity of our students' experiences and understandings of rape culture, sexualized violence, and consent before we can design responses that will successfully speak to students. Otherwise, the tools we develop to respond and intervene risk failing to achieve the "broad culture change" that we believe necessary.

This chapter describes a project that reveals the complex context in which we work to reduce campus sexual violence and promote a safer campus culture.[1] I have collected over 400 narratives from students on two Nova Scotia campuses. They recounted stories related to consent, rape culture, and bystander interventions in unsafe situations. I take students' interpretations of their own stories to both elucidate the cultural context in which we work and show how our current efforts to intervene will have limited effects.

CONTEXT

In response to sexualized violence and campus rape culture, post-secondary institutions have designed programs and policies that target the problems (Anderson and Whiston 2005; Banyard, Plante, and Moynihan 2004; Berkowitz 2001; Davis and Liddell 2002; Lonsway 1996; McMahon, Postmus, and Koenick 2011; Hensley 2003).[2] The programs typically aim to educate students, change their attitudes, and thus (hopefully) their behaviour. Some explicitly target rape culture, and most are geared towards victims and potential victims and perpetrators (McMahon and Banyard 2012). Many aim to dispel "rape myths" and help students see the link between sexist and degrading language and sexual assault (McMahon and Banyard 2012; Foubert 2000; Lanier 2001, cited in Hayes-Smith and Levett 2010).

Despite the proliferation of programs, reports of sexual violence and manifestations of rape culture continue to take place. Researchers have proposed several explanations. Hayes-Smith and Levett (2010) suggest that while programs raise awareness of the issue, they fail to increase the visibility of the problem, in the sense that students can dismiss what they have learned as applicable only to other students. Other researchers have suggested that programs are based on common sense, but are not well grounded in theory (McMahon and Banyard 2012). and they have not incorporated theories about changing attitudes (Hayes-Smith and Levett 2010).

Consent programs have been developed without much research having been done on how students understand sex and how they understand and negotiate consent (Jozkowski and Peterson 2013). Consent training is premised on research that conceptualizes sex as either wanted or unwanted and it sometimes fails to recognize a more complex model in which women (or men) may want sex but not its potential consequences (e.g., pregnancy). Muehlenhard and Peterson (2005) have proposed a model that moves beyond a simple binary of wanted and unwanted sex or consensual sex and rape. They argue, for example, that we should distinguish between wanting sex and consenting to sex.

COMPLEXITY

Dave Snowden and Mary Boon (2007) outline three types of problem relevant to the research proposed here: simple, complicated, and complex. Simple problems are characterized by repeating patterns. They can be understood in terms of easily identifiable cause-and-effect relationships. These problems may be addressed based on facts and "best practices." Complicated problems require expertise to uncover the less obvious cause-effect relationships and underlying patterns, but they are still made up of the sum of their parts (Keogh 2018). While there may be more than one solution to a complicated problem, the resolution is still driven by facts. Complex problems present as "fluid and unpredictable" (Snowden and Boon 2007, 7). They require us to probe the problem, uncover patterns, and develop creative interventions that emerge from our understanding of the context. To illustrate, Snowden and Boone (2007) suggest that fixing a Ferrari is a complicated problem, but fixing a rainforest is complex.[3]

Given the context described above, the culture in which campus sexual violence occurs is more like a rainforest than a Ferrari. It constitutes a complex problem that does not present with identifiable causes and effects, and how it will respond to interventions is unpredictable. Yet programs and policies to address campus problems are pitched at the simple or complicated realm. Our responses have relied on facts, best practices, expertise, and the search for cause-effect relationships. Responses to university rape culture have tended to assume linear relationships between causes (e.g., students' adherence to rape myths) and effects (e.g., sexist comments and sexual harassment). We teach students facts about rape, we try to counter the myths, and we expect their behaviour to change accordingly.

Many program and policies address the simple and complicated aspects of campus sexual violence. An example of the former is designing a mobile app for students that gives them easy access to information about who to contact in case of an assault, or which provides user-friendly information could help fill a gap in students' knowledge. If students simply do not know who to call, an app can help them find out. Bystander training addresses campus sexual violence at a more complicated level. The programs do not prescribe only one way to intervene, and encourage a more nuanced understanding of situations that may require action, but still assume a linear relationship between bystander intervention and preventing sexual violence.

Both approaches will be necessary to fully address the problem of campus sexual violence. Nonetheless, neglecting to address the complex realm will limit our ability to create the "broad culture change" that is needed. As Liz Keogh (2018) suggests, culture change cannot be imposed. It instead emerges from small positive changes, the effects of which need to be amplified over time. From a complexity perspective, our responses have failed to recognize that complex problems do not respond well to solutions that assume static, cause-effect relationships. For this reason, they also do not respond well to traditional research methods. I argue that taking a complexity perspective will help us better understand the limitations of our current responses and help direct us to new ones.

CURRENT APPROACHES TO RESEARCHING CAMPUS SEXUAL VIOLENCE

Much research about campus sexual violence relies on quantitative methods, particularly campus climate and victimization surveys. Climate campus surveys measure campus characteristics expected to relate to sexual violence. These typically include individual characteristics, such as gender, and situational ones related to campus culture. Victimization surveys capture the incidence of various experiences such as rape or sexual harassment. Some researchers have included questions to generate numbers about how many people have perpetrated sexual violence. Others include various scales to measure adherence to rape myths among students.

These efforts are critical to documenting the extent of problems on campuses. But there are limitations to how well these data can lead us to effective interventions. Questions about rape myths may mask some less overt but perhaps even more problematic attitudes (Hayes-Smith and Levett 2013). Questionnaires measuring attitudes are also susceptible to social desirability bias and respondents who are able to guess the "right" answer.

Qualitative researchers have gotten more nuanced pictures of how campus culture relates to sexual violence. Some ethnographic work and analysis of "talk" has been particularly insightful (Sanday 1990; Jozkowski and Peterson 2013). But Jazkowski and Peterson (2013) point out a limitation of their own research, relevant to the project described in this chapter. Their study explored how students negotiate consent and asked them direct questions about how they get consent and how they communicate it. The researchers produced a thematic data analysis. They describe the "imprecise semantics" in students' responses, which featured language ambiguities that could be interpreted in different ways. For example, many male students said that the way they sought consent was by telling a woman that they were going to have sex. The researchers point out that they cannot tell whether this meant the men thought they were ordering women to have sex, or beginning a dialogue with a statement.

COLLECTING CAMPUS NARRATIVES

This chapter draws on insights from students' narratives about consent, rape culture, and bystander interventions in unsafe situations. The research reported here has been informed by ideas related to complex social problems.

In winter 2017, a research team collected 412 micro-narratives, or very short anecdotes, from students on two campuses in Nova Scotia. Research assistants walked around the campuses and invited students to fill out a paper questionnaire. They then entered the data into SenseMaker®, a software package developed by Snowden (2010) that allows researchers to collect and analyze large amounts of narrative data (Webster 2012).

The sample is quite varied. Most stories, 73 per cent, come from women, and participants' median age fell between twenty and twenty-four years old. Almost all students who responded were undergraduates (96 per cent), with half (48 per cent) registered in the Faculty of Arts. Business students represented 26 per cent of those who responded, and science students 24 per cent. Given these numbers, women are overrepresented in the sample (they constitute 48 per cent of students on campus); business students are somewhat underrepresented; and Arts students overrepresented. The age distribution of students in the sample is close to the age distribution of students on campus, although the sample is somewhat younger.

SenseMaker® questionnaires differ from traditional surveys in two major ways.[4] First, a SenseMaker® "signification framework," as the questionnaire is called, begins with a story prompt. It asks research participants to recount a micro-narrative, a short paragraph or a few sentences, about an experience related to the issue being explored. Next, the signification framework invites participants to code, or signify, their own story: research participants tell the researcher what they think their story is about. The software provides triangles, described in more detail below, that allow a research participant to indicate their story's meaning by putting a dot in a triangle labelled with options that could describe some aspect of the story they told.

SenseMaker® data analysis begins with the researcher looking for patterns in how participants indexed their own stories. The researcher maps the ways stories have been "signified," or indexed, rather than looking first at the stories themselves. The software produces various graphical representations of the data to show distributions, correlations, and clusters, essentially plotting how respondents signified their stories (Snowden 2010). The software provides cross-tabulations along various axes and indices, including demographics and other questionnaires included on the instrument. The researcher can also compare how different types of participants indexed their stories.

This approach to data collection and analysis allows quantitative data to be "supported by the rich context of self-interpreted narrative," and "provides a more objective basis for qualitative interpretative processes by the researcher" (Snowden 2011, 228). As Snowden states, "because stories carry with them ambiguity, their meaning can be interpreted in different ways in different contexts. While few would disagree that narrative creates meaning, the question arises as to how it should be interpreted" (ibid., 227). The patterns revealed in SenseMaker® offer insight into what the stories meant to the people who told them.

The questionnaire included prompts related to three domains: consent, rape culture, and bystander intervention. Students were asked to choose one prompt and describe an experience relating to the issue raised in the prompt. The *consent prompt* aimed to elicit stories about intimate encounters and consent negotiation. Just under half of students (45 per cent) answered this prompt. The prompt was worded as follows:

> *Describe a time when you, or someone you know, had physical or sexual contact with someone on campus but were unsure about whether it was fully consensual. What happened?*

OR

> *Describe a time when you, or someone you know, had physical or sexual contact with someone on campus and were sure that it was fully consensual. What happened?*

The *rape culture prompt,* answered by 31 per cent of students, explicitly used the term "rape culture" to provide insight into what experiences students categorized as exemplifying "rape culture":

> *Describe something that happened to you, or someone you know, that shows that rape culture is alive and well on campus. What happened?*

OR

> *Describe something that happened to you, or someone you know, that shows that worries about campus rape culture are exaggerated.*

The third prompt sought stories related to safety more broadly and about bystander intervention in particular. A quarter of students responded to the *bystander prompt,* which asked:

> *Think about a time when you were worried about your safety or someone else's safety on campus. Describe a time someone successfully intervened, and everyone was kept safe. What happened?*

OR

> *Describe a time when no one intervened and something bad happened. What happened?*

Students could answer one prompt, and since each prompt included two options, students could tell either a story they thought was positive or a story they thought was negative.[5]

INTERPRETING CAMPUS NARRATIVES

The questionnaire asked students several multiple-choice questions about their stories. These questions constitute one way for students to index their stories. Their answers provide descriptive data about the stories and experiences they chose to write about. Almost all stories (95 per cent) involve students, and half describe an experience that happened to someone other than the student who answered the questionnaire (i.e., a story about "someone else"). In 40 per cent of the stories, the characters were friends, acquaintances, or friends of friends. Close to one-third of the stories involve encounters between strangers, while few stories (11 per cent) related to encounters between intimates. While the stories are not described as being widely known (59 per cent are known to only "a few others"), neither are they rare events: more than half involved something that happened regularly or all the time. Students characterized their stories as overwhelmingly negative – less than 10 were associated with positive emotions. The most common emotions that students associated with their stories included anger, powerlessness, and shame. Most positive stories involved consensual sexual encounters.

The relationships between which story prompt a student answered and the characteristics of the story they told provide more insight into the context in which these stories took place. Table 17.1 shows several patterns. The rape culture and bystander stories more evenly split between being about either the storyteller or someone else, whereas two-thirds of the consent stories were about someone else. While not surprising, the most striking pattern about the relationship between story prompt and characters in the stories relates to how few rape culture and bystander stories were about intimates. In addition, these stories more often involved strangers. The consent stories were more typically about friends, acquaintances, or intimates. This pattern shows that students tend to think about stories between people who know each other when they think about consent. In contrast, they rarely think about stories about intimates when thinking about rape culture or bystander intervention.

Table 17.1 also shows the relationship between story prompt and the impacts of the story, from the students' perspectives. The students

Table 17.1
Relationships between story prompt and characteristics

	Story prompt		
WHOSE EXPERIENCE WAS THIS?	Consent	Rape culture	Bystander intervention
Someone else	64%	57%	56%
Me	36%	43%	44%
Total	100%	100%	100%
n	(165)	(98)	(90)
HOW WOULD YOU DESCRIBE THE RELATIONSHIP BETWEEN THE MAIN CHARACTERS?			
Friend/acquaintance	46%	41%	35%
Intimate	23%	6%	9%
Stranger	31%	53%	57%
Total	100%	100%	100%
n	(142)	(79)	(81)
HOW LONG WILL THE EFFECTS OF THIS EXPERIENCE LAST?			
Forever	11%	17%	0%
A very long time/long time	35%	50%	28%
Not long	19%	14%	27%
Very briefly/already forgotten	34%	18%	46%
Total	100%	100%	100%
n	(148)	(98)	(79)
HOW COMMON IS THIS KIND OF SITUATION?			
All the time/regularly	57%	65%	55%
Occasionally/rarely	43%	34%	45%
Total	100%	100%	100%
n	(155)	(102)	(83)
WHO KNOWS/KNEW ABOUT WHAT HAPPENED?			
Me and a lot of others	15%	38%	18%
Me and a few others	67%	54%	70%
Me and one other	14%	6%	8%
Only me	4%	3%	4%
Total	100%	100%	100%
n	(171)	(117)	(91)
RATE THE EMOTIONAL INTENSITY OF THIS EXPERIENCE FOR YOU.			
Strongly negative/negative	60%	73%	70%
Neutral	31%	26%	23%
Strongly positive/positive	9%	1%	7%
Total	100%	100%	100%
n	(181)	(195)	(186)

indicated that rape culture stories were the most memorable, most frequently occurring, and most widely known. Many stories recounted for this prompt involve incidents widely reported in the media, in particular the incidents that occurred locally at Saint Mary's and Dalhousie. Such incidents would be widely known due to media reporting, but the pattern here suggests that incidents receiving media attention are the tip of the iceberg for students who regularly see examples of similar behaviours, and that they see these incidents as evidence of rape culture.

In terms of emotional impact, table 17.1 shows that rape culture and bystander stories had more negative impact on storytellers than consent stories. This seems somewhat odd given that the stories related to consent more often involved sexual assault. Perhaps the negative impact was muted because so many of the latter stories recounted someone else's experience, and the question asked students to rate their own emotional intensity. Importantly, though, these incidents are still having a negative emotional effect on students who told the stories, even if the storytellers had not been directly involved.

The questionnaire included another set of questions that allowed students to indicate what their stories meant to them or how they interpreted their stories. The questionnaire used "triads" to do this. A triad, as in figure 17.1, depicts a triangle with each point labelled with a different word or phrase that might fit or describe a story. One triad, reproduced below, asked students what motivated the people in their story to act. If the student felt that the event was motivated only by individual attitudes, they put a dot in the top of the triad. If the student felt that their story was exclusively motivated by cultural norms, they put a dot in the bottom right point of the triad. Students put a dot in the centre if they felt that their story was equally motivated by individual attitudes, cultural norms, and university rules/polices. Each dot on the triad represents how one student labelled the story they wrote on the questionnaire.

The students' thoughts on motivation tell us something about their understanding of how these events can happen. Figure 17.1 shows that very few students identified university rules/polices as having motivated people in their story. The stories in that section of the triad seem unrelated. One described a lockdown and another recounted the university's failure to act about a reported rape because the students had graduated. A third story involved a professor who lectured their class about the rape chant mentioned earlier in this paper. What is notable is the lack of stories tagged as motivated by rules/policies, and that most dots on the triad are associated with individual attitudes and the space in between individual attitudes and cultural norms.

While few students tagged their story as motivated exclusively by cultural norms, in the bottom right of the triad, many stories here related to incidents that happened while students were drinking.

A large proportion of stories in this triad were tagged at the top of the triad, classifying them as being motivated by individual attitudes or a mix of individual attitudes and cultural norms. The stories characterized as exclusively motivated by individual attitudes were diverse, but fewer involved alcohol than those characterized as motivated by cultural norms, and about one-quarter involved positive outcomes of experiences involving alcohol. These positive stories typically involved someone helping a drunk person. Interestingly, many students characterized stories about consensual sex as being motivated by individual attitudes as well. Most stories about consensual sex were tagged as motivated by individual attitudes. Many, 28 per cent, of students identified the people in their stories as being fairly equally motivated by individual attitudes and cultural norms. Many stories from that area of the triad involve sexual harassment by strangers, sexual assault, and the incidents reported in the news that happened at local universities.

The overall pattern in this triad suggests that students see people in their stories as motivated mainly by individual attitudes, sometimes in combination with cultural norms. Consensual sex, according to the patterns in the data, is motivated intrinsically by individual attitudes. Students tended to associate experiences related to alcohol with cultural norms, rather than individual attitudes.

Figure 17.2 shows a triad in which students situated their story as being about relations between genders, sexualized culture, and individualized beliefs. The pattern is somewhat less stark than in figure 17.1, but we see the dots clustered around one side of the triad. In this triad, however, we see fewer dots at the extremes and a larger proportion in the middle. The stories in the middle, tagged as being equally about gender relations, individualized beliefs, and sexualized culture, vary considerably.

The stories tagged as being exclusively about individualized beliefs involved more harassment – not always sexual – and less alcohol than those tagged as exclusively sexualized culture. In fact, stories relating to alcohol and sexual assault tended to be tagged closer to sexualized

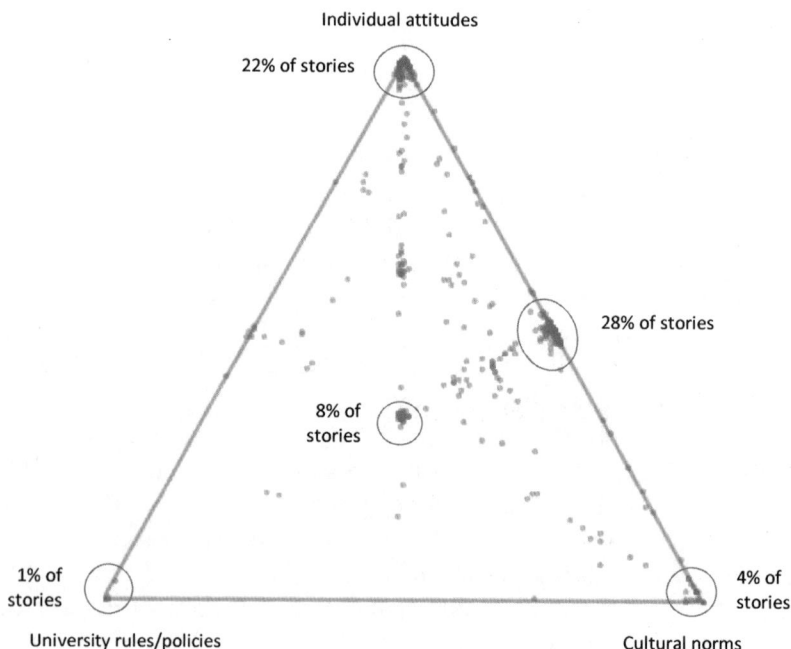

17.1 What motivated people in your story to act the way they acted?

culture and away from relations between genders and individualized beliefs. The stories tagged as being about individualized beliefs were more often about harassment than assault. Finally, a larger proportion of stories tagged as being about relations between genders described consensual sexual encounters than elsewhere in the triangle. Several stories relating to physical violence also appear at the triangle's apex. These patterns suggest that students associate alcohol and sexual violence with a sexualized culture, but consensual encounters and physical violence with relations between genders.

COMPLEXITY AND CONTEXT

Students witness or have heard about many negative experiences related to consent, rape culture, and bystander intervention. Students regularly see examples of the kinds of events that make the news and they do not feel good about it. These findings are not surprising. Campus surveys have described high levels of sexual violence and its negative impacts. But the patterns here reveal more about how students

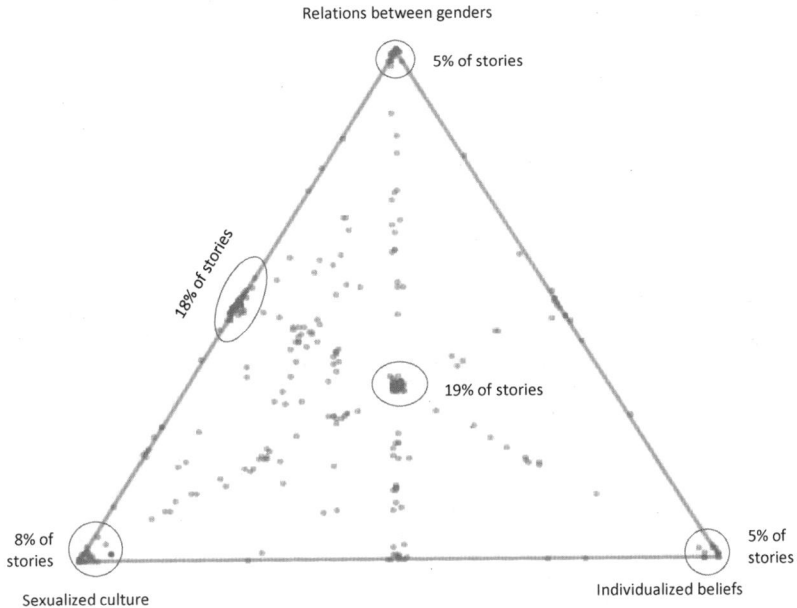

17.2 The experience I wrote demonstrates something about ...

understand the context in which their stories happened and the complexity of the context in which universities work to intervene.

Students rarely think about stories involving intimates when thinking about rape culture or bystander interventions. They are not inclined to think about encounters between intimates as part of rape culture, or to see opportunities to intervene in incidents that occur between intimates. Programs that describe incidents between intimates as illustrative of rape culture may, therefore, not align with how students interpret their own experiences or the experiences of others around them. In addition, we know that bystander training cannot help students intervene with incidents that happen behind closed doors and between intimates. But given how students categorized their narratives, it may be that they will find it difficult to recognize red flags when people are intimate or in dating relationships.

Students described stories about sexual encounters, good and bad ones, as happening between people who know each other rather than between strangers (table 17.1). This reflects the empirical reality: the people we know put us at more risk than strangers. But the students' indexing of their stories tells us more than that. When it comes to stories about consensual sex, the students indicated that these experiences were motivated mainly by individual attitudes, sometimes in combination with cultural norms (figure 17.1) and relations between genders (figure 17.2). This tells us something about how we might go about amplifying the conditions for consensual sex. This finding suggests that consent programs should, therefore, work to strengthen individual attitudes related to consensual sex rather than focus on the broader cultural context. The idea of "consent culture," for example, may not make sense or be efficacious in this context. These patterns also suggest that programs about consent should directly address relations between genders. This might constitute discussions about gender roles and inequality.

In addition, the parts of both triads in which we find the stories about consent tended to involve fewer stories about alcohol. Of course, we know that alcohol creates circumstances in which consent becomes more tenuous and sexual assault more likely. But, looking at how the students indexed more stories related to alcohol – as motivated by cultural norms and as about sexualized culture – gives some insight into the nature of the problem. We know that drinking is a cultural norm on campus. What this data suggests, though, is that having negative sexual experiences while drinking is also a norm: students expect these experiences. This finding speaks to the need to address drinking, and the negative sexual experiences that come with it, as extrinsically motivated and perhaps even taken for granted. Students have a shared expectation that drinking and negative sexual experiences happen together. This finding suggests ways of framing the problem of alcohol and sexual violence that may resonate with students' understandings of their own experiences.

Another way to look at each triad is to associate each point with the three contexts described earlier: simple, complicated, and complex. Each point in the triad in figure 17.1 aligns with characteristics of each context. University rules/policies can address only the simple realm where relationships between causes and effects are easy to identify. Individual attitudes are more complicated. Identifying ways to affect individual attitudes, or their underlying causes, requires expertise and good practice. But, as Liz Keogh (2018) suggests, we can still "analyze the problem, closing the gap between where you are and where you want to be." Good educational programs, that remain flexible and responsive as opposed to scripted and rigid, may help change individual attitudes. Cultural norms lie in the realm of the complex. The relationship between causes and effects cannot be identified and interventions may have unintended positive or negative effects. In the language of complexity theory, then, students view motivations in the complicated or complex realm. Simple interventions, like rules, will not change their motivations. In addition, given the distribution of stories related to alcohol, we cannot assume that rules or education programs targeting individual attitudes will have an impact on negative experiences related to drinking and sexual violence.

Like in figure 17.1, the points on the second triad (figure 17.2) align with simple, complicated, and complex contexts. In this case, individual beliefs are simpler than relations between genders, and sexualized culture lies in the realm of the complex. The pattern in figure 17.2 shows a similar tendency for students to tag stories more as belonging to the complicated and complex contexts. Likewise – and perhaps most tellingly in relation to universities' efforts to change culture – stories involving alcohol lay in the complicated and complex realm: we find more stories related to alcohol and sexual violence on the left side of this triad. Again, stories related to alcohol are tagged as demonstrating something about culture, not individuals.

CONCLUSIONS

The patterns in the narratives described above reveal the context in which we work to change campus culture. They show how students interpret experiences related to consent, rape culture, and bystander intervention. Unlike other research methods, the narrative approach gets at students' "tacit culture knowledge" (Goh 2011) about the context, rather than their opinions. The patterns in the narratives show their underlying orientation to the context rather than their explicit beliefs about it. The patterns reveal the disposition of the context to change in particular ways.

We are seeing a deep desire to commit to culture change among those interested in reducing campus sexual violence.[6] The promise in this language lies in how it has framed the issue as embedded in culture. Having said that, if we learn anything from complexity theory, we should recognize that the kinds of recommendations embedded in these reports will have limited effects.

The data reported in this chapter goes some way toward exploring campus culture and how students understand the context in which sexual violence and harassment occur. The data point to experiences that lie in the realm of the complex and will therefore be unresponsive to changes in rules and policies. Experiences related to alcohol and negative sexual experiences, in particular, will require change processes that account for complexity. These stories will not change if universities' interventions focus only on changing individual behaviours.

RECOMMENDATIONS FOR POLICY AND FUTURE RESEARCH

Universities should focus less on changing rules and polices and turn their attention to interventions that might produce more meaningful culture change. This change will not come from doing more of the same kinds of programs and policies that we have relied on for years; it will come only with interventions developed through a deep understanding of campus cultures. Universities should include in policies expectations around engagement and participatory processes to effect culture change, rather than focusing on rules, policies, and education or training.

To catalyze this type of change, more research should involve students as ethnographers of their own experiences, and more attention should be paid to the cultural norms related to alcohol and sex. It will not be enough to remind students of the relationship between drinking and sexual assault. Learning more about how students understand and make meaning of their experiences needs to guide future policy and program development.

NOTES

1 The project, *Methods Matter: Integrating Complexity into Research on Rape Culture*, was funded by the Social Sciences and Humanities Research Council (grant # 430-2015-00410) and the Nova Scotia Department of Community Services.
2 See Nelund's chapter in this volume for an overview of Canadian university policies.
3 For a further explanation of this framework see Cognitive Edge (2019a).
4 For information on SenseMaker® see Cognitive Edge (2019b).
5 I designed the story prompts based on several group interviews and workshops with students that pretested potential prompts.

6 The report from my own institution emphasized culture change (Saint Mary's University President's Council 2013) and a recent report from the Council of Nova Scotia University Presidents (n.d.) is titled *Changing the Culture of Acceptance*. In addition, a Universities UK Task Force has produced a report that addresses violence against women, harassment, and hate crimes on UK campuses (UUK 2016).

REFERENCES

Anderson, Linda A., and Susan C. Whiston. 2005. "Sexual Assault Education Programs: A Meta-Analytic Examination of their Effectiveness." *Psychology of Women Quarterly* 29 (4): 374–88.

Banyard, Victoria L., Elizabeth G. Plante, and Mary M. Moynihan. 2004. "Bystander Education: Bringing a Broader Community Perspective to Sexual Violence Prevention." *Journal of Community Psychology* 32 (1): 61–79.

Berkowitz, Alan D. 2001. "Critical Elements of Sexual Assault Prevention and Risk Reduction Programs for Men and Women." In *Sexual Assault in Context: Teaching College Men about Gender*, edited by Christopher Kilmartin and Alan D. Berkowitz, 75–99. New York: Taylor and Francis.

Choate, Laura Hensley. 2003. "Sexual Assault Prevention Programs for College Men: An Exploratory Evaluation of the Men against Violence Model." *Journal of College Counselling*. 6 (2): 166–76.

Cognitive Edge. 2019a. "Cynefin Framework Introduction." https://cognitive-edge.com/videos/cynefin-framework-introduction/.

– 2019b. "SenseMaker." http://cognitive-edge.com/sensemaker/.

Council of Nova Scotia University Presidents. n.d. "Changing the Culture of Acceptance: Recommendations to Address Sexual Violence on University Campuses." https://novascotia.ca/lae/pubs/docs/changing-the-culture-of-acceptance.pdf.

Davis, Tracy L., and Debora L. Liddell. 2002. "Getting Inside the House: The Effectiveness of a Rape Prevention Program for College Fraternity Men." *Journal of College Student Development* 43 (1): 35–50.

Foubert, John D. 2000. "The Longitudinal Effects of a Rape-Prevention Program on Fraternity Men's Attitudes, Behavioral Intent, and Behavior." *Journal of American College Health* 48 (4): 158–63.

Goh, Zhen. 2011. "Narrative and the Ethnographic Inquiry." www.cognitive-edge.com.

Hayes-Smith, Rebecca M., and Lora M. Levett. 2010. "Student Perceptions of Sexual Assault Resources and Prevalence of Rape Myth Attitudes." *Feminist Criminology* 5 (4): 335–54.

Jozkowski, Kristen N., and Zoë D. Peterson. 2013. "College Students and Sexual Consent: Unique Insights." *Journal of Sex Research* 50 (6): 517–23.

Keogh, Liz. 2018. "Cynefin for Everyone." https://lizkeogh.com/cynefin-for-everyone/.

Lanier, Cynthia A. 2001. "Rape-Accepting Attitudes: Precursors to or Consequences of Forced Sex." *Violence against Women* 7 (8): 876–85.

Lonsway, Kimberly A. 1996. "Preventing Acquaintance Rape through Education: What Do We Know." *Psychology of Women Quarterly* 20 (2): 229–65.

McMahon, Sarah, and Victoria L. Banyard. 2012. "When Can I Help? A Conceptual Framework for the Prevention of Sexual Violence through Bystander Intervention." *Trauma, Violence, and Abuse* 13 (1): 3–14.

McMahon, Sarah, Judy L. Postmus, and Ruth Anne Koenick. 2011. "Conceptualizing the Engaging Bystander Approach to Sexual Violence Prevention on College Campuses." *Journal of College Student Development* 52 (1): 115–30.

Muehlenhard, Cynthia L., and Peterson, Zoë D. 2005. "Wanting and Not Wanting Sex: The Missing Discourse of Ambilvalence." *Feminism and Psychology* 15(1): 15–20.

Saint Mary's University President's Council. 2013. *Promoting a Culture of Safety, Respect and Consent at Saint Mary's University and Beyond: Report from the President's Council.* Halifax: Saint Mary's University.

Sanday, Peggy Reeves. 1990. *Fraternity Gang Rape: Sex, Brotherhood and Privilege on Campus.* New York: New York University Press.

Snowden, David. 2010. "Naturalizing Sensemaking." In *Informed by Knowledge: Expert Performance in Complex Situations*, edited by Kathleen L. Mosier and Ute M. Fischer, 223–34. New York: Taylor and Francis.

Snowden, David J., and Mary E. Boone. 2007. "A Leader's Framework for Decision Making." *Harvard Business Review* 85 (11): 68–76.

UUK. 2016. "Changing the Culture: Report of the Universities UK Taskforce Examining Violence against Women, Harassment and Hate Crime Affecting University Students." https://www.universitiesuk.ac.uk/policy-and-analysis/reports/Documents/2016/changing-the-culture.pdf.

Webster, L. 2012. "SenseMaker® Basics." Paper presented at Cognitive Edge training workshop, Albany, NY.

Moving toward Transformation

Diane Crocker

This book opened with an anecdote that reveals a certain disappointment with a lack of change around campus sexual violence. A friend and I attended a public meeting about what happened at a neighboring university when some female students discovered the sexist and misogynist Facebook page set up by their male colleagues. The panel led my friend to worry that, since her undergraduate days in the 1990s, "nothing had changed." My friend's point can be read in several ways that reverberate throughout this book's chapters.

"Nothing has changed" can be read as a comment on behaviours that have remained stubbornly persistent. Sexual violence and harassment continue in spite of early campus awareness campaigns, like "No means no" among others. While social media has provided new ways for violence and harassment to proliferate, there were always gossip networks, predatory professors, and fraternity parties.

That this book needed (and others need) to be written tells us that this aspect of campus life has not fundamentally changed. The incidents and events that have happened across Canada, and which are mentioned throughout this text, illustrate that university campuses are still not always the safe places that we would hope and expect them to be. The work that has been done has not had the desired effects. We need more transformative solutions.

My friend's comment can be read in another way – namely, that our analysis of the problem has not changed much. Several chapters provide some evidence for this. As Del Gobbo argues in his chapter, we see remnants of the "sex wars" in debates about how to respond to campus sexual violence. Harkening back to feminist conflicts related to sexual violence and the role of law, Del Gobbo sees parallels in debates over how universities should respond to sexual violence and harassment. Del Gobbo suggests that feminists should be able to rethink the poles of this conflict and agree on using a "complainant-centred" approach. Further, Radtke and colleagues discuss some feminist concerns about the EAAA program. They argue that in order to dismantle rape culture we need to focus not only on men and masculinity but on what it means to be feminine and female. The EAAA resistance program can help women undermine norms and expectations about being female that effectively prop up the longstanding meanings of sex/gender and sexuality embedded in rape culture.

Several other chapters point to limitations in our current thinking and conceptualization of campus sexual violence. Tuulia Law provides a cogent critique of two concepts central to campus sexual violence work: consent and rape culture. Law argues that we need to allow for ambiguity in what these terms mean if they are to be mobilized in a way that resonates with students: their current mobilization reinforces normative understandings and sex and sexuality and does not provide space for an intersectional analysis. Along similar lines, Malinen and Tobin reveal that feminist work on hazing and sexual violence explores the problems through a "homosocial lens." They urge us to explore the sexual violence inherent in male-on-male hazing rituals, and name it as such, in order to strengthen our analysis of the issues to be addressed on campus.

Both these chapters challenge us to be vigilant about the effects of how we mobilize concepts in our work. Jeffrey's chapter points out how this problem manifests among students themselves, and how some of their fears are driven by stereotypes and traditional sexual scripts. Their research reveals the strengths of these beliefs.

"Nothing has changed" could also describe the institutional context in which campus sexual violence and harassment take place. Women faculty still represent fewer than half of the full professors at Canadian universities and make less than their male colleagues (Statistics Canada 2018, 2019). And, of course, this says nothing about the even worse conditions faced by part-time faculty, our racialized colleagues and students, or those who do not adopt binary gender identities. Our institutions have not done much to change the systems and structures that support gender inequity on campuses. Jochelson and his colleagues' experience of having the university reject the union's proposal to put some policy in place around faculty-student relationships illustrates this point. The authors point to a sad irony that the union wanted policy, but the university did not. This experience shows that universities are more willing to regulate the sex lives of students, when in relationship with each other, than those of faculty. The authors' experience with a specific case on their campus also suggests that universities seem willing to resist examining and changing the power structures that surround faculty status and which are deeply embedded in institutional structures.

The chapters in this book challenge us to promote change in several ways. First, many challenge universities to ensure that they have appropriate policies to help prevent and respond to campus sexual violence. Both legal and ethical reasons should drive this work. In very recent years we have seen a major push in this regard. Universities in some provinces have been legislated to develop stand-alone sexual violence policies. But meeting the legal and ethical obligation to have policies does not mean that they will be good ones.[1]

Sharrif and Bonhumeur address some of the legal dilemmas associated with policy-making in this realm. They argue that policies must carefully incorporate what has been learned in the scant case law and embed principles around privacy that conform with privacy legislation in each province. The chapter by Rossiter and colleagues provides guidance to help ensure that campus sexual violence policies are "survivor centred." This approach can help universities to avoid replicating the shortcomings of criminal justice responses to sexual violence (Craig 2018). In her piece reviewing existing policies, Nelund raises related questions and points to the risks that policies create a site for "alternative justice" that actually may reflect the less desirable aspects of both criminal and restorative justice, without gaining the benefits of either. Finally, Vemuri describes the sometimes contentious role of student activists in policy design. This chapter documents the role of student associations who flip "call out culture" as a means of criticizing university administrator's work on sexual violence policy. The piece draws attention to the need to include student voices in this work. Transformation might begin with universities paying careful attention to how these author promote change.

Of course, even the best policies get played out in a particular context that may not be amendable to suitable responses. Sibley and

Moore show how victims/survivors tend not to want to avail themselves of formal reporting "architecture" laid out in university policy.
The implication is that a policy can be called "survivor-centred" and
still not serve victims/survivors well. Oliver et al. echo some of the
same themes and evoke the metaphor of "institutional walls" to
describe students' experiences seeking support from the university.
Those working to transform campus culture must be careful to avoid
policies that adopt the right language but fail to undermine the structures that make it difficult for survivors to come forward or find
appropriate support. They must also be careful to avoid what Buss
and Majury describe as operating in the "shadows," and to understand
that policy is made in more than the formal texts that describe it.
Policy is also shaped in the shadows of social relations and systems
of meaning. My own chapter pushes these points one step further to
argue that policy, by its very nature, will never be able to transform
culture in a meaningful and sustainable way.

Policies alone do not make for a survivor-centric culture or transform the systemic root causes embedded in the institution itself. And,
indeed, transformation is what is in order here. Garcia et al. show how
arts-based interventions can be transformative. They argue that art
always has the potential to challenge norms. Other existing programs
show promise in this regard. Harrigan et al.'s work is important in its
exploration of how to mobilize bystander training to most effect by
understanding who is likeliest to intervene. Dunn et al. explore
bystander interventions using an intersectional lens and show how
this approach can address institutional power structures. These are
important contributions to help push bystander training, sometimes
a palatable and politically uncontroversial program, to produce more
transformative change. The EAAA program described by Radtke and
colleagues directly confronts rape's cultural scaffolding. The
approaches described in these chapters provide an optimistic antidote
to much of the rest of the work collected in this book.

The chapters in this book include specific policy and research recommendations. These will push us past doing more work better and
toward doing different work altogether. While the chapters here do
not map a path forward, they describe its contours. Taken as a whole,
the chapters document varied locations for work in this field.
Universities must address survivors' needs, hear their voices, and be
informed by their experiences. Universities must think hard about
how processes to respond to complaints constitute important justice

work. And institutions must acknowledge that their own structures, narratives, and the social relations embedded in them are part of the problem. The power structures that keep institutional norms in place will need to be shaken up before real change will occur.

Thirty years ago, Peggy Reeves Sanday (1990) wrote about rape-supportive culture on university campuses. Features of this culture included a lot of exclusively male bonding events and an explicit expectation that brothers "score." Sanday continued to explore the theme of "rape prone" and "rape free" cultures in her second edition of the book (2007), but in this more recent incarnation, she described a fraternity explicitly founded on "rape-free values" (ibid., 4). Maybe something can change after all. This book provides a starting point for moving in the right direction, toward change that can be truly transformative.

NOTE

1 For a thorough discussion related to complaint policies see Busby and Birenbaum (forthcoming).

REFERENCES

Busby, Karen, and Joanna Birenbaum. Forthcoming. *Achieving Fairness: A Guide to Campus Sexual Violence Complaints.* Toronto, ON: Thomson-Reuters Canada.

Craig, Elaine. 2018. *Putting Trials on Trial: Sexual Assault and the Failure of the Legal Profession.* Montreal, QC: McGill-Queen's University Press.

Sanday, Peggy Reeves. 1990. *Fraternity Gang Rape: Sex, Brotherhood, and Privilege on Campus.* New York: New York University Press.

– 2007. *Fraternity Gang Rape.* New York: New York University Press.

Statistics Canada. 2018. "Number and Salaries of Full-Time Teaching Staff at Canadian Universities (Final), 2017/2018." https://www150.statcan.gc.ca/n1/daily-quotidien/181115/dq181115b-eng.htm.

– 2019. "Number of Full-Time Teaching Staff at Canadian Universities, by Rank, Sex." https://www150.statcan.gc.ca/t1/tbl1/en/tv.action?pid=3710 007601&pickMembers%5B0%5D=1.1&pickMembers%5B1%5D=3.1.

Contributors

JANE BAILEY is professor in the Common Law Section (English) at the University of Ottawa Faculty of Law, who teaches cyberfeminism, technoprudence, contracts, and civil procedure. She and Valerie Steeves co-lead The eQuality Project, a seven-year SSHRC-funded research initiative that explores the ways in which the big data environment shapes young people's online interactions and relationships, including cyberviolence against girls and young women. She is also a co-investigator on "A Multi-sectoral Partnership to Investigate and Develop Policy and Practice Models to Dismantle 'Rape Culture' in Universities," a SSHRC-funded Partnership Grant project headed by Shaheen Shariff.

PAULA BARATA is associate professor in the Department of Psychology at the University of Guelph. Her research is explicitly feminist and has largely focused on violence against women. She has examined women's experiences with the criminal justice system, minority women's definitions of abuse, housing discrimination against survivors, housing programs for women who have experienced abuse, and programs for pre-schoolers who have witnessed violence against their mothers. She has also collaborated on a successful multi-site randomized clinical trial evaluating the effectiveness of a sexual assault resistance program, and she continues to work on the wider implementation of the program.

LORI BEAVIS identifies as being of Mississauga (Anishinaabe) and Irish-Welsh settler descent. She is a band member of Hiawatha First Nation at Rice Lake, Ontario. Lori is a curator and art educator/art historian based in Montreal. Her PhD (2016) investigated the inter-sections between life-long art experiences and cultural identity in the lives of four contemporary Indigenous women artists. Her cura-torial work and art practice reflect the importance of cultural identity and self-representation, which is often articulated in the context of family and personal and cultural history. Presently at McGill University, Beavis is the P. Lantz Art Hive (MAHI) coordinator and the Faculty of Education liaison for Turtle Island Reads (2018); she also serves on the Aboriginal Curatorial Collective's Tiohtià:ke Project Advisory Committee.

JULIA BELLEHUMEUR is a BCL/LL.B candidate in the McGill Faculty of Law. Upon graduating, she will begin her career in criminal prosecution at the Crown Attorney's Office in Thunder Bay, Ontario. Julia is a co-founder of "Elevation: Equality, Inclusivity, Empowerment Inc.," a consulting organization that develops policies, procedures, and programs for sports organizations. She has worked in Malawi, Africa, for the Equality Effect, assisting in the preparation for a con-stitutional claim regarding sexual assault cases, and organizing a community based capacity-building conference. She has written inde-pendent legal research papers on sexual assault and workplace sexual harassment. She has also worked at the Student Advocacy Office, where she represented students facing university policy issues, includ-ing cases regarding sexual violence policies.

DORIS BUSS teaches and researches in the areas of international law and human rights, women's rights, global social movements, and femi-nist theory. Her research examines how gender equality and women's rights norms are framed and contested in various international legal, regulatory, and policy sites. In this work, she explores international law and policy-making on women's international human rights in various UN arenas, as well as the international responses, including criminal prosecution of conflict-related violence against women.

MINDY R. CARTER (PhD, University of British Columbia) is assistant professor in teacher education, curriculum studies, and arts education at McGill University. Carter's funded research focuses on using cur-ricular inquiry and drama education to engage with socially relevant issues (i.e., sexual violence on university campuses, Indigenous topics, and education for sustainable development).

SARA CRANN is a postdoctoral fellow in the Department of Psychology at the University of Windsor, Ontario. She received her MA and PhD in applied social psychology from the University of Guelph. Her research uses mixed methods and community-engaged approaches to examine issues related to gender and health, with a focus on male violence against girls/women. In her current position, she is leading a longitudinal project to adapt and evaluate a sexual assault resistance program for adolescent girls.

DIANE CROCKER is professor in the Department of Criminology at Saint Mary's University. Her work explores the use of law to address social problems, particularly those that disproportionately affect women. Crocker is currently working on a five-year evaluation for Circles of Support and Accountability, a community-based restorative justice initiative to help reintegrate those convicted of sex offences into the community. A second project explores sexual violence and "rape culture" on university campuses. She is currently a member of the Canadian Domestic Violence Prevention Initiative and the Gender-Based Violence Prevention Network and regularly advises government and community agencies on projects related to gender-based violence.

DANIEL DEL GOBBO is an SJD candidate at the University of Toronto Faculty of Law and an adjunct professor at Osgoode Hall Law School, York University. His research interests lie at the intersections of alternative dispute resolution, feminist and queer legal theory, access to justice, and equality law. He has recently published in the *Ohio State Journal on Dispute Resolution, Osgoode Hall Law Journal, Cardozo Journal on Conflict Resolution*, and *Canadian Journal of Law and Jurisprudence*. Previously, Daniel earned an LLM from Harvard Law School and JD from Osgoode Hall Law School.

MISHA DHILLON is the research and projects coordinator at the Ending Violence Association of BC (EVA BC). She earned a Master of Arts in Sociology from the University of British Columbia, where her research explored sexuality and sexual violence in the lives of young South Asian women in Canada. In her role at EVA BC, she contributes her expertise to numerous projects and initiatives aimed at preventing and improving responses to gender-based violence, including community-based research and the development of training and resources for the anti-violence, health, justice, and education sectors.

SUZANNE DUNN is a PhD student at the University of Ottawa Faculty of Law. Her research focuses on technology-facilitated violence, with a particular focus on harms caused by impersonation and artificial intelligence such as deepfakes. She is a research fellow with the eQuality Project and has been a policy advisor at the Digital Inclusion Lab at Global Affairs Canada.

MISHA ELIASZIW is associate professor of public health and community medicine at Tufts University. She is a biostatistician who seeks out opportunities to apply mathematical and probabilistic methods to solve clinical and public health questions through numbers. She has been a member of the EAAA project team since 2009.

SANDRA ERB is a PhD candidate in the clinical child and adolescent psychology program at the University of Guelph. She completed her undergraduate degree at the University of Waterloo where she examined the experience of mature students in higher education. Sandra's current research focuses on the experience of negative self-conscious emotions and resilience in survivors of intimate partner violence (IPV). Her master's thesis research examined the relationship between self-compassion, shame, and self-blame in IPV survivors. She is currently collecting data for her dissertation project that involves the development and validation of a trauma-related shame and guilt scale.

MARIA EZCURRA (MFA, PhD) is an artist and educator whose research interests include collaborative art practices, dress and textiles, gender-based violence, memory, identity, and immigration.

CHLOE KRYSTYNA GARCIA is a PhD candidate in the Department of Integrated Studies in Education at McGill University. Her research interests include sexualities education, sexual and gender-based violence, and as media and digital literacies.

REBECCA GODDERIS is associate professor of health studies and social and environmental justice at Wilfrid Laurier University. She is serving a three-year term as Gendered Violence Faculty Colleague working with senior leaders in the university to address gendered and sexual violence on campus. Her research and teaching is broadly in the areas of gender, sexuality, and health, and her community-based work focuses on articulating and promoting feminist intersectional approaches to the prevention of sexual violence, and on addressing inequities faced by LGBTQ+ communities.

MALLORY HARRIGAN graduated with her MA in community psychology from Wilfrid Laurier University. During her time at Laurier she worked as a research assistant for the Gendered Violence Task Force on the 2016 Campus Safety Survey: Students' Perceptions and Experiences with Sexual and Gendered Violence. She has conducted other research focused largely on sexual health. In addition to these areas of study, Mallory's research interests include community-based participatory research methodologies, and knowledge translation strategies for making findings accessible to audiences beyond academia. She is currently working in the HIV sector.

KAREN L. HOBDEN is a social psychologist and research manager in the Department of Psychology at the University of Windsor. She has been overseeing the EAAA sexual assault resistance program evaluation studies since 2011.

DAVID IRELAND works at the Faculty of Law at the University of Manitoba. A graduate of both the LL.B. and LL.M. programs at Robson Hall, Professor Ireland practised criminal law as both Crown and defence counsel before joining the faculty in 2016. His graduate thesis, "Bargaining for Expedience? The Overuse of Joint Recommendations on Sentence," supervised by Debra Parkes, highlighted the prevalence of cultural joint recommendations in the plea-bargaining process in Manitoba. Professor Ireland is a frequent presenter in the criminal justice community, regularly speaking at conferences for judges, lawyers, and law enforcement officers.

NICOLE JEFFREY is currently a research associate in the Department of Psychology at the University of Windsor in Ontario, Canada. She received her MA and PhD in applied social psychology from the University of Guelph. She uses mixed methods and feminist social-psychological theories to study men's sexual and intimate partner violence against women. She is mainly interested in the social and systemic forces that contribute to men's use of violence and women's experiences of violence. In her current position, she is collaborating on various projects related to sexual violence among university students and sexual violence resistance education.

RICHARD JOCHELSON works at the Faculty of Law at the University
of Manitoba. He holds his PhD in law from Osgoode Hall Law School
at York University, a master's in law from the University of Toronto
Law School, and a law degree from University of Calgary Law School
(Gold Medal). He is a former law clerk who served his articling year
at the Alberta Court of Appeal and Court of Queen's Bench, before
working at one of Canada's largest law firms. He worked for ten years
teaching criminal and constitutional law at another Canadian university prior to joining Robson Hall. He has published peer-reviewed
articles dealing with obscenity, indecency, judicial activism, police
powers, criminal justice pedagogy and curriculum development,
empiricism in criminal law, and conceptions of judicial and jury rea-
soning. He is a member of the Bar of Manitoba and has co-authored
and co-edited several books. He has recently co-authored *Criminal
Law and Precrime: Legal Studies in Canadian Punishment and
Surveillance in Anticipation of Criminal Guilt* (Routledge, 2018).

LEON LAIDLAW is a PhD student in sociology at Carleton University,
where he is conducting his dissertation research on the topic of transgender prisoners. His research interests fall within the scope of Trans*
studies, gender and trans theory, sex work, critical and feminist criminology, and intersectionality. Leon has headed several research projects, including his SSHRC-funded master's thesis, which revealed the
experiences of trans women in the sex industry, and an independent
project analyzing how trans students navigate institutional cisgender-
ism within universities.

DEBRA LANGAN is associate professor in criminology at Wilfrid
Laurier University. Her research interests are in the areas of policing,
women police, gendered violence, families and intimate relations, and
the scholarship of teaching and learning. Her most recent publications
appear in: *Feminist Criminology, Women and Criminal Justice, Gender
and Society, Studies in Social Justice,* and *Media, Culture and Society.*

TUULIA LAW is assistant professor in the criminology program of
York University's Department of Social Science. A key focus of her
research and teaching is the interplay of gender norms with the legal
and social governance of sexual conduct. In this broad area, Law is
currently undertaking research about students' application of anti-
sexual assault education in sexual interactions; her longstanding

involvement in research about the performance of gender in the sex industry is also ongoing.

KELLEYANNE MALINEN is professor in the sociology and anthropology department at Mount Saint Vincent University. She does research in the area of sexual violence, and has published articles about woman-to-woman sexual violence in journals such as *Symbolic Interaction* and *Affilia*. She is the editor of a volume entitled *Dis/Consent: Perspectives on Sexual Consent and Sexual Violence* (2019).

DIANA MAJURY teaches in the Department of Law and Legal Studies at Carleton University. A long-standing feminist, her teaching, research, and activism are primarily in equality theory and practice, human rights, women's health, and violence against women. She is a founding member of Women Healthsharing, the Women's Court of Canada, and the Feminist History Society.

JOANNE MINAKER received a PhD in socio-legal studies from Queen's University. She is associate dean, academic in the Faculty of Arts and Science at MacEwan University. A sociologist, qualitative researcher, and ardent mother, Minaker's body of work centres around care, human connection, and social (in)justice. An emphasis on knowledge for social transformation resonates deeply and underscores her scholarly, creative, and pedagogical contributions, which include the book *Youth, Crime and Society: Issues of Power and Justice* (2009), co-authored with Bryan Hogeveen; *Criminalized Mothers, Criminalized Mothering* (2015), co-edited with Bryan Hogeveen; and numerous articles that call into question marginalizing processes that exclude, silence, and dehumanize groups such as young women, criminalized youth, and survivors of sexual violence. In 2016, she spoke at TEDxUAlberta, "The Power of Meaningful Connections," on the transformative power of relationships inside and outside academia.

CLAUDIA MITCHELL is a James McGill Professor in the Faculty of Education, McGill, and director of the McGill Institute for Human Development and Well-Being. She works in the area of participatory visual and other arts-based methodologies, particularly in relation to gender-based violence in a variety of contexts, including Ethiopia, South Africa, and Mozambique. She also works with Indigenous girls and young women in Canada.

DAWN MOORE is associate professor in law and legal studies at Carleton University. She is the lead researcher on two SSHRC projects. "Seeing Crime" explores the use of visual evidence in cases of domestic violence. The Prison Transparency Project deploys Participant Action Research to document human rights abuses in Canadian prisons. Moore is the author of three books and has recent publications in *Theoretical Criminology*, *Punishment and Society*, *Socio-Legal Studies*, and *New Criminal Law Review*.

YAMIKANI MSOSA is a grassroots feminist anti-violence advocate and support worker. For the last decade, she has worked towards ending gender-based violence. Most of her work has been grounded in the rape crisis movement, including the Ottawa Coalition to End Violence against Women, Immigrant Women Services, and Ryerson University's Office of Sexual Violence Support and Education. She has sat on the executive of the Ontario Coalition of Rape Crisis Centres.

AMANDA NELUND is assistant professor in the sociology department at MacEwan University. She is interested in bringing together feminist and other critical criminologies in order to explore possibilities for better criminal and social justice. She is particularly interested in imagining different ways to think about and practise justice both in the context of responses to criminalized women and responses to sexual violence.

IAN NEWBY-CLARK is professor of psychology at the University of Guelph. He is a social psychologist with expertise in social cognition, attitudes, behaviour change, and methodology and statistics.

MILKA NYARIRO is a PhD candidate in the Department of Integrated Studies in Education at McGill University. Her research focuses on studying gender violence in and around schools and adopts participatory visual methodologies as intervention.

MARCIA OLIVER is associate professor in law and society at Wilfrid Laurier University. Her research and teaching cover a range of themes in global governance and development, sexuality and gender, and inequality and justice. Her most recent journal publications appear in *Refugee Survey Quarterly*, *Global Social Policy*, *Studies in Social Justice*, and *International Feminist Journal of Politics*.

TRACY PORTEOUS, RCC, is the executive director of the Ending Violence Association of BC (EVA BC). She has established herself as a leader in the Canadian anti-violence movement, having spent thirty-five years working to address the issue of gender-based violence through policy and program development, training, and cross-sector collaboration. She began her career volunteering in a sexual assault centre, and has been a driving force in the development of the award-winning, gender-based violence prevention program, Be More than a Bystander. She recently co-founded the Ending Violence Association of Canada (EVA Canada), a national organization dedicated to addressing the issue of gender-based violence.

H. LORRAINE RADTKE is professor of psychology at the University of Calgary. Her research interests include feminist theory and methods, discourse analysis, violence against women, mothering, and women's identities.

KATE ROSSITER is the research and projects manager at the Ending Violence Association of BC (EVA BC) and coordinator of the Safe Choices LGBT2SQ+ Support and Education Program. She earned her PhD in the School of Criminology at Simon Fraser University (SFU), where she was associate director at the FREDA Centre for Research on Violence against Women and Children. As a subject matter expert on gender-based violence, Kate led the development of EVA BC's campus sexual violence guidelines, and facilitates training on responding to disclosures of sexual violence to staff, faculty, and student leaders at post-secondary institutions across BC. Kate is an adjunct professor in the School of Criminology at SFU and a co-investigator for the Canadian Domestic Homicide Prevention Initiative with Vulnerable Populations.

CHARLENE SENN is professor of psychology and women's and gender studies and a Tier 1 Canada Research Chair in sexual violence at the University of Windsor. She is a long-time VAW activist and an expert on effective sexual violence interventions. She developed the Enhanced Assess, Acknowledge, Act (EAAA, a.k.a. Flip the Script™) sexual assault resistance program. With her colleague, Anne Forrest, she has worked since 2010 on another important piece of the campus sexual assault prevention puzzle to institutionalize effective bystander education for men and women and to study its impact in the short and longer term.

SHAHEEN SHARIFF is a James McGill Professor at McGill University. Her work is grounded in the intersection of law and education, with a focus on human rights and constitutional issues, diversity, legal pluralism, and civil society. She is an associate member of McGill's Faculty of Law and its Center for Human Rights and Legal Pluralism, and an affiliate scholar at Stanford University Law School's Center for Internet and Society. She is a founding director of the Institute for Human Development and Well-Being in McGill's Faculty of Education. Shariff is best known for her expertise on institutional responses and legal obligations to address intersecting forms of discrimination and reduce toxic learning environments that foster cyberbullying and sexual misconduct in schools and university contexts on campuses and social media.

MARCUS A. SIBLEY is a PhD candidate in the Department of Law and Legal Studies at Carleton University. His research focuses on the historical, legal, and political implications of governing sexual violence through discursive and affective attachments to the idea that we live in a "rape culture."

WILFREDA E. THURSTON is professor emerita in the Department of Community Health Sciences, University of Calgary. Before academia she worked in the social service sector, including government services, a women's centre, and a shelter for women. Feminist analysis and advocacy for women's health and gender equality in medicine and society generally shape her career. Her research has included prevention of violence against girls and women, especially those marginalized by racialization.

CHELSEA TOBIN is a graduate of Mount Saint Vincent University where she majored in sociology and family studies. She has collaborated with KelleyAnne Malinen as a research assistant on various projects pertaining to sociological issues. These projects explore sexual assault on university campuses, the racial achievement gap in education, and the impact of public education systems on the students who attend them. Her understanding of these issues is reinforced by her work with Kids Help Phone and Restorative Justice. Chelsea's future plans are to complete a PhD in social work and pass her knowledge on to future generations of students.

ANNA TOURTCHANINOVA began her articles in law in 2019. She is a graduate of Robson Hall Law School. She has an interest in public law and has conducted legal research across a number of areas including sexual misconduct, nuclear proliferation, and corporate/commercial challenges.

AYESHA VEMURI is a PhD student in communication studies at McGill University. Her research focuses on the intersections of feminist activism, social media platforms, and transnational, feminist solidarity networks.

CIANN L. WILSON is assistant professor of community psychology at Wilfrid Laurier University. Her teaching, research, and community service, along with her lived experience as an Afro- Indo- and Euro-Caribbean woman, inform her commitment to student mentorship and support; her relations with black, Indigenous, and people of colour communities; and her art- and community-based scholarship in health. She specializes in intersectionality and anti-colonial theories, social determinants and political economy of health, health promotion, HIV/AIDS, community-based research, and qualitative research methodologies. She combines these theories, approaches, and frameworks to conduct interdisciplinary research focused on the health and well-being of marginalized communities.

MICHAEL R. WOODFORD is associate professor of social work at Wilfrid Laurier University. Michael was a Gendered Violence Faculty Colleague with Laurier's Gendered Violence Taskforce from 2014–2017. His research addresses the inclusion and well-being of LGBTQ individuals. Guided by minority stress, resilience, and socio-ecological theories, much of his work addresses the nature and outcomes of campus climate for LGBTQ+ university students, including the relationship between heterosexist and cisgenderist microaggressions and students' mental health and academic development. Recent work has applied an intersectional lens to students' experiences. Michael was the principal investigator for Laurier's 2016 Campus Safety Survey.

Index